The **Rough Guide** to

Fiji

written and researched by

Ian Osborn

NEW YORK · LONDON · DELHI

www.roughguides.com

Contents

Underwater Fiji
colour section
following p.112

Visiting a Fijian village
colour section
following p.240

◀◀ Navala village, Viti Levu ◀ Seaplane, Yasawas Islands

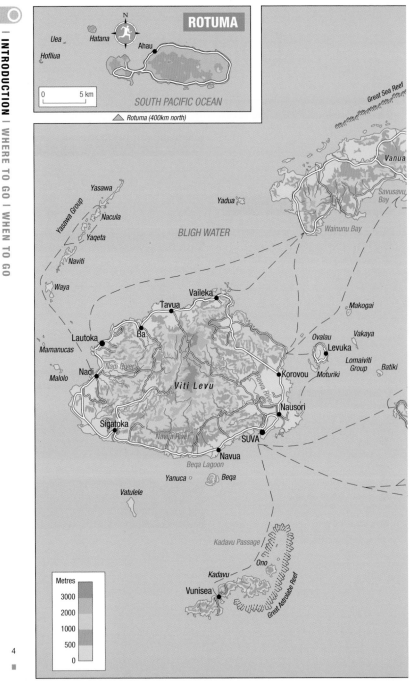

ROTUMA

Uea
Hatana
Hofliua
Ahau

N

0   5 km

SOUTH PACIFIC OCEAN

Rotuma (400km north)

Great Sea Reef

Vanua

Savusavu
Bay

Yasawa

Yadua

BLIGH WATER

Nacula

Wainunu Bay

Yaqeta

Yasawa Group

Naviti

Waya

Vaileka

Tavua

Makogai

Lautoka   Ba

Mamanucas

Ovalau   Vakaya

Levuka

Nadi

Nadi River

Lomaiviti
Group   Batiki

Malolo

Korovou   Moturiki

Viti Levu

Rewa River

Nausori

Sigatoka

Navua River

SUVA

Navua

Beqa Lagoon

Yanuca   Beqa

Vatulele

Kadavu Passage

Ono

Metres

3000

2000

1000

500

0

Kadavu

Vunisea

Great Astrolabe Reef

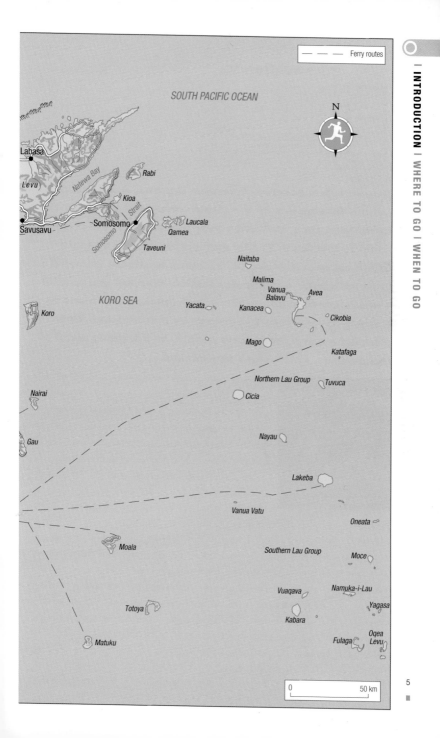

Introduction to

Fiji

Sun-drenched beaches, turquoise lagoons, swaying palm trees – Fiji supplies all the classic images of paradise. No wonder, then, that every year thousands of travellers come to this South Pacific archipelago for the ultimate island escape. With over 300 islands to choose from, Fiji is an amazingly versatile destination. Whether you're after a luxury honeymoon retreat, a lively backpacker island or a family-friendly resort you won't be disappointed. You'll also find a warm, hospitable people, an intriguing blend of Melanesians, Polynesians and Indians.

With a reliable tropical climate, a good tourist infrastructure, English as its main language and no jabs or pills to worry about, travelling in Fiji is as easy as it gets. As the hub of South Pacific tourism, the country attracts over half a million visitors a year, mostly from Australia and New Zealand, its largest "neighbours" lying over 2000km southeast. Of the northern hemisphere travellers who arrive, many are backpackers from Europe or surfers and scuba divers from North America.

While it can be tempting to spend your whole time in Fiji sunbathing and sipping cocktails from coconuts, there are plenty of **activities** to lure you away from the beach. Within a ten-minute boat ride of most resorts you can find yourself **snorkelling** with dolphins and manta rays or **scuba-diving** at pristine coral reefs. In addition, at the exposed edges of the reefs are some of the world's finest and most consistent **surfing breaks**. **Nature lovers** are also spoilt for choice, both underwater and on dry land and wildlife-spotting opportunities are plentiful, whether you are seeking turtles, exotic birds or three-metre-long tiger sharks.

Away from the resorts is another Fiji waiting to be discovered: a land of stunning mountains, rainforests and **remote villages**. Here you'll find

Beach scene, Mamanucas

Fact file

• Fiji is made up of 330 islands and many tiny islets. Two thirds of Fiji's islands remain uninhabited.

• The name Fiji is an adaptation of the Tongan pronunciation of "Viti", orginally written by Europeans as "Feejee".

• Of a total population of 827,900, 473,983 are ethnic Fijians, 311,591 Fiji-Indians and the remainder Chinese, Europeans and various Pacific islanders.

• Fiji ended 96 years of British colonial rule on October 10, 1970. Officially a republic, it has retained Queen Elizabeth II as its highest ranking chief. An interim government currently adminsters the country in the wake of the 2006 coup.

• Fiji's main export is sugar, followed by fish and mineral water. Tourism is the country's largest foreign income earner.

• Around a fifth of ethnic Fijians live a mostly subsistence lifestyle on tribally owned native land (87 percent of all land in the country).

fantastically hospitable Fijians living a similar lifestyle to their tribal ancestors. Staying a night or two at a village homestay will give you an authentic insight into ethnic Fijian culture as well as the chance to sample **yaqona** or *kava*, the national drink. Fiji is also home to a large **Indian community** and their influence is seen in the delicious Indian food served in almost every town, Bollywood films showing in the cinema and vibrant Hindu festivals celebrated throughout the year. While Fiji is not renowned for its towns or **cities**, three are definitely worth taking the time to explore: quaint, colonial-era Levuka, yachting hotspot Savusavu, and Suva, the lively capital city and the best place to party in the South Pacific.

However long you spend in the country you'll notice an unhurried, good-humoured lifestyle. This is the essence of **Fiji Time** – an attitude that can be both inspiring and infuriating.

Boat transfer, Yasawas

7

Away from the highly organized upmarket resorts, life runs at a different pace – bus and ferry timetables serve more as guidelines and a simple meeting in a village can last for days. It's best to leave your inner control freak at home – you never know, you may come back a calmer person.

Where to go

The vast majority of travellers arrive at Nadi International Airport on **Viti Levu**, the biggest island in the archipelago. Most stay around the suburban tourist hub of **Nadi** for a day or two to organize travels to other parts of the country, or use it as a convenient base for exploring the surrounding countryside and offshore islands. The most popular destination in Fiji lies visible off Nadi's coastline – a gorgeous collection of islands known as the **Mamanucas**. Here you'll find sublime beaches and tiny coral cays with suitably exotic names such as "Bounty" or "Treasure Island". Extending north of the Mamanucas is the **Yawawas Group**, a string of larger, volcanic islands home to a mixture of budget beach resorts and upmarket boutique accommodation.

Almost as popular as the Mamanucas and Yasawas, especially with families, are the beach resorts of the **Coral Coast** along the south coast of Viti Levu. Around an hour's drive from Nadi, these larger resorts offer good value all-inclusive packages and a great choice of sightseeing tours. Inland is the rugged **rural interior of Viti Levu**. This region was once home to

◀ Parliament House, Suva

Six of the best

Fijian resorts range from simple beachside **bures** (traditional thatched huts) with cold-water showers to opulent **villas** with hardwood floors and private spa pools. With almost a hundred resorts throughout the islands the choice can be overwhelming. To help you decide, we've whittled them down to six of the best, each aimed at a different type of traveller.

Luxury *Vatulele Island Resort*, Vatulele. See p.180
Backpackers *The Beachouse*, Coral Coast, Viti Levu. See p.129
Romance *Matangi Island Resort*, off Taveuni. See p.238
Families *Plantation Island Resort*, Malolo Lailai, Mamanucas. See p.96
Divers *Matava Hideaway*, Kadavu. See p.187
Eco-adventure *Tui Tai Cruise*, Vanua Levu and Taveuni. See p.218

fierce, cannibalistic hill tribes and is crisscrossed with **hiking trails** including the route to Fiji's highest peak, **Mount Tomanivi**. Heading east along Viti Levu's south coast brings you to **Pacific Harbour**, Fiji's adventure tour capital offering whitewater rafting, jet-ski safaris and the world-renowned shark dives off the nearby island of **Beqa**. Beyond is **Suva**, Fiji's cosmopolitan capital city and the hub for sea transport throughout the archipelago.

Of the outer islands, the most accessible are in the **Lomaiviti Group**, a short trip by boat from the east coast of Viti Levu. Here you'll find the quirky former capital of Levuka on the island of Ovalau and a good range of budget island resorts – a less commercial alternative to the Mamanucas and Yasawas. Spreading west for hundreds of kilometres is the vast **Lau Group**. Reached by cargo boat from the mainland, these islands provide a true adventure for the intrepid traveller and the chance to sample Polynesian culture. South of Viti Levu is the snaking shape of **Kadavu**, a magnet for scuba-divers thanks to the impressive Great Astrolabe Reef.

Fiji's second largest island, **Vanua Levu**, is in the northern part of the archipelago. On its south coast is the beautiful sailing anchorage of Savusavu while to the east is **Taveuni**, Fiji's lush "Garden Island". Half of Taveuni is protected as a national park and it's the best place to hike through rainforest and encounter the country's rare, native birdlife. Offshore is the stunning Rainbow Reef, aptly named after its colourful soft corals. Far north of Vanua Levu is the tiny Polynesian island of **Rotuma**, politically part of Fiji but so isolated it feels like a different country with its own language, culture and traditions.

When to go

◄ Climbing for coconuts, Kadavu

The most comfortable time to visit is during the **dry season** between May and October when temperatures hover around 25°C by day and drop to a pleasant 19–20°C at night. At this time of year the southerly **trade winds** bring cool breezes off the sea and sometimes blustery conditions on the south and eastern coasts. Coinciding with the southern hemisphere winter, the dry season is also the **busiest** time to visit, with holiday makers from New Zealand and Australia flocking to Fiji to escape the cold. Hotels in the popular resort areas are often booked out months in advance, especially around the **school holidays** between June and July.

The summer months from November to April are known as the **wet season** when temperatures rise to a fairly constant 31°C but with greatly increased humidity. Rainfall during these months is substantially higher,

The art of the Fijian coup

A recent Fijian newspaper cartoon depicted tourists arriving at Nadi airport below a sign reading "Welcome to Fiji – under new management". With wry humour it summed up the political experience of the country in recent times. Fiji has suffered no less than four **coups d'etat** since 1987, the most recent in December 2006. One of the reccurring themes of the coups has been ethnic tension between Fijian nationalists and the large Indian community. In contrast, the most recent coup, led by army chief **Frank Bainimarama**, was aimed at weeding out corruption in government and, ironically, putting an end to the vicious cycle of coups. Support for this coup was widespread across racial lines although it was swiftly condemned by local political heavyweights Australia and New Zealand. For **tourists** out on the island resorts, the coup might as well not have happened for all the impact it had. The military were keenly aware of the consequences of scaring off Fiji's main foreign income earner, with the odd roadblock being the only reminder of the event. More worrying were the travel advisories issued by Western governments warning against all travel to Fiji. These have since been relaxed as the country moves slowly towards fully democratic elections in 2009.

◄ Cooling off, Mana Island

although most of it falls in sudden torrential **tropical downpours** usually in the mid-afternoon. Mornings and late afternoons generally remain sunny and the sea is often beautifully **calm** – a great time for scuba divers. During the wet season the islands are lush with vegetation and waterfalls are at their most impressive; however, note that walking trails can get slippery and dirt roads impassable. Low pressure between December and April sometimes brings stormy weather from the northwest lasting around five days. In extreme cases **tropical cyclones** can develop. Direct hits on the islands are infrequent and damage quite localized. In 2007, a cyclone flattened most homes on the outlying island of Cikobia but left nearby islands relatively untouched.

Another aspect of Fiji's weather are the **microclimates** found on the leeward and windward sides of the main islands. For example, Nadi, on the dry west side of Viti Levu, has reliably sunny weather while Suva, on the opposite side of the island but barely 100km away is often drenched by showers rolling in off the ocean.

Fiji climate chart

	Jan	Feb	Mar	Apr	May	Jun	Jul	Aug	Sep	Oct	Nov	Dec
Nadi												
Max. temp (°C)	32	32	31	31	30	29	29	28	29	30	31	32
Min. temp (°C)	23	23	23	22	20	19	18	19	20	21	22	22
Rainfall (mm)	343	292	341	160	89	65	45	65	70	102	132	178
Suva												
Max. temp (°C)	31	31	31	30	29	28	27	26	27	28	29	30
Min. temp (°C)	24	24	24	23	22	21	21	20	21	22	23	24
Rainfall (mm)	371	265	374	366	270	163	136	158	177	221	245	277

things not to miss

It's not possible to see everything that Fiji has to offer in one trip – and we don't suggest you try. What follows is a selective and subjective taste of the island's highlights: from lush rainforests and quaint villages to the best activities on and off the water. They're arranged in five colour-coded categories to help you find the very best things to see, do, eat and experience. All highlights have a page reference to take you straight into the Guide, where you can find out more.

01 **Navala Village** Page **135** • Fiji's most picturesque village set deep in the highlands of Viti Levu and home to over two hundred traditional handcrafted *bures*.

02 **Snorkelling** See *Underwater Fiji* colour section and Page **37** • With vibrant coral reefs found off almost every beach, Fiji is a fantastic place to slip on a pair of fins and dive in.

04 **Cruise the Mamanucas** Page **73** • Take a day cruise around the tiny islands of the Mamanucas or pamper yourself at one of the islands' exclusive resorts.

03 **Meke dance night** Page **70** • The classic Fijian night out – traditional dancing accompanied by a feast of roast pig cooked in an underground oven.

05 **Levuka** Page **194** • Fiji's most beguiling town, a colonial museum piece full of stories and colourful locals.

06 **Hiking, Waya Island** Page **107** • Circumnavigate beautiful Waya Island and hike to the summit for stunning views.

07 **Spending a night in a village** See *Visiting a Fijian village* colour section • Get to know the locals over a nightly brew of *yaqona* in one of Fiji's many rural villages.

09 **Savusavu** Page **228** • Sipping an ice-cold beer overlooking this stunning bay at sunset is hard to beat.

10 **Climbing Mount Tomanivi**
Page **138** • Conquer Fiji's highest mountain and visit the notorious nearby village of Nubutautau.

12 **Sea-kayaking** Page **184** •
Paddle your way round Kadavu island, stopping at fishing villages and camping under the stars.

11 **Fiji-Indian culture** Page
36 • Fiji's Hindu temples come alive throughout the year with vibrant festivals often featuring wince-inducing fire walking.

13 **River rafting** Page **133** •
Head deep into the mystical Namosi Highlands on a white-water rafting trip.

Basics

Getting there

Fiji is the travel hub for the South Pacific, and a popular stopover on round-the-world tickets. The majority of direct flights arrive from New Zealand, Australia or Los Angeles and travellers from North America or Europe usually must connect through one of these. Arriving by boat is only possible on a privately chartered yacht, by taking one of the few cruise liners calling in on Lautoka or Suva or by finding passage on a container ship.

If flying from Australia or New Zealand, Fiji's main tourism market, you're likely to find heavily discounted airfares and package deals, particularly in the low season between January and April. The majority of travel agents focus on the ever-popular resorts in the Mamanucas, the large hotels along the Coral Coast on the main island and the occasional outer-island boutique retreat.

From North America, the UK or continental Europe, options are more limited although you should find Fiji as a stopover on many round-the-world tickets. The main tour operators in these regions tend to offer only the large international hotels around Nadi as package holidays. Searching for the best-priced flights, or using frequent-flyer points, then booking more desirable accommodation independently is likely to give you the most options at the lowest price.

Flights from the US and Canada

Fiji-bound travellers from **North America** have two choices for a direct flight to Nadi Airport: Air New Zealand or Air Pacific (Fiji's international airline). Both have daily flights from **Los Angeles**, with Air Pacific also having twice weekly flights from **Vancouver via Honolulu**. The eleven-hour nonstop flight from Los Angeles costs from US$1000 return, or US$1500 from Vancouver.

Flights from the UK and Europe

From the **UK**, you have the choice of travelling west via North America or east via Asia – it's 16,000km either way. Fares follow the high and low seasons between Europe and North America or Europe and Australia, with June to August and the Christmas holidays being particularly busy with fewer discounted deals available. Air New Zealand offers a convenient nonstop flight to Fiji **via Los Angeles** departing daily (except Fri) from Heathrow and costing £800–1300 – the flight takes 26hr including a four-hour connecting stopover at Los Angeles (unfortunately you have to clear US customs and immigration then re-enter which makes the transit a little frustrating). Air New Zealand also offers a daily eastern route from London Heathrow **via Hong Kong** and New Zealand, although this journey takes 28hr with two stopovers and costs from £1000. Some of the cheapest direct flights to Fiji from London are **via Seoul** with Korea Air costing from £650 if booked via an agent with the outward journey taking 24hr but the return leg requiring an overnight stop in Seoul with hotel and transfers included in the flight price. Otherwise, your best option is to find a cheap flight on the extremely competitive route between the UK and **Australia** which costs from £550 and then buy a return flight from either Brisbane or Sydney to Nadi with budget operator Pacific Blue, which adds around £300.

Flights from Australia, New Zealand and South Africa

Flights to Fiji are most frequent from **Australia and New Zealand** and both offer competitively priced deals. You won't find the ludicrous discounts offered on the trans-Tasman route, but you should discover reduced fares on the Internet and special offers bundled with accommodation packages.

Two airlines operate flights from **Australia**: the highly competitive Pacific Blue, an offshoot of Virgin Blue; and Air Pacific, which is co-owned by Qantas which operates all its flights. Both airlines depart daily from Brisbane and Sydney, taking about 4hr 30min with deals often available from A$450 return; Air Pacific also has four flights a week from Melbourne (6hr), costing roughly A$200 more.

The shorter, 3hr 5min hop from **New Zealand** is generally more expensive and monopolized by Air Pacific and Air New Zealand, with daily flights from Auckland starting from NZ$700 – there's also a twice weekly flight from Christchurch operated by Air Pacific taking 4hr.

The most direct route for travellers from **South Africa** is to fly to Sydney or Auckland and then on to Fiji.

Flights from elsewhere in the Pacific

Flying to Fiji from elsewhere in the South Pacific is not always practical, and often quite expensive, despite Fiji being the main travel hub for the region. Fiji's national airline, Air Pacific, flies to Fiji from: Upolu, **Samoa** (3 weekly; 1hr 30min; F$452 one way); Honolulu, **Hawaii** (2 weekly; 8hr; F$863 one way); Christmas Island, **Kiribati** (1 weekly; 4hr; F$677 one way); Tarawa, **Kiribati** (2 weekly; 3hr; F$677 one way); Port Vila, **Vanuatu** (3 weekly; 1hr 30min; F$392 one way); Tongatapu, **Tonga** (2 weekly; 1hr 20min; F$357 one way).

Other regional airlines serving Nadi include: Air Fiji from Funafuti, **Tuvalu** (2 weekly; 2hr 30min; F$780 one way) and from Vavau, **Tonga** (2 weekly; 2hr; F$430 one way); Aircalin from Noumea, **New Caledonia** (3 weekly; 2hr; F$739 one way); Air Vanuatu from Port Vila, **Vanuatu** (1 weekly; 1hr 40min; F$389 one way); Solomon Airlines from Honiara, **Solomon Islands** (2 weekly; 3hr; F$525 one way). There are no direct flights between Fiji and the Cook Islands, Tahiti or Easter Island – the easiest way to get to Fiji from these eastern Polynesian destinations is via Auckland or Los Angeles.

Airlines, agents and operators

Online booking

ⓦ www.expedia.com
ⓦ www.lastminute.com

Fly less – stay longer! Travel and Climate Change

Climate change is perhaps the single biggest issue facing our planet. It is caused by a build-up in the atmosphere of carbon dioxide and other greenhouse gases, which are emitted by many sources – including planes. Already, **flights** account for three to four percent of human-induced global warming: that figure may sound small, but it is rising year on year and threatens to counteract the progress made by reducing greenhouse emissions in other areas.

Rough Guides regard travel as a **global benefit**, and feel strongly that the advantages to developing economies are important, as are the opportunities for greater contact and awareness among peoples. But we also believe in travelling responsibly, which includes giving thought to how often we fly and what we can do to redress any harm that our trips may create.

We can travel less or simply reduce the amount we travel by air (taking fewer trips and staying longer, or taking the train if there is one); we can avoid night flights (which are more damaging); and we can make the trips we do take "climate neutral" via a carbon offset scheme. **Offset schemes** run by climatecare.org, carbonneutral .com and others allow you to "neutralize" the greenhouse gases that you are responsible for releasing. Their websites have simple calculators that let you work out the impact of any flight – as does our own. Once that's done, you can pay to fund projects that will reduce future emissions by an equivalent amount. Please take the time to visit our website and make your trip climate neutral, or get a copy of the *Rough Guide to Climate Change* for more detail on the subject.

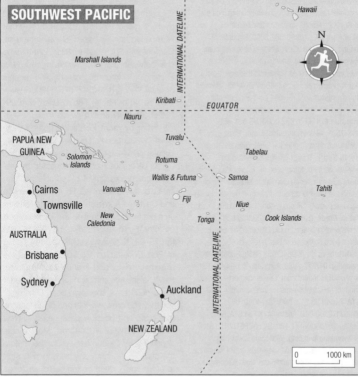

SOUTHWEST PACIFIC

Hawaii

Marshall Islands

Kiribati

EQUATOR

Nauru

PAPUA NEW GUINEA

Solomon Islands

Tuvalu

Tabelau

Rotuma

Wallis & Futuna

Samoa

Cairns

Vanuatu

Fiji

Niue

Tahiti

Townsville

New Caledonia

Tonga

Cook Islands

AUSTRALIA

Brisbane

Sydney

Auckland

NEW ZEALAND

INTERNATIONAL DATELINE

0   1000 km

ⓦ www.opodo.com
ⓦ www.orbitz.com
ⓦ www.travelocity.com
ⓦ www.zuji.com

Airlines

Aircalin Australia ☎02/9299 8854, New Zealand ☎09/308 3363; ⓦwww.aircalin.com.

Air Fiji US ☎1-877/247-3454, New Zealand ☎09/308 5206, Australia 02/8080 5646; ⓦwww.airfiji.com.fj.

Air New Zealand ☎0800/737000, Australia ☎0800/132 476, UK ☎0800/028 4149, USA ☎1800-262/1234, Canada ☎1800-663/5494; ⓦwww.airnz.co.nz.

Air Pacific US ☎1-800/227-4446, Australia ☎1800/230 150, New Zealand ☎0800/800178, UK ☎0870/572 6827; ⓦwww.airpacific.com.

Air Vanuatu Australia ☎1300 780 737, New Zealand ☎09/373 3435; ⓦwww.airvanuatu.com.

Korean Air US and Canada ☎1-800/438-5000, UK ☎0800/413 000, Republic of Ireland ☎01/799 7990, Australia ☎02/9262 6000, New Zealand ☎09/914 2000; ⓦwww.koreanair.com.

Pacific Blue Australia ☎13 16 45, New Zealand ☎0800/670000, Worldwide ☎+61 7/3295 2284; ⓦwww.flypacificblue.com.

Qantas Airways US and Canada ☎1-800/227-4500, UK ☎0845/774 7767, Republic of Ireland ☎01/407 3278, Australia ☎13 13 13, New Zealand ☎0800/808 767 or 09/357 8900, SA ☎11/441 8550; ⓦwww.qantas.com.

Solomon Airlines US and Canada ☎1-800/677-4277, Australia ☎02/9244 2189, New Zealand ☎09/308 3380, UK ☎0845/838 7947; ⓦwww.flysolomons.com.

Agents and operators

Beautiful Pacific Fiji ☎672 2600, US ☎619/618 0229, UK ☎020/8123 8622, Australia ☎02/8005 1232, New Zealand ☎09/889 0909;

ⓦwww.beautifulpacific.com. South Pacific travel specialist based in Fiji offering discounted rooms at most beach resorts and adventure retreats.

ebookers UK ☎0800/082 3000, Republic of Ireland ☎01/488 3507; ⓦwww.ebookers.com, ⓦwww.ebookers.ie. Low fares on an extensive selection of scheduled flights and package deals.

Fiji Adventures US ☎1-866/755 3453, ⓦwww .fijiadventures.com. Guided tours and adventure packages for North American travellers.

Impulse Fiji Fiji ☎672 0600, US ☎1-800/ 953-7595; ⓦwww.impulsefiji.com. Postings for last-minute special offers at larger resorts.

North South Travel UK ☎01245/608 291, ⓦwww.northsouthtravel.co.uk. Friendly, competitive travel agency, offering discounted fares worldwide. Profits are used to support projects in the developing world, especially the promotion of sustainable tourism.

Tailor Made Travel UK ☎0800/988 5887, ⓦwww.tailor-made.co.uk. UK-based travel agent with a good collection of beach resorts.

Trailfinders UK ☎0845/058 5858, Republic of Ireland ☎01/677 7888, Australia ☎1300/780 212; ⓦwww.trailfinders.com. One of the best-informed and most efficient agents for independent travellers.

STA Travel US ☎1-800/781-4040, UK ☎0871/2300 040, Australia ☎134 STA, New Zealand ☎0800/474 400, SA ☎0861/781 781; ⓦwww.statravel.com. Worldwide specialists in independent travel; also student IDs, travel insurance, car rental, rail passes, and more. Good discounts for students and under-26s.

Getting to Fiji by boat

Although a romantic proposition, arriving **by boat** is tricky unless on a private yacht – it's a five- to ten-day journey up from New Zealand depending on weather or at least a month's sailing across the Pacific from the US west coast. Several large cruise liners visit Fiji but usually spend only a day at port, either at Lautoka, Suva or Savusavu before cruising around the islands, perhaps dropping anchor for snorkelling trips, and then heading back to the open seas.

Finding passage on a **container ship** was once one of the great adventures of the Pacific, but most companies no longer

take passengers due to heightened security concerns since September 11, compounded by Fiji's recent political turmoil. For further information try Fiji-based shipping agents, Carpenters Shipping (☎331 2244) who sail between Fiji and Australia and New Zealand, or international shipping agents Andrew Weir (UK ☎020/7575 6480, ⓦwww .aws.co.uk) or Pacific Forum Line (NZ ☎09-356 2333, ⓦwww.pflnz.co.nz).

If visiting **by yacht**, Fiji has four ports of entry: Suva (ⓕ330 2864), Lautoka (ⓕ666 7734), Levuka (ⓕ344 0425) and Savusavu (ⓕ885 0728). Clearance must be requested at least 48 hours before arrival by completing form C2-C obtained from the Fiji Inland Revenue and Customs Administration website (ⓦwww .frca.org.fj) and faxing it to the intended port of entry. For detailed sailing info, Yacht Help (☎675 0911, ⓦwww.yachthelp.com) based at Port Denarau on Viti Levu publishes the extremely useful and free *Fiji Marine Guide*; they'll also try and find a yacht charter if you don't have your own boat. Otherwise, you may find **crew work** at one of the marinas (see p.39) and possibly passage on to New Zealand, Australia or California. Most yachts depart Fiji by September or October before the start of the hurricane season and start to arrive again, often having sailed via Tonga or Tahiti, from May to August.

Cruises

P&O Cruises Australia ☎13 24 69, New Zealand ☎0800/951 200; ⓦwww.pocruises .com.au. Large passenger cruise ships departing Sydney, Brisbane and Auckland and visiting various ports including Suva, Lautoka and Savusavu as well as Beqa and the Yasawa Islands, usually on twelve-day itineraries.

Soren Larsen NZ ☎09/817 8799; ⓦwww .sorenlarsen.co.nz. New-Zealand-based tall ship adventure cruise broken into twelve independent legs across the South Pacific. The Fiji leg arrives in Levuka from Samoa/Tonga in August and spends six days cruising around the islands before heading on to Vanuatu.

Getting around

Fiji is spread over a huge chunk of the southwest Pacific, covering almost 1.3 million square kilometres. On a map, the islands may look close enough together to hop between, but with limited infrastructure this can be a time-consuming process, often involving back-tracking to either Nadi or Suva. Viti Levu, the main island, is extremely well connected by public transport and easy to explore, as are the popular beach destinations of the Mamanucas and Yasawa Islands, connected by fast catamaran. Exploring further afield, though, requires patience and a sense of adventure with cumbersome passenger ferries and cargo boats visiting the outer islands on a weekly or monthly basis and flights in small propeller planes landing on gravel and sometimes even grass airstrips.

Nadi, on the main island of Viti Levu, is the nation's tourist hub, home to the international and main domestic airport and with sea access to the Mamanucas and Yasawa Islands. **Suva**, 120km away on the opposite side of the mainland, is the transport hub for all outer-island shipping as well as having air access to ten outer-island airstrips.

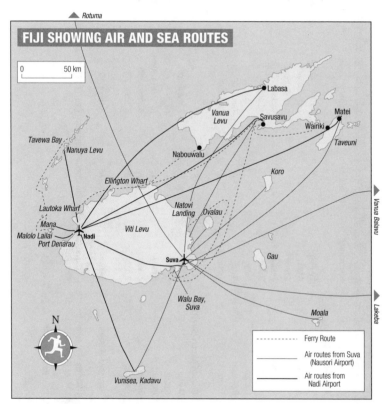

FIJI SHOWING AIR AND SEA ROUTES

0   50 km

Rotuma

Labasa

Vanua Levu

Savusavu

Matei

Wairiki

Taveuni

Tavewa Bay

Nanuya Levu

Nabouwalu

Koro

Ellington Wharf

Lautoka Wharf

Natovi Landing

Ovalau

Vanua Balavu

Mana

Malolo Lailai

Port Denarau

Nadi

Viti Levu

Suva

Gau

Lakeba

Walu Bay, Suva

Moala

N

Vunisea, Kadavu

- - - - - - - - - - Ferry Route

—————— Air routes from Suva (Nausori Airport)

—————— Air routes from Nadi Airport

Internal flight schedule

Route	Frequency	Airline	Departs	Returns	Duration	Fare (one way)
Nadi Airport to:						
Suva	10 daily	PS, AF	6.10am–8.15pm	6am–9.15pm	25min	F$175
Malolo Lailai	4 daily	PS	7am–5.05pm	7.30am–5.25pm	10min	F$83
Mana	4 daily	PS	8am–5.05pm	8.25am–5.35pm	15min	F$101
Turtle Island	1 daily	TA	Varies	Varies	35min	F$299
Kadavu	Daily	PS	12.40pm	1.45pm	45min	F$180
Labasa	Daily	PS	9.45am	11.10am	1hr 5min	F$254
Savusavu	5 daily	PS, AF	7am–3.30pm	8.20am–4.45pm	1hr	F$248
Taveuni	4 daily	PS, AF	7am–2pm	9am–4pm	1hr 30min	F$304
Nausori Airport (Suva) to:						
Ovalau	2 daily	AF	7.15am, 5pm	7.40am, 5.30pm	15min	F$88
Kadavu	Daily	AF	noon	12.45pm	30min	F$139
Labasa	6 daily	PS, AF	5.45am–4.30pm	8.45am–5.15pm	35min	F$198
Savusavu	2 daily	PS, AF	8.30am, 2pm	9.30am, 3pm	45min	F$171
Taveuni	2 daily	PS, AF	8.30am, 2.30pm	9.30am, 3.30pm	45min	F$210
Savusavu to Taveuni	Daily	PS, AF	3.10pm	3.40pm	20min	F$118

Other **weekly** routes from Nausori (Suva) (all AF only): Gau (Tues; F$89); Koro (Wed; F$125); Moala (Tues; F$164); Cicia (Thurs; F$167); Vanua Balavu (Fri; F$178); Lakeba (Mon; F$182); Rotuma (Wed; F$411).

PS = Pacific Sun; AF = Air Fiji; TA = Turtle Airways

On the two largest islands of **Viti Levu** and **Vanua Levu**, as well as on **Taveuni**, exceptionally cheap buses travel around the coast and countryside on a fairly regular basis and carrier vans or taxis can be hired for private tours. On all other islands, though, getting around usually involves a boat journey, often in a small, ten-passenger fibreglass boat with a 60HP single engine, and these, when chartered, are expensive. Hitching a ride with the locals is much cheaper but more often than not boats are filled to the brim, sometimes with as many as twenty large Fijians plus their luggage.

By air

Fiji's **domestic flight network** is monopolized by the government-owned Air Fiji (☏347 6324, ⓦwww.airfiji.com.fj) and Air Pacific-owned Pacific Sun (☏672 0888, ⓦwww.pacificsun.com.fj). Consequently, domestic flights rank among some of the most expensive in the world by distance covered and are served by small twin-propeller planes only; Pacific Sun operating ageing Twin Otters to smaller destinations and more modern ATRs between Nadi, Suva and Labasa, with Air Fiji flying mostly Chinese-made Harbin Y-12s. Whilst flying in such aircraft may cause a little nervousness, it is by far the quickest way to get around and there are often excellent **deals** available via the airlines' websites, with discounts of fifty percent or more available on the main tourist routes. This can make flying almost as cheap as travelling by passenger ferry. Availability is seldom a problem, except at Christmas when flights can be booked out months in advance. **Baggage allowance** on internal flights is a meagre 15kg per person (unless flying internationally with Air Pacific when you're permitted an additional 5kg on all Pacific Sun flights). If you plan on travelling with your own scuba diving equipment or surf board check with the airline in advance.

There are also two **seaplane** companies operating in Fiji: Turtle Airways based at Wailoaloa Beach in Nadi (☏672 1888, ⓦwww.turtleairways.com) and Pacific Island Seaplanes (☏672 5644, ⓦwww.fijiseaplanes.com) based at Nadi Airport. Turtle Airways offer a **daily public flight**

to Turtle Island in the northern part of the Yasawa Islands for US$299 one way with a minimum of two passengers but you must pre-arrange a boat to transfer you on to your intended destination – departure times vary and can only be advised the day before based on sea conditions. Island Hoppers (☏672 0410, ⓦwww.helicopters .com.fj) shuttles guests to upmarket resorts by **helicopter**. Baggage allowance on seaplanes and helicopters is 15kg per person, with excess charges thereafter.

By cargo boat and passenger ferry

Cargo boats have been plying Fiji's waters since the pioneering days of the late nineteenth century, bringing in trade, exporting copra and connecting the people with the outside world. It is still common practice for passengers to join cargo boats supplying the outer islands, usually sitting and sleeping on deck amidst barrels of oil, boxes of tinned meat and bunches of bananas; for those with a little time and a spirit of adventure, it's a chance to rub shoulders with Fijians from all walks of life. For more information see p.208 and the chart on p.28.

The busy tourist destinations of the Mamanucas and Yasawa islands are graced by fast **passenger catamarans** offering fabulous views from their upper decks and enclosed air-conditioned seating on the lower levels. By contrast, the bulky and ageing **vehicle and passenger ferries** visiting Kadavu, Vanua Levu and Taveuni suffer particularly from sea swell, and often meander around an erratic schedule. Christmas is especially hectic with over-laden boats common during the summer school break from early December to late January while rough seas often disrupt schedules between December and April. See the box on p.26 for routes and costs.

By bus

With no rail service and few people owning cars, **buses** are the only practical way for the public to affordably get around the large islands of Viti Levu and Vanua Levu. Both islands have reliable, frequent and **exceptionally cheap** bus services operating out of the all town centres, usually with open-sided

Passenger ferry schedule

Destination	Company	Departs	Frequency	Time	Duration	Fare (one way)
Mamanuca Islands						
South Sea, Bounty, Treasure, Beachcomber, Mana, Castaway & Malolo	South Sea Cruises	Port Denarau, Nadi	3 daily	9am, 12.15pm & 3pm	20min–1hr 45min	F$63–78
Matamanoa & Tokoriki	South Sea Cruises	Port Denarau, Nadi	2 daily	9am & 3pm	2hr 20min	F$178
Malolo Lailai	Leeward Services	Port Denarau, Nadi	3 daily	10.30am, 2pm & 5pm	1hr	F$55
Yasawa Islands						
South Sea, Bounty, Beachcomber, Kuata, Waya, Naviti, Matacawalevu, Nanuya, Tavewa & Nacula	Awesome Adventures	Port Denarau, Nadi	Daily	8.30am	20min–5hr	F$65–110
Kadavu						
Vunisea	Venu Shipping	Walu Bay, Suva	Tues	10.30pm	7hr 30min	F$45–55
Lomaiviti Group						
Levuka, Ovalau	Venu Shipping	Walu Bay, Suva	Weekly	varies	6hr	F$20
Levuka, Ovalau	Patterson Bros	Suva bus stand via Natovi Landing	4 weekly	1.30pm	5hr	F$25
Levuka, Ovalau	Turtle Transport	Suva bus stand via Natovi Landing	4 weekly	8am	5hr	F$18
Koro	Consort Shipping	Walu Bay, Suva	Mon, Fri	6pm	8hr	F$46
Vanua Levu & Taveuni						
Labasa, via Nabouwalu	Patterson Shipping	Suva bus stand via Natovi Landing	6 weekly	5am, 7am	10hr, 8hr,	F$60 & F$55
Savusavu & Taveuni	Consort Shipping	Walu Bay, Suva	Mon, Wed & Fri	6pm	12hr & 16hr	F$55 & F$64
Savusavu & Taveuni	Bligh Water Shipping	Walu Bay, Suva	Mon, Wed & Fri	4pm & 6pm	12hr & 16hr	F$63 & F$79
Savusavu	Bligh Water Shipping	Lautoka	Wed & Sun	6pm	12hr	F$63

windows and visiting almost every rural location imaginable, be it along a dirt road, up a steep mountain or over narrow wooden planks bridging rivers and stopping when requested. **Express buses** run between major towns on Viti Levu. The five-hour journey between Nadi and Suva costs F$10. Most buses are rather dated with hard cushioned seats and sliding windows but the tourist operator Coral Sun runs a modern air-conditioned soft-seated coach for double the price. You should also consider the air-conditioned tourist bus operator Feejee Experience (see p.121) which circumnavigates the main island on a four-day adventure journey. A very limited bus schedule operates on Ovalau and Taveuni, mostly for shuttling kids back and forth from school, but on all other islands buses are non-existent.

Minivans and carrier vans

Also running in urban centres and speeding along the main roads are ten-seater **minivans** which stop by the roadside to pick up waiting passengers for the same fare as a bus. Many operate illegally and drive carelessly but if your only consideration is to get from A to B quickly and cheaply, they're a good option. More basic **carrier vans**, with an open back usually covered by tarpaulin and with a wooden bench along each side, travel along the rural dirt roads carrying people and their produce between the villages and town markets.

By car

On the main island of Viti Levu **a car** is without doubt the best way to explore the countryside. Although buses and carrier vans travel to most regions, the freedom to stop at will for photos, to chat with locals along the way and simply to travel at your own convenience is both pleasurable and time saving. **Renting a car** is straightforward using your home licence, but you must be aged 21 or older. Rates are relatively cheap, starting at F$85 per day including insurance (twenty percent more on Vanua Levu and Taveuni due to less competition and poor road conditions), but the relatively high cost of fuel makes longer trips quite expensive. Prices are fixed by the government – at the

time of writing this was F$2.15 per litre for unleaded and F$1.95 for diesel.

It's a good idea to rent a **4WD**, or, at the very least, a car with high clearance – most roads off the coastal highway are unsealed, of compacted dirt and often littered with crater-sized pot holes; with rain, and it often rains in the mountains, these roads become very slippery and sometimes impassable without a 4WD. Rental companies tend to void insurance for breakdowns or accidents on dirt roads so check in detail beforehand.

The same facts apply to Vanua Levu, but renting is not so straightforward with only a couple of rental firms in Savusavu and Labasa, and these with only a few cars available, so pre-booking is advisable. The only other island where you can rent a car is Taveuni.

Driving tips

Driving between towns along the sealed coastal road of Viti Levu is very straight-forward; but turning off this road can be intimidating with absolutely no **signposts** and roads splitting and veering in every direction. Keep an eye open for the tiny white roadside markers which indicate distance from set points, usually from major towns or turn-offs and the main connecting roads. There are no decent maps available to help navigation in the countryside – the only option is to ask for directions along the way. The most common **hazards** apart from the potholes are mindless pedestrians and stray animals. Driving is on the left with the speed limit generally set at 40kmph through towns, 60kmph in the suburbs and 80kmph elsewhere. If you break down, call your car rental company which should provide you with a 24hr service number – but be warned there are few telephones along the roadside and mobile phone coverage is pretty sporadic in rural areas.

Car rental agencies

The following major **car rental** companies have offices at Nadi Airport where you can arrange a rental before your trip – most also have outlets in Suva enabling you to drop off the car after a one-way journey. For details of independent local companies, see "Listings" throughout the Guide.

Cargo boat schedule

Destination	Company	Departs	Frequency	Duration	Fare (one way)
Kadavu	Western Shipping	Walu Bay, Suva	2 monthly	9hr	F$50
Lau Group					
Lakeba, Oneata, Moce, Komo, Namuka, Vanua Vatu	Salia Basaga	Walu Bay, Suva	2 monthly	1–5 days	F$175
Moala, Totoya, Matuku.	Salia Basaga	Walu Bay, Suva	Monthly	1–3 days	F$85
Kabara, Fulaga, Ogea Vatoa, Ono-i-Lau	Seaview Shipping	Narayan Jetty, Suva	Monthly	2–6 days	F$100
Yaqata, Vanua Balavu, Tuvuca, Cicia, Lakeba	Western Shipping	Walu Bay, Suva	2 monthly	1–5 days	F$98
Rotuma	Western Shipping	Walu Bay, Suva	Monthly	2 days	F$98–125

Schedules are managed by Fiji Shipping Corp located beside Walu Bay roundabout on Edinburgh Drive in Suva (☎331 9383, ✉fscl@unwired.com.fj).

Avis US and Canada ☎1-800/331-1212, UK ☎0870/606 0100, Republic of Ireland ☎021/428 1111, Australia ☎13 63 33 or 02/9353 9000, New Zealand ☎09/526 2847 or 0800/655 111; ⒲www.avis.com.
Budget US ☎1-800/527-0700, Canada ☎1-800/268-8900, UK ☎0870/156 5656, Australia ☎1300/362 848, New Zealand ☎0800/283 438; ⒲www.budget.com.
Europcar US & Canada ☎1-877/940 6900, UK ☎0870/607 5000, Republic of Ireland ☎01/614 2800, Australia ☎393/306 160; ⒲www.europcar .com.
Hertz US & Canada ☎1-800/654-3131, UK ☎020/7026 0077, Republic of Ireland ☎01/870 5777, New Zealand ☎0800/654 321; ⒲www .hertz.com.
Thrifty US and Canada ☎1-800/847-4389, UK ☎01494/751 500, Republic of Ireland ☎01/844 1950, Australia ☎1300/367 227, New Zealand ☎09/256 1405; ⒲www.thrifty.com.

Taxis

Getting about **by taxi** in Nadi and Suva is cheap and practical, regulated by the government with flag fall set at F$1.50 between 6am and 10pm (F$2 outside these hours), plus 10 cents for every 200m travelled, all calculated by meter – unfortunately the practice is not enforced in Nadi

so you'll probably have to negotiate with the driver beforehand. Competition is fierce, with unlicensed minivans scouring the streets and picking up passengers along the way, charging 50 cents for an inter-urban journey. Hiring a taxi for rural **sightseeing** or travel between towns is a good option if you don't want to drive yourself, and works out as a cheap alternative if travelling with three or more people. Negotiate a rate beforehand and expect to pay F$25–35 per hour depending on how far you want to travel.

Bicycles and motor scooters

There are few **cyclists** to be found on Fiji's shoulder-less, potholed roads, and good reason for it – cyclists are shown little courtesy from motorists. However, exploring rural Viti Levu or Vanua Levu by bicycle will certainly draw attention and conversation when passing through villages and should be a great adventure for those confident enough to try. Unless you bring your own bike though, you'll have to buy one in Nadi, Suva or Labasa, but don't expect quality. The only place you're able to rent **bicycles** is at a few large resorts, with Denarau Island off Nadi and Malolo Lailai in the

Mamanucas being the main contenders. **Motor scooters** are extremely rare except in Nadi where they are something of a novelty – travelling along the busy town roads is practical though not particularly safe and you should certainly expect the unexpected with motorists who seem to be blind to anything on two wheels. Travel beyond the town area is not recommended.

Accommodation

For a developing country, Fiji is a fairly expensive place to visit, with room prices and standards closer to those in Australia than Southeast Asia. However, at many budget island resorts and some of the more remote, upmarket boutique resorts, meals and some activities are included making the price seem more expensive than it actually is. On the outer islands there's usually nowhere else to eat other than the resort restaurant, which can inflate the cost of staying. Nevertheless, there's great diversity around the islands with some resorts dedicated to scuba diving, surfing or ecotours while others specialize in relaxation and fine dining.

Outside of the main towns, almost every place to stay is on a beach or overlooking the sea and called a **resort**, regardless of its amenities. The highest concentrations of accommodation are in Nadi and along the south coast of Viti Levu which are the **best-value** places to stay, and in the Mamanucas and Yasawa Islands, which are graced with delightful beach resorts from budget to upmarket. There are slimmer but adequate sprinklings of hostels, retreats and boutique resorts around rural Viti Levu and on the outer islands of Kadavu, Ovalau, Vanua Levu and Taveuni, the latter also being popular for longer stays and holiday homes. Beyond, in the remote outliers of the Lomaiviti Group, the Lau Group and Rotuma, accommodation is scarce and provisions and general infrastructure are basic.

For those travelling on a **budget**, there are plenty of affordable beach resorts all around the islands with cheap hotel rooms and dorm beds in most towns. Obtaining **discounts** direct from the resorts is difficult although the large international hotels usually run tempting website promotions. The best bet is to seek out accommodation-only deals via the Internet.

Several companies specialize in diving, kayaking, surfing and ecotour holidays in Fiji. See "Sports and outdoor activities", p.37 for information on these niche operators.

Rates

The majority of resorts quote everything in the **local currency** of Fijian dollars (F$), although a few of the upmarket resorts, particularly

---

Accommodation price codes

All accommodation reviewed in this guide has been graded according to the following **price codes** in Fijian dollars. Unless noted otherwise, the prices refer to the least expensive double or twin room at standard rack rates including all taxes.

❶ Under F$50	❹ F$151–200	❼ F$351–500
❷ F$51–100	❺ F$201–250	❽ F$501–650
❸ F$101–150	❻ F$251–350	❾ Over F$651

percent for Hotel Turnover Tax (HTT) – only a couple of resorts don't include these taxes and these are noted in the Guide. Once in Fiji, **walk-in rates** at some resorts are given if requested, although seldom at the backpacker hostels. To encourage longer stays, many resorts offer a "stay six/pay five" incentive or similar. Rooms overlooking the beach and ocean are sold at a premium but note that terminology is often ambiguous – a "beachfront" bure may not be right on the beach and an "ocean view" room may only have a partial glimpse of the sea through trees or other buildings.

For the most part, everything from food to activities within a hotel or resort is charged to your room and paid for at the end of your stay by **credit card**, though usually only Visa and MasterCard are accepted, sometimes with a small card-service fee, so check beforehand. Paying **tips** to individuals is not encouraged, but communal staff fund boxes are usually left on reception counters and distributed to staff as a Christmas bonus or used for community projects.

Hotels and inns

On the main island of Viti Levu, particularly on Denarau Island and along the Coral Coast, you'll find a dozen or so large **hotel complexes**. Facilities include air-conditioned rooms with flat-screen TVs, huge swimming pools with swim-up bars, multiple restaurants with international cuisine, souvenir shops, spas, gyms, tennis courts, kids' clubs and jet-skis. Unlike the huge US all-inclusive resorts, the majority are "pay as you go" giving you the freedom to eat where you want and to do as little or as much as you wish. You'll also find smaller, cheaper **hotels and inns** around

those focusing in on the US market, quote in US\$. **Rates** start from around F\$15 (£5/US\$10) for a dorm bed in town centres, F\$60 (£20/US\$40) per person including meals in the budget resorts, F\$60 for a basic hotel room in urban centres and anywhere from F\$200 to over F\$500 (£165/US\$330) at a beach resort. The small, exclusive boutique resorts on private islands cost from F\$800 (£270/US\$540) per night and up.

All rates in Fiji are quoted **per room** and not per person, unless for dorm beds – only a few places, mostly urban hotels and hostels, offer single-person room rates. Almost all published prices include local **taxes** which are currently 12.5 percent for VAT and 5

Bures

The most common style of accommodation in Fiji is a **bure**, an open-plan traditionally styled building with high ceilings and thatch roofing ensuring natural ventilation. At the upmarket resorts, bures are exquisite handcrafted palaces, usually with king-sized beds, walk-in showers and wood floors while at a backpacker resort you can expect thin bamboo walls, a simple foam mattress, no electricity and a shared communal bathroom. At some of the mid-range and larger resorts, a bure is often an A-frame wooden structure split into two or four rooms and referred to as a duplex or quad bure.

Tying the knot

Fiji is a beautiful and relatively stress-free place to get married and most resorts offer **wedding packages** with ceremonies held on the beachfront. For those with large groups in attendance, getting married on the main island of Viti Levu is more convenient, but the atmosphere on the offshore islands is far more intimate and a much better option for smaller parties. The best options are *Octopus Resort* (see p.108) and *Oarsman's Bay Lodge* (see p.113) in the Yasawa Islands; *Matamanoa Island Resort* (see p.101) and *Treasure Island Resort* (see p.93), in the Mamanuca Islands. If getting married on the **beach**, find out about the tides and sun direction before fixing a time. Early-morning weddings are worth considering as it's not only cooler and less windy, but also less likely to rain – there's nothing more dampening than reciting your vows in a makeshift alter in the resort restaurant.

The practicalities of obtaining a **marriage licence** are very straightforward and all resorts will help with the paperwork. For more information contact ⓦwww .weddingspacific.com or ⓦwww.fijinet.com.

the Coral Coast, some offering self-catering air-conditioned rooms, others small restaurants but usually with few water sports or amenities available except for a swimming pool. Apart from two large beach hotels in the Mamanucas, the majority of places to stay in the outer islands are small, intimate boutique resorts.

Boutique resorts

A small **boutique resort** spanning a secluded beach on a remote island is Fiji's specialty. Some have as few as three bures, others up to fifty, but all focus on providing exceptional service. A few of the more upmarket boutique resorts are all-inclusive affairs, some even including alcoholic beverages in the price. The majority have 24hr reception, small shops, room service, nightly turn-down, restaurants and sunset bars as well as scuba diving and spa/massage facilities. Perhaps the only drawback is the lack of freedom to sightsee or choose where to eat although for most people this simply makes the experience more relaxing.

Guesthouses and homestays

Guesthouses in Fiji tend to be colonial-style wooden buildings with simple rooms, communal lounges and shared bathrooms. They are usually cheap, with rooms costing less than F$40 and make convenient bases for travellers wanting to explore off the tourist trail; note that guesthouses are

often used by government contract workers in the outer islands or remote settlements. More appealing to tourists are the handful of **bed and breakfasts** around the country, those in Nadi and Suva on the main island attracting business travellers, whilst several charming homestays and self-contained cottages in the small towns on Vanua Levu, Ovalau and Taveuni are mostly operated by expatriates and charge from F$100 per night and up.

Homestays are operated by local families who either open up their homes to travellers (offering absolute immersion into Fijian culture), or build tourist bures just outside the village which gives both parties a little privacy. Homestays commonly cost F$50 per person per night including meals, sometimes served with the family and laid out on the floor, Fijian style. See the *Visiting a Fijian village* colour section for more about village stays.

Hostels and backpacker resorts

There's a huge amount of **budget accommodation** in Fiji although those expecting Southeast Asian prices are likely to be disappointed. Although the more shambolic operations don't last for long, standards are variable. Members of the Fiji Backpacker Association (ⓦwww.fiji-backpacking.com) are usually reliable, as are those promoted by Awesome Adventures (ⓦwww .awesomefiji.com), although by staying at these established places you'll be missing out on the quirky places which offer a real insight into Fiji. Spending a few days in Nadi and meeting other travellers is a sure way to get on the grapevine and suss out where's new and happening.

The term "hostel" usually refers to a town boarding house aimed specifically at locals. A more common name is **"backpacker resort"**, and these can be found throughout the islands and even in Nadi. Most have rooms or lodges crammed with dorm beds but often the price of a simple double room or bure is the same as two dorm beds.

Student discount cards are not widely accepted – if you've travelled around Australia or New Zealand and already have one you may be able to save yourself around ten percent at certain places – the Australian operated Nomads (Ⓦwww.nomadsworld .com) and VIP backpackers (Ⓦwww .vipbackpackers.com), both have affiliates in Nadi but there's no YHA.

Camping

Camping is not encouraged in Fiji – it's perceived by Fijians as an insult, as if you're saying the local village is not good enough to sleep in. However, several backpacker resorts permit pitching of tents within their resort grounds and several organized tours, with the consent of village landowners, make temporary camp on secluded beaches.

Food and drink

Until recently, Fiji was a bit of a culinary backwater, with very basic Indian and Chinese restaurants dominating the high streets and most resorts serving unimaginative international cuisine. However much has changed over the past ten years: both Nadi and Suva boast stylish and reasonably priced restaurants serving everything from Italian to Japanese food and it's also now easier to find well-presented traditional Fijian cuisine. Out on the resorts, internationally acclaimed chefs have been brought in to raise the cooking standards expected by upmarket travellers.

Fijian cuisine

Fijian cuisine includes plenty of locally caught bony reef fish cooked in rich coconut cream, and sometimes *kai* mussels, mud crabs and even lobster, but little meat except for slow-cooked pig *(taro)* on a special occasion. When the seas are rough or the season's pickings are slender, Fijians resort to imported fatty mutton and tinned corned beef, the latter perceived as something of a delicacy and often served up by the carton at ceremonial functions.

Appearing at every mealtime is a hefty portion of starchy **rootcrop**, either cassava (a bland and extremely dry tuber), *dalo* (known as *taro* in Polynesia, a large corn) or yams (huge tubers, sometimes two metres long, and the most flavoursome of the three rootcrops). **Vegetables** are less common with the most popular being: *bele*, a green, sometimes slimy, leaf; and *rourou*, the leaf of the *dalo* crop which if cooked too quickly causes an itchy sensation to the throat. The availability of **fruit** is dependent on the season (see below).

Traditional Fijian dishes include: **kokoda** made from a large fish, usually tuna or wahoo, chopped into chunks, marinated overnight in lime juice and chillies, seasoned with coconut cream and served cold; **palusami**, coconut cream wrapped up in the leaf of *dalo* and slow cooked (delicious); and the kids' favourite **vakalolo**, a sticky pudding

The lovo

In pre-European times, the Fijian islanders cooked food in bamboo strips on an open fire but, with increased trade with the Tongans, the underground oven or "**lovo**" was adopted. To make a *lovo*, a hole is dug in the soil, laid with wood over which black volcanic stones are placed. A fire is lit, the stones are heated and the food, wrapped carefully in banana leaves or tin foil, is placed on top. The main constituents are usually a whole pig at the bottom with *dalo*, yam, chicken, fish and *palusami* laid on top in order to give each the correct amount of cooking. The hole is covered with coconut leaves with soil spread on top sealing in the heat and cooking the food slowly (anything from an hour to five hours depending on size). Most Fijian families prepare a *lovo* early Sunday morning before heading to church so it is ready for eating at lunch. *Lovos* also form the heart of ceremonial feasting at weddings, funerals and any other communal gathering.

made from cassava mixed with sugar and thick coconut cream and best served with ice-cream and bananas. Fish in *lolo* (coconut cream) with cassava or *dalo* is served as counter food in most high-street restaurants but finding the more delicate dishes of *kokoda*, *palusami*, *vakalolo* or *lovo* suckling pig is more challenging: *Nadia's* in Nadi (see p.68) and *Old Mill Cottage* in Suva (see p.165) are two of the few restaurants serving traditional Fijian cuisine.

Fiji-Indians tend to be more adventurous in taste, relying on home-cooked curries, often made of freshly picked vegetables seasoned with hot chillies and other spices accompanied by home-made chutney but usually drowned in oil or ghee.

Seasonal fruit and vegetables

While they are available in supermarkets, **imported fresh ingredients** are often too expensive for Fijians and the resorts have been encouraged by successive governments to source more produce locally. The results are slowly being realized, giving Fijians a new source of income.

The availability of **fruit** and some vegetables is determined by the seasons, with local produce extremely cheap when in abundance – **bananas**, **pawpaw** (also known as papaya) and **coconuts** are available year-round. Expensive imports including apples, oranges and melons bolster lows in productivity. The following is a list of fruits grown extensively in Fiji:

January Watermelon, pineapple, *vi* (Tahitian apple), avocado, *vutu* (small nut, similar to almond), guava, lemon.
February Pineapple, *vi*, avocado, guava, lemon, *lvi* (Tahitian chestnut).
March Guava, lemon, *lvi*, mandarin, orange.
April Guava, lemon, *lvi*, mandarin, orange.
May Lemon, mandarin, orange, *daruka* (Fijian asparagus).
June Mandarin, orange, passionfruit, *tarawao* (small, round and crunchy with a hard seed), *dawa* (Fijian lychee), watermelon, *soursop* (large spiky looking fruit with lots of hard seeds, creamy in texture).
July Passionfruit, *tarawao* (tiny hard, sour fruit), *dawa*, watermelon, soursop.
August *Kavika* (wax apple), soursop.
September Mango, pineapple, *kavika*, soursop.
October Mango, pineapple, *kavika*, jackfruit.
November Mango, pineapple, jackfruit, *vi* (Tahitian apple), breadfruit, *vutu*.
December Watermelon, pineapple, *vi* (Tahitian apple), breadfruit, avocado, *vutu*.

Breakfast and lunch

Breakfast at resorts inevitably includes fresh fruit and a continental style buffet with freshly baked breads and cereals. In the Fijian home it's often a much heartier affair, with a large plate of boiled rice or cassava, fish if caught the night before, heavy pancakes, sweet tea and plain biscuits.

Lunch is the most commonly overlooked meal in Fiji, and many tourists often find it too hot to consider eating anything substantial, with salads and quick snacks most popular.

Dinner and eating out

Dinner is usually taken early, and you'll find all restaurants open by 6pm and often winding down by 9pm, or perhaps 10pm on busy nights. At independent restaurants mains start from F$7 and seldom rise above F$30 even in Nadi and Suva.

Dinner at **resort restaurants** is always more expensive, and at most island resorts it's your only option, with mains starting around F$15 and often reaching F$50 or more. **Buffet dinners** are popular at the large resorts, particularly the weekly Fijian *lovo* night when a suckling pig and root crops are cooked in an underground oven and usually preceded by a traditional dance, costing from F$40–70 a person.

Drink

Fijians have a reputation for enjoying a **drink**, always in company and often to excess, be it the national drink, **yaqona** (known as *kava* in Polynesian countries; see the *Visiting a Fijian village* colour section), beer or local dark rum. Drinking sessions are invariably all-male affairs with a single glass or cup passed around in rotation and the contents swallowed in one gulp – a sure way of ending up drunk quickly. If out at a bar or nightclub, **closing time** is usually 1am, although on Saturday everything must close by midnight to avoid being open on a Sunday.

The four labels of local **beer** are passable, all highly carbonated lagers brewed in Suva under a subsidiary of the Australian Fosters Group. Fiji Bitter (4.6 percent alcohol) is the most palatable. Lighter in taste but of similar strength are Fiji Gold, Fiji Export and Fiji Premium, all more popular with tourists. Fiji Bitter comes in two sizes: 375ml "stubbies" and the larger 750ml "long necks", popular with the locals; Gold comes in stubbies only, Export in cans and Premium in clear bottles. In the shops a stubby costs around F$2, in the local bars it's anything from F$2.50 to F$5 and in the resorts it starts at F$5. Draft Fiji Bitter can be found at the more upmarket bars and resorts and is infinitely better tasting. Imported bottled beer, mostly lagers from Australia, cost a few dollars more. If you thirst for a draft Guinness you'll need to head to *O'Reillys Bar* in Suva.

Rum, brewed from local sugar in Lautoka, is popularly referred to as "wash down", drunk after a *yaqona* session to sweeten the palate. The smooth, mellow Bounty Dark Rum brand has won several international awards and costs around F$37 for a 750ml bottle. Both dark and white rum are regular ingredients in the gorgeous **cocktails** concocted by resort barmen – these usually cost anywhere from F$15 to F$25 although happy-hour prices are substantially discounted. Locally brewed gin and vodka are less appealing. **Wine** is usually imported from Australia and New Zealand – a reasonable bottle will cost F$20 in a bottle shop, and perhaps double that in a restaurant. BYO is not a common practice but some restaurants do permit this with a corkage fees around F$10. In the villages, **home-made wine** made from pineapples, watermelon or oranges is worth trying if offered.

It's worth noting that you can buy two bottles of **duty-free liquor** on arrival at Nadi Airport beside the luggage carousel before clearing customs.

Soft drinks

Despite the abundance of fruit, freshly squeezed **fruit juices** and smoothies are seldom sold in towns or even resort bars. However, you will find that Fijians are amazingly adept at shinning up tall palm trees, felling a **coconut**, slicing its top off and offering the milky contents as a refreshing drink. Trying one is something of a must-do in Fiji.

Tap water in towns is filtered and chlorinated and on the whole safe to drink although it's best avoided after heavy rains when sediment often appears. Chilled, sweetened tap water mixed with fresh limes is sold from glass tanks at all town markets. At rural and outer-island resorts, water is sourced from natural springs or wells although for drinking purposes, **rainwater** collected in tanks is preferable. Brackish well water is sometimes a problem, and in places of scarcity, especially in the Mamanucas and Yasawa Islands, desalination plants have been installed which often give a slightly saline taste to the water and anything made from it. **Bottled water**, for which Fiji is globally renowned, costs between F$2 to F$3 for a large 1.5-litre bottle in the shops, depending on brand, but at least triple that in the resorts. Fiji Water, owned by a private American company and hugely popular in the US, is sourced from a deep well beneath the Nakauvadra Range in northern Viti Levu, with a multi-million dollar bottling plant at Yaqara. Other local brands include VTY, a pun on Fiji Water (*Viti* is Fiji and *Wai* is water in Fijian), Island Chill and Aqua Pacific, all sourced on Viti Levu.

The media

Fiji's media, expressed vocally through newspaper, radio and television, has often been suppressed under military rule, but nevertheless strives to keep the public informed and entertained. When conventional media has been censored, the Internet has proven invaluable in distributing the views of Fijians, notably through blogs often written by critical emigrants living outside of Fiji.

Newspapers and magazines

Of the three English-language daily **newspapers**, the *Fiji Times* (🌐www.fijitimes.com), owned by Rupert Murdoch's News Corporation, is the most respected and dominant, with the broadest international coverage. Its closest rival is the locally owned *Fiji Sun* (🌐www.sun.com.fj), a slightly more tabloid style publication, while the government-owned and somewhat biased *Fiji Daily Post* (🌐www.fijidailypost.com) is not greatly read. Two foreign weekly newspapers, *The New Zealander* and the *International Express*, can be bought from the larger Morris Hedstrom supermarkets in Nadi and Suva, and at Yees Supermarket and Newsagency, both at Port Denarau in Nadi for F$7.50. Otherwise, international embassies in Suva usually stock foreign newspapers for browsing.

Local **magazines** have improved significantly in recent years, with several excellent publications including *Fiji Living* (lifestyle), *Marama* (women) and the long-standing *Islands Business* (current affairs), as well as several rugby-orientated titles. Local magazines can be purchased from Post Shops, part of the post office, at Morris Hedstrom supermarkets and most bookstores. Foreign magazines, mostly women's weekly's but also *Time* and *The Economist* are imported from Australia and New Zealand and sold at a slightly inflated price and usually a week old.

Radio

The part-government-owned Fiji Broadcasting Corporation operates six **radio stations**, two each in Fijian, Fiji-Hindi and English; of these, one focuses on news and community issues, the other music and chat. For Fijian music try Bula FM (FM102.4 in Nadi) – all stations have varying FM frequencies depending on location. The independent Communications Fiji Limited broadcast five mostly music stations, two Fiji-Hindi, one Fijian and the popular English music and gossip stations – FM96 and Legend FM (FM106.8).

Television

After broadcasting Fiji's only free-to-air **television** channel, Fiji One, since 1987, Fiji TV's monopoly was broken in 2007. However, the hotly awaited second channel has yet to materialize. Fiji One's programming is almost exclusively in English with only a few locally produced shows, the rest being sourced from the US, UK and New Zealand. The informative one-hour *Fiji News* is shown daily at 6pm with mostly local content and a smattering of international headlines. Other programmes to watch out for are *The Pacific Channel*, shown on Fiji One daily from 2pm–3pm; *Noda Guana*, an informative cultural show broadcast on Monday evening at 7pm; *Close Up*, a weekly current affairs chat show shown on Sunday at 6.30pm; and the community-orientated *Dateline* or *Pacific Way* every Sunday at 4pm. At midnight, programming switches to Australia Network which broadcasts until 2pm. Sky Pacific, also owned by Fiji TV, offers twelve channels, two of which are Indian, showing Bollywood movies, one Chinese, the others include BBC and CNN.

Festivals

Ethnic Fijians tend to express their culture in day-to-day life rather than through specific festivals. By contrast, Fiji-Indians celebrate most events with gusto, whether it's a local wedding, religious festival or one of the many fascinating fire walking ceremonies held around the country. The country enjoys twelve public holidays; the most likely of these to feature traditional dance and other public displays are Ratu Lala Sukuna Day on May 30 and Fiji Day on October 10.

The main **towns** of Nadi, Lautoka and Suva each have a commercially driven week-long **festival** (see calendar below) with fairground rides, food stalls, parades, beauty-queen crowning and an alternative Priscilla night when gays and transvestites take centre stage. The town festivals held in Levuka and Savusavu are more culturally inclined. **Indian festivals** are commonly celebrated in public and with great fanfare, with Diwali the biggest and loudest for Hindus and Eid a serious affair for Muslims – towns with a large Fiji-Indian population are naturally the best, especially Lautoka and Tavua on Vanua Levu or Labasa on Vanua Levu. There are over forty Indian **firewalking** ceremonies held around the country between April and September. These are fascinating and very spiritual experiences – ask around at local temples to find out where one is being held. The two largest are listed below:

January

Coconut Tree Climbing Competition (1 Jan). Held at Denarau Island, this zany event tests the skills of Fiji's most daring personalities.

Thaipusam Festival (end Jan with main day being the last Sat). This ten-day Hindu festival at the Nadi temple (see p.65) has devotees piercing their bodies and dragging chariots using meat hooks.

March

Holi (one day after full moon usually early March). Hindu festival celebrated with throwing of coloured turmeric powder, feasting and the singing of religious poems.

April

Indian fire walking (First Sun after the full moon). Held at the Malolo Temple south of Nadi, devotees walk across a pit of burning wood embers.

May

Rotuma Day (13 May). Dance and feasting amongst Rotumans throughout Fiji to celebrate Rotuma's cession to Fiji and Britain.

Ratu Sir Lala Sukuna Day (30 May). Public holiday remembering statesman Ratu Sukuna (see p.266), sometimes with organized dance and fundraising events in urban centres, but generally a family holiday with *lovo*.

July

Bula Festival Mid to end of the month (☎670 0133). Nadi's yearly week-long celebrations at Koroivoli Park.
Fiji Swims (🌐www.fijiswims.com). Three ocean races from 1km to 18km centred around Beachcomber Island in the Mamanucas.

August

Indian firewalking (first Sun after the full moon). Largest of the Fiji-Indian firewalking event is held at the Mahadavi Temple on Howell Rd, Suva (see p.163).
Hibiscus Festival mid Aug, coinciding with school holidays (☎331 1168). Suva's yearly week-long celebrations at Albert Park.

September

Fiji Regatta Week Musket Cove Marina, Mamanucas (🌐www.musketcovefiji.com). Pirate trips, races (in small hobie-cat boats) and general yachty hoo-ra.
Sugar Festival Usually the first week of Sept (☎666 8010). Lautoka's yearly week-long celebrations at Churchill Park.

October

Fiji Day (10 Oct). Public holiday celebrating the day when Fiji was both ceded to Britain (1874) and given independence (1970). Dance performances are sometimes held in Albert Park, Suva.
Back to Levuka Week (10 Oct). Traditional re-enactments of cession, art displays and agricultural shows.
Diwali (late Oct to mid Nov – depending on lunar calendar). Fireworks and lights are the star attractions of this Hindu celebration.
Rising of the Balolo (mid Oct to mid Nov depending on moon). Naturally occurring event at a dozen or more coral reefs around the islands – the tail of a mysterious worm rises to the surface, is collected and eaten as a delicacy (see p.279).

November

Savusavu Music Festival (🌐www.fiji-savusavu .com). Local musicians and dance troupes perform throughout this week-long event.

December

Fara (1 Dec to mid Jan). Door-to-door dancing and merry-making on the outer island of Rotuma, known as *fara* (see p.253). Sometimes indulged in by Rotumans living in urban centres, particularly Suva.

Sports and outdoor activities

With endless beaches, teeming coral reefs and water temperatures averaging 27°C, Fiji is renowned for its scuba diving, snorkelling, surfing and other water sports. But adventure also awaits in the sultry tropical rainforests with fabulous hiking, river rafting and ecotours on offer.

Scuba diving and snorkelling

Fiji offers superb **scuba diving** and **snorkelling** with exceptionally colourful and easily accessible reefs as well as plenty of diverse fish species including sharks. Diving is excellent year-round with visibility usually at least 30m – the very best months are October and November, after the trade winds have subsided and before the tropical wet season begins.

Almost all resorts offer scuba diving with dive sites normally between five and forty minutes by boat. Many resorts offer **dive training**, with PADI Open Water courses the most popular and costing F$550–800 for

Sea kayaking

Every resort seems to have **sea kayaks** for guest use, usually as a complimentary activity; note that it's always wise to wear a life jacket and inform somebody of your intended journey in case you get caught in a dangerous current or a squally storm suddenly descends. Two companies (see below) offer week-long kayaking expeditions between May and October, snorkelling in the lagoons and camping on beaches or overnighting in remote fishing villages. Another good option is the half-day trip along the Lavena Coastline (see p.241) within the Bouma National Heritage Park on Taveuni.

Kayaking operators

Tamarillo Tropical Expeditions (☎360 3043, ⓦwww.tamarillo.co.nz/fiji). New-Zealand-based company exploring the rugged and remote coastline of Kadavu with support boats. Seven-day packages from NZ$2,150 per person.
South Sea Ventures (☎02/8901 3287 in Australia, ⓦwww.southernseaventures.com). Australian-run group trips exploring the northern Yasawa Islands in either single or twin sea kayaks. Seven-day packages from A$1,925.

Fishing

Fishing is a way of life for many Fijians, using nets, spear guns and fish traps in the shallow lagoons and simple hand lines along the river banks as a matter of subsistence. Commercial fishermen with small wooden fishing boats head to the deeper waters for tuna, mahi-mahi and wahoo. For tourists, **game fishing** is an exciting prospect, particularly in pursuit of **billfish** in the deep waters off Taveuni and Savusavu in the north and in the rich fast-flowing currents between Beqa and Kadavu in the south. Fishing licences aren't required but you'll need to find a reputable fishing charter with a proper game-fishing boat, good equipment and most importantly, a knowledgeable skipper – charters are usually available at Savusavu on Vanua Levu and at Pacific Harbour on Viti Levu, with more casual game fishing from Port Denarau in Nadi; otherwise, recommended resorts include *Matangi Island* (see p.238) off Taveuni; *Makaira by the Sea* (see p.237) on Taveuni; or *Matava* (see p.187) on Kadavu; rates start from F$700 for half a day.

Casting into the fringing reefs from small boats is usually excellent with snapper, barracuda and trevally the prize catches; fly fishing in the shallow lagoons is good in places although there are few opportunities to land the highly prized bone fish, prolific in other parts of the South Pacific, and you'll definitely need to bring your own gear. Fishing in the **rivers** is seldom practised as a sport although a couple of lodges along the south coast of Vanua Levu are idyllically set up for this (see p.231).

Hiking

Compared to its South Pacific neighbours, Fiji stands out as a great **hiking** destination. There are fine tropical rainforest walks in the Namosi Highlands, mountain treks on Viti Levu and Kadavu and stunning coastal walks on Waya island. Of the national parks, Koroyanitu and Bouma on Taveuni are the best for hiking. For less avid walkers, there are usually short trails leading to hilltop lookouts overlooking islands and lagoons. Resorts offering excellent local hikes include *Walu Beach Resort* (see p.98), *Matamanoa Island Resort* (see p.101), *Botaira Beach Resort* (see p.109), *Naveria Heights* (see p.226) and *Matangi Island Resort* (see p.238).

Horse riding hasn't really developed as an attraction, although the potential is excellent – you can rent saddled horses along the wild beachfront at the Sigatoka Sand Dunes (see p.124).

River rafting and adrenaline sports

River rafting is a fun way of exploring the remote regions of Viti Levu, with the Grade III rapids of the upper Navua River on the south coast of Viti Levu the only place with established operators (see p.133).

For adrenaline seekers there's **skydiving** available from Nadi Airport (see p.60), **jet boating** up the mangroves from Port Denarau (see p.72), **canopy zip lines** in the rainforest at Pacific Harbour (see p.134) and **mountain biking** at Savusavu (see p.229).

Golf

Fiji is beginning to establish itself as a major **golfing** holiday destination, thanks to its great year-round weather and affordable

National Parks and Heritage Parks

Fiji's only official national park, protected by law, is the **Sigatoka Sand Dunes National Park** (see p.124) on the southwest coast of Viti Levu. The fragile sand-dune ecosystem has an informative visitor centre and two managed trails for exploring.

Of more appeal to ecotravellers are two community-based projects assisted by the National Trust of Fiji and New Zealand Overseas Development Aid: The **Bouma National Heritage Park** (see p.240) encompassing almost half of Taveuni; and **Koroyanitu National Heritage Park** (see p.83) inland from Lautoka on Viti Levu. Both offer managed walking trails to waterfalls, village interaction and community-run accommodation.

Other projects managed by the **National Trust of Fiji** (☎330 1807) include Momi Guns (see p.77), south of Nadi, Levuka Town (see p.194) on Ovalau, Muanakaka Reserve in Kadavu (see p.185), Yadua Taba Island (see p.224) and Waisali Reserve in Vanua Levu (see p.230).

---

green fees. There are presently championship golf courses at Denarau (see p.66) and Pacific Harbour (see p.131) with two major international golf developments outside of Nadi in the making: Momi and Natadola.

Ecotours and village visits

Fiji is well positioned as an ecotour destination, with **village-based cultural visits** and **marine biology** the main focus. There are no specific ecotour holiday packages but most resorts, especially those in the outer islands, can organize village visits, plantation tours and guided hikes.

Visiting a village is more often than not an overwhelmingly positive experience. Apart from relishing the tourist-orientated *yaqona* ceremony, travellers can usually visit people's homes, sample foods, learn to weave, go fishing and generally immerse themselves in daily Fijian life. Several villages have set up **community resorts**, usually located at the parameters of the village so as not to disrupt village affairs. For more background on village visits see our colour section. For a more thorough introduction into Fijian life, consider joining one of the internationally organized **gap-year education programmes** where you assist in teaching at a remote village school and live with the people (see below for details).

Boasting numerous diverse and unchartered coral reefs, Fiji is also the focus for several global institutions conducting scientific **marine research**. It's possible to join one of these groups on a working holiday, volunteering in research and gathering information, often on remote islands.

Organizations for working holidays

American Institute for Foreign Study US ☎1-866/906-2437, ⊛www.aifs.com. Language study and cultural immersion combined with Australian programmes.

Earthwatch Institute US ☎1-800/776-0188 or 978-461/0081, UK ☎01865/318 838, Australia ☎03/9682 6828, ⊛www.earthwatch.org. Scientific expedition project that spans over fifty countries with environmental and archeological ventures worldwide.

Frontier ☎020/7613 2422 (UK), ⊛www.frontier .ac.uk. English teaching project based on the outer island of Gau. £895 for four weeks includes a weekend of TEFL training.

Gap Year Diver ☎0845/257 2392 (UK), ⊛www .gapyeardiver.com. Four-to ten-week marine conservation projects off the south coast of Vanua Levu costing from £1,500 to £2,300.

Greenforce ☎020/7470 8888 (UK), ⊛www .greenforce.org. Six- to ten-week programme assisting in the survey of coral reefs on behalf of the World Conservation Society. From £2000 per person. No dive experience required.

Madventurer ☎0845/121 1996 (UK), ⊛www.madventurer.com. A range of opportunities based around Lautoka on Viti Levu from teaching sport to working in healthcare. Two weeks from £800.

Peace Corps ☎800 424 8580 (US), ⊛www .peacecorps.gov. Over fifty volunteers work all around Fiji assisting in a wide scope of community projects from environmental and health awareness to teaching information technology.

Culture and etiquette

Any discussion of Fijian culture must take account of the split between ethnic Fijians and their Fiji-Indian adopted neighbours. Fiji-born Indians are forbidden by law to call themselves Fijians with an almost apartheid-styled constitution being the country's greatest barrier to building a unified nation. On the street level, the two races get on well enough, but with vastly different cultures and aspirations they tend not to mix socially. Considering them as a whole is thus difficult, although you'll find Fiji's peoples are generally extremely hospitable, generous and forgiving; they tend also to be deeply religious with church, temple and mosque well attended.

In **rural areas**, both amongst Fijians and Fiji-Indians, men and women have distinct roles and seldom mix in social settings. Macho behaviour is common and women travellers may find they experience unwanted attention. Amongst indigenous Fijians a strong heritage of tribal customs influence day-to-day life. For more information on these traditional customs see p.274.

Smoking is socially acceptable in public places although it has been officially banned on public transport. Some restaurants and a few bars have self-imposed smoke-free zones. **Public toilets** are few and far between, although there's usually one beside the town bus stand – they tend to be quite filthy though so it's wise to seek out the nearest hotel instead. Littering, and rather off-puttingly, spitting, is common practice both in towns and in the villages where it's wise to wear shoes.

As for **dress codes**, local women dress quite modestly. Shorts, sleeveless tops and short skirts are quite acceptable in town centres although they may draw undesired attention. Bikinis are fine at the pool or the beach, but not out and about. Bathing topless in public is strictly forbidden. Most restaurants and resorts are pretty casual but upscale eateries generally expect you to dress for dinner by donning trousers and a collared shirt for men; trousers, skirts or dresses for women. The most conservative environment for dress is in the villages where it's expected for women to cover shoulders and for both men and women to wear *sulus* or at least shorts covering the knees – sunglasses and hats should also be removed.

Fijians tend to go to bed early and wake up early so don't expect much to be going on after 9pm. When meeting, locals are eager to shake hands and ask you where you're from, and usually exchange pleasantries when passing – a hearty "**bula**" being almost mandatory in rural areas, although in town centres this greeting is usually a ruse for selling you something. Fijians do not, as a rule, shout at each other or demand service. Visitors often become frustrated at the often glacial speed at which things move and the detached attitude when a problem arises – **sega na leqa** rules, a mix of *mañana* of Latin America and the "no worries mate" of Australia. There is little you can do about it and the more anxious or frustrated you get the less sympathy or assistance you'll be shown. Slow down, relax and take it Fiji time.

Shopping

Fiji is not a great shopping destination, hindered by its isolation and heavy import duties and starved by lack of individual creativity in design and fashion. With a dearth of boutique shops and art galleries, your best bet is to head to the urban municipal markets which ooze character, overflow with local produce and have the most authentic collection of handicrafts.

Both Nadi and Suva have special **handicraft markets**, although both are burdened with pushy sales people – try to pick out the artisan traders who are often busy weaving, polishing or sewing their wares. Woodcarving items include beautifully polished and patterned rimmed *tanoa* bowls, war clubs, cannibal forks and totemic items such as turtles and face masks. Bags woven from *pandanus* leaves and styled with *tapa* cloth are often eye-catching, as is jewellery made from coconut shells, and hand-woven mats costing from F$60 and up, depending on the fineness of the weave, make practical souvenirs.

The best places to buy **local crafts** direct from the artisans are from the Flea Market in Suva (see p.158) or, if your timing is right, at one of the craft fairs in Nadi organized by the Western Arts & Craft Society every few months – some of these artisans set up stall on Saturdays at the Namaka Market in suburban Nadi. Otherwise, Jacks Handicraft or Nadi's Handicraft both have quality crafts, a large variety of scented **coconut** oils, creams and soaps, locally harvested **black pearls** (see p.238), colourful ranges of clothing and other knick-knaks often sourced from overseas – they also provide a shipping service.

The shopping experience can be hampered by shopkeepers standing in their doorways pestering tourists to come in and look, particularly in Nadi. You'll need to **haggle** at all small Indian-owned shops – even at the big chain stores if you ask politely for a discount you'll probably get something off. Bargaining, though, is not a Fijian custom so if buying from an indigenous Fijian the asking price will invariably be realistic. You should avoid buying **shells**, especially turtle and triton shells which are both banned as export items, as is the *tabua* **whale's tooth**.

Shops are few and far between on the outer islands so it's wise to **stock up** on provisions before you depart Viti Levu. In an emergency, most outer-island resorts have small shops selling sun cream and other essentials at greatly inflated prices.

Travelling with children

Often viewed as a romantic escape for couples, Fiji is in fact a popular family holiday destination, especially amongst Australians and New Zealanders. With enormous empathy and affection for children, Fijians make fabulous hosts and those with infants will find the locals eager to entertain your children at every opportunity. Most resorts have complimentary kids' clubs and plenty of family-orientated water activities.

Soft sand and gentle waves are a great formula for family holidays with the beach resorts along the **Mamanucas** and **Yasawa Islands** a particular favourite, notably *Plantation Island*, *Amunuca Island* and *Treasure Island* in the Mamanucas; and the more budget-orientated *Octopus*, *Korovou* and *Oarsman's Bay* in the Yasawas. The large resorts along the **Coral Coast** are also popular, with several good family attractions including the Kula Eco Park as well as adventure activities around **Pacific Harbour** for older children.

Most resorts allow kids under a certain age to **stay for free** if sharing a room with their parents – some even offer free meals as incentives. The exception are the upmarket boutique resorts which often have a strict **no-child policy** to ensure a romantic atmosphere for their guests; the exception is *Cousteau Resort* (see p.226) on Vanua Levu which is one of the very best luxury resorts for families; others may allow kids only during dedicated holiday periods. Other outer-island resorts which actively encourage families are *Naigani Island Resort* (see p.201) in the Lomaiviti group and *Papageno Resort* (see p.186) on Kadavu. For those on a budget,

many of the backpacker resorts have family rooms, especially in Nadi.

Rural **villages** are a fascinating environment for children of all ages and they'll most likely be enthusiastically welcomed by the village kids, encouraged to play and generally well looked after.

Minor **health issues** are the greatest concern for parents travelling with young children, especially from the adverse effects of high humidity, intense sun and mosquito bites. Medicated baby powder for the prevention of rashes and sores is an essential item to carry. In the main towns, high-quality baby formula, nappies and children's medications imported from Australia are readily available. **Breast feeding** in public is fairly commonplace, especially so in rural environments although baby-changing facilities are rarely offered.

If travelling by car or taxi, seat belts, let alone dedicated infant **car seats**, are difficult to find, although the major car rental companies do provide them. **Prams** in general are not that practical to travel with and at many of the resorts, pathways are sandy – even around towns, pavements are not pram friendly.

Travel essentials

Costs

For travellers most items will appear very affordable, especially public transport, dining out and buying local food. If frugal, you can survive on F$50 (£17/€22/US$34) per day, staying in dorms, preparing your own meals and travelling on public transport. Stay in private rooms and eat out regularly and you'll need around F$100 (£33/€44/US$65), although extras such as alcohol, car rental scuba diving and sightseeing tours will all add to your costs. Travelling around the two largest islands of Viti Levu and Vanua Levu offer the best value with prices on the outer islands usually inflated by at least 20 percent. Note that **tipping** is not expected and in traditional Fijian society causes embarrassment.

Hostel **accommodation** will set you back around F$20 a person for a dorm bed, or F$65 per person including meals at the popular Yasawa backpacker resorts. Town hotel rooms start from around F$60, with double or twin rooms often the same price as a single. A moderate beach resort starts from F$180 for a room, the more popular holiday resorts cost from F$300 and a luxury boutique resort is anything from F$500 to F$2000 per night.

Food on the whole is reasonably cheap, with local produce offering by far the best value, especially when purchased from the roadside or at municipal markets. Supermarket shelves tend to be dominated by more expensive imported food items, mostly canned and restricted in variety. Dining out is affordable with cheap restaurant counter food costing from F$4 a serve, main dishes ordered from a menu from F$8 to F$20 – resort restaurants are invariably more expensive.

Travelling around Viti Levu by public transport is especially cheap with the five-hour journey from Nadi to Suva costing just F$10 and local journeys starting from 65 cents. Visiting the offshore or outer islands is going to eat up a larger chunk of your budget. For example, the hop-on, hop-off boat pass along the Yasawa islands costs F$269 for seven days; and a domestic flight to Taveuni can cost up to F$200 one way, although discounted fares are usually available via airline websites and can almost match passenger ferry rates which cost F$75 between Suva and Taveuni.

Every traveller over twelve years of age departing Fiji must pay a **departure tax** of F$30, although this should be pre-paid in the cost of your airline ticket.

Crime and personal safety

As in any society **crime** exists in Fiji but it's certainly not rife and not nearly as common as in most European or North American cities. **Petty theft** stems from a cultural trait where the individual owns few possessions, shares everything freely and is bound by the beliefs of *kerekere*, a form of asking for something with the owner being obliged to give. It's especially common among hotel workers and you may find clothes or small change frequently going mssing from bures and communal resort areas. Bring in clothes and shoes at night and certainly don't leave money or jewellery lying about as an invitation.

With machismo entrenched in Fijian culture, **sexual harassment** can be an issue for female travellers – a firm "not interested" should ward off any unwanted attention while all the usual precautions apply, such as avoiding walking alone at night. If in need of assistance contact the Fiji Women's Crisis Centre (🌐www.fijiwomen.com) in either Nadi (☎670 7558), Ba (☎667 0466), Suva (☎331 3300) or Labasa (☎881 4609). Domestic violence or **"wife bashing"**, as it's rather crudely known in Fiji, is also disturbingly prevalent, and a bruised eye is seldom concealed or reported to the authorities At the same time Fijians are a respectful society and treat each other and especially visitors with kindness.

Emergencies

☎911 is the free **emergency** telephone number to summon the police, ambulance or fire service.

Although commonly smoked by young urban Fijians, **marijuana** possession is strictly illegal and is strongly discouraged in more traditional rural areas where it is perceived as a dangerous evil – if a village youth is caught smoking more than once, public floggings may result; the official penalty for marijuana possession is three months in jail, so consider wisely before indulging.

The **Fijian police** are for the most part helpful, with police stations in all towns and major settlements. Larger towns have additional posts in busy areas. See the "Listings" section in each chapter for local contacts.

Electricity

Fiji's electrical current is 220–240 volts, (50Hz) with a **three-pin plug** common with Australia and New Zealand. Fluctuation in current and surges are common, especially in the outer islands where electricity is run by diesel generator, so it's advisable to have a **surge protector** if using electrical equipment. In many resorts, 110 volt outlets for shavers and hairdryers are provided.

Entry requirements

All visitors to Fiji must hold a valid passport for at least six months beyond the intended period of stay and proof of onward travel to another country. Adhering to the above, a four-month **tourist visa** is issued on arrival to most nationals including those of Australia, New Zealand, South Africa, the US, Canada and EU member states. For a complete list, check the Fiji Visitor Bureau website (®www.bulafiji.com). A maximum **two-month visa extension** may be made on application with the Immigration Department at Nadi Airport or Suva, but there are no provisions for stays beyond six months for any overseas nationals unless obtaining resident status or work/student visas. All visitors are required to fill out standard immigration cards upon arrival. The card must be surrendered to Fiji immigration authorities upon departure.

Fijian embassies abroad

Australia High Commission of the Republic of Fiji, 19 Beale Crescent Deakin ACT 2600 ☎06/260 5115.

Belgium Embassy of the Republic of Fiji, 92-94 Square Plasky, 1030 Bruxelles ☎32-2/736-9050.

New Zealand High Commission of the Republic of Fiji, 31 Pipitea St, Thorndon, Wellington ☎04/473 5401.

UK and Ireland High Commission of Fiji, 34 Hyde Park Gate, London SW7 5DN ☎020 7584 3661.

US Embassy of the Republic of Fiji, 2000 M St NW, Suite 710, Washington DC 20036 ☎202/466-8320.

Embassies and consulates in Fiji

Australia High Commission, 37 Princes Rd, Tamavua, Suva ☎338 2211.

European Union Commission, 4th floor, Development Bank Centre, Suva ☎331 3633.

Federated States of Micronesia 37 Loftus Rd, Suva ☎330 4566.

Kiribati 38 McGregor Rd, Suva ☎330 2512.

New Zealand Pratt St, Suva ☎331 1422.

Tuvalu 16 Gorrie St, Suva ☎330 1355.

UK High Commission, 47 Gladstone Rd, Suva ☎322 9100.

US Embassy 31 Loftus St, Suva ☎331 4466. Moving in late 2009 to 158 Princes Rd, Tamavua ☎337 1110.

Gay and lesbian travellers

Gay and lesbian travellers shouldn't feel any sort of discrimination in Fiji, especially within resort environments where many outwardly homosexual staff work. However, gay behaviour is far more evident than lesbian and open affection between women may generate curiosity. In urban areas, homosexuality and cross-dressing appear to be quite open although contradictory to this, any homosexual engagement is illegal, punishable with prison sentences of up to two years. It's also frowned upon in the conservative Christian-dominated village environment where discretion is advisable.

Health

Fiji presents few major health issues for visitors. The most common **problems** are sunburn and/or heat stroke caused by overexposure to the tropical sun; fungal ear infections from swimming, which are easily cured with ear drops; mosquito or sand fly **bites**; and on rare occasions, fish poisoning.

No **vaccinations** are required to enter Fiji unless you are coming from a yellow fever area, in which case you need to have an International Health Certificate indicating that you have been immunized against yellow fever sometime in the past ten years. Vaccination against Hepatitis A is often recommended by independent medical advisories although the last reported case in Fiji was in 1997. Isolated outbreaks of typhoid have occurred on Vanua Levu in recent years during the wet season.

Heat stroke

Heat stroke is a serious and sometimes fatal condition that can result from long periods of exposure to high temperatures and high humidity. The wisest approach is to always wear a high SPF **sunscreen** (over 35), even in cloudy weather, not forgetting your lips, ears, feet and back; wear a wide-brimmed hat and sunglasses; **drink plenty of water**, generally a litre every two hours, bearing in mind that room-temperature water is better for you in the tropics and that drinking alcohol is going to add to your dehydration; and **cover up** when out snorkelling by wearing a T-shirt to protect your back, still with sun cream on, and wear a long-sleeve shirt with a collar when out walking. Better still, stay in the shade.

Symptoms of heat stroke include nausea and general discomfort, fatigue, a high body temperature, severe headache, disorientation and/or little or no perspiration despite the heat. Eventually the sufferer can become delirious and fall into convulsions, and rapid medical treatment is essential. First aid is to seek shade, remove the victim's clothing, wrap them in a cool, wet sheet or towels and fan around them.

Drinking water

Although urban **tap water** is filtered, chlorinated and safe to drink, travellers with sensitive stomachs should consider boiling it first or buying bottled water, especially after heavy rains when tap water can appear murky. In rural Viti Levu and the outer islands water is mostly sourced from natural springs which may appear extremely pure but can cause upset stomachs – most travellers are encouraged to buy bottled water or drink rain water which is usually supplied to guests free of charge from large tanks and which is less likely to be contaminated. Drinking from a pristine stream whilst

Dengue fever

Although there is **no malaria** in Fiji, very occasionally **dengue fever** outbreaks occur, a similar but not nearly as threatening disease – the last widespread outbreak was in 1998. Outbreaks are usually restricted to urban areas after prolonged heavy rains and are acted upon swiftly by the authorities with spraying to kill the dengue-spreading mosquitoes – it's only the black and white striped **day-biting mosquito** that causes dengue infection. If you become infected, tell-tale signs include **aching joints** accompanied by intense headaches, a sudden high fever, chills, nausea and sometimes a red rash which usually first appears on the lower limbs or chest. The symptoms will last from anywhere from five to fifteen days. Although the recommended cure is simple – stay in bed, drink plenty of water and wait it out – it's advisable to consult a doctor. In more severe cases, a doctor will administer intravenous fluids to prevent dehydration and acetaminophen to reduce fever. **Avoid aspirin** as this can often cause complications. Whilst the fever is rarely life-threatening in fit adults, the elderly and children are prone to complications and death can result – if an outbreak is present, take extra precautions against being bitten by mosquitoes.

out walking in the forests might be tempting but it's not recommended as water-borne diseases such as bilharzia and leptospirosis can be present.

Bites and stings

Mosquitoes can easily spoil an otherwise perfect evening under the stars not just with their itching **bites** but also the high-pitched buzzing sound they make. They are most widespread during the **wet season** from December to April, although even during these times you may not be bothered by them. Most resorts spray gardens to keep mosquitoes at bay, but in less-developed parts of the islands they can be voracious, almost unbearable at dusk and dawn when it may be wise to stay indoors or sit by the sea, preferably facing a stiff wind. Most resorts have well-screened windows, but if these are not present, a **mosquito net** and/or mosquito repellent should be used. Mosquito nets are quite romantic to sleep under but do add to the stuffiness, especially in the humid nights of summer. The best type of **repellent** is the Good Knight electric mat heaters which cost F$4 from supermarkets, plus F$1.50 for a packet of ten mats, one mat being sufficient per night. You'll need constant electricity to use them and when this isn't available, you may have to resort to mosquito coils which can be slightly noxious on inhalation. **Roll-on mosquito repellent** works for both mosquitoes and sand flies on a temporary basis, and there are now brands that are more environmentally sensitive and safer on your skin – try Rid, an Australian product costing around F$10 a bottle and available from most pharmacies.

Sand flies can cause irritating rashes through their bites, usually spreading over a larger area than a mosquito bite, and are found not surprisingly along sandy beaches, appearing at dusk and dawn. **Sea lice** can also cause a small rash and appear on occasions in sandy-bottom shallow lagoons between December and April.

Ciguatera fish poisoning

Ciguatera fish poisoning is a fairly common ailment amongst rural Fijians and can be caught by **consuming reef fish** which have been feeding on toxic algae. Although seldom life threatening, the poisoning causes nausea, diarrhoea, vomiting and a numbness or tingling sensation often in the fingers and usually commences within 24hr of consumption. If you believe you have the symptoms of ciguatera, head straight to a doctor or local hospital where you can receive treatment via an injection. Although not confined to any particular fish, it is most common in older and larger reef fish, typically grouper, red snapper, Spanish mackerel and barracuda. Most villagers know which fish to avoid at certain times of the year.

Medical resources for travellers

US and Canada

CDC ☎1-877/394-8747, ⊛www.cdc.gov/travel. Official US government travel health site.
International Society for Travel Medicine ☎1-770/736-7060, ⊛www.istm.org. Has a full list of travel health clinics.
Canadian Society for International Health ⊛www.csih.org. Extensive list of travel health centres.

Australia, New Zealand and South Africa

Travellers' Medical and Vaccination Centre ⊛www.tmvc.com.au, ☎1300/658 844. Lists travel clinics in Australia, New Zealand and South Africa.

UK and Ireland

British Airways Travel Clinics ☎0845/600 2236, ⊛ww.britishairways.com/travel /healthclinintro/public/en_gb for nearest clinic.
Hospital for Tropical Diseases Travel Clinic ☎0845/155 5000 or ☎020/7387 4411, ⊛www .thehtd.org.
MASTA (Medical Advisory Service for Travellers Abroad) ⊛www.masta.org or ☎0870/606 2782 for the nearest clinic.
Travel Medicine Services ☎028/9031 5220.
Tropical Medical Bureau Republic of Ireland ☎1850/487 674, ⊛www.tmb.ie.

Insurance

You should always have **travel insurance** that covers you against theft, illness and injury. Most policies exclude so-called dangerous sports unless an additional premium is paid:

in Fiji this can mean snorkelling, surfing or scuba diving. If you need to make a claim, you should keep all receipts for medicines and treatment as well as transport and any additional accommodation bills whilst recuperating. In the event of having anything stolen, you must obtain an official statement from the police confirming this.

Internet

Almost all large hotels and boutique resorts offer **Internet access** – a few of the larger hotels around Viti Levu also have wireless (Wi-Fi) access or broadband sockets in rooms. On the outer islands, Internet access is not always available, especially at the budget resorts in the Yasawa Islands; when it is available it's generally slower and more expensive than elsewhere. Prices are typically at least F$25 an hour at the luxury hotels and outer-island resorts, F$4 to F$8 an hour at the backpacker hostels and around F$2 to F$4 an hour at private Internet cafés which can be found in most town centres, especially in Nadi, Lautoka and Suva where competition is fierce and prices sometimes fall below F$2 an hour, usually charged by the minute. Listings for each region in the Guide contain addresses for local internet access points.

Laundry

Most hotels and resorts provide a **laundry service** for guests, although self-service machines are seldom available. Independent laundries, which tend to be better value, can be found in the larger towns, or at several of the larger marinas – listings for laundries can be found in each chapter.

Living in Fiji

Due to high levels of unemployment, it is difficult to obtain a **work permit** for Fiji. However, there are a few options if you want to really sink your teeth into the culture and stay a while. There is, for example, a shortage of teachers and nurses and you could contact schools or hospitals directly for possible work opportunities. Many expatriates work in the hospitality industry and if you have relevant work experience or **specific skills** such as languages or scuba-diving qualifications, you may find resort work. A prospective employer in any field must demonstrate that they have conducted an exhaustive but unsuccessful search for a qualified Fijian candidate and must post a bond to cover the costs of shipping you home if you become incapacitated. Few are willing to go through this process unless your skills are particularly desirable.

International students may apply for enrollment at the University of the South Pacific (ⓦwww.usp.com.fj, ☏323 1000) on either a cross-credit semester or a full-time course providing you have attained a High School certificate pass or similar from your home country. There's no age limit for enrollment and a student visa is granted to all successful applicants providing a clean police record and clear medical including a negative HIV test.

Alternatively, a variety of marine conservation organizations offer unpaid or even you-pay **internships** for periods lasting a week to several months; see p.41. Otherwise, if you have a large chunk of money you're willing to invest and you can find a local partner who must hold at least a fifty-percent shareholding, you can set up or purchase a **business**. Specific questions should be addressed to the Fiji islands Trade and Investment Board (☎331 5988; ⓦwww.ftib.org.fj) with headquarters at Civic Tower on Victoria Parade in Suva or on Naviti Street in Lautoka.

Mail

Post Fiji operates all **post offices** (Mon–Fri 8am–4pm, Sat 8am–noon) and offers a stamps, telegraphic and fax services, with larger branches selling stationery and post cards. All post offices have telephones and sell phone cards for calling internationally and locally.

Post can be slow, especially **posting items to Fiji** and it's not uncommon for letters to take three weeks from North America or Europe, with delivery to the outer islands often taking an additional week. **Posting items from Fiji** is cheap and somewhat quicker, with letters to Europe commonly taking less than ten days. Postcards to all destinations cost 40¢, airmail letters up to 15g cost 90¢ to North America and F$1.20 to Europe – all letters and postcards should be labelled with an airmail sticker otherwise they may go by boat, taking months to arrive. UPS, DHL and Federal Express all have offices in Suva and Nadi, although Post Fiji's in-house courier service, EMS, is considerably cheaper.

Stamps are available from most hotels and gift shops, as well as some bookstores. Public mail boxes are very rare, and you should always find the nearest post office to mail important items – most resorts, especially those on the outer islands, will post letters for you. Postage within Fiji costs a standard 20¢ for up to 50g. Local courier companies offer a next-day delivery service around Viti Levu from $2.50.

Poste restante is available at all post offices. Letters should be marked "General Delivery, Poste Restante" followed by the location of the post office and your name. Letters will be held for two months – for post sent to Nadi, be sure to specify either Nadi Town or Nadi Airport. To receive a parcel in Fiji, you must clear it through the post office's customs counter (Mon–Fri 10am–11am & 2pm–3pm), and pay a service charge of F$2.20 plus any customs or import duty.

Maps

Navigating between towns is very straightforward with just one or two main roads on each island. General-purpose town or island **maps** are hard to come by, the most useful being the free Jason's Travel Media map available from most hotel tour desks. A slightly more detailed folded sheet map is published by Hema and available in bookstores and large chain stores around Nadi and Suva for F$12.95. For detailed 1:50,000 **topographical maps** of the individual islands and 1:15,000 street maps, contact the Lands and Survey Department (☎321 1395, ⓦwww.lands.gov.fj; F$7.88 each; you can buy either at the Map Shop on the ground floor and at the back of Government Buildings in Suva or from the Government Bookshop on Rodwell Road also in Suva.

Money

Fiji's currency is the **Fiji dollar** (F$) divided into 100 cents. Notes come in F$2, F$5, F$10, F$20, F$50 and F$100 denominations,

Addresses

Fijian **addresses** are something of an enigma. There is no door-to-door postal service so anybody wanting to receive mail uses a PO Box number; consequently few people know their residential address or display a house number. In towns, the majority of shops and businesses don't have a shop number, although street addresses are mostly signposted. On Viti Levu, the main road around the island – called the Queens Road along the south coast and the Kings Road along the north coast – passes through most towns where it more commonly reverts to "Main Street" or "High Street". On outer islands, addresses are a complete unknown except identifying a village or settlement. Directions are equally vague and you shouldn't necessarily take someone's earnest advice as fact.

the latter hard to trade with, especially at small shops. All notes and coins proudly feature Queen Elizabeth II along with other traditional and iconic symbols. Any foreign currency should be exchanged at one of the five bank chains including ANZ and Westpac or with one of the many currency exchange outlets found in the main towns and at Nadi Airport.

Travellers' cheques tend only to be accepted by hotels or cashed at banks, but **credit cards** are widely accepted, although only Visa and MasterCard, and very occasionally AMEX; all usually incur a service charge of around 4 percent. If visiting the Yasawa Islands, bear in mind some resorts are cash-only environments whereas others insist everything is payable by credit card at the end of your stay; it's wise to check with the resort beforehand.

ATM machines are available in all towns on Viti Levu except Tavua and Korovou, in Levuka on Ovalau, at Savusavu and Labasa on Vanua Levu and at Naqara on Taveuni, as well as at Nadi Airport, the Nadi branch of *McDonald's*, the shopping mall in Port Denarau and several of the large hotel chains in Nadi and along the Coral Coast. If you plan on using your debit card or credit card at an ATM, make sure you have a personal identification number (PIN) that's designated to work overseas.

Having **money wired** from home is never convenient or cheap and should only be considered as a last resort. The post office acts as general agents for Western Union (Ⓦwww.westernunion.com) which has branches at Nadi Airport, Nadi Town, Lautoka and Suva; MoneyGram (Ⓦwww.moneygram.com) operate via Westpac Bank and some Morris Hedstrom supermarkets. Direct bank transfers are also possible but you'll need the address and swift code of the bank branch where you want to pick up the money and the address and swift code of the bank's Suva head office which will act as the clearing house;

Public holidays

The following are **public holidays** in Fiji, when government offices, banks, schools and most shops are closed. Note some public holiday dates vary from year to year – see Ⓦwww.fiji.gov.fj for official dates.

New Year's Day January 1.
National Youth & Commonwealth Day March 10.
Prophet Mohammed's Birthday March 17.
Good Friday
Easter Saturday
Easter Monday
Ratu Sir Lala Sukuna Day May 30.
Queen's Birthday Third Monday in June.
Fiji Day October 10.
Diwali Late October/early November.
Christmas December 25.
Boxing Day December 26.

money wired this way usually takes two working days to arrive and costs around £25/US$40 per transaction.

Opening hours

Business hours at government and private offices are Mon–Fri 8am–5pm with offices generally closed for at least an hour for lunch, sometimes two. Regular **banking hours** are Mon–Fri 9am–4pm, although banks have slightly varying times on Mondays and Fridays; specific bank details are listed throughout the Guide. Most high street shops are open Mon–Sat 8.30am–5pm, although some, particularly the larger hardware shops, close on Saturday at noon; some **supermarkets** and local grocery shops open as early as 7am and don't close until 8pm. Most **restaurants** are open seven days a week, the most likely time of closure being Sunday lunch and for a couple of hours from 3pm to 5pm.

Phones

Telephone and email costs in Fiji have reduced significantly since deregulation of the communication industry in 2007. There still remains a monopolistic player in the landline communication industry, Telecom Fiji, but currently there are three **mobile** phone companies: Vodafone and Inkk which operate using the same network and the independently transmitted Digicel.

Mobile/cell phones

Before travelling, contact your mobile network provider to ensure you can use your phone in Fiji. Alternatively you can **rent a mobile phone** from Rentafone (℡672 6226, ⓌYwww .vodafonerental.com.fj; daily 5am–10.30pm) based at Nadi Airport in the arrivals concourse. Costs are F$5.99 per day for the phone, F$1.99 per day for the SIM card and 52¢ per minute local call charges which are automatically billed to your credit card on a weekly basis. For stays of more than a few days, it will almost certainly work out cheaper **buying a SIM card** for your phone along with pre-paid calling time, available from many retail outlets around the islands; even if you don't have a mobile you can pick up a simple model with SIM card in Nadi for under F$100. Mobile phone **coverage** around the main islands of Viti Levu and Vanua Levu is poor once outside the main urban areas and certainly in the highlands – in the Mamanucas and Yasawa Islands you will probably have to climb a hill to get the faintest of signals.

Public phones and phone cards

Public phones remain a good option for calling, with over 1500 distinctly styled *drua* phone booths around the country operated by **TeleCard**. Cards, available in F$3, F$5, F$10 and F$20 denominations, can be purchased from all post offices, from many retail outlets and can be used from private

Calling home from Fiji

Note that the initial zero is omitted from the area code when dialling the UK, Ireland, Australia and New Zealand from abroad.
Australia 00 + 61 + city code.
Republic of Ireland 00 + 353 + city code.
New Zealand 00 + 64 + city code.
South Africa 00 + 27 + city code.
UK 00 + 44 + city code.
US & Canada 00 + 1 + area code.

landlines, although they are often barred from being used in hotel rooms.

Local calls have become substantially cheaper in recent years, with regional calls costing 12¢ per call and national calls costing 20¢ per minute. If calling overseas, landline costs remain prohibitive with most destinations costing 75¢ per minute, often with a hefty surcharge billed when calling from hotel rooms. Consider buying a **telephone charge card** from your phone company back home. Using a PIN number, you can make calls from most hotel, public and private phones that will be charged to your account, but check to see Fiji is covered and bear in mind that rates aren't necessarily cheaper than calling from a public phone.

Perhaps the cheapest option, though, is taking advantage of **VoIP** (Voice over Internet Protocol) calls (for example ⓌYwww.skype .com) from an Internet café.

Radio phones

Radio telephone, where callers take turns to speak, remains the only source of contact on many outer islands including parts of the Yasawa Islands. Many resorts in outer-island locations have installed private satellite phones or have dedicated Telecom signalling.

Photography

Fiji is a photographer's paradise with wonderful scenery and vivid colours. If in a village, it's polite to ask before taking photographs. As Fijians tend to pose for the camera it can be difficult to get natural and spontaneous expressions – after snapping a few posed pictures, wait until the scene becomes more naturalistic before shooting again. The most dramatic **light** is experienced early in the morning and late in the afternoon, although taking pictures of beaches and lagoons is good when the sun is high in the sky and the blues are pronounced. Film and **memory cards** are available in Nadi, Lautoka and Suva, although at higher prices than in the US or Europe.

Time

Although Fiji straddles the 180° meridian on which the International Dateline is based, the line diverts east around both it and Tonga.

The country thus has a single **time zone** being twelve hours ahead of Greenwich Mean Time (GMT), an hour ahead of Sydney and twenty hours ahead of Los Angeles. Fiji doesn't participate in daylight saving adjustments. The sun has a minimal variation from summer to winter, rising between 5am and 6am and setting from 6pm to 7pm, always with only a brief period of twilight.

Tourist information

The only official **tourist information** office in Fiji is in downtown Suva (see p.154). However, almost every hotel, resort and hostel in Fiji has its own privately operated tour desk offering brochures and a booking service. The government-funded **Fiji Visitor Bureau** (FVB) provides basic tourist information through its website ⓦ www.bulafiji.com. Its head office (☏ 672 2433, Mon–Thurs 8am–4.30pm, Fri 8am–4pm) is sited in an obscure location at the Colonial Plaza in Namaka, Nadi where you can pick up several useful tourist publications including *Affordable Guide* and *Fiji Dive Guide* but there are no staff on hand to help with travel enquiries or bookings. Three of the outer-island regions have established their own privately funded tourism organizations: the Savusavu Tourism Association (ⓦ www .fiji-savusavu.com); the Taveuni Tourism Association (ⓦ www.puretaveuni.com); and the Kadavu Tourism Association (ⓦ www .kadavutourism.com).

Fiji Visitor Bureau offices overseas

Australia Level 12, St Martin's Tower, 31 market Street, Sydney ☏ 02/9264 3399.
New Zealand 35 Scanlan Street, Grey Lynn, Auckland ☏ 09/376 2533.
UK Albany House, Albany Crescent, Claygate, Esher, Surrey, KT10 0PF ☏ 0800/652 2158.
US 5777 West Century Boulevard, Suite 220 Los Angeles, CA 90045 ☏ 310/568-1616.

Useful websites

ⓦ **www.fijiguide.com** Information on travelling around the islands including sections on diving and surfing as well as entertaining anecdotes.

ⓦ **www.fiji-island.com** Interactive picture maps enabling you to visualize the islands' beaches, scenery, towns and hotels.
ⓦ **www.fijituwawa.com** Aimed primarily at Fijians, this website gives a good overview of culture and everyday issues.
ⓦ **www.islandsbusiness.com** Current events and issues affecting Fiji and its Pacific Island neighbours.
ⓦ **www.pacific-resorts.com** Huge variety of accommodation searchable by style and region with pictures and reviews.
ⓦ **www.roughguides.com** Post any of your pre-trip questions – or post-trip suggestions – in Travel Talk, our online forum for travellers.
ⓦ **www.spto.org** Useful website for sourcing hotels, tours, travel agents and cultural events throughout the South Pacific.

Government sites

Australian Department of Foreign Affairs ⓦ www.dfat.gov.au, ⓦ www.smartraveller.gov.au.
British Foreign & Commonwealth Office ⓦ www.fco.gov.uk.
Canadian Department of Foreign Affairs ⓦ www.dfait-maeci.gc.ca.
Irish Department of Foreign Affairs ⓦ www .foreignaffairs.gov.ie.
New Zealand Ministry of Foreign Affairs ⓦ www.mft.govt.nz.
US State Department ⓦ www.travel.state.gov.

Travellers with disabilities

Fiji has a poor infrastructure for **travellers with disabilities** with no provision for wheelchairs on public transport and pavements rarely in a fit state for wheelchairs or the visually impaired – holes, ledges and cracks are all too common and there are few ramps at street corners. Moreover, many resort pathways are made of sand making mobility extremely difficult. Fortunately, Fijians will go out of their way to make your travels comfortable, assisting whenever possible and even building temporary ramps for disabled guests at resorts. The following organization can offer general advice and information:
Fiji National Council for Disabled Persons Qarase House, Brown St, Suva ☏ 331 9045, ⓦ www.fncdp.org.

Guide

Guide

Nadi and around

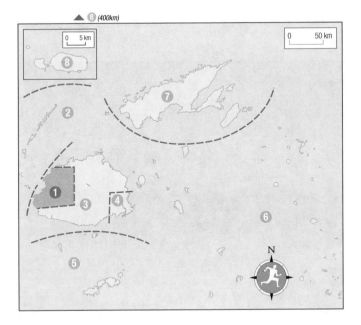

▲ 8 *(400km)*

CHAPTER 1

Highlights

✳ **Sri Siva Subrahmanya Swami Temple** The largest Hindu edifice in the Southern Hemisphere is a riot of colours and beautiful carving. See p.65

✳ **Wailoaloa Beach** Enjoy a sunset stroll along the beach at this travellers' hotspot and grab a cool beer at the *Ghostship* bar. See p.66

✳ **Day Cruising** Enjoy a day under sail cruising around Nadi's offshore islands. See p.73

✳ **Heaven's Edge** Head to this highland retreat above Nadi for waterfalls, stunning views and sheer relaxation. See p.78

✳ **Shopping in Lautoka** Go bargain hunting amongst Lautoka's bustling Indian shops for clothes and craft souvenirs. See p.80

✳ **Koroyanitu National Park** Take an overnight trek to this stunning region and sleep in a small hut on the top of Mount Batilamu. See p.83

▲ Sri Siva Subrahmanya Swami Temple

Nadi and around

A lmost all of Fiji's half a million annual visitors get their first glimpse of the country descending towards Nadi International Airport. Tiny tropical islands glint in the ocean off Nadi Bay while Viti Levu's spectacular mountains loom inland. Given this introduction, **NADI** (pronounced *Nan-dee*) itself can come as a slight anticlimax. Despite boasting Fiji's third largest population, it's not really a city, more a loose collection of villages surrounded by sugarcane fields, and you may be forgiven for thinking you've arrived at a quaint, tropical suburbia. Where Nadi excels, though, is in its choice of **accommodation**, with everything from five-star resorts to beachside backpackers dotted along the nearby coastline. You'll also find all the **facilities** you need to plan the rest of your trip including banks, travel agents, a good range of shops as well as a few excellent restaurants.

Nadi Airport, 10km north of the Downtown area, has a small cluster of hotels but is otherwise surrounded by farmland. Heading south along the congested Queens Road is **Namaka**, a frenetic shopping parade, while further south in the suburb of **Martintar** are several ethnic and international restaurants, Nadi's best nightlife and a couple of affordable hotels. South of here is **Downtown Nadi**, the terminal for buses with the municipal market, Internet cafés, boutique shops and cheap Chinese restaurants but virtually no accommodation. The southern point of town, where sugarcane fields take over, is guarded by Nadi's sole iconic attraction, the **Sri Siva Subrahmanya Swami Temple**, or more simply "Nadi Temple". A few kilometres east off the Queens Road are the beaches of **Nadi Bay**, home to the budget hotspot of **Wailoaloa Beach** as well as **Denarau Island**, an exclusive luxury enclave.

Just offshore from Nadi, the stunning islands of the Mamanucas (see Chapter 2) are accessible on numerous **day cruises** with sailing, snorkelling, diving and island-hopping available. Inland, the serene mountains of the **Nausori Highlands** and **Koroyanitu National Park** make a fabulous alternative adventure with tropical waterfalls, traditional villages and some breathtaking walking trails. The utilitarian port of **Lautoka**, just twenty minutes' drive north of Nadi airport, is a pleasant spot to shop and mingle unmolested by the tourist touts.

Some history

Nadi before the 1870s was a wild, unchartered region, seldom visited by the tyrants of Eastern Viti or Lau and hardly documented by European explorers or missionaries. In 1870, a small British community, known as the **Nadi Swells** for their broad-brimmed hats and affluent demeanour, set up cotton and cattle farms along the Nadi River. Soon after, with the establishment of **sugarcane** as a viable crop and with indentured labourers from India, the region began its

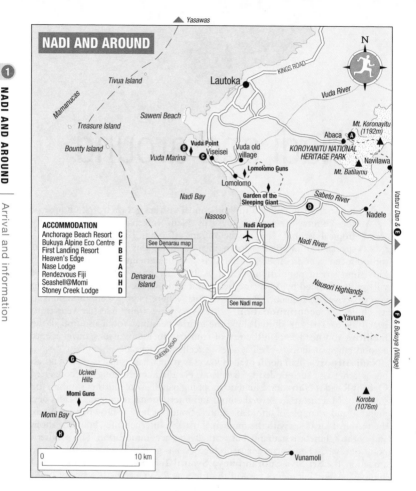

NADI AND AROUND

N

Yasawas

Tivua Island

Lautoka

KINGS ROAD

Vuda River

Mamanucas

Saweni Beach

Treasure Island

Abaca

Mt. Koronayitu
(1192m)

A

Bounty Island

B Vuda Point

Vuda Marina **C**

Viseisei

Vuda old
village

KOROYANITU NATIONAL
HERITAGE PARK

Navilawa

Lomolomo Guns

Mt. Batilamu

Lomolomo

Nadi Bay

**Garden of the
Sleeping Giant**

Sabeto River

D

Nadele

Nasoso

Nadi Airport

Vaturu Dam & **E**

ACCOMMODATION

Anchorage Beach Resort	**C**
Bukuya Alpine Eco Centre	**F**
First Landing Resort	**B**
Heaven's Edge	**E**
Nase Lodge	**A**
Rendezvous Fiji	**G**
Seashell@Momi	**H**
Stoney Creek Lodge	**D**

See Denarau map

Nadi River

Denarau
Island

See Nadi map

Nausori Highlands

& Bukuya (Village)

Yavuna

QUEENS ROAD

G

Uciwai
Hills

Momi Guns

Koroba
(1076m)

Momi Bay

H

0   10 km

Vunamoli

transformation to an Indo-Fijian dominated market centre. During World War II, the Royal New Zealand Air Force lengthened and strengthened the tiny Nadi airstrip, the US military constructed a major **airbase** and two large British gun batteries were erected either end of Nadi Bay to protect the Navula Passage. The Japanese invasion never came, but the paved runway was certainly big enough to receive the first jet planes and, with a slight expansion in the 1960s, Nadi established itself as the **tourist hub** of Fiji.

Arrival and information

Nadi International Airport (☎673 1615, ⓦwww.afl.com.fj) handles both international and domestic flights in a single terminal building with two wings known as the arrivals concourse and the departures concourse. To slightly confuse matters, all **domestic flights** depart from and arrive at the departures concourse, a one-minute walk away from international arrivals. There is no official **tourist information** at the airport. However, just after passing customs on the right-hand side, you'll find an accommodation **bulletin board** where you can make free calls to advertised hotels around Nadi. Once inside the general public area, a **help desk** manned by Airport Fiji Limited can point you in the right direction for taxis, buses, tour operators and travel agents. Unfortunately the airport has a bad reputation for accommodation touts – a firm "no" should suffice if being pestered. If you need **booking assistance**, call in on the reliable Sun Vacations (℡672 4273, open 24hr) on the right-hand of Western Union currency exchange.

Two **duty free** shops beside the luggage carousel in the arrivals concourse sell cheap alcohol, perfumes and cigarettes. The airport has free basic showers at both the domestic and arrival concourse toilets and you can **leave luggage** in a secure 24-hour storage room at the far corner of the departures concourse (F$4.10 per day per suitcase or backpack).

Express buses running between Lautoka and Suva call in at the departures concourse and will drop you in Downtown for F$1.10, twenty minutes to the south. Regular **local buses** stop along the Queens Road opposite *Raffles Gateway Hotel*, a two-minute walk from the arrivals concourse, between 6am and 6pm and cost 85 cents into town. Bear in mind most hostels and hotels offer complimentary **pick-ups** for international flight arrivals. **Taxis** wait directly outside the arrivals concourse and charge a fixed F$7 to Martintar, F$10 to Wailoaloa or Downtown or F$22 to Denarau Island or Vuda. There are also five **car rental** firms immediately after clearing immigration (see Listings p.75).

Buses or **minivans** from elsewhere on the mainland will drop you at the main terminus in Downtown, with many continuing on to the airport. Arriving by **sea** you will likely be pulling into Port Denarau (see p.67), served by fast catamarans from the Yasawas or Mamanucas, or if travelling by yacht, Vuda Marina (see p.79).

City transport

A constant stream of cars, minivans and buses impatiently dart along the main Queens Road between Nadi Airport and Downtown, and picking up **public transport** here is a breeze. Travelling **off the main road**, though, usually involves taking a taxi, with only an infrequent bus service to the busy tourist areas of Wailoaloa and Denarau, and these only from Downtown. The suburban layout of Nadi with gaping farmland between attractions makes exploring by foot impractical. You can bypass the whole of suburban Nadi by taking the **Nadi Back Road** from the roundabout south of Nadi Airport to the southern end of Downtown, a journey which takes less than ten minutes.

Buses and minivans

Local buses operate between 6am and 6pm travelling every fifteen minutes or so along the Queens Road between Downtown Nadi and Nadi Airport, costing 90 cents a ride, with about half of these travelling on to Lautoka and the other half diverting off the Queens Road to rural settlements. Local buses also head to all suburban areas off the main road roughly five times a day, including to the popular beach areas of Wailoaloa and Denarau Island, departing from the **bus station** in Downtown – ask the bus drivers for assistance as it's not always clear where buses are heading to. **Minivans**, many of them illegally operated, run constantly along the Queens Road picking up passengers by the roadside for 50 cents a trip – the legal operators usually have a business name and telephone number stencilled on their bodywork.

Taxis

Taxis are based at most hotels, or can be called by reception staff. Nadi International **Airport taxis** are painted yellow and wait immediately outside both the international and domestic arrivals concourses at all hours. If you need to call a taxi, good options are: Airport Taxi (☎672 2887) at Nadi Airport; Taxi 2000 (☎672 1350) in Martintar; or Safeway Tours (☎670 3280) in Downtown. Otherwise you can **hail a cab** on the street with an outstretched arm and a flap of a hand. Although bound by law to charge **fares** by the meter, with a flag fall of F$1.50 (F$2 from 10pm to 6am) plus 10 cents for every 200m travelled, few do. Instead journeys are charged a fixed rate which is often inflated for tourists. Make sure you know the price before you get in the taxi, and bargain down if necessary. Downtown Nadi to Denarau or the airport should be F$10, to Wailoaloa Beach F$7 or to Martintar F$4. You could insist the meter is switched on which, if you're lucky, will happen reluctantly – if the driver flatly refuses, it's your right to take down the licence number and driver's name and report the matter to the Land Transport Authority (☎672 8622, Mon–Fri 8am–4.30pm) in Beddoes Circle, Namaka, although whether the driver will be cautioned is uncertain.

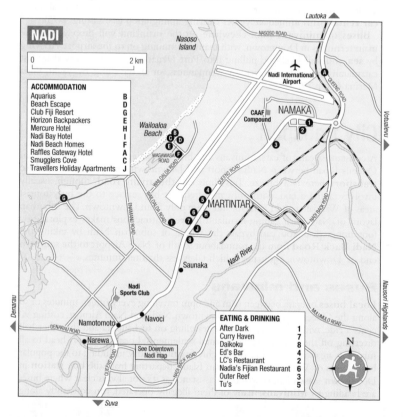

Car, bicycle and scooter rental

If you're planning to explore Nadi and Viti Levu, **renting a car** is more economical than hiring a taxi and a lot more convenient than waiting for sporadic buses along the Queens Road, especially in rural locations. Rates range from F$65 to F$150 per day (plus F$20 a day for insurance). All agencies will drop the car off for free at any hotel in the Nadi area. See Listings p.75 for reliable operators.

Scooter rental is offered by Westside Motorbike (℡672 6402; F$79/24hr) in Namaka Industrial Estate and is OK for buzzing around town but is neither pleasant nor safe on the main highways. Off-road flexible cycling day tours and general **bike rental** are offered by Stinger Bicycles (℡628 3771; bike F$50 per 24hr including bike delivery to Nadi hotels, mountain tour including lunch F$68; minimum 2 people).

Accommodation

There are a handful of affordable hotels along the main road between **Nadi Airport** and **Downtown**. However, to get a view of the ocean, you need to stay at the more isolated regions of either Wailoaloa Beach, Denarau Island or Vuda Point, all several kilometres off the Queens Road on Nadi Bay. **Wailoaloa Beach**, the budget and backpacker centre, is the most central of these and has a laid-back atmosphere with stunning views along the coast but the beach itself is by no means postcard-worthy with greyish sand and murky water. The opulent man-made creation of **Denarau Island**, 5km west of Downtown with its five-star resorts, luxury homes and a modern shopping centre has an intuitively hollow, plastic feel. **Vuda Point** (see p.79), twenty minutes' drive north of the airport, has a couple of mid-range boutique beach resorts and is closer to Lautoka.

For **longer stays**, try *Nadi Beach Homes* (℡672 7999, ⓦwww.nadibeach.com; studio rooms ❸, apartments ❹, holiday homes ❺–❻) with excellent-value weekly and monthly rates in three-bedroom private holiday homes with swimming pools, modern one- and two-bedroom air-conditioned beach apartments, or studio-style homestays.

Nadi Airport and Downtown

Mercure Hotel Nadi Queens Rd, Martintar ℡672 2255, ⓔreservations @mercurenadi.com.fj. Great location for dining out and visiting a few of Nadi's local bars which are within walking distance. The 85 modern rooms are bland in design but very comfortable, located in two blocks, each three stories high, overlooking a small central swimming pool. ❹

Nadi Bay Hotel Wailoaloa Rd, Martintar ℡672 3599, ⓦwww.fijinadibayhotel.com. The largest backpacker hostel in Nadi is set in a mundane suburban location just off the main Queens Rd. Once inside, though, it's a pretty oasis with a large swimming pool. The cosy restaurant serves the best food of all the backpacker places in a plant-filled courtyard with wooden decking.

Dorms, standard rooms and apartments are all a bit pokey though and light sleepers will curse at being directly in the flight path of the early morning 747s. 14-bed dorm F$29, a/c 4-bed dorm F$30, rooms ❷–❸

Nadi Downtown Backpackers Queens Rd, Downtown Nadi ℡670 0600, ⓦwww.fijihostels .com. One of the few options in Downtown Nadi, this poky building is located along the seedier southern end of the main street but offers the cheapest backpacker rooms in Nadi. The eight-bed dorm rooms and double rooms are identical in size, each with en-suite cold-water bathrooms but bedding is grubby. Dorm F$15–22, rooms ❶–❷

Raffles Gateway Queens Rd Nadi Airport ℡672 2444, ⓦwww.rafflesgateway.com. Smack opposite Nadi International Airport with a spacious garden setting, large family pool with water slide and tennis courts, this is a good choice for families. Rooms boast floral decor and wicker furniture but are clean and with air con – the family rooms can sleep two children who, if under 16 and accompanied by two adults, stay for free. Day rooms between 6am and 6pm are handy for late flights. ④–⑤

Travellers Holiday Apartments Queens Rd Martintar ☎ 672 4675. Centrally based apartments on the main road with small basic rooms, tiny hot-water bathrooms but most with air con, TVs and kitchenettes. If you're after something cheap but soulless, this is a good option. ②

Wailoaloa Beach

Aquarius Wasawasa Rd, New Town Beach ☎ 672 6000, ⓦ www.aquarius.com.fj. A converted homestead facing the beach and ocean, this place feels homely with lots of hammocks, a small pool, communal lounge and wide staircase leading to the slightly old-fashioned rooms. The cramped dormitories are squashed at the back but a/c, with either two, four or twelve beds and en-suite bathrooms. Dorms F$28–30; rooms ②–③

Beach Escape Wasawasa Rd, New Town Beach ☎ 672 6000, ⓦ www.beachescape.com.fj. Excellent-value accommodation in twelve multi-purpose pine bungalows, available as either private villas or dorms with shared rooms. The interiors are dark and the villas very squashed together but face a nice pool and dining courtyard a few blocks back from the beach. Dorms F$19–26, rooms ①, villas ②

Club Fiji Enamanu Rd, Wailoaloa South ☎ 670 2189, ⓦ www.clubfiji-resort.com. Quiet beach setting at the secluded southern end of Wailoaloa. The restaurant and bar has an island style atmos-phere. Rooms are in duplex cottages with polished wooden floors and spacious bathrooms with a slightly out-of-place two-storey cement block with cheaper hotel style rooms. ③–⑥

Horizon Backpackers Wasawasa Rd, New Town Beach ☎ 672 2832, ⓦ www.horizonbeachfiji .com. Set one block back from the beach, the reception, lounge and pool table extend from the driveway but there's a quiet pool area for lazing. The tiny rooms and dorms are hidden within a

warren of corridors but are essentially the cheapest at Wailoaloa. Dorm F$15–F$22, rooms ①–②

Smugglers Cove Wasawasa Rd, New Town Beach ☎ 672 6578, ⓦ www.smugglersbeachfiji .com. A stark modern cement building hides one of Wailoaloa's liveliest spots on the beachfront. Guitarists and *kava* drinking keep the bar humming and the open-sided kitchen serves tasty food. There's a small pool and large deck area facing the beach. The modern a/c rooms are clean albeit small and most have tiny bathrooms and the large mixed dorm is partitioned into four-bed areas with lockers. Internet, laundry and a 24hr reception make this a popular choice and it's often full. Dorm F$28, rooms ②–④ includes light breakfast.

Tropic of Capricorn Wasawasa Rd, New Town Beach ☎ 672 3089, ⓔ mamas@mamastropic .com. The dorm rooms in the old building at the back are a bit basic but the modern three-storey cement building facing the beach has clean simple rooms and the best balcony views, especially the deluxe ocean-view rooms at the top. Dorm F$18–F$28, ③–④

Denarau Island

Golf Terraces Port Denarau ☎ 675 0557, ⓦ www .golfterraces.com.fj. Fully equipped and spacious one-, two- and three-bedroom apartments overlooking the golf course and mountains. 2min walk to Port Denarau's shops, restaurants and marina. ⑦–⑧

Sofitel Fiji Resort North Beach ☎ 675 1111, ⓦ www.sofitelfiji.com.fj. Beautifully landscaped five-star resort with most of the 296 rooms having ocean views, although they are small for the price. The beach outlook is pretty with plenty of water sports available and a serene spa centre. ⑧–⑨

The Westin North Beach ☎ 675 0000, ⓦ www .westinfiji.com. Classically designed with traditional style architecture, dark timber and a streamlined swimming pool, with rooms recently refurbished to achieve Starwood's five-star Westin brand. Like all resorts on Denarau, rooms are over three-storey cement blocks. Half the resort faces a seawall with the other half on black sand. ⑧–⑨

Downtown Nadi

With a population of just 12,000, split almost evenly between indigenous Fijians and Fiji-Indians, Nadi has a laid-back rural charm, enhanced by an almost constantly sunny climate. The twin Fijian villages of Navoci and Namotomoto and the murky Nadi River separate **Downtown Nadi** from its northern

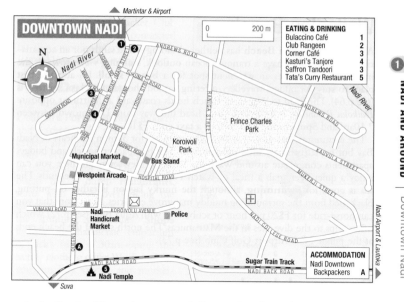

DOWNTOWN NADI

Martintar & Airport

Suva

Nadi Airport & Lautoka

EATING & DRINKING

Bulaccino Café	1
Club Rangeen	2
Corner Café	3
Kasturi's Tanjore	4
Saffron Tandoori	3
Tata's Curry Restaurant	5

ACCOMMODATION

Nadi Downtown Backpackers	A

suburbs. South of here, the congested Queens Road is referred to as **Main Street**, lined with fashion and accessory shops and with a lively market square off to one side. The post office and police station are located on the opposite side of the market between Hospital Road and Koroivolu Avenue. North of the market and beyond the **bus stand** is a tiny grandstand overlooking Prince Charles Park, venue for Nadi's football and rugby games.

The **northern side** of town is by far the most pleasant, with several excellent restaurants serving Indian dishes and interesting boutique handicraft stores, although persistent taxi drivers vying for attention distract from its charm. The busiest part of town is off Main Street, down Clay Street and into Market Road towards the lively **Nadi Municipal Market**. It's a good place to pick up local produce and *yaqona* roots and to mingle with the locals – if you're after a snack, Indian boys usually sell peanuts, curried beans and roti parcels for 50 cents each at the main entrance on Market Road.

The farther south you walk along Main Street, the seedier things become and by **Westpoint Arcade** beyond Hospital Road, the sidewalk touts take over, hassling tourists with "Bula mate!" followed by a "smoke weed?" or "best prices in my shop!". Opposite the arcade in the Children's Park are twenty wooden stalls which make up the **Nadi Handicraft Market** where you can pick up reasonably priced wooden carvings and woven baskets; you'll need to negotiate on prices. From here on, the road is dominated by *kava* saloons where the locals gather to play pool. It's worth continuing on to visit the impressive **Sri Siva Subrahmanya Swami Temple** (daily 6am–7pm; tourists are charged F$3.50 to enter and take photographs). In 1994 this Hindu temple moved from beside the flood-prone Nadi River to the southern end of town where an evocative three-tower complex was finely created over a ten-year period by eight specialist craftsmen brought in from India. The Dravidian temple is dedicated to the deity Murugan whose statue, specially carved in India, is housed within the twelve-metre-high main pryramidal *vimanam* with a rectangular toped roof. The two towers at the rear of the temple with colourful domed shaped roofs are dedicated to Ganesh and Shiva.

65

cakes for F$12.50 and daily blackboard specials including an excellent-value Sun BBQ (F$10). Daily 11am–11pm.

Dance shows

Hilton Fiji Resort Denarau Island ☎675 6800. Fijian *meke* performed beside the pool for diners on Sat at 8.30pm.

Smugglers Cove Wailoaloa Beach ☎672 6578. Informal beach setting with a mix of Fijian and Polyneisan dance plus enthralling fire dances performed by the Helava Group. Sunday 8pm.

Sheraton Fiji Resort Denarau Island ☎675 0777. Traditional Fijian *meke* at the *Veranda Restaurant* on Sat at 8pm.

Sofitel Fiji Resort Denarau Island ☎675 1111. Fijian *meke* performed beside the beach every Thurs at 5pm.

Travellers Beach Wailoaloa Beach ☎672 3322. Polynesian show with the Sowea Group every Fri at 7.30pm.

Westin Denarau Resort Denarau Island ☎675 0777. Impressive Fijian fire walking set in a staged amphitheatre every Wed 7.30pm (F$24).

Shopping

Nadi has a decent selection of **shops** and is one of the few places in Fiji stocking **electronic goods** such as memory cards for digital cameras. General shopping hours are from 8.30am – 5.30pm weekdays, and 8.30am to 1pm on Saturday. Most shops at the open-air Port Denarau shopping centre are open daily from 7am – 7pm, closing at 9pm on Friday and Saturday. For **food** shopping, Morris Hedstrom has the largest variety, found at both Namaka and opposite Jack's Handicrafts in Downtown. For gourmet food, try Yee's at Namaka at the end of Hillside Road, or at Port Denarau.

Souvenirs

For many, wood carvings or woven mats, baskets and fans are the **souvenir** of choice. These are available from many handicraft stores in town. War clubs, *tanoa* bowls and priest dishes are authentic Fijian designs while face masks are simply tourist gimmicks and mostly imported from Asia. Nad's and Jack's handicraft

▲ Nadi Handicraft Market

stores, both at the north end of town and the latter also at Port Denarau, offer good-quality workmanship and will pack and post worldwide. If you're good at haggling you may find better bargains at the local Handicraft Market beside Koroivolu Lane. **Jewellery** is another popular item although local shops tend to cater to the Indian community with bright shiny and laced gold items being most desirable. **Black and multi-hued pearls** are harvested at several places in Fiji (see p.43) and make fine necklaces and earrings but quality and prices vary immensely – the cheapest disfigured pearls cost as little as F$20; perfect ones, opaque, smooth and of a deep colour fetch as much as F$1000. Some pearls are imported from Cook Islands and Tahiti, the biggest producers of black pearls in the world. The best place to buy jewellery is at **Tappoo's**, the closest Nadi has to a department store, with four levels at the north end of Downtown; there are also branches at several resorts.

Clothes and books

Clothes shopping in Nadi is cheap and of reasonable quality – Sogo, midway down Main Street, has colourful *sulus* and swimwear for women, Origin 66 is good for dresses and blouses while Aladdin's Cave in the arcade beside Nadi River at the north end of town offers ethnic-style accessories; men should try S. Nagindas midway down Main Street for shirts and board shorts. There are no specific **bookstores**. The best place to buy novels is at either Prouds or Tappoo's – you'll also find romantic novels, classics and magazines at Devia (Shop 262 on Main Street just before Hospital Lane).

Snorkelling and fishing gear

It's worth buying your own set of **snorkelling gear**, especially as many budget island resorts either don't supply them or have rather old leaky kit. It will set you back about F$60 for the snorkel and mask and F$40 for a pair of fins. A good selection is available at Viti Watersports in Martintar (℡670 2413; Mon–Fri 8am–5pm, Sat 8am–noon). When you're done, the gear makes a fantastic gift to a local villager and saves lugging them home. For **fishing gear**, Sports World on Main Street have a selection of rods as well as hooks and hand line which also make practical gifts if you are visiting coastal villages.

Tours and activities

Nadi offers a huge range of **tours** and **activities** allowing you to sample the nearby islands of the Mamanucas and Yasawas, hike inland to remote villages, or try out scuba diving or deep-sea fishing, all within a day. If you just need to kill a few hours, Denarau Island offers excellent golf, tennis and jet-ski rides. You'll be able to book day-trips and activities at your accommodation but note that hotel and resort **tour desks** always give preference to operators, paying them the highest commissions, or even promote private tours with family and friends. If in doubt, contact the operators listed below direct or try Sun Vacations at Nadi Airport (see p.60) or Travel Fiji in central Nadi (see p.66).

Tour operators offer complimentary pick-up and drop-off from all Nadi hotels. Bear in mind that if you're staying near the airport the journey to Port Denarau (departure point for island trips) takes over an hour meandering around the suburbs and town picking up other guests. To save time, you may want to travel by taxi which will cost F$18 one way and take twenty minutes.

Adrenaline sports

Adrenalin Watersports Denarau Island ℡ 675 1111, Ⓦ www.adrenalinfiji.com. Parasailing (F$100) and jet-ski safaris (F$350 solo, F$195 tandem; 3hr) from the beach in front of *Sofitel Fiji*.
Jet Fiji Port Denarau ℡ 0800 675 0401, Ⓦ www.jetfiji.com. Thrilling ride along the tight mangrove estuaries of the Nadi River with 360-degree spins along the way. Daily 10am–3pm, F$79, max 12 people.
Tandem Skydive Nadi Airport ℡ 672 8166, Ⓦ www.skydivefiji.com.fj. Tandem freefall from over 4000m with a pro sky diver, landing on the beach at Wailoaloa or Denarau. F$348–498 depending on height jumped.

Deep-sea fishing

The Malolo Barrier Reef, 20km southwest of Port Denarau is a great spot for deep-sea fishing, best in the early hours of the morning. Sailfish, Tuna, and Walu are the prize game, with Giant Trevally and Barracuda good casting fish.

Crystal Blue Adventures Port Denarau ℡ 675 0950, Ⓦ www.crystalbluefiji.com. Five fast sports fishing vessels capable of 25–30 knots with a maximum of four anglers or eight sightseeing passengers. Half day F$770, full day F$1150 includes fishing gear, snorkelling equipment, snacks, soft drinks and lunch. Also offers day-cruises spending two hours with spinner dolphins and a BBQ lunch on Malolo Island; Mon, Wed & Sat; depart 9am; F$160 per person.
Reel Time Charters Port Denarau ℡ 999 3454. Predominantly fishing charters to the Malolo Barrier Reef on a ten-metre game-fishing boat capable of 22 knots. Will also take sightseeing charters, snorkelling trips and island hopping. Half day F$775, full day F$1100 includes all gear, lunch and soft drinks.

Diving and snorkelling

Nadi Bay's murky waters, spoiled by run-off from the surrounding hills, are unsuitable for **diving** or **snorkelling**. For both, you need to travel at least twenty minutes offshore which takes you to the excellent dive sites of the Mamanucas – the further away from the mainland, the better the water clarity and more vibrant the coral reefs. Dive boats depart from Port Denarau, Wailoaloa Beach and Vuda Marina.

Aqua Blue Wailoaloa Beach ℡ 672 6111, Ⓦ www.aquabluefiji.com. Budget operator, boats depart Wailoaloa Beach, handy for backpackers. PADI Open water course F$600, two-tank dive F$200.
Subsurface Vuda Marina ℡ 666 6738, Ⓦ www .subsurfacefiji.com. Serving both Anchorage and First Landing resorts with daily direct runs out to Beachcomber in the northern Mamanucas taking 20min where you join up with the Beachcomber guest divers. PADI Open water course F$690, two-tank dive F$230, minimum two divers; 3hr snorkelling trip with divers F$50 per person.
Sun Splash Vuda Marina ℡ 628 3666. Small group dedicated snorkelling trips to the sand spit in the northern Mamanucas with a BBQ lunch at Bounty Island where you can also snorkel off the beach. F$90, min 3 people; 9am–4pm, complimentary Nadi and Lautoka hotel pick-up.
Viti Watersports Corner of Queens Rd and Kennedy St ℡ 670 2413, Ⓦ www.vitiwatersports. com. Operating fast covered boats from Denarau with state-of-the-art dive gear and complimentary Nadi hotel pick-ups. PADI Open water course F$695, 2-tank dive F$225, snorkellers F$70. Also sell snorkel and dive equipment.

Hiking

To explore the countryside **around Nadi**, the best hiking opportunity is at Koroyanitu National Park (see p.83), a thirty-minute drive inland from Lautoka. Otherwise, there are short walking trails at the Nausori Highlands lookout (see p.77) with breathtaking views overlooking Nadi Bay. Another option is to head down to Sigatoka, an hour by bus, and join in the tours along the Coral Coast (see p.128) and Pacific Harbour (see p.130). Most tour

▲ Denarau Golf Course

companies listed in those regions offer pick-ups from Nadi hotels but this can make a long day out.

Golf and tennis

Visitors to Nadi have three public **golf courses** to choose from. The **Denarau Golf Club** (☎675 9710; daily 6.30am–6.30pm; F$125 including compulsory golf cart, club hire F$55, shoe hire F$12) has slightly discounted rates for guests staying at any of the Denarau resorts. It's a long flat course, well manicured with virtually no rough but lots of fish-shaped bunkers, canals coming into play and large fast greens. The course is rarely busy, making it a joy to play. The public nine-hole **Nadi Airport Golf Club** (☎672 2148; daily 10am–6pm; F$20 for 18 holes) is at Wailoaloa Beach. This slightly undulating course is quite challenging with rough and tricky greens. There's also a pitch-and-putt nine-hole course at the *Novotel Nadi* at Votualevu (☎672 2000; daily 7am–5pm; F$12). The Peter Thompson designed **Momi Golf Course** at Momi Bay, thirty minutes' drive south of Nadi, has nine holes currently completed and is playable through membership only or by staying at the *JW Marriott Resort*.

The Denarau Golf and Racket Club (☎ 675 9710, daily 7am–9pm; F$20 per hr, F$25 per hr for grass) has four all weather synthetic **tennis courts** and six grass courts, with lessons available by the hour. The Nadi Sports Club (☎670 0239; daily 6am–9pm) at Navakai has one hard court available to non-members costing F$5.50 per hr per person and two **squash courts** at the same price.

Island cruises

Exploring the **offshore islands** of the Mamanucas on a day-trip can either be experienced aboard an elegant yacht or by zooming out to the island resorts by fast catamaran.

Sailing cruises
Coral Cat Port Denarau ☎651 3475 or ☎992 0076. Small twenty-metre catamaran with boom net across middle for sunbathing; heads to the Malolo Barrier Reef for dolphin watching and snorkelling at nearby Black Rock. 10am–5pm; F$145 includes BBQ lunch at Musket Cove marina.

Ra Marama Port Denarau ☏ 670 1823. Most affordable of the sailing cruises aboard a charming square-rigged vessel and cruising along the Viti Levu coast to the tiny coral island of Tivua where you can spend five hours day dreaming, lounging in the lagoon and snorkelling. F$97 includes BBQ lunch; 10am–5pm.

Seaspray Port Denarau ☏ 675 0500; ⓦ www.ssc.com.fj. Two-part tour with the first leg catching the South Sea Cruise fast catamaran to Mana Island where you transfer to a double-mast schooner venturing to the outer Mamanucas. It takes almost three hours travel time from Nadi but you get to walk on the fine white sands of Modriki, location of the film *Castaway*, starring Tom Hanks. You also visit the traditional fishing village of Yanuya where a shell market and *kava* ceremony are put on by the locals (daily except Sun). 9am–6pm, F$175; includes BBQ lunch, local beer and wine.

Whale's Tale Port Denarau. ☏ 670 2443 This beautiful 33-metre schooner offers a day of indulgence – sipping wine whilst sightseeing around the protected waters of the inner Coral Islands and anchoring at an uninhabited island for a gourmet lunch and snorkelling. F$169 per person includes champagne breakfast, lunch and all drinks; 10am–6pm.

Valentino Sailing Safari Port Denarau. ☏ 675 0611 For private charters of up to ten people, this can work out to be a good deal. The eleven-metre catamaran sailing yacht offers a footloose adventure cruise around the Mamanucas taking in snorkelling, handline fishing or island sightseeing. Half-day cruises leave at 8am or 1pm, F$750 includes lunch and drinks, 5hr; full-day departs 9am, F$1350 includes lunch and drinks; 8hr 30min.

Motorboat cruises

Awesome Adventure Port Denarau ☏ 675 0499; ⓦ www.awesomeadventures.com. Take a 2hr 30min cruise to Waya Island in the southern Yasawas for a village visit and snorkel around the gorgeous sand spit, or head 30min further north to the beautiful beach setting at Botaira. Daily 8.30am–6pm; F$130 includes lunch.

Fiji Sea Travel Port Denarau ☏ 672 5523, ⓦ www.fijiseatravel.com. Offers two exciting day safaris on alternate days: the first is a sight-seeing cruise past seven islands in the Mamanucas with dolphin watching and snorkelling along the way (Mon, Wed & Fri; 9am–4.30pm); the second whizzes up to the Yasawas allowing you to swim and snorkel with manta rays (May–Sept only, Tues, Thurs & Sat; 8.30am–4.30pm). Both cruises cost F$175 which includes lunch and soft drinks.

Mala Mala Island Sunsail Port Denarau ☏ 670 5192. Time out at an uninhabited coral cay just 25min from Port Denarau with good snorkelling for beginners. The "early bird" tour gives you a couple of hours of peace before the masses arrive. Early bird F$85, 8am–3pm; Full day F$89, 10am–5pm; Half day F$79, 10am–3pm; includes BBQ lunch and soft drinks.

South Sea Combo Cruise Port Denarau ☏ 675 0500. Good sightseeing introduction to the small island resorts of the Mamanucas – the best views are from the top-level open-air deck and you pull up sufficiently close to three tiny coral cays to see into the bures. BBQ lunch is served on South Sea Island before heading back. Daily 9am–5.45pm; F$95. Alternatively, you can hop off the cruise at any of the resorts along the way to spend a few hours on the island, lounging on the beach or snorkelling. Beachcomber F$95, South Sea Island F$99, Bounty F$120, Treasure F$125, Castaway F$135, Mana F$125, Malolo F$130.

Scenic flights

Island Hoppers Nadi Airport ☏ 672 0410, ⓦ www.helicopters.com.fj. The best views of the islands and mountains are on large-window scenic helicopter flights. F$220 per person for 20min, F$330 per person for 35min, minimum two people or you can try the tag-along deal which accompanies resort transfers to an unspecified destination for F$200. Adventurous, remote "heli-drop" hiking trips are in the pipeline.

Surfing

Surfing on the Malolo Barrier Reef is easily accessible from Momi Bay or Uciwai (see p.99) where there are two surf-oriented budget resorts for experienced surfers. Beginners should contact the Fiji Surf Co (☏ 670 5960, ⓦ www.fijisurfco.com) on the corner of Hospital Road above Raniga Jewellers for transfers to surfing breaks, surf equipment and surf instruction at Natadola Beach or Sigatoka Sandunes, both breaks accessible from the beach and not crashing over hazardous coral reefs.

Village tours

Adventure Fiji ☎672 2935 (part of Rosie Holidays). Full-day scenic tour to the Nausori Highlands with a two-hour downhill trek to Yavuna Village provides an excellent rounded introduction into Fijian life. Mon–Sat departs 8am, F$83 includes lunch in village, minimum two people; 8hr.

Great Sights ☎0800 672 0455 or ☎672 3311. Two half-day 4WD village tours to either Abaca (F$105; 3hr) or Navilawa (F$110; 4hr), both north of Nadi. Also operate coach tours: Discover Nadi (F$65; 3hr) and Discover Suva (F$90; 12hr).

Naks Tours (☎672 8335) Anand, a local Indo-Fijian driver, operates his own taxi and provides knowledgeable private tours of the Nadi area for F$15–20 per hour.

Pehicle ☎672 4086. If you're interested in Indian culture, this is the only tour visiting an Indian settlement where you can sample curries, roti and chutneys (daily on demand, F$45; 2hr). There's also a full-day tour to Lauwaki Village on the road to Lautoka with a *kava* ceremony, lovo lunch and weaving instruction (departs 9.30am daily; F$100 minimum two people; 7hr)

Viti Eco Tours ☎672 4312. The two-hour drive to delightful Navala Village is well worth the effort just to walk amongst the 200 traditional thatch houses (Mon–Sat, departs 9am; F$175 includes picnic lunch, minimum two people; 7hr) but there's also pleasant sightseeing along the way. A shorter half-day tour visits Nalesutale Village, 30min drive from Nadi along the Sabeto Valley with a short forest hike to a small waterfall and village lunch (Mon–Sat, departs 9am; F$79 includes lunch; 4hr).

Listings

Airlines Most airlines are based at Nadi International Airport arrivals concourse. Air Fiji (☎672 2521), also agents for Pacific Blue and Air Vanuatu, daily 5am–8pm; Air New Zealand (☎672 2955) 1st floor Mon–Fri 8am–5pm; Air Pacific, also for Pacific Sun (☎672 0888) Mon–Fri 8am–5pm; AirCalin (☎672 2145) Mon, Wed, & Fri 8am–5pm, Tues 6.30am–3.30pm, Thurs 7am–4pm, Sat 8am–6pm; Solomon Airlines, 1st Floor Williams & Gosling Building, beside the post office at Nadi Airport (☎672 2831) Mon–Fri 8am–1pm & 2pm–5pm.

Banking All the following have ATM machines, but expect lengthy queues on Thurs afternoon and Fri after payday, and also on Sat morning. Machines sometimes run out of cash in which case try the ATM inside *Macdonald's* Restaurant in Saunaka Village between Martintar and Downtown or beside the boat transfer check-in counter at Port Denarau. Westpac Corner of Main St and Vunivau Rd Mon–Thurs 9.30am–3pm, Fri 9.30am–4pm, also at Namaka Lane and Port Denarau; ANZ Bank Queens Rd Mon 9.30am–4pm, Tues–Fri 9am–4pm, also at Namaka Lane and Nadi International Airport Arrivals Concourse (24hr).

Car rental Aims, Shortlane St, Namaka ☎672 8310; Budget, Nadi Airport ☎672 2735, also at Denarau Island ☎675 0888; Carpenters Rentals, Waqadra ☎672 2772; Khans, Nadi Airport ☎672 3506 also Downtown ☎995 1738; Sharma's, Nadi Airport ☎672 1908, also Downtown 670 1055.

Hospital Nadi Hospital Nadi College Rd, Downtown ☎670 1128 is where to head in cases of emergency.

Internet access Click, Park St, opposite Hospital Lane Mon–Fri 8am–7.30pm, Sat 8.30am–7pm, Sun 10am–6pm with fast gaming machines and the cheapest braodband at F$2.80 per hr with further discounts before 11am Mon–Fri. My Internet, 1st Floor, Asgar Complex Main St, adjacent to *Kasturi's Tanjore*; Mon–Sat 7.30am–8pm, Sun 9am–4pm; F$3 per hr.

Laundry Kennedy Laundry, Corner of Queens Rd and Kennedy Ave, Martintar ☎670 2402, daily 8am–5pm, serviced laundry F$15 half load, F$25 full load.

Medical Namaka Private Medical Centre, Namaka ☎672 2288, can perform some surgical procedures. Mon–Fri 9am–6pm and 7pm–9pm, Sat 9am–1pm and 7pm–9pm, Sun 10am–1pm and 7pm–9pm. Zens Medical Centre at 30 Lodhia St Downtown Nadi ☎ 670 3533 is best for minor ailments; doctor open 24hr, dentist open Mon–Fri 8am–6pm, Sat 8am–1pm.

Optician Zens Medical Centre 30 Lodhia St Downtown Nadi ☎ 670 3533; Mon–Fri 8am–5pm, Sat 8am–1pm.

Pharmacy Namaka Medisure Pharmacy ☎672 8851, Namaka Lane, daily 8am–10pm; Thakoral's, Main St Downtown Nadi Mon–Fri 8am–6pm, Sat 8am–3pm, Sun 9am–1pm.

Police Emergencies ☎917; The main police station is at Koroivolu Lane in Downtown ☎670 0222; There are suburban stations at Nadi Airport

672 2172 and Totogo Lane in the CAAF
Compound, Namaka ☎ 672 2222.
Post office Koroivolu Lane, Downtown and
Airport Complex, Nadi Airport Mon–Fri 8am–4pm,

Sat 8am–noon; both offer Poste Restante
(see p.50).
Telephone Public phones at Nadi Airport and in
front of the post office in Downtown.

Around Nadi

The area **around Nadi** offers access to Viti Levu's rural interior as well as the surfing breaks of the nearby Malolo Barrier Reef. The latter can be sampled by staying at one of the two surfing resorts around **Momi Bay**. Inland, the flats of the Nadi River eventually yield to the **Nausori Highlands**, an alpine environment home to one of Fiji's best eco-resorts.

North towards Lautoka, the Queens Road passes the scenic **Sabeto River Valley** before reaching **Vuda Point**, home to a small marina and two boutique resorts. A few kilometres further, the busy industrial port of **Lautoka** offers good shopping and access to the north coast. In the distance, the shapely **Koroyanitu National Park** beckons through the haze.

South to Momi Bay

Twenty minutes' drive south of Nadi along the Queens Road is the turn-off to **Uciwai Hills**, the closest spot on the mainland to the surfing breaks along the Malolo Barrier Reef (see p.99). You can stay along the remote coast here at the budget **surf resort** *Rendezvous Fiji* (☎ 628 4426, ⓦ www.surfdivefiji .com, camping F$45, dorm F$60, rooms ❹ including meals) run by a local Fijian surfer and his Japanese wife. Accommodation here is clean and simple, either in private en-suite rooms sleeping up to four, doubles with shared facilities or a six-bed dorm. Daily **surf trips** (guests F$55; non-guests F$65) take just twenty minutes to get to Malolo Barrier Reef and spend between two and

---

Moving on from Nadi

The easiest way of **moving on** from Nadi is by bus, with a frequent services heading north to Lautoka and south to Suva from Downtown Nadi and Nadi Airport. There's roughly one express bus heading every hour to Lautoka (7am–6pm; 45min; F$2.35) while local buses (F$2.10) depart every ten to fifteen minutes, stop frequently along the Queens Road and take double the time. Of the **express buses**, easily the most comfortable is the air-conditioned Coral Sun (☎ 672 3105 or ☎ 672 6392; daily departures from Nadi Airport to Suva at 7.30am & 1pm; 30min later from Downtown Nadi; F$19; 4hr) with large cushioned seats and big windows. Other options include Sunbeam Transport (☎ 666 2086; 6 daily from Nadi Airport to Suva, 9am–2.15pm; F$13.50; 5hr) and Pacific Transport (☎ 670 0044; 5 daily from Nadi Airport to Suva, 6.50am–5.50pm; F$12.95; 5hr). **Minivans** cost F$15 to Suva, departing from Hospital Road beside the bus stand in Downtown Nadi. These can be substantially quicker but are often hair-raising experiences and you won't get to see much of the scenery along the way. A **taxi** will set you back F$50 to Lautoka or F$200 to Suva.

▲ Surfing Malolo Reef

four hours surfing; both short and long boards can be rented with a few secondhand boards normally for sale.

Around the headland to the south is **Momi Bay**, the site for a new resort development hoping to rival Denarau Island as the most exclusive real estate in Fiji. Plans include a *Marriot* hotel with overwater bungalows, a manicured USPGA Championship **golf course** as well as artificial beaches and lagoons. In the meantime you can stay at the beach-less *Seashell@Momi* (⊤670 6100, Ⓦwww.seashellresort.com.; dorm F$80 includes meals, rooms ❸, cottage ❹, apartments ❺; surf trips F$57.75) a quiet seaside retreat on the south side of the bay. As with *Rendevous Fiji,* most guests are surfers although there's also excellent scuba diving and game fishing on offer. The resort is spacious but plain, with ageing bures and lodge rooms set out pleasantly in the gardens. The air-conditioned one-bedroom apartments are squashed at the back but have modern interiors and fully equipped kitchens. Note that few buses run out here and it takes fifteen minutes by taxi to reach the Queens Road.

Just before the turn-off for the new Momi Bay development, a small track leads to the **Momi Guns** (daily 9am–5pm; F$3; ⊤997 1580), two six–inch World War II coastal artillery guns aimed at Navula Passage in anticipation of Japanese invasion. The site is administered by the National Trust and has a lovely view of the southern Mamanuca Islands.

Inland to the Nausori Highlands

Towering over the coastal flats of Nadi are the high peaks of Koromba to the south and Kornonayitu in the north, both over 1000m and forming part of the spectacular **Nausori Highlands**. A stunning **drive** into these dry hilly grasslands starts from halfway along the Nadi Back Road at the turn-off known as Mulomulo Road. Head inland along this road for 14km. After a steep hairpin bend, keep an eye out for a walking track on the left-hand side (you can park 50m beyond at a roadside clearing on the right). The track leads up past a triangular survey marker to a steep cliff with superb views over the Sabeto River Valley and out over Nadi to the offshore islands.

The road continues climbing through pine forests to Nausori Village. Five kilometres beyond is a fork in the road – the left track marked Natewa Road heads over to Vaturu Dam (see below) but it's a rough 4WD trail and at the time of writing was closed due to a landslide. The right fork leads to **Bukuya Village** where you can **stay** at the *Bukuya Alpine Eco Centre* (☎620 7088; F$60 includes meals), a blue wooden lodge perched high above the village with breathtaking views across the highlands. The owners Jim and Mereani can arrange a variety of activities including pig hunting and horse riding to Naivilavila waterfall (both around F$50). You can also reach Bukuya by **public carrier van** from Nadi market for F$8 (ask for Bukuya or Nanoko), normally departing mid-morning, but there are no public buses.

From the crossroads in Bukuya you can turn right for the Valley Road all the way to Sigatoka Town on the south coast (3hr), or turn left, up the hill and through the sparse alpine wilderness to **Navala Village** (see p.135), with its beautiful traditional thatch bures, and on to Ba Town on the north coast (2hr 45min). Both tracks are remote and bumpy, best suited to 4WD vehicles with high clearance.

North to Lautoka

The most scenic region around Nadi lies along a rural fifteen-kilometre stretch of the Queens Road north of the airport towards Lautoka. Inland is the beautiful **Sabeto River Valley** and the botanical **Garden of the Sleeping Giant**. Further on the road passes through the historic villages of Lomolomo and Viseisei before reaching the tranquil coastal setting of **Vuda Point**, halfway between Nadi Airport and Lautoka.

The Sabeto River Valley

The lush **Sabeto River Valley**, 4km north of the airport towards Lautoka, is accessed along a five-kilometre sealed road which thereafter turns to dirt for another 30km. The valley is flanked on its north side by the distinct outline of the **Sleeping Giant** rock formation with its pointy nose facing the sky. As the road turns to dirt, just beyond Masimasi Hindu Temple, you'll find *Stoney Creek Lodge* (☎672 2206, ⓦwww.stoneycreekfiji.net; camping F$33, dorm F$28, rooms ❷, bure ❸–❹). This delightful **rural retreat**, with dreamy views looking north up the valley, is only fifteen minutes from Nadi Airport and boasts a lovely swimming pool, excellent restaurant and quiet bar. Activities on offer include a trip to hot springs and mountain treks. The dirt road continues on, winding its way up the steep Sabeto Hills to the utterly remote **Vaturu Dam**. This is the location of the spectacular ⚐ *Heaven's Edge eco-resort* (☎670 3986, Ⓔedgefiji@connect.com.fj; 12-bed dorm F$60, bure ❸ includes meals; 2hr 4WD transfers from Nadi F$30). Seemingly at the top of the world, the restaurant, dorm lodge and shared bathrooms sit on a flat grassy plateau with steps leading down to five simple shared thatch bures overlooking the dam. Surrounding and feeding the dam's reservoir are verdant tropical valleys which can be explored by horse-back or on foot to visit caves and waterfalls; bird-watching and fishing from the lake are also available.

The Garden of the Sleeping Giant

One kilometre beyond the Sabeto Valley turn-off, the Wailoko dirt road turns inland off the Queens Road towards the **Garden of the Sleeping Giant** (℡672 2701; Mon–Sat 9am–5pm; F$12). The entrance is 2km further on. These botanical gardens boast a wonderful collection of orchids and other flowering plants as well as several trails meandering through the landscaped grounds and into the lowland rainforest abutting the Sleeping Giant escarpment.

Lomolomo and Viseisei villages

Eight kilometres north of the airport, the rocky tongue of the Sabeto Hills descends dramatically to the base of **Lomolomo** village. From here you can explore a delightful walking track over the hills and back to the Wailoko dirt road. The trail starts from the unsignposted Esivo Road, 1km beyond the village just beyond the timber mill. Three hundred metres down this dirt road, a small track leads uphill following the ridge inland towards the seldom visited **Lomolomo Guns**. It takes thirty minutes to walk to these World War II artillery guns from the main road and there's a fine view overlooking Nadi Bay and the surrounding mountains. For a longer two-hour trek, continue walking along the ridge, bearing right towards the telecommunication antennae. From here the trail meanders around boulders and overhanging caves to the rocky summit of Khan's Farm where you'll notice plenty of goats. From the summit you can follow the access road south to Wailoko Road, 3km inland from the Queens Road and close to the Garden of the Sleeping Giant (see p.79).

Heading north towards Lautoka and just after the Vuda River, the old Queens Road branches off left through the chiefly village of **VISEISEI**. According to Fijian legend this was where **Lutunasobasoba**, the first inhabitant of Fiji, landed his canoe, the *Kaunitoni*, having sailed all the way from Tanganyika (modern-day Tanzania). Today, Fijians around much of the country still claim descent from Lutunasobasoba. Vuda, the **ancient village** that Lutunasobasoba is said to have founded, is a couple of kilometres inland along the Vuda River at the foot of a massive boulder. You can visit by turning right off the Queens Road just before the river, along the the Vuda–Vaivai Road. The site is signposted on the right and may be attended in which case you need to pay a F$5 fee which includes a guided tour. Otherwise, you're free to explore the overgrown paths around the old village site. Keep an eye out for ancient **rock platforms** where homes were built and clearings with accumulated pottery sherds and *kai* shells where the common people cooked. The high chiefs, and supposedly Lutunasobasoba himself, lived atop the rocky bluff for added security; any invaders would have to pass through a rock doorway guarded by warriors. Several **tour companies** incorporate a visit to Viseisei in their itineraries (see p.75).

Vuda Point

On the brow of the hill past Viseisei Village, a scenic three-kilometre road turns left to **Vuda Point**, home to a marina and two small boutique resorts. *Anchorage Beach Resort* (℡666 2099, ⊛www.anchoragefiji.com; rooms ❹–❺, cottages ❻) is perched on a hillside with great views of the offshore islands and inland to Mount Koroyanitu. The resort rooms are colourfully decorated with spa bathrooms, while the beachside villas are spacious albeit in duplex fashion. Between June and November, sugar trains run right past the resort swimming pool, which can be interesting during the day but off-putting at night.

A kilometre further down the road, and beyond the unattractive oil storage tanks, is **Vuda Marina** (℡666 8214, ⊛www.vudamarina.com.fj; VHF Channel

16), considered the safest anchorage for yachts in Fiji. There's a general store and **café** (daily 7.30am–6pm) and the *Yacht Club* is a popular spot on Sundays for a BBQ lunch with live musicians playing jazz and reggae. Adjacent to the marina is *First Landing Resort* (☏ 666 6171, ⓦ www.firstlandingfiji.com; bures ⑥–⑦, villas ⑧ includes cooked breakfast), fronting a pretty coral-sand beach. The gardens here are magnificently mature with huge rain trees and decorative mosaic pathways and there's an excellent restaurant overlooking the beach serving wood-fired pizzas. Bure accommodation is in 33 duplex plantation-style cottages with dark interiors and polished wood floors. The luxury two-bedroom holiday villas have plush, modern furnishings and private swimming pools.

Lautoka and around

Half an hour's drive north of Nadi is **LAUTOKA**, Fiji's second largest city and an important port. It's a surprisingly low-key affair – the city centre doesn't feel any bigger or busier than Downtown Nadi, with most of the 53,000 population living amongst the light industrial suburbs. Although there is little to admire architecturally, Lautoka is a good place to wander with plenty of leafy avenues and diverting **Fiji-Indian stores** and market stalls – the latter a far cry from Nadi's touristy souvenir shops. Looming inland are the hills of the **Koroyanitu National Park**, a worthwhile day-trip.

Lautoka established itself around the **sugar industry**. In 1903 the Australian-owned Colonial Sugar Refinery Company set up headquarters here, attracted by a deep-water harbour that almost rivals Suva's. The **sugar mill** they built is still the largest in Fiji and employs over two thousand people, mostly from the surrounding Fiji-Indian sugarcane farms. In recent years, Lautoka has become a second home for the indigenous people of the **Yasawas** who, without secondary schools or work opportunities, send their children here for education – today, more Fijians live in the city than Fiji-Indians.

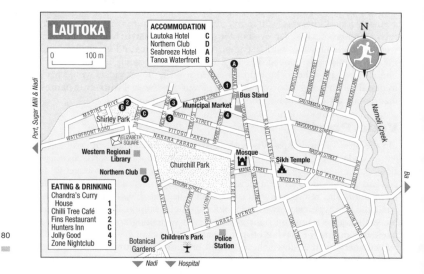

Arrival and orientation

If **arriving** by bus or minivan, you'll be dropped at the bus stand between Tukani and Naviti streets behind the Municipal Market in the heart of the city. Approaching from Nadi, the Veitari roundabout, full of mango sellers from August to December, splits the Queens Road in two. The right fork, along **Drasa Avenue**, passes through Lautoka's residential area, bypassing downtown and joining the Kings Road to Ba Town at the north end of the city. The left fork heads down Navutu Road along the industrial section of Lautoka into downtown. The road passes South Pacific Distilleries (where Fiji's famous rum is concocted), the fishing port and the sugar mill. The rambling corrugated sheds and chimney stacks of the **sugar mill** are fed by an endless parade of cane trucks and trains between June and December, eventually pumping raw molasses along pipes to container ships moored at **Lautoka Port**. It's not a place to linger with the stench of sugar sludge filling the air.

The Town

Beyond industrial Lautoka, the organized city centre is laid out in a grid pattern with one-way streets, flanked by beautiful tree-lined Vitogo Parade and parallel Naviti Street. A walk around this one-square-kilometre centre takes in the majority of **shops**, the municipal market bursting with food produce and an impressive **mosque**. Opposite the mosque, the pick of the endless parade of fashion stores along **Vitogo Parade** include S. Naginda's for men's clothing, Deoji's at #123 for shoes and the department store Jack's on the corner of Vidolo Street which has an extensive selection of women's saris from F$30. Opposite Jack's on Vidolo Street is the tiny boutique shop Silver Age, crammed with ornate Indian costume jewellery. Most of the shops along **Naviti Street** sell a bizarre array of odds and ends, mostly cheap imports from China, but you'll find plenty of colourful **fabrics** sold by the roll. For quality made-to-measure clothing, try Sunil's Tailoring (☎651 1605; Mon–Fri 8am–5.30pm, Sat 8am–2.30pm) upstairs at 54 Naviti Street where a blouse costs F$15 or trousers F$20. Across Naviti Street is the **Municipal Market** (Mon–Fri 7am–5.30pm, Sat 5am–4pm), one of the most spacious and least claustrophobic markets in Fiji – you can sample *yaqona* here for 50 cents a cup, or browse the handicraft stalls which flank the north side alongside Naviti Street.

For a pleasant detour away from the downtown shopping area, head south of Elizabeth Square down Tavewa Avenue. Midway down you can stop for a swim (F$2.50) or a beer at the colonial style **Northern Club** (see below) before continuing on past the government offices and elegant Hari Krishna Temple to Lautoka's superbly kept **botanical gardens** (Mon–Fri 8am–6pm, Sat & Sun 10am–6pm; free). Opposite the gardens is the Children's Park, busy with swings, slides and monkey bars, while up above is the city hospital.

Accommodation

Lautoka Hotel Corner of Naviti and Tui sts ☎666 0388, ✉ltkhotel@connect.com.fj. Handy location and best spot for backpackers. The budget rooms and ten-bed dorms are simple windowless boxes with plywood walls but the good-value deluxe rooms surrounding the pool are pretty with air con and Sky TV. Can get noisy at weekends when two nightclubs operate in the premises. Dorm F$14–17, rooms ❶–❷.

Northern Club Narara Parade ☎666 2469, ✉northernaccom@yahoo.com.au. This pleasant colonial-style establishment is a bit of a gentleman's watering hole and popular with families at weekends but it's close to downtown and set in nice landscaped gardens. The six studio units in a separate two storey cement building are a bit old-fashioned and the bathrooms are tiny but with air con, TV, cooking stove and fridge this is excellent value. ❸.

Seabreeze Hotel 5 Bekana lane Ⓣ666 0717, Ⓕ666 6080. Tucked down a lane from the bus stand and overlooking the ocean, the location is great and the rudimentary rooms are cheap albeit with worn carpets and flowery bedspreads. ❷.

Tanoa Waterfront Marine Drive Ⓣ666 4777, Ⓦwww.tanoahotels.com/waterfront. Located adjacent to Shirley Park and across the road from the ocean, this is Lautoka's only upmarket hotel. A recent facelift included a large landscaped swimming pool but it remains predominantly frequented by business people. ❹–❺.

Eating and drinking

Cafés and restaurants

Chandra's Curry House Tukani St. Simple Indian restaurant serving the usual mix of lamb and chicken curries as well as chicken chow mein and chop suey; mains all around F$4. Grab a table overlooking the bustling bus stand.

Chilli Tree Café 3 Tukani St. Lautoka's most atmospheric place to eat, serving delicious cakes for around F$4, good coffee for F$3.50, a full breakfast for F$10 or kebabs and wraps for F$8. Mon–Sat 7.30am–7pm.

Fins Restaurant Marine Drive Ⓣ666 4777. At the *Tanoa Waterfront* hotel, this is Lautoka's only fine-dining restaurant. A handful of outdoor tables boast ocean views although the modern interior is café-style. The broad but overpriced menu includes curry of the day at F$20, local beef fillet at F$32 or pan-fried tuna at F$29. Daily 6.30–9am, 11.30am–2.30pm, 6–10.30pm.

Jolly Good Corner of Naviti and Vakabale sts. Convenient café if your're after a quick bite with counter-cooked food served from a large trailer and covered outdoor tables overlooking the market. The fish and chips are excellent value at F$3 and the F$1.20 ice cream is worth savouring. Mon–Wed 9am–9pm, Thurs–Sat 8am–10pm, Sun 8am–9pm.

Bars and clubs

Hunters Inn Tui St at the *Lautoka Hotel*. This dark, dungeon-like night club has free entry throughout the week and plays popular Fijian-style hits.

Northern Club Narara Parade Ⓣ666 0184. The bar of this social club is a good place to meet a few locals over a F$1.90 draught beer, the cheapest in Fiji; alternatively play snooker on a full-sized table for 50 cents a game. Also serves bar snacks and F$2.50 meat pies.

Zone Nightclub Naviti St. Popular with a young, predominantly Fiji-Indian crowd. There are DJs on Fri & Sat nights, pool tables and satellite TV showing sports or music. F$3.

Listings

Banking All banks listed have 24hr ATM machines. ANZ Bank 165 Vitogo Parade, Mon 9.30am–4pm, Tues–Fri 9am–4pm, Sat 9am–1pm, also with Currency Express; Westpac 175 Vitogo Parade, fronting Shirley Park Mon–Thurs 9.30am–3pm, Fri 9.30am–4pm.

Cinema Village Four Cinemas 25 Namoli Ave Ⓣ666 3555, daily 10am–11pm; F$5.50. Shows the latest Hollywood blockbusters.

Internet access *Rohit's*, 2nd floor Kamil Building on Narara Parade just off Elizabeth Square, is the cheapest in town at F$1 per hr (Mon–Sat 8am–6pm). *Click Internet* opposite the market on Naviti St is the largest with 20 terminals at F$2 per hr (Mon–Sat 8am–6pm, Sun 9am–5pm).

Laundry Narsey's Laundry Ⓣ666 0363, 5 Yasawa St (Mon–Fri 8am–5pm).

Library Western Regional Library Ⓣ666 0091, Tavewa Ave off Elizabeth Square (Mon–Fri 10am–5pm).

Medical Lautoka Hospital Ⓣ666 0399 off Thompson Crescent caters for emergencies or several general practitioners are based at the Bayly Clinic, 4 Nede St Ⓣ666 4598, (Mon–Fri 8am–1pm & 2pm–4.30pm, Sat 8am–1pm for private doctor or dentist).

Pharmacy Hyper Pharmacy Ⓣ665 1940, 101 Vitogo Parade, Mon–Sat 8am–8pm, Sun 9am–2pm & 6–8pm.

Police Ⓣ666 0222, at Drasa Ave opposite Yawini St. There's also a police post in the city centre on Tui St beside Shirley Park.

Post office Elizabeth Square, Mon–Fri 8am–4pm, Sat 8am–noon.

Sports Club Northern Club Ⓣ666 0184, Narara Parade. Social club with swimming pool (F$2.50), tennis (F$1.50 per hr) and squash (50 per cents per 30min).

Taxi City Cabs Ⓣ666 3950, Tukani St, opposite bus stand.

Telephone At the post office on Elizabeth Square.

The story of Abaca

Abaca got its name by accident. The original village was called Nagara but in 1931 a **landslide** hit the village leaving only three survivors. Thankful to be alive, the three went in search of a new home. On their journey they came across a large stone emblazoned with the letters ABC. The letters had been painted by a missionary in the 1830s while teaching the alphabet to the people of Nagara. Inspired by this prophetic sign, the survivors decided to name their new village "Abaca", an acronym in the local dialect for "the beginning of eternal life after a miracle".

Koroyanitu National Park

Around 10km southeast of Lautoka, **Koroyanitu National Heritage Park** (F$8 admission) has the most accessible walking trails of Fiji's two National Heritage Parks. The park was created in 1992 to preserve the area's natural forests and endemic birdlife from clearing for pine forest and encroaching grasslands. Access to the park is by 4WD from Lautoka via Tavakubu Road off Drasa Avenue. It takes thirty minutes to reach **Abaca** village, headquarters for the park, travelling up a steep dirt road past the dramatic volcanic escarpment of **Castle Rock**. There are no public buses to Abaca but a carrier van from opposite Lautoka bus stand will cost F$25.

At the entrance to Abaca is a small **visitor centre** (Mon–Sat 8am–5pm, Sun 8am–10am & noon–5pm; ☎666 6644 after beep dial 1234) where you can pick up pamphlets and local information. There are two **walking tracks** from here. The most challenging is the Batilamu Track which snakes uphill through forest for two hours until it reaches the summit of the 1,163-metre **Mount Batilamu**. The mountain forms the belly of the Sleeping Giant (see p.79) and from the summit you can see all the way back to Lautoka and across to the Yasawa Islands. Alternatively, an easy two-hour loop trail follows a grassy ridge to **Savuione Falls** which tumbles 80m in two tiers to a deep swimming pool. From the falls, the trail descends into thick dakua forest back to Vereni Falls close to Abaca Village. You can **stay** overnight in the park at the remote wilderness setting of *Nase Lodge* (dorm bed F$30) arranged through the visitor centre. The lodge has two large bunk rooms, communal lounge and kitchen – you're likely to be the only guest unless there's a school group in residence.

If you're interested in exploring the park further, guides from Abaca can accompany you on an **overnight trail** deep into the forest. This involves a tough five-hour walk to the remote village of Navilawa, although at the time of writing a landslide and a precariously hanging boulder has made the trail dangerous. Alternatively, **guided trekking tours** are offered by *Mount Batilamu Trek* (☎664 5747, ✉batilamu@yahoo.com; day tour departs 8.30am; F$100 includes Nadi hotel transfers, lunch and all fees; overnight trek F$200 includes meals and all fees) based in Lautoka.

Travel details

As a tourist hub, **Nadi** is a major centre for travel with the international and domestic airport and the main ferry terminal for the Mamanucas and Yasawa Islands at Port Denarau. Public buses around Viti Levu orginate from either Lautoka and Suva and pass through all towns.

Buses

Lautoka to: Ba (16 daily; 30min–1hr); Nadi (40 daily; 25min–50min); Suva via Rakiraki (6 daily; 6hr); Suva via Nadi and Sigatoka (5hr 30min). Nadi to: Lautoka (40 daily; 25min–50min); Sigatoka (18 daily; 1hr–1hr 45min); Suva via Pacific Harbour (13 daily; 5hr).

Ferries

Port Denarau, Nadi to: Beachcomber (4 daily; 45min); Bounty (4 daily; 35min); Castaway (3 daily; 1hr 50min); Mana (3 daily; 1hr 25min); Malolo (3 daily; 2hr); Malolo Lailai (3 daily; 55min); Matamanoa (2 daily; 1hr 30min); South Sea (4 daily; 30min); Tokoriki (2 daily; 1hr 45min); Vomo (daily; 1hr 15min); Yasawa Islands, Kuata to Nacula (daily; 2–5hr). Wailoaloa Beach, Nadi to: Mana (2 daily; 50min) Vuda Marina to: Beachcomber (daily; 25min); *Nanuya Island Resort* (daily; 2hr 15min); *Octopus Resort* (daily; 1hr 30min); Treasure (daily; 20min).

Flights

Nadi to: Kadavu (daily; 45min); Mana (4 daily; 15min); Malolo Lailai (4 daily; 10min); Matei, Taveuni (2 daily; 1hr 30min); Labasa (daily; 1hr 5min); Savusavu (5 daily; 1hr); Nausori, Suva (10 daily; 25min).

The Mamanucas and Yasawa Islands

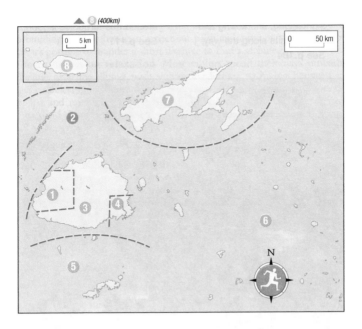

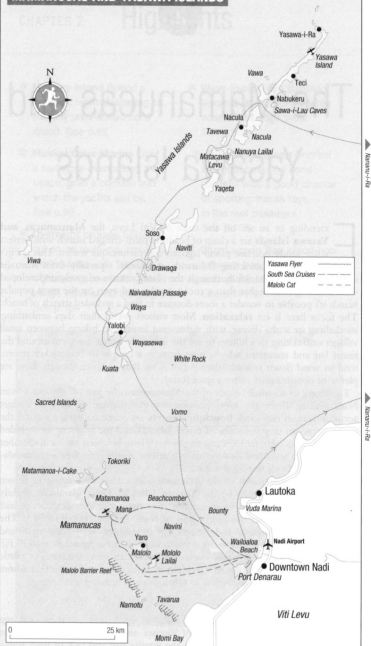

MAMANUCAS AND YASAWA ISLANDS

N

Yasawa-i-Ra

Yasawa
Island

Vawa

Teci

Nabukeru

Sawa-i-Lau Caves

Nacula

Tavewa   Nacula

Nanuya Lailai

Matacawa
Levu

Yaqeta

Soso

Naviti

Viwa

Drawaqa

Naivalavala Passage

Waya

Yalobi

Wayasewa

White Rock

Kuata

Sacred Islands

Vomo

Tokoriki

Matamanoa-i-Cake

Matamanoa   Beachcomber

Mana   Bounty

Mamanucas   Navini

Yaro

Malolo   Mololo
          Lailai

Malolo Barrier Reef

Namotu   Tavarua

Momi Bay

Yasawa Islands

Lautoka

Vuda Marina

Wailoaloa
Beach   Nadi Airport

Downtown Nadi
Port Denarau

Viti Levu

Nanu-i-Ra

Nanu-i-Ra

Yasawa Flyer ....
South Sea Cruises ———
Malolo Cat   — — —

0   25 km

Only three of the larger volcanic islands, Malolo, Yanuya and Tavua, supported **fishing villages**. With poor farming conditions, life was extremely tough and the majority of islanders sought out new opportunities on the mainland. Today, with a reversal of fortunes, every village household earns money through hotel land rent and has at least one family member working in the tourist industry. Food supplies are now shipped in on fast boats from the mainland.

Conditions were better on the larger Yasawa Islands. Thanks to the presence of natural spring water and more fertile soils a greater number of coastal villages established here. The southernmost islands of the chain, Kuata and Wayasewa, are aligned to the mainland village of Viseisei, being part of its *yavusa* or district. All other islands give allegiance to the high chief or **Tui Yasawa** who resides in Yasawa-i-rara Village at the northernmost tip of the group. Little is known about the early history of the Yasawa people except that they were deeply feared as warriors by the inhabitants of eastern Fiji. In 1789 **Captain William Bligh** (see p.262), having been cast adrift in a small rowing boat by the *Bounty* mutineers, rowed through the Yasawas and was chased by several war canoes. Fortunately for him, a squall blew in and the pursuing Yasawans retreated. The passage through which he escaped is known as Bligh Water.

The Mamanucas

Clearly visible from Nadi, the **MAMANUCAS** are a stunning collection of 32 small islands surrounded by 35 square kilometres of translucent ocean strewn with coral reefs. Situated in the lee of the main island of Viti Levu, the islands boast the finest weather in Fiji – year-round sunshine, calm seas and gentle breezes. Given the ease of travel and the wide choice of resorts this is the prime beach holiday destination in the South Pacific.

The **coral islands**, lying immediately offshore from Nadi and Lautoka, comprise a dozen picturesque tiny **coral cays**, which feature heavily in the tourist brochures and boast several world-class surfing breaks. More prominent, though, from the mainland are the larger volcanic islands of the **Malolo Group** with rolling grassy hills framing beautiful **beaches** and the surrounding seas bobbing with yachts and ferries. There are plenty of **activities** here to keep tourists busy, including game fishing, jet skis, and kayaking as well as excellent **scuba diving**.

Forming the western border of Fiji, the remote **Mamanuca-i-Cake Group** is also volcanic in appearance but with more rugged coastlines and steeper hills covered in light forest. Being further from the mainland – it takes ninety minutes by boat from Nadi – these islands are less busy with just three small boutique beach resorts appealing mostly to the honeymoon market; they are also a popular stop on **overnight cruises**.

Those looking to save money on their accommodation might consider staying in Nadi where rooms are far more competitively priced and instead visiting the islands on a series of **day cruises** (see p.73).

Arrival and island transport

There are plenty of options for getting to the Mamanucas. The bulk of visitors arrive on the **fast catamarans** running from Port Denarau at the southern end of Nadi, although there are also **water taxis** and a dedicated service to Mana from **Wailoaloa Beach**. To make the most of fantastic sightseeing along the way you could also consider transferring out to the islands **by air**, returning to Nadi by sea. Two islands, Mana and Malolo Lailai, have airstrips while the rest can be reached by seaplane or helicopter.

Once in the Mamanucas, all resorts have speedboats for **inter-island transfers** but these are expensive – the short ten-minute hop between Malolo and Malolo Lailai for example will set you back F$75 one way. It's a lot cheaper catching one of the fast catamarans between the islands; South Sea Cruises have the most frequent connections.

Fast catamarans

The following companies all offer free hotel pick-ups and drop-offs in the Nadi area. Note that some resorts operate their own speedboat transfers and this will be arranged when you book.

Awesome Adventures (Yasawa Flyer) Port Denarau ☎ 675 0499, ⊛ www.awesomefiji.com. The two-hundred passenger *Yasawa Flyer* departs Port Denarau daily at 8.30am calling in at South Sea Island (F$45), Bounty Island (F$55) and Beachcomber Island (F$60) before heading up to the Yasawas.
Leeward Services Port Denarau ☎ 675 0205. Operates the fast *Malolo Cat I & II* between Port Denarau and Malolo Lailai for *Plantation Island Resort* and *Lomani Resort*. Services depart Port Denarau at 10.30am, 2 & 5pm (F$55 one way, 1hr) and leave Musket Cove Marina on Malolo Lailai at 8.45am, 12.15 & 3.15pm. Guests staying at *Funky*

Fish Resort on adjacent Malolo Island will be picked up from Musket Cove Marina.
South Sea Cruises Port Denarau ☎ 675 0500, ⊛ www.ssc.com.fj. Runs services to most Mamanucas resorts. Their large catamaran ferry departs Port Denarau at 9am, 12.15pm and 3pm calling at: Bounty, Treasure and Beachcomber islands (F$63 one way); Malolo Island (F$73); Castaway Island (F$73) and Mana Island (F$78). A second fast catamaran departs Port Denarau at 9am & 3.15pm for Matammanoa and Tokoriki (F$100). Air-conditioned seating in the Captain's Lounge will set you back an additional F$20.

Water taxis and small boats

Mana Flyer Wailoaloa Beach ☎ 997 1885. Small covered wooden boat serving the backpacker resorts on Mana Island, departing Wailoaloa Beach at 10am and returning from Mana at 12.30pm; F$55 one way. Travellers heading on to the Yasawa Islands can arrange transfers from Mana to Beachcomber Island in order to meet up with the *Yasawa Flyer*.
Sea Fiji Port Denarau ☎ 672 5961, ⊛ www .seafiji.net. 24hr water taxi service from Port

Denarau to all island resorts in distinctive bright orange catamarans and mono-hulls. Transfers to the inner islands start from F$445 for up to eight people. Island-hopping tours and game fishing charters are also available (F$795 half-day, F$1,295 full-day; includes soft drinks, fishing equipment and snorkelling gear).

Flights

Island Hoppers Nadi Airport ☎ 672 0410, ⊛ www .helicopters.com.fj. Provides helicopter flights to most islands in the Mamanucas from Nadi Airport, Denarau Island, Vuda Point and various resorts along the Coral Coast. Prices start from F$200 per person one way (minimum two passengers). Fabulous aerial sightseeing tours (35min; F$330) run on demand.

Pacific Island Seaplanes Nadi Airport ☎ 672 5644, ⊛ www.fijiseaplanes.com. Offers five- and ten-seater seaplanes, taking off from Nadi Airport and splashing down in the resort lagoons. Prices start from F$193 and you're allowed 20kg of luggage.
Pacific Sun Nadi Airport ☎ 672 3016, ⊛ www .pacificsun.com.fj. Five daily scheduled flights from Nadi Airport to Malolo Lailai (7am–5pm; F$66 one

way) and four daily flights from Nadi Airport to Mana Island (8am–4pm; F$79 one way). Flights are in small five- to twelve-seater propeller aircraft and take just 10min.

Turtle Airways Wailoaloa Beach, Nadi ⓣ 672 1888, ⓦ www.turtleairways.com. Sea planes depart from their base at Wailoaloa Beach, a 15min drive from

Nadi Airport. As well as a daily service to Turtle Island (35min) Turtle Airways also offer charter flights to all island resorts in the Mamanucas with sheltered lagoons. Prices start from F$299 per person one way (minimum two passengers). Departure times are dependent on sea conditions and flights are subject to short-notice cancellation.

Scuba diving

With fast boat transfers and a wide choice of dive operators, **divers** can easily sample all dive sites in the Mamanucas while staying at a single resort. The islands are a great spot to **learn to dive** with sheltered lagoons, water temperatures seldom dropping below 24°C and excellent visibility, usually at least 30m.

The dozen or so shallow patch coral dive sites in the northern **coral islands** are ideal for beginners. More advanced divers come here for the two popular **wrecks** – a partially intact World War II B26 bomber at 26m; and the forty-metre-long cruise ship, *Salamander*, lying at 12–28m and covered in soft corals and anemones. In the southwest of the Mamanucas, the thirty-kilometre-long **Malolo Barrier Reef** has several deep drop-offs suitable for experienced divers – turtles, lion fish, rays and large sharks are common. The reef is a fifteen-minute boat ride from Malolo Lailai.

The reefs surrounding **Mana** have some exceptional sites for beginner to intermediate divers. The most raved about site is "Supermarket" offering regular **shark encounters** from white tips to greys as well as a drift dive along a wall with an abundance of lionfish and moray eels. Other sites include "Gotham City" named for its abundance of batfish and "Barrel Head" a wide bommie where you can drift along a wall with massive sea fans and plenty of turtles. Heading west to the Mamanuca-i-Cake Group, **Tokoriki** has several interesting sites with gorgonian **sea fans** featuring prominently at "Sherwood Forest" along with a fine selection of soft corals, nudibranchs and anemones.

Dive operators

AquaTrek Mana ⓣ 666 9309, ⓦ www .aquatrekdiving.com. Highly organized outfit based at *Mana Island Resort*. Four-day PADI Open Water Course F$700, two-tank dive F$195.
Ratu Kini's ⓣ 666 9309. Budget operator for the backpackers on Mana Island. Four-day PADI Open Water Course F$590, two-tank dive F$160.
Reef Safari ⓣ 675 0950, ⓦ www.reefsafari .fj. Text. International operator with bases at South Sea Island and Tokoriki. Four-day PADI Open Water Course F$545, two-tank dive F$175.
Subsurface Fiji ⓣ 666 6738, ⓦ www .subsurfacefiji.com. Dominant dive operator with

bases at Bounty, Treasure and Beachcomber, Navini, Namotu, Tavarua, Malolo Lailai and Malolo as well as at *First Landing Resort* and *Anchorage Beach Resort*, both at Vuda Point on Viti Levu (see p.79). One-tank dive for day-trippers F$130, two-tank dive for resort guests F$230, three-day PADI Open Water Course F$690.
Viti Watersports ⓣ 670 2413, F$ ⓦ www .vitiwatersports.com. Based at Matamanoa but also operates fast covered boats for day-trippers from Denarau Island to the Malolo Barrier Reef. PADI Open Water course F$695, two-tank dive F$190 from Matamanoa, F$225 from Denarau.

The coral islands

The **CORAL ISLANDS** comprise twelve tiny cays, surrounded by a shallow lagoon. These islands seldom rise more than five metres above sea-level, are covered with light scrub vegetation and until recently were all uninhabited.

Island names

Resorts on the smaller coral islands have a higher profile than the islands themselves and in most cases the **traditional Fijian name** has been ditched in favour of an alluringly exotic title. We've used the **resort names** throughout as this is what you will see on transport information and timetables.

Resort name	Fijian name
Beachcomber Island	Tai
Bounty Island	Kadavu
Castaway Island	Qalito
Mystery Island	Tivua
South Sea Island	Vunivadra
Treasure Island	Elevuka

Apart from the resorts that are now built on them, there's not an awful lot to distinguish one from another except for Namotu and Tavarua in the southeastern tip of the Malolo Barrier Reef, which have world class **reef surfing**. The northern coral islands are the most accessible with transfers from both Port Denarau and Vuda Marina in less than twenty minutes.

South Sea Island

The tiny speck of **South Sea Island** (T675 0500, Wwww.ssc.com.fj; dorm F$89 includes meals) is the smallest of the coral islands and takes just 25 minutes to reach from Port Denarau. This is the first stop on both the South Sea Cruises and the *Yasawa Flyer* routes making it a busy little place with both day-trippers from Nadi and backpackers heading to and from the Yasawas. It's a rather cramped island, not even a hundred paces in width, and takes less than five minutes to walk around. Accommodation is in one large wooden dorm room above the restaurant with two toilets and an open sink smack in the middle making it devoid of privacy. If you like snorkelling you'll be disappointed – this close to Nadi Bay the reefs have been damaged by runoff from the sugarcane farms and rivers on Viti Levu. There's not much to do except bask on the beach and cool off in the swimming pool – **day-trippers** are enticed by the offer of unlimited beer or house wine.

Bounty Island

Five minutes northwest of South Sea Island is **Bounty Island**, the largest of the coral cays in the Mamanucas at forty-eight acres and the best for exploring. The laid-back 𝓣 *Bounty Island Resort* (T666 7461, Wwww.fiji-bounty .com; dorm F$42 with ceiling fan, F$47 with air conditioning, bures ⑤) is located on its north beach. It's a popular spot for **backpackers** heading back and forth from the Yasawas and benefits from sound ecological management. The 22 simple wooden and bamboo huts come with air conditioning and en-suite bathrooms and are strung out along the beachfront whilst dorm rooms are set back in a large cement building and share hot-water showers. There's a restaurant and swimming pool with wooden decking beside the beach with kayaks and catamarans for rent. Kayakers can circumnavigate the island in an hour paddling in a crystal clear lagoon. The north lagoon facing the resort has reasonable snorkelling, with shallow waters good for beginners, and there are several massive coral heads with plenty of small reef fish barely 30m from shore. You'll also find walking trails meandering under light scrub for bird-spotting and interesting **beachcombing** with lots of shells, driftwood, hermit crabs and wonderful views looking back to Vuda Point and the mountains of Viti Levu.

Treasure Island

Three kilometres to the west of South Sea Island is **Treasure Island** measuring just over fourteen acres in size and home to family-orientated *Treasure Island Resort* (T 666 6999, W www.fiji-treasure.com; ❸–❾, includes breakfast) with its fantastic all-day kids' club. Accommodation is in 66 air-conditioned family rooms set 30m back from the beach with mini-putt golfing and a **turtle sanctuary** (see below) in the centre of the island. A few hundred metres off the south beach is a tiny sand islet with some good snorkelling.

Beachcomber Island

Facing Treasure Island, less than a kilometre to the west, is **Beachcomber Island** home to the hedonistic *Beachcomber Island Resort* (T 666 1500, W www .beachcomberfiji.com; dorm F$85, rooms ❻, bures ❼, includes meals). Organized party nights with pumping music, limbo dancing, crab races and lots of young gap-year travellers may not be everyone's idea of fun but the island raves past midnight, something of a rarity in Fiji. There are also plenty of activities to fill the days including parasailing, sailing, water-skiing, jet skis and banana-boat rides, all of which can be sampled on an action-packed day cruise. Accommodation is in two stuffy 84-bed dormitories and 22 more comfortable bures with en-suite hot-water bathrooms.

Mystery Island

Ten kilometres northeast of Beachcomber and just a few kilometres off Lautoka on the Viti Levu coast is **Mystery Island**. Leased by Captain Cook Cruises, the island is used as a picnic stop on its day-trips from Nadi and a stop on its three-and seven-day small ship cruises (see p.104). The snorkelling reefs are at least 300m from the beach and best accessed on the organized snorkelling trips by boat.

THE MAMANUCAS AND YASAWA ISLANDS | The coral islands

Sea turtles in the Mamanucas

Three of the world's seven species of **sea turtle** can be found in Fiji and all three lay their eggs on the small coral islands of the Mamanucas. The green and hawksbill are very similar in appearance and average around 1.2m in length whilst the endangered leatherback can reach over 2m. Female turtles reach sexual maturity around the age of 25 and return to the same beach where they hatched to lay their eggs, burying them deep in the sand in batches of up to two hundred. This happens at night, some time between September and January. After sixty to seventy days, the eggs **hatch** en masse, again at night, and the hatchlings make their way to the sea. As few as one in a thousand reach full maturity, and the odds of survival are being reduced further by light and noise pollution from resorts.

Despite a national ban on **hunting turtles** for their meat – which for Fijians is both a delicacy and an essential ingredient in ceremonial feasting – locals in the outlying islands continue to do so. In an effort to revive populations and promote ecological awareness, *Treasure Island Resort* has set up a small **turtle sanctuary** to nurture baby sea turtles for a year before releasing them back into the ocean. If your timing's right you may be able to participate in their release which generally occurs between November and March.

to the Won Ket family who worked the land as a successful copra plantation for 63 years using Chinese labourers – a Chinese cemetery can be seen in the hills. In 1966, with the collapse of copra prices, the island was sold to its present owners, the Smith and Raffe families, both of whom pioneered the region's tourism industry building successful **holiday resorts**.

Accommodation

Lomani Resort ℡666 8212, @www .lomaniisland.com. With just twelve Mediterranean-style whitewashed suites with four-poster beds and a lovely swimming pool with decked outdoor restaurant, this is a good choice for honeymooners. The serene plantation-style setting with open lawns is at the quieter end of Malolo Lailai's main beach with a lagoon deep enough for swimming and snorkelling. ❽–❾

Plantation Island Resort ℡666 9333, @www .plantationisland.com. Large resort bustling with young families. The palm-fringed beach is stunning and there's a specially cordoned-off lagoon area as

well as three swimming pools and windsurfing boards and kayaks to borrow. The restaurant is a bit out-dated but overall it's a great place to have some fun. ❼–❽

Reef House ℡664 0805, @www.afijiholiday.com. Secluded three-bedroom bungalow tucked behind a hill on the northern point of the island along a rocky coastline. The pine-panelled rooms are small and distinctly unfashionable with pastel furniture but as they sleep up to eight people this can make for excellent value. It's a 5min walk to *Musket Cove Resort* where you can rent kayaks, bicycles or snorkel equipment. ❽

Eating and drinking

One of the delights of staying on Malolo Lailai is its choice of **restaurants**. For food shopping *Ananda's* has a small **supermarket** (daily 7am–8.30pm) and The Trader (daily 8am–7pm), beside Musket Cove Marina, stocks a good selection of groceries but no alcohol. Expect to pay double mainland prices. You can buy

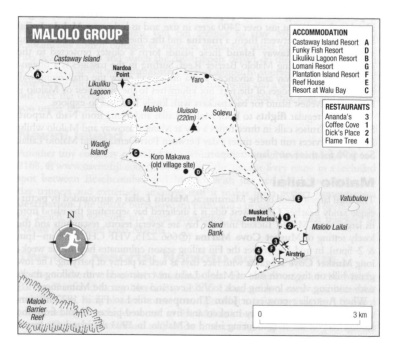

MALOLO GROUP

Castaway Island

Nardoa Point

Likuliku Lagoon

Malolo

Uluisolo (220m)

Yaro

Solevu

Wadigi Island

Koro Makawa (old village site)

Vatubulou

Musket Cove Marina

Sand Bank

Malolo Lailai

Airstrip

N

Malolo Barrier Reef

0   3 km

ACCOMMODATION	
Castaway Island Resort	A
Funky Fish Resort	D
Likuliku Lagoon Resort	B
Lomani Resort	G
Plantation Island Resort	F
Reef House	E
Resort at Walu Bay	C

RESTAURANTS	
Ananda's	3
Coffee Cove	1
Dick's Place	2
Flame Tree	4

ready-to-cook meat and fish packs at The Trader (F$20) and wander over to *Ratu Nemani Island Bar* to cook on the supplied wood-fired BBQs.

Ananda's *Plantation Island Resort* ☎ 666 9333. Located on the beach beside the airstrip midway between *Plantation* and *Musket Cove*. Fijian chef Buli's F$28 three-course BBQ is a winner with a choice of fish fillet, boneless chicken or sirloin steak, cooked in front of you but with a long line of diners waiting in turn behind. Otherwise there's a blackboard full of alternatives: from fettuccine to curry chicken. Come early to ensure a beachside table. Daily 6pm–9pm.

Coffee Cove Musket Cove Marina, accessed from The Trader. Pretty setting and overlooking the marina but the staff are rushed off their feet so don't expect a quick snack. The pie of the day is good value at F$10 including chips and salad, or try the F$14 gruyère quiche. Otherwise, sit admiring the view over a F$3.50 cappuccino. Daily 10am–6.30pm.

Dick's Place *Musket Cove Resort* ☎ 664 0805. Excellent menu from delicious New Zealand lamb shanks to *ika vakalolo* (traditionally cooked fish in coconut cream) to risotto, with mains around F$30.

If you're here on Thurs you'll be treated to the sumptuous Pig on the Spit for F$36. The kids' menu portions are huge and very reasonably priced. Daily 7.30am–10pm.

Flame Tree *Lomani Resort* ☎ 666 8212. This is a fantastic choice if you want to get away from the hordes, and kids – it's adults only here. The food is excellent and the setting thoroughly romantic with just fourteen candlelit tables under a large flame tree. Mains are around F$32 with the lamb rack an excellent option and there's a choice of fourteen wines. It's a good 20min walk along the beach from Musket Cove, but if you call ahead they'll happily pick you up by golf cart. Daily lunch and dinner.

Ratu Nemani Island Bar Musket Cove Marina. Atmospheric bar on an aritificial island connected to the marina by pontoon and overlooking Malolo Bay. A great spot to sip a beer, wine or local spirit (all F$4) or try one of the multicoloured exotically named cocktails (from F$12). Daily 10.30am–11pm.

Activities

Activities at both *Musket Cove Resort* and *Plantation Island Resort* are available to non-guests and include water-skiing, parasailing, banana rides, sport fishing, island-hopping trips and surfing. Subsurface Fiji (see p.91) offer a full range of **scuba diving** courses including PADI Bubblemaker for kids and Nitrox. Thousands of tiny reef fish congregate around the sand bar, a kilometre offshore in Malolo Bay, but you'll need to join the **snorkelling trip** by boat to get there, organized by all resorts on Malolo Lailai.

For **sailing** or speedboat charters, the best option is Dulcinea (☎938 2232; F$420 for 4hr, up to six people), based at Musket Cove Marina. The owner of Dulcinea, Captain Dave, occasionally offers lessons in sailing a small-keeled yacht (from F$60 an hour). The activity bure (daily 8am–5pm) beside Musket Cove Marina rents out **bicycles** for F$15 per day. There's a flat nine-hole **golf course** behind *Plantation Island Resort* (F$15.50 a round or F$26 including golf clubs and balls). Several holes run parallel to the beach (the longest is only 329 yards) and with nice sea views it makes for a pleasant walk.

Malolo

Malolo is the largest island in the Mamanucas, home to two budget resorts as well as the most luxurious resort in the region. On the north coast, backed by grassy sunburnt hills with patches of ironwood trees, is the chiefly village of **Yaro**. Twenty minutes' walk along the tidal beach down the east coast is **Solevu** promoted as "shell village" to tour groups although many of the shells on sale here are imported from Asia. Fifteen minutes further south is the tiny settlement of **Cubi**, inhabited by a community from Fulaga (see p.211) in the Lau Group – the men are renowned wood carvers and you should be able to find fine samples of *tanoa* bowls and war clubs. From Cubi, you can follow the inland trail to Uluisolo (see p.98) or it's a ten-minute walk to the southern point of Malolo

▲ Windsurfers off Malolo Lailai

which juts out into the shallow lagoon almost touching Malolo Lailai – you can walk between the two islands at low to mid tide.

Although not practical for swimming or snorkelling (the reefs have been extensively damaged by fishing), the southern lagoon is great for **kitesurfing**, especially off *Funky Fish Resort* which picks up the southeasterly trade winds creating almost perfect conditions between May and October, although guests must bring their own equipment.

The real beauty of Malolo lies inland. There are plenty of **walking tracks** around the island including several ascending to the 220-metre Uluisolo. At the summit is a US-built World War II **lookout post** offering fabulous views of the entire Mamanucas and as far north as Matacawalevu in the northern Yasawas. The easiest ascent is from *Funky Fish Resort* from where it takes just under an hour to reach the top although note that there is little shade along the way. There's also an excellent walking track along the fire break at the northwestern point of the island. The path winds its way over several bluffs with lovely panoramas from **Naroba Point** and looks down on the exclusive *Likuliku Lagoon Resort* (see below). From Naroba Point, you can scramble down to shimmering **Navutu Beach** and walk east along the north coast all the way to the southern point of Malolo past Yaro and Solevu villages – if coming from Yaro the track ascending Naroba Point is difficult to find.

Accommodation

Funky Fish Resort ☏ 651 3180, ⓦ www
.funkyfishresort.com. Small backpacker resort run by Brad Johnston, ex Fiji rugby coach. The 16-bed dorm lodge backs onto the swimming pool and also has six tiny double rooms inside. Ten equally small beach huts with en-suite bathrooms line the narrow beachfront and there are two spacious family bures sleeping five. The restaurant and bar take pride of place on the hill overlooking the lagoon and beyond to the surfing breaks along the Malolo Barrier Reef making it popular with surfers. Dorm F\$35, rooms ❷, bures ❷–❻.

Likuliku Lagoon ☏ 672 0978, ⓦ www
.likulikulagoon.com. In a delightful crescent-shaped bay with tidal beach, this resort oozes elegance. The eighteen hand-crafted beachfront bungalows are exquisite with massive bathrooms with indoor and outdoor showers. The very pricey box-like overwater bungalows have good snorkelling direct from the steps leading down into the lagoon but are a long walk from the main resort area. ❾

Walu Beach Resort ☏ 665 1777,
ⓦ www.walubeach.com. Rebuilt as part of a reality TV series, *Walu Beach* has an unfinished

feel to it. However, the modern whitewashed beachfront bures are the best value in the Mamanucas while the six ocean-view lodges perched up a steep hill are exceptionally spacious (sleeping up to six) and double as dorms. With a reasonable beach and swimming pool, plenty of water sports as well as dolphin-watching and surfing trips, it's a great budget option. Dorm F$90 includes breakfast and dinner, lodge ❹, bure ❺.

Castaway Island

Lying less than a kilometre off the northwest tip of Malolo, steep rocky **Castaway Island** has a stunning powdery sand point and gorgeous turquoise lagoon. *Castaway Island Resort* (☎666 1233, ⓦwww.castawayfiji.com; ❾) offers 66 traditional thatch bures located on the point. It's a popular choice for families as well as older couples. There's a tennis court, swimming pool and spa in the landscaped gardens as well as exceptional snorkelling from the beach.

The island also boasts one of the best **walking trails** in the Mamanucas. Starting at the back of the resort a narrow path climbs for five minutes before levelling out and meandering through light natural forest. After twenty minutes, the trail emerges on the rocky slopes of the east side of the island where you're graced with wonderful views overlooking the small uninhabited Mociu Island and beyond to Mana and Matamanoa. The trail ends here but it's worth continuing for ten minutes, picking your way over the boulders until you reach the eastern tip of the island. Here there's another stunning view overlooking Likuliku Lagoon and the western end of Malolo Island. You can return via the north beach – look out for a trail on the right within a minute's walk back down through the forest. Follow this to the beach and then continue north and around Monkey Rock, which resembles a monkey's head, and back to the resort.

Surfing Malolo on the cheap

Surfing at **Malolo Barrier Reef** is exceptional with waves up to five metres high, crystal clear water and smooth right- and left-hand breaks. The most famous breaks are the left-handers "Cloudbreak" and "Restaurants" facing Tavarua where the Globe Pro Fiji championships are usually held. However, unless you fork out mega-bucks to stay at one of the two surf resorts in the area, you can only surf them on a Friday when there's public access. Fortunately, there are several excellent **non-exclusive breaks** which can be surfed any day of the week. These include the right barrel of "Wilkes" and "Desperations". One of the best ways to experience them is with Small John (☎930 2262) from Solevu village on Malolo island. He and his brother Suji offer **surfing trips** (F$45 for 2hr, minimum two people), picking up guests from resorts around the Malolo Group. Both are skilled boatmen and have surfed the reefs at Malolo for over fifteen years without incident. You'll find Small John in person at the activities hut at *Plantation Island Resort* on Malolo Lailai (see p.95) whilst Suji works at the adjacent *Musket Cove Resort*. The brothers share a selection of long and short boards available for rent at F$30 per day. Other resorts offering boat trips to the reefs include *Funky Fish Resort* (15min), *Castaway Island* (20min) or *Mana Island* (35min). There's also direct access from *Seashell at Momi* (25min) and *Rendezvous Surf Resort* (25min) both on the mainland, a twenty-minute drive south of Nadi (see p.76).

Note that most of the breaks are at their best in the **morning** before the winds freshen up and the prime season for monster waves is between April and November. Surfing here is not for beginners – waves can be huge and, with **sharp coral heads** just a few metres below the surface, any untimely wipeout could lead to severe cuts or grazes.

Mana

Mana is one of the best islands in the group to explore with several hilly peaks and outstanding views of the surrounding islands. Flanked by gorgeous sweeping beaches, this 569-acre island is home to the largest resort in the Mamanucas, plus four small backpacker resorts. It lies on the outer edges of the Malolo Group, twenty five minutes by boat from Malolo and Castaway Island.

The island is split by the *Mana Island Resort* which occupies the entire western side of the island, and the **backpacker hostels** squashed in amongst the Fijian village on **South Beach**. The two areas are separated by a high wire fence which runs from the jetty across to the north side of the island. The fence was erected in the 1990s when a dispute broke out between the resort and the backpacker hostels. For the time being both parties get along and visitors can wander back and forth although backpackers are not permitted to use the *Mana Island Resort* facilities. The **lagoon** off South Beach has copious amounts of seaweed, but swim fifty metres out and you'll reach a nice drop-off with great visibility for snorkelling, coral heads teaming with fish and the chance to spot the occasional turtle.

Past the rocks enclosing either side of South Beach are fine stretches of secluded sand. It's possible to walk around the entire island in about two hours, mostly along the beachfront, but make sure it's close to low tide as crossing the rocky points between beaches when wet can be difficult. The beaches on the north side of Mana have even better **snorkelling** with a steep drop-off just 50m from shore, particularly off **Dream Beach**, location of the US *Shipwreck* television series in 2007.

There are also several nice walks along the hilly ridges: two signposted trails depart from the *Mana Island Resort*, both a fifteen-minute amble through light forest and offering great sunset views; the other trailhead starts behind the blue lodge at *Ratu Kini's* and follows the eastern ridgeline to the sixty-metre summit of Delai Koro Navoku with superb views overlooking the rocky islands of the Mamanuca-i-Cake Group.

Accommodation

Mana Lagoon ☎929 2337. Cheapest of the Mana backpackers with a large and lively sand-floor beach-front restaurant and two rather stuffy dorm lodges at the back. Dorm F$55, rooms ❸, includes meals.

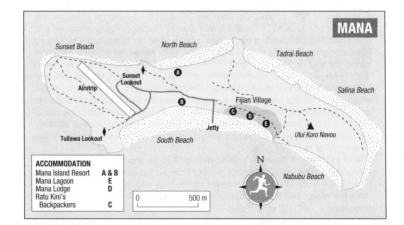

The destruction of Solevu village

In July 1840 a flotilla of six **US Navy warships** was sent to the South Pacific to survey the islands and assure the safety of American whalers in the region. Having toured Tonga, Samoa, New Zealand and most parts of Fiji, the ships arrived at Malolo island. A small boat was sent to Solevu village to bargain for much needed food provisions but the crew was ambushed and two officers killed. Outraged by this unprovoked attack, the captain of the flotilla, John Wilkes, set about revenge. First, the bodies were recovered and buried in an unmarked grave on tiny Kadavu island (presently home to *Bounty Island Resort*); then the village of **Solevu** was swiftly burned to the ground, garden plantations ripped apart, canoes sunk and 57 men slaughtered. The attack proceeded to neighbouring Yaro where the village elders hastily surrendered by prostrating themselves as a sign of humility. Wilkes ordered the villagers to supply his ships with water, yams, a dozen pigs and three thousand coconuts – a huge task considering the damage caused by the attack and the poor farming conditions of the region. Wilkes was subsequently court-martialled for his severe actions – the first military strike in Fiji carried out by Western forces.

Mana Lodge ☎620 7030, ✉ manalodge2@yahoo .com.fj. The three shared cottages and dorm lodge all look cheerful from the outside but have rather dingy interiors with tired windowless bathrooms. They're virtually on the beach though, and with exceptionally cheap rates it makes a tempting option for the more laid-back traveller. Basic meals are served in the communal restaurant. The owners offer surf tours, scuba diving and excellent value island-hopping boat trips. Dorm F$60, rooms ❸, bures ❹, includes meals.
Mana Island Resort ☎665 0423, ⓦwww .manafiji.com. With 150 rooms and bungalows, this is the largest of the Mamanuca resorts, but spread out over three hundred acres of landscaped gardens and fronting both South and North Beaches you wouldn't think so. There are loads of amenities and water activities and a wide range of accommodation options from rooms, apartments and bungalows. ❻–❾
Ratu Kini's Backpackers ☎672 1959, ⓦwww.ratukini.com. Long-established but rather disjointed backpacker hostel. The restaurant and bar are right on the beach, the new units set in a cement building thirty metres behind and the lodge rooms and dormitory at the back of the village abutting the hill. Interiors are clean and there's a lively atmosphere at night with themed entertainment. Tent F$35, dorm F$45–55, rooms. ❸

Mamanuca-i-Cake Group

The enchanting **MAMANUCA-I-CAKE GROUP** lies beyond the fast catamaran route from Port Denarau although there are regular connections by smaller outboard boats. Only two of the thirteen islands have resorts, **Matamanoa** and **Tokoriki**, and there are traditional fishing villages on **Tavua** and **Yanuya**. Otherwise, the islands are completely uninhabited – **Modriki** and its equally stunning neighbour **Monu** were made famous in the 2001 film *Castaway* starring Tom Hanks but the remote **Sacred Islands** remain well off the tourist trail, only visited briefly by an overnight cruise company or by private yachts.

Matamanoa

Rocky **Matamanoa** is covered in thick forest with a gorgeous beach on its eastern flank. The twenty spacious thatch bures at ⚴ *Matamanoa Island Resort* (☎672 3620, ⓦwww.matamanoa.com; ❼–❽) are raised slightly from this beach giving fabulous ocean views, with fourteen air-conditioned rooms at the back in a single storey cement block. If you're looking for a good-value romantic getaway this is the place to stay. Bird Rock, a few hundred metres off the southern coast teems with sea birds, mostly noddies, terns and frigates, and is a fantastic spot for snorkelling and scuba diving operated by Viti Watersports (see p.91).

A steep trail from the resort, starting behind the tennis court, winds its way up to the island's summit where several huge boulders seem to balance precariously; it's easy to scale these for one of the most impressive **views** in Fiji – a 360-degree panorama with small islands in all directions. Directly north is **Tavua**, the third largest island in the Mamanucas with a single village on its west coast, lined with lush coconut trees which stick out amongst its sunburnt barren hills. If you come in the evening or early morning, there's a good chance of spotting fruit bats and doves which feed in the forests and possibly the elusive crested iguana, which is usually well camouflaged in the canopy.

Tokoriki

Surrounded by a fringing reef, hilly **Tokoriki** has two resorts either side of a rocky outcrop dividing a long stretch of beach on the west side of the island. 𝕁 *Amunuca Island Resort* (☏664 0640, ⓦwww.amunuca.com; ⑨–⑧) has a contemporary feel with affordable one- and two-bedroom whitewashed units perfect for families. The resort overlooks a turquoise lagoon and offers wakeboarding, banana-boat rides and parasailing. Neighbouring *Tokoriki Island Resort* (☏672 5926, ⓦwww.tokoriki.com; ⑨) is an upmarket retreat for honeymooners. The resort has a gorgeous infinity pool overlooking the ocean and several beach bures. Perched against the hillside at the far end of the property are a series of **private villas** ranking amongst the most delightful in Fiji, each with handcrafted wooden interiors and their own plunge pools.

In recent years Tokoriki has suffered from beach erosion and large amounts of seaweed washing up on certain tides and giving off a pungent smell. The locals believe this is due to the lack of hurricanes over the last decade and when one eventually hits the seaweed will be washed out. Thankfully, the offshore reefs are unaffected and **snorkelling** is excellent about 200m from the beach at both resorts. From May to July the lagoon teems with tiny bait fish attracting both **seabirds** which circle and dive bomb from above, and locals from the neighbouring villages casting fishing nets from small boats.

Yanuya, Monu and Modriki

Tokoriki is owned by the people of neighbouring **Yanuya**, a long thin island with several knolls. The village here is renowned for its **pottery making** and you can visit on a day-trip from either resort, or on the daily *Seaspray* sailing cruise from Mana island (see p.100) which comes ashore for a traditional *kava* ceremony and village craft market. Off the west side of the village are the islands of **Monu** and **Modriki** used as the setting for the film *Castaway*. With steep craggy rock faces and thick forests, its difficult to explore these islands but with a guide it's possible to reach the summit of the long flat rock face of Modriki from where Tom Hanks looked out in despair seeing nothing but ocean. In reality you can see six islands directly in front of you to the east, the Sacred Islands and the southern Yasawas to the north, as well as most islands in the Mamanucas. The beaches on the eastern side of both islands are beautiful with fine white sand piled deep on a point backed by tall palm trees.

The Sacred Islands

Ten kilometres north of Tokoriki, the seven uninhabited **Sacred Islands** (or Mamanuca-i-Ra) rise out of the ocean in breathtaking splendour. Between May and September a handful of yachts are usually anchored in the protected bays here enjoying the solitude. Apart from the weekly visit by Captain Cook Cruises, few other people venture this way except the occasional TV crew who have filmed four series of *Survivor* on the islands. The reef alongside the picturesque two-hundred-metre sand spit on Vanua Levu has fantastic **snorkelling** with extensive coral gardens but the beach is difficult to land on. Neighbouring Navadra is more accessible with a good swimming beach. The islands are important nesting grounds for migrating sea birds, particularly terns and noddies.

The Sacred Islands are owned by the people of Tavua. In their oral history, the **legend** of the canoe *Rogovaka*, arriving with Fiji's first inhabitants led by Tui Na Revurevu, is still recalled in dance. The new arrivals are said to have settled on the largest of these islands and called it Vanua Levu, translating to "big island" (not to be confused with its much larger namesake in northern Fiji). The legend goes on to tell of a second wave of immigrants that found Vanua Levu already settled, and continued on to Vuda on Viti Levu (see p.79). A village thrived on Vanua Levu for a while, but as the island has no source of spring water, it was later abandoned. An archaeological excavation revealed ancient **Lapita pottery** which seems to justify the legend's authenticity. The people of Tavua hold the island sacred and to this day, it's expected that anyone setting foot on Vanua Levu should lay a traditional gift of *yaqona* roots in a small cave found behind the row of coconut palms on the eastern side of the sand spit.

The Yasawa Islands

The volcanic **YASAWA ISLANDS** attract thousands of visitors drawn to their dramatic jagged peaks, tranquil bays and stunning beaches. Connected by a fast daily catamaran service from Nadi the islands are easy to hop between and have developed into a popular **backpacker trail**.

The group of thirty islands has three distinct zones. **Kuata**, **Wayasewa and Waya**, in the southern part, are similar in nature to the outer Mamanucas with high mountain peaks, dramatic rock faces and fantastic walking tracks. These three islands are the closest to the mainland, only two hours by fast catamaran, and are by far the most interesting to visit with deep bays and pretty villages providing regular stops for **overnight cruises**. To the north is the largest island in the group, **Naviti**, with rolling grassy hills and a dozen small offshore islands where **manta rays** congregate between May and October. Fifteen minutes north of Naviti are the **northern Yasawas**, home to a cluster of budget resorts and three super-exclusive retreats.

Arrival and island transport

The efficient *Yasawa Flyer* **catamaran** (☎675 0499, ⓦ www.awesomefiji.com) departs from Port Denarau daily at 8.30am and returns at 6pm stopping in either direction at all Yasawa resorts as far north as Nacula as well as several islands in the Mamanucas (see p.89). Tickets start at F$90 for a one-way trip to Kuata (2hr). You can also buy transfers between islands, although if you're going to island-hop, the best option is to purchase the **Bula Pass** (F$269 for

The rise of the resort

Barely twenty years ago, travellers who wanted to explore the Yasawas had to obtain a special visitor pass from the District Office in Lautoka. However in 1987, the government decided to open up the region to independent travel. A few **backpacker resorts** initially sprang up on Tavewa and these were soon followed by similar developments on Waya and Wayasewa. Passage to the islands was by small fishing boat, usually without radio or life jackets and often with dubious engines. Having witnessed the success of these early resorts, the government opened an **ecotourism** start-up fund offering F$50,000 worth of materials to local landowners. The result was an explosion of budget resorts. Since 2001, with the introduction of the *Yasawa Flyer*, the region has changed dramatically and the romantic days of exploratory tourism have given way to a thriving commercial industry with over thirty resorts now operating across the area.

seven days, F$389 for fourteen days or F$419 for 21 days) allowing unlimited trips on the *Flyer* until you return to Port Denarau. Note that you and your luggage will be transferred from the *Yasawa Flyer* to your resort by a small outboard-motor boat and some resorts charge F$5–15 for this service.

A few resorts try to compete with the *Yasawa Flyer* by offering quicker **direct transfers** from Lautoka on the mainland for around the same price. While these can shave some time off the journey, the boats are often too small for the somewhat choppy waters and best avoided. The only exceptions are the comfortable resort speedboats taking guests to *Navutu Stars* or *Nanuya Island Resort* in the **northen Yasawas**. These boats reach their respective islands in about two hours thirty minutes, half the time of the *Yasawa Flyer*.

The only **airstrip** in the Yasawas is on the northernmost island, Yasawa Island, but the grass runway with a steep inclination is used exclusively by the upmarket *Yasawa Island Resort*. Turtle Airways (☎672 1888; F$299 one way; daily, times vary) provides **seaplane transfers** (35min) between Wailoaloa Beach in Nadi and Nanuya Levu in the northern Yasawas but you must pre-arrange with your chosen resort for them to pick you up by boat from Nanuya Levu.

Cruise trips

Taking a multi-day **cruise** may not appeal to everyone, but it can be the most convenient way to experience the Yasawas. All the cruises listed below anchor at sublime open-water snorkelling reefs, take time out at secluded beaches and visit traditional villages with great sightseeing from the boat along the way.

Blue Lagoon Cruises ☎666 1622, ⓦwww .bluelagooncruises.com. Offers a range of cruises to the Yasawas from the two-night "Club Cruise" (from F$617 per person) aboard a 39m *Nanuya Princess* to the six-night "Gold Club Cruise" (from F$1770 per person) on a deluxe 60m catamaran. Prices include all meals. Departures are from Lautoka Wharf (Club Cruise every Wed & Sat 10am; Gold Club Cruise every Mon & Thurs 3pm). **Captain Cook Cruises** ☎670 1823, ⓦwww .captaincook.com.fj. With a maximum of ninety guests and spanning four levels with swimming pool, sauna and sun deck and lively entertainment, this rather square-looking cruise ship is surprisingly spacious on board and cabins are comfortable. Four-night Northern Yasawa Cruise departs Port Denarau at 2pm every Tues (from F$1468 per person for cabin bunks includes all meals). **Windjammer Sailing Safari** ☎670 1823, ⓦ www.fijisailingsafari.com.fj. Probably the most romantic way to travel around the Yasawas, this 35m double-mast schooner sets sail to reefs, caves and fishing spots each day returning to *Barefoot Lodge* on Drawaqa Island for the night. Departs Port Denarau at 9pm every Mon & Thurs (3 nights F$535, 4 nights F$713 per person including accommodation at *Barefoot Lodge* and all meals).

Backpacker resorts

The majority of **backpacker resorts** in the Yasawas are run by the islanders themselves, either as individual businesses or as community projects. Services and hygiene have improved over the years although you're still likely to run into the odd creepy crawly especially in the thatch bures. Bathrooms are usually shared and only offer cold water although a couple of resorts now offer en suites. **Meals** at the more basic resorts remain hopelessly inadequate, consisting of huge dollops of rice with boiled boney fish or tinned spaghetti – it's definitely worth bringing some snacks. At the larger resorts you may get to choose from a limited menu.

Compared to the mainland, **costs** are inflated but by no means expensive. Most resorts charge F$60 for a dorm bed including three meals while a small bottle of beer costs around F$4. Snorkelling gear costs F$5 a day to rent so it's definitely worth bringing your own set. There's little else to spend money on – organized **activities** are limited to fishing trips and village visits which work out at F$15–45 per person. Around half of the backpacker resorts don't accept **credit cards**, and most won't accept travellers' cheques so you should bring plenty of cash. Those that do accept credit cards usually apply an additional five percent charge to your bill.

Whirring diesel generators provide **electricity** and tend to run from 6pm to 10pm only. There is no television or Internet access. While a few resorts have installed satellite phones the majority rely on one-way radio phones. **Mobile phone** coverage reaches all islands, but in the north, particularly on the west coasts, you'll need to climb a hill to get reception.

Kuata, Wayasewa and Waya

The three volcanic islands of **Kuata**, **Wayasewa** and **Waya** are the most striking of the Yasawa Islands and on a clear day can be seen from Nadi jutting out on the distant horizon. The fifty-kilometre journey by boat from Port Denarau takes just under two hours.

▲ Snorkellers off Kuata island

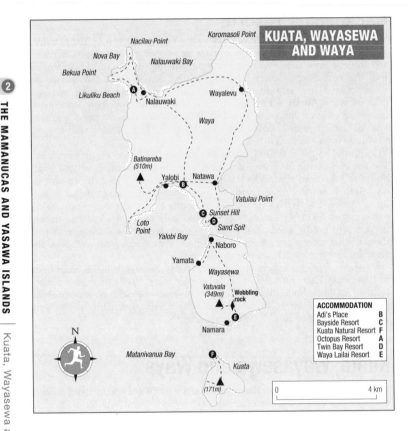

Map: KUATA, WAYASEWA AND WAYA

Nacilau Point
Koromasoli Point
Nova Bay
Nalauwaki Bay
Bekua Point
Likuliku Beach
Nalauwaki
A
Wayalevu
Waya
Batinareba (510m)
Yalobi
Natawa
B
Vatulau Point
Loto Point
C
Sunset Hill
D
Sand Spit
Yalobi Bay
Naboro
Yamata
Wayasewa
Vatuvala (349m)
Wobbling rock
E
Namara
Matanivanua Bay
F
Kuata
(171m)
N

ACCOMMODATION
Adi's Place — B
Bayside Resort — C
Kuata Natural Resort — F
Octopus Resort — A
Twin Bay Resort — D
Waya Lailai Resort — E

0   4 km

Kuata

Kuata, the most southerly island of the Yasawas, has been designated a **nature sanctuary** by its owners on adjacent Wayasewa. The only civilization is at *Kuata Natural Resort* (☏666 9020; dorm F$65, bures ❸, includes meals) a lively backpacker resort popular among the Bula Pass crowd. The thatched-roof dorms are a tad tired looking, but the en-suite bungalows with tiled floors are spacious and clean.

Pleasant walking trails meander around the oddly shaped hills and rocky outcrops but, unless you're very lucky, you're unlikely to see any of the **crested iguanas** that hide in the forest trees. A deep ocean wall immediately off the island's west coast has fantastic **scuba diving** with an unusual figure-of-eight swim through pinnacles and caves off the east coast. There are dive operators at both *Kuata Natural Resort* and neighbouring *Waya Lailai Resort* or you can dive with Captain Cook Cruises (see p.104). Snorkelling is also very good here and there's a popular reef reached by boat where you're likely to see quite a few reef sharks.

Wayasewa

Across the passage from Kuata, **Wayasewa** is dominated by the towering 350-metre-high twin peaks of Vatuvula and Vatusawalo with the old village of Namara and a **backpacker resort** sitting precariously beneath. In 1985, after heavy rain, a landslide brought several huge boulders tumbling down the hillside to within inches of people's homes. The village was declared unsafe and relocated to the north side of the island at Naboro. It didn't take long, though, for a few stubborn families to return and when the adjacent backpacker resort opened in 1995, more villagers moved back. Today, over half of the houses are occupied, although most families with young children prefer living close to the new primary school at Naboro.

Waya Lailai Resort (☏651 2292, ✉wayalailai@connect.com.fj; dorm F$70, bures ④, includes meals) is one of the more organized backpacker resorts in the Yasawas with a lot of activities, yet it's managed to retain a charming laid-back Fijian style atmosphere. Set over three terraced levels with spacious lawns, the two dorm lodges sit at the top overlooking ten small en-suite bures which look down onto the beach and ocean. There's a large wooden-deck restaurant abutting the hill with stunning views over to Kuata and unobscured stargazing.

The forty-minute **hike** from the back of the resort to the summit of Vatuvula is a must, especially at sunset. The well-trodden track ascends steeply through forest and up a narrow crag before opening out onto a rocky escarpment that leads to the summit. It's hard going after rain and crossing the ten-metre-long boulder to reach the sheer-cliff summit is a little nervy, but for conquerors there are fabulous views looking directly down on the resort and over the bay to Kuata and the Mamanucas. The return leg passes another island icon, the **wobbling rock**, a giant boulder you can rock from side to side. It's also worth hiking across to Naboro Village on the north coast (3hr) – the resort will arrange to pick you up by boat. If you plan to move on, ask them to take your luggage by boat to Naboro – from there you can walk across the two-hundred-metre sand spit to *Twin Bay Resort* (see below) on neighbouring Waya island or around the point to the beautiful retreat *Bayside Resort* (see p.108).

Waya

Dramatic **Waya** has a strange, contorted appearance with knife-edge ridges, monumental rock protrusions and several unbelievably photogenic **beaches**. From its western coast, a giant's face seems to peer out from the island, slanting back as though floating in the sea. Almost oblong in shape, a fishing village lies in each corner. All are connected by **walking trails**, making it a paradise for hikers. Although Waya is connected to Wayasewa by a **sand spit** exposed at low tide, the islands' inhabitants have very different roots – the people of Waya look north to the high chief of Yasawa Island while Wayasewa is inhabited by the people of Vuda from Viti Levu.

For **hikers**, the southern side of Waya, with its two budget resorts, is a great base from which to explore the island. From here walking trails head along the cliff edge and into the undulating hills and it's possible to scale the pointed 510-metre Mount Batinareba. Local **guides** (around F$30 per half day) are essential for all but the short twenty-minute trail to Sunset Hill as the paths can be difficult to follow and are treacherous after rainfall; the locals also believe dangerous spirits lurk in the hills; make sure you carry plenty of water.

Sitting directly on the sand spit is the budget *Twin Bay Resort* with a curved beach extending either side. There are pretty **coral reefs** in both bays although the west side is more sheltered. A twenty-minute walk along the west beach past the *Bayside Resort* brings you to **Yalobi**, one of the most stunningly located villages in Fiji. Set in a deep bay, fronting a sandy beach, it's backed by a series of massive contorted cliffs almost 500m high with green veins of rainforest growing in the fissures and valleys. Yalobi is the chiefly village of Waya island home to around five hundred people, a health centre and a primary school.

Along the west coast are the pretty twin bays of Liku and Likuliku each with a small resort. The most established of these, *Octopus Resort*, faces a delightful long crescent-shaped beach backed by coconut palms with extensive coral gardens offshore. There's a great coastal hike from here – walk to the north end of **Likuliku Beach** and around the rocky ledge of Bekua Point to secluded Nova beach. At low tide, you can rock-hop around Nacilau Point for a sweeping view of the north coast of Waya island. Just before you reach Nalauwaki Village climb over the hills and back down to *Octopus Resort* – the complete circuit takes two to three hours.

Accommodation

Adi's Place Yalobi ☎ 665 0573 or 992 6377. This family-run guesthouse located between Yalobi village and the primary school is a great choice if you want to interact with the local community. The basic wooden lodge rooms with a simple outdoor bathroom are set on an open lawn area slightly separated from the village. There's also a quaint tiny bungalow available with an en-suite bathroom. Cash only. Dorm F$60, rooms ❸, bungalow ❹, includes meals.

Bayside Resort Yalobi ☎ 620 9565, ⓦ www.baysideresortfiji.com. With just two thatched bures overlooking a secluded beach and sharing a bathroom between them, kerosene lamps for light and no electricity, this place couldn't be more intimate. The home-cooked meals are extremely filling but drinks can be limited so bring your own (along with snorkelling gear). Cash only. Bures ❸, includes meals.

Octopus Resort Nalauwaki, ☎ 666 6337, ⓦ www.octopusresort.com. Appealing to families, couples and the more refined backpacker, this resort has a gorgeous beach location with swimming pool and excellent food selected from a blackboard menu. Note that local taxes are not included in their online rates. Book in advance. Dorm from F$94, bures ❻–❼, including meals and taxes.

Twin Bay Resort Natawa, ☎ 651 6773. Although it's terribly disorganized (the village selects a new manager every year) and the staff seem unmotivated, this resort has an undeniably fabulous setting. The pretty thatched bures all have small en-suite bathrooms but, in most, either shower heads or basins are missing and water pours out of a plastic pipe. Bring your own snorkelling gear and snacks. Cash only. Dorm F$65, bures ❸, includes meals.

Naviti

Less intriguing than Waya island but blessed with delightful secluded beaches, **Naviti** is the largest of the Yasawa Islands, home to five villages and the region's only boarding school. The island is shaped somewhat like a lobster with two elongated arms reaching out to the north and a cluster of small islets forming a tail to the south. The best of the **beaches** is alongside *Botaira Beach Resort* on the southwest side.

A gradual climb from Botaira into the hills and along a grassy ridge to the southern point of the island presents an inspiring view looking down on the lagoon around **Drawaqa island** with its thousand hues of blue. The lagoon offers excellent **snorkelling** and between May and October it's possible to swim with **manta rays**, which feed around the rich current-fed passages. Your best chance of seeing them is one hour after high tide. You can visit from *Botaira Beach Resort*, a ten-minute boat ride away, or swim directly from *Barefoot Lodge* or from the aptly named *Mantaray Island Resort*, on the adjacent island of Nanuya Balavu. Otherwise it's possible to swim with the manta rays on a day trip from Nadi with Fiji Sea Travel (see p.74).

A little over halfway along the west coast of Naviti is **Natuvalu Bay**, a beautiful long stretch of sandy beach peppered with tall coconut trees and three evenly spaced resorts. The lagoon here is very shallow but if you walk ten minutes over

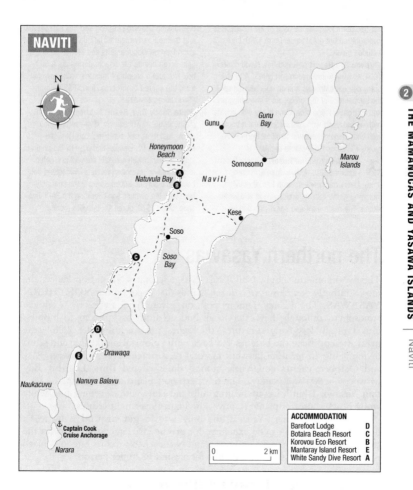

the point at the north end of the bay you'll find **Honeymoon Beach**, a great swimming and snorkelling spot. For even more seclusion, continue walking north around the rocky bluff to find a series of charming sandy cove beaches. On your way back, just past the summit of the small hill leading down to the resorts, a track on the right leads off along a promontory which after ten minutes opens out to a lookout with fabulous **views** of both Natuvalu Bay and Honeymoon Beach.

Accommodation

Barefoot Lodge Drawaqa ℡ 670 1823, www
.fijisailingsafari.com.fj. Set on a stunning point
with beaches on both sides and lined with thatch
bures, this is the overnight resting place for the
Windjammer Sailing Safari (see p.104). You can
also visit independently and, although prices are on
the high side for shared bathroom accommodation,
the food is excellent. Bures ❹, includes meals.

Botaira Beach Resort Soso, Naviti
℡ 666 2266, www.botaira.com. One of
the original Yasawas eco-resorts, *Botaira* couldn't
have a nicer beach with hammocks strung
between palm trees, deep white sand and good
snorkelling. The ten thatch bures are spacious with
en-suite hot-water bathrooms and neat verandas
shielded from the beach by vegetation. A small

ten-bed dorm lodge at the back of the reception is underutilized but great value. Dorm F$90, bures ❼, includes meals.

Korovou Eco Resort Natuvalu Bay, Naviti ☎665 1001, ⓦwww.korovouecoresort.com.fj. A tad too many cement pathways and an ugly seawall spoil the appearance of this place, but a swimming pool and affordable lodge rooms and bures with private bathrooms, albeit with cold water, make it popular with both backpackers and families. Dorm F$70, rooms ❹, bures ❹, includes meals.

🏃 **Mantaray Island Resort** Nanuya Balavu ☎664 0520, ⓦwww.mantarayisland .com. Lively backpackers with lots of activities including game fishing, scuba diving and water-skiing. The restaurant and bar is perched on a hill overlooking Drawaqa Lagoon and has satellite TV and themed party nights. The quaint jungle bures are raised on wooden stilts and hidden amongst light scrub beside the beach; dorms are a bit box-like and a couple of minutes' walk downhill from the shared bathrooms. Tents F$36, dorm F$41, bures ❸–❹.

White Sandy Dive Resort Natuvalu Bay, Naviti ☎666 4066, ⓔwhitesandy_diveresort@yahoo .com. Just three self-contained cottages, one sleeping up to five people, and a pretty thatch dorm lodge sleeping twelve. Meals are well presented and served on a wooden veranda overlooking the beach and sunset. Scuba diving is the speciality here with the owner's son operating the PADI dive shop. Dorm F$70, bures ❹, includes meals.

The northern Yasawas

The five-kilometre choppy Naivalavala Passage separates Naviti from Yaqeta, the most southerly of a cluster of a dozen islands that make up the **NORTHERN YASAWAS**. The islands' remote position gives them an exotic, exclusive atmosphere although they cater to all budgets from backpackers to business class. Typically low-lying in nature – the highest point is just under 300m – the main attractions are the beaches and bays, with colourful snorkelling and scuba diving along an intricate network of coral reefs never far away. Between May and October, **yachts** congregate around the sheltered **Blue Lagoon Bay** between Tavewa and Nanuya. The northernmost island of the group, the long thin **Yasawa Island**, has undulating hills and cliffs with sweeping fine white sandy beaches used as picnic stopovers by luxury overnight cruises.

Once in the northern Yasawas, the only way to **get around** is by resort outboard boat. These can be expensive for private charter, costing F$75 for the short ten-minute hop between Tavewa and Nacula. Most resorts offer organized island sightseeing trips or village visits for around F$20 per person.

Yaqeta and Matacawalevu

Shaped like a hammerhead shark, **Yaqeta** has an extremely fertile and flat middle, stretching from the west to east coast where the solitary Matayalevu village is located. On the north side of the island facing an outstanding turquoise lagoon is the elegant *Navutu Stars* resort (☎664 0553, ⓦwww.navutustarsfiji.com; ❻–❾). Run by a young Italian couple, the food here is superb, using herbs and fruits grown from the organic gardens. There are little corners of solitude everywhere including a treehouse-style yoga platform and a simple spa hut. The contemporary whitewashed villas have a Balinese feel and the grand bures on the hill have beautiful sunken spa baths and wonderful views of the bay.

Just across the lagoon from Yaqeta is the hilly island of **Matacawalevu** home to the laid-back 🏃 *Long Beach Resort* (☎666 0198, ⓦwww.longbeachfiji.com; dorm F$65, bures ❸, cottages ❹, includes meals; cash only). This small retreat, located along a beautiful one-kilometre stretch of powdery white sand, is run by welcoming hosts from the local village. You can stay overlooking the beach either in a quaint thatch bure (quite small and with shared outdoor bathrooms about 50m away) or opt for one of the reasonably priced modern en-suite cottages with ceiling fans and tiled floors. One of the cottages is used as an eight-bed dorm. Just offshore from the resort is the triangular rocky island of Deviulau, which can be climbed for fantastic views overlooking the beach and bay and offers good snorkelling along its southern point.

A twenty-minute track from the resort leads across to the east coast village of **Vuake**. The village's picturesque **Catholic Church** is perched on a hill overlooking the shallow tidal waters of Nasomo Bay. It makes a wonderful place to experience the full volume of a Fijian Sunday church service. From Vuake, walking tracks lead up into the hills where village gardens are planted with *dalo* and *yaqona*, or you can walk north to the island's second village, the Methodist enclave of Matacawalevu, also on the east coast.

Blue Lagoon Bay

Flanking the north and east coast of Matacawalevu are the small islands of Nanuya and Tavewa with the larger island of Nacula to the north forming the **Blue Lagoon Bay**. The bay is named partly for its dream-like turquoise waters but also to capitalize on the semi-erotic 1980 film, *The Blue Lagoon* starring Brooke Shields, filmed partly on Nanuya Levu. Around this sheltered bay is the

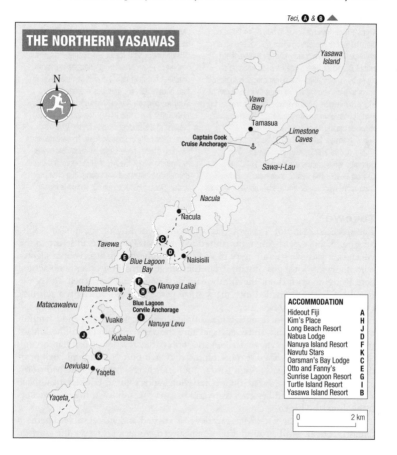

Teci, **A** & **B** ▲

THE NORTHERN YASAWAS

N

Yasawa Island

Vawa Bay

Tamasua

Limestone Caves

Captain Cook Cruise Anchorage

Sawa-i-Lau

Nacula

Nacula

Tavewa

Blue Lagoon Bay

Naisisili

Matacawalevu

Nanuya Lailai

Matacawalevu

Blue Lagoon Corvile Anchorage

Vuake

Nanuya Levu

Kubalau

Deviulau

Yaqeta

Yaqeta

ACCOMMODATION	
Hideout Fiji	A
Kim's Place	H
Long Beach Resort	J
Nabua Lodge	D
Nanuya Island Resort	F
Navutu Stars	K
Oarsman's Bay Lodge	C
Otto and Fanny's	E
Sunrise Lagoon Resort	G
Turtle Island Resort	I
Yasawa Island Resort	B

0	2 km

highest concentration of **backpacker resorts** in the Yasawas making it a handy place for island-hopping.

Nanuya Levu and Lailai

Nanuya Levu (big Nanuya) is strictly off-limits unless staying at the ultra-exclusive *Turtle Island Resort* (☎672 2921, ⓦwww.turtlefiji.com; ❾). The fourteen handcrafted bures here are offered to couples only on a minimum six-night package costing over US$11,000. There's more down-to-earth **accommodation** (see below) on Nanuya Lailai (little Nanuya), the northern of the two islands. Enandala Beach on the windswept east coast is edged with four budget resorts run by the same extended family. The best beach on Nanuya Lailai is on the sheltered west coast, although sea grass around the northern point is becoming more invasive. There's decent snorkelling a hundred metres offshore along a thirty-metre-deep coral wall drop-off. At the northern end of the beach, adjacent to *Nanuya Island Resort* is Westside Watersports (☎ 666 1462, PADI open water course F$625, two-tank dive F$165) which services all resorts in the northern Yasawas. This is the only place you can rent a surf board for the reef breaks off the north point of Tavewa.

Accommodation

Kim's Place Nanuya Lailai ☎666 6644 (after beep dial 1019). For something more quirky, this little place perched on a grassy bluff at the southern end of Enandala Beach has its beds hanging on ropes from the ceiling like a hammock, with sand floors in case you fall off. At night though, it can be tricky to navigate from the five hillside bures to the shared bathroom beside the beach. Cash only. ❸, includes meals.

Nanuya Island Resort Nanuya Lailai ☎666 7633, ⓦwww.nanuyafiji.com. Fantastic value on the northern end of Blue Lagoon beach. The centrepiece here is its huge open-plan, wooden-floored restaurant and lounge bar where delicious meals are served. Simple wooden treehouse bures are perched on a steep hillside under light forest emanating a peaceful ambience – the beachfront cottages are more practical for older couples and can sleep up to four people. ❺–❼, includes breakfast.

Sunrise Lagoon Resort Nanuya Lailai ☎666 6644 (after beep dial 9484). The largest and liveliest of the budget resorts on the east coast, aimed distinctly at backpackers. Three small huts abutting the hill have basic en-suite cold-water bathrooms whilst the five thatch bures and three dorm lodges all share bathrooms in a cramped space. Dorms F$60, bures ❸, includes meals.

Tavewa

The freehold island of **Tavewa** was originally owned by the people of neighbouring Nacula, but being uninhabited in the late 1800s, and of little use to the villagers, it was given as a dowry to William Dougherty, a Scottish copra planter who married a local girl of status from the village. Over time, other Scots settled here bringing with them the family names of Bruce and Campbell. Today the island has been subdivided into many small parcels of land distributed amongst Dogherty's descendants.

There's no village on Tavewa, but a couple of backpacker resorts and a handful of resident shacks and holiday cottages line the eastern beachfront. The best of the two resorts is 🏃 *Otto and Fanny's* (☎666 6481, ⓦwww.ottoandfanny.com; dorm F$40, bures ❷–❸). Otto has built five thatch bures set slightly back from the beach. Two are big enough for families and there's a small eight-bed dorm appealing to the more sedate budget traveller. Fanny's home-cooked meals have a good reputation and her chocolate and banana cakes draw in the backpackers from along the beach.

The west coast, as with Matacawalevu, is rugged and inaccessible. There's a fantastic **coral wall** around the northeastern point of Tavewa but surface

Underwater Fiji

A huge part of Fiji's appeal lies below the surface of the waves. Don a mask and snorkel and you will find coral reefs shimmering with colourful fish, sea fans dancing in the current and manta rays and reef sharks cruising the lagoons. Throw in crystal clear water and temperatures that rarely fall below 25°C and you have one of the world's greatest snorkelling and diving destinations.

Detail of coral polyps with starfish ▲

Fringing reefs, Mamanucas Islands ▼

Coral reefs

Fiji's ten thousand square kilometres of **coral reef** twist and turn around every island and sprout from the ocean in circular patches or elongated barriers. These amazing structures provide habitats for thousands of species of fish, plants and animals and are comparable with rainforests in terms of biodiversity.

The building block of all coral reefs is the **coral polyp**, a small spineless animal similar to an anenome with a series of six or eight tentacles. In **hard corals**, the polyp uses calcium carbonate from seawater to build itself a tough, cup-shaped skeleton. Polyps grow together in colonies of thousands, gradually constructing the reefs we see today. **Soft corals**, particularly common in Fiji, do not build skeletons and are soft or leathery in texture. They are found only in rich nutrient-fed currents and at lower light intensities.

Fiji's top dive sites

Jacques Cousteau put Fiji on the diving map when he declared it "the **soft coral capital of the world**". Divers will also find big shark encounters, exciting drift dives and plenty of wrecks to explore.

Fiji is the perfect place to **learn to dive** with calm lagoons, excellent visability (20 metres plus) and a wide range of dive centres to choose between. The following are some of the islands' top-rated dive sites:

Beqa Lagoon, Pacific Harbour: the best open-water shark dive on earth.

Rainbow Reef, Taveuni: gorgeous soft corals and fast drift dives.

E6, Bligh Water: the photographer's favourite, acccessed by live-aboard boat.

Naiqoro Passage, Kadavu: beautiful drift dive on the Astrolabe Reef.

The Salamander, Mamanucas: a 36-metre wreck now home to puffer fish.

Coral reefs are extremely sensitive to climatic conditions, partly due to their symbiotic relationship with a type of algae known as **zooxanthellae**. These algae live within the coral polyp and convert ocean nutrients through photosynthesis into food. Zooxanthellae also produce a range of pigments which give the otherwise clear, white coral its beautiful colour. Zooxanthellae depend on **light** for photosynthesis which is why corals can only thrive in clear waters less than fifty metres deep. Ideal water temperatures range between 24°C and 29°C, hence the large profusion of reefs in Fiji. If water temperatures suddenly change, the polyps stop growing and may expel the zooxanthellae, leading to the effect known as **coral bleaching**.

The three most common types of reef found in Fiji are: **fringing reefs**, which are attached to an island and offer snorkelling direct from the shore; **patch reefs**, individual coral reefs found within a lagoon and usually attracting great numbers of reef fish; and **barrier reefs**, which are separated from the shore by a deep channel and feature steep drop-offs and strong currents. Fiji's Great Sea Reef found off the north coast of Vanua Levu is the world's third longest barrier reef.

Respecting the reef

Lying at the crossroads of the Pacific, Fiji's reefs are recognized as a globally important area of **biodiversity** and make up four percent of the world's total area of coral reefs. As well as attracting thousands of tourists, they protect the islands from hurricanes and provide an income for fishermen. Despite their often vast size, coral reefs are fragile and complex ecosystems that require care and respect from snorkellers and

▲ Corals provide habitats for thousands of reef fish

▼ The characteristic ridge shape of brain coral

scuba-divers. It's imperative you **do not touch** the reef, or try to stand or tread water close to coral heads. Even a brief contact is likely to destroy the delicate coral polyps which can take years to grow back. Brushing against the reef is also likely to result in cuts or grazes which can take weeks to heal.

Although they make tempting souvenirs, **shells** should not be removed from the reef as they play a vital role in providing homes for invertebrates. Avoid buying shells from the village markets, especially tritons, or trumpet shells, the only natural predators of the coral-destroying crown of thorns starfish.

Snorkeller with linkia starfish ▲

Spotted moray eel ▼

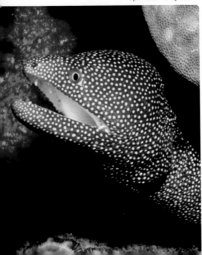

Snorkelling essentials

▶▶ It's worth investing in your own mask, snorkel and fins. Snorkel gear provided by resorts may not fit and masks often leak. The most comfortable fins are those worn over wetsuit "booties".

▶▶ Avoid snorkelling at low tide – with less water between you and the reef, collisions can be common.

▶▶ Remember you can still get sunburnt underwater. Your best option is to wear a lightweight surf top or "rash vest".

▶▶ To ensure your mask doesn't steam up, rub some spit around the lens. To prevent leaks, pull back your hair to get a good seal around your face.

▶▶ When diving down, hold your nose and blow out to "equalize" the pressure on your ears. Note that ear infections are common – consider rinsing your ears with warm water after a dive.

▶▶ If you're not a confident swimmer, try a guided snorkel tour – many resorts offer them and it's a great way to learn about underwater wildlife.

▶▶ Consider buying a waterproof case for your camera. These are now relatively affordable, especially for small digital cameras, and will provide much better results than cheap disposables.

Reef fish

In almost every lagoon you'll find a huge range of small **reef fish**, some darting in and out of the coral, others coalescing in great schools. The following is a brief guide to the most common varieties.

Perhaps the most iconic reef fish is the orange and white **clown anenomefish**. Clownfish are found weaving through the tentacles of stinging sea anenomes with which they form a symbiotic relationship. Although they live in pairs as lifetime partners, you may notice a third, smaller clown fish hanging around. This is a non-mating male who functions as a kind of insurance policy. If the female clown fish dies, the dominant male changes sex and the smaller fish takes over as the male. Surprisingly feisty, clown fish will rush up to your mask if you get too close.

Closely related to the clownfish is the ubiquitous **damselfish**. Only around 5cm from nose to tail, damselfish come in a huge range of colours, the most vivid being the golden and black-and-white striped versions. Larger but just as colourful are the elegant **butterflyfish** and **angelfish**. Difficult to tell apart, these species both whizz around the reef in pairs. If you can get up close you may notice a small spine by the gills which indicates an angelfish rather than a butterflyfish. Also possessing a sharp spine is the aptly named **surgeonfish**, a streamlined version of the angelfish often found in large schools.

One of the few fish you can hear underwater is the **parrotfish** who munch away at the reef making a distinctive scraping sound with their sharp, beaked mouth. Larger reef fish found in lagoons include the thick-lipped, grumpy-looking **grouper** and the long, streamlined **barracuda**, who often file past in squadrons.

▲ Clown anenomefish

▲ Double-saddle butterflyfish

▲ Picasso triggerfish

▼ Blue surgeonfish

Golden damselfish at a reef wall ▲

Blacktip reef shark on the prowl ▼

Sharks

Of the dozens of shark species found in Fijian waters, by far the most common are the smaller **reef sharks** (blacktips, whitetips and, to a lesser extent, grey reef). These elegant shallow-water predators seldom reach over two metres in length and feed on small reef fish, squid and crustaceans. Of the **big sharks**, bulls, tigers and hammerheads are present in Fiji but rarely enter the lagoons, preferring the deep current-fed passages along the outer edges of the reefs, or, as is the case with bull sharks, lurking in the murky coastal waters and mangrove estuaries. Bull sharks have beady eyes and a blunt snout and are considered the most aggressive shark species, owing to their high levels of testosterone. Tiger sharks have a distinct mottled skin tone and are occasionally encountered on the shark-feeding dives carried out in Beqa Lagoon. Hammerheads are the most timid of the three and stick to deeper waters. **Shark attacks** in Fiji are incredibly rare. Those that have occurred have almost always involved local spear fishermen carrying bloody, injured fish.

Rays

Three types of rays are found in Fiji. The largest are the bat-like **manta rays** that can grow to over four metres in width and are often seen around the Yasawas Islands. The smaller **stingray** is harder to spot, preferring to bury itself in the sandy bottom of lagoons. Armed with a razor-sharp venomous barb, stingrays only present a danger when stood upon – always look before settling on a patch of sand. The rarest type of ray in Fiji is the beautiful **spotted eagle ray**. This species, which features numerous white spots on an inky blue body, hunts in the open ocean.

Invertebrates

Marine **invertebrates** include crustaceans, molluscs and starfish as well sponges and sea anemones. One of the most fascinating is the colourful **nudibranch** or "sea slug". Tiny creatures, barely the width of a fingernail, nudibranchs come in over three thousand varieties. Their latin name means "naked gills" and refers to the feather-like appendages above their bodies. Also found crawling across the reef are tiny **coral shrimps**. Certain species of shrimp creep into the mouths of reef fish to clear away parasites. Found on the bottom of shallow lagoons is the leathery **sea cucumber**. Also known as "bêche de mer", sea cucumbers are considered a delicacy in China and are gathered by local fisherman for export.

▲ Diver drifting past a sea fan

▼ Manta ray

▼ Nudibranchs

Kayaking in the Yasawas

A fantastic way of seeing the remote side of the northern Yasawas is to join one of the **kayaking trips** run by South Sea Ventures (℡02/8901 3287 in Australia, ⓦwww .southernseaventures.com; 7-nights for A$1,925). Group trips run between May and October with between three and four hours of paddling a day in either single or twin sea-kayaks. Of the eight-day trip, five days are spent paddling between Mataca-walevu and Sawa-i-Lau camping on beaches in two-man tents. Trips are equally suitable for novice or experienced kayakers, although a reasonable level of fitness is expected.

conditions can be windy. If you head a little further out, there's a good chance you'll see reef sharks and sometimes tons of harmless jellyfish. The nicest swimming beach is around the sheltered Savutu Point at the southern tip of Tavewa facing both Matacawalevu and Nanuya. For **anglers**, there's good casting here into the offshore reefs, and Trip-N Tour (℡666 6481) next to *Otto and Fanny's* organizes half-day trips to the Sawa-i-Lau Cave and Blue Lagoon Bay (F$50), snorkelling trips to the outer reef (F$15) and a relaxing sunset cruise to Nanuya Lailai (F$15).

Nacula

Hilly **Nacula** is the third largest of the Yasawa Islands with the chiefly village, also named Nacula, on the west coast. The southern side of the island has lovely beaches including the kilometre-long crescent sands alongside *Oarsman's Bay Lodge* (℡672 2921, ⓦwww.oarsmansbay.com; tents and dorms F$79.50, bures ❻–❼, includes meals). This picturesque resort with wonderfully accessible snorkelling is popular with all age groups from backpackers and couples to families and pensioners. The simple wooden cottages have tiled floors with hot-water en-suite bathrooms although they are beginning to show signs of wear and tear. It's excellent value, though, and the new-look wooden-decked restaurant serves decent food. A twelve-bed dorm, located above the restaurant, has low slanting ceilings and is usually packed and stuffy.

At low tide you can walk south around **Sandy Point** to the even longer stretch of beach, home to *Nabua Lodge* (℡ 666 9173 or 999 7294; camping F$40, dorms F$60, bures ❸–❹, includes meals), a delightful family-run retreat. Six of the nine bures overlook the beach, three of them have en-suite bathrooms and sleep up to four people. Over the eastern bluff from *Nabua Lodge* is the fabulous beach setting fronting *Safe Landing Resort* where you'll find some of the nicest budget bures in Fiji. Unfortunately, at the time of writing the resort was closed due to a land dispute with its financial backer.

A scenic **walking trail** along the grassy inland ridges connects the village of Naisisili on the southeast coast with the island's namesake, Nacula, on the west coast. About halfway across the island, the trail breaks off and leads up to the 238-metre summit of Naisau from where, on a clear day, you can see the entire Yasawa chain.

Sawa-i-Lau

Lying off the north coast of Nacula, the island of **Sawa-i-Lau** lies in a pretty bay hugging the south point of Yasawa Island and is home to some partially flooded **limestone caves**. The passage to the south of the island is probably the windiest place in Fiji with gusts ripping in and churning the seas – backpackers usually get drenched and somewhat shaken getting here. Nevertheless, it's touted as the best sightseeing trip in the Yasawas. Locals believe the ten-headed **snake god**, Uluitini, resides deep inside the caves and folklore warns that any pregnant woman, however slight, will be unable to fit through the entrance. The main chamber is 15m high with limestone pillars and natural sunlight streaming in from above. Boys from nearby Nabukeru village usually climb to the very top and jump into the crystal clear **pool** here; the other challenge is to swim underwater for ten seconds to a series of smaller darker chambers where **petroglyphs** can be seen incised on the walls.

Yasawa Island

The long thin **Yasawa Island** has impressive **cliffs** and pristine powdery white sand beaches along the west coast, several of which are leased to one of the two cruise companies which visit almost daily (see p.104). The island is synonymous with the luxury *Yasawa Island Resort* (☎ 672 2266, ⓦ www.yasawa.com; ⑨) beautifully positioned on a secluded stretch of beach on the northeast coast. Bures here start at US$850 per night with the honeymoon suite going for a cool US$1800 per night. Air transfers from Nadi airport to the resort's airstrip cost an extra US$235 per person.

Six traditional villages are found on the east coast. The fishing village of **Teci** is one of the most authentic in Fiji with over half its homes being traditional thatch-roof bures. At the northern tip is the chiefly village of **Yasawa-i-Rara** facing several rocky islands with hundreds of nesting seabirds. You can stay here at *Hideout Fiji* (☎ 628 3803; ⓦ www.hideoutfiji.com; dorm F$80, bure ④, includes meals) a small **budget retreat** close to Vulawalu Beach. It takes over an hour by outboard boat to reach the resort from the *Yasawa Flyer* drop-off point at Nacula (which adds F$300 onto the transfer cost). Depending on the seas, this transfer can either be a glorious adventure with lovely scenery or an endurance test; however, it's worth it for those looking to escape the well-trodden backpacker path further south.

Travel details for the Mamanucas and Yasawa Islands are covered in Basics, p.26 and Chapter 1, p.84.

Rural Viti Levu

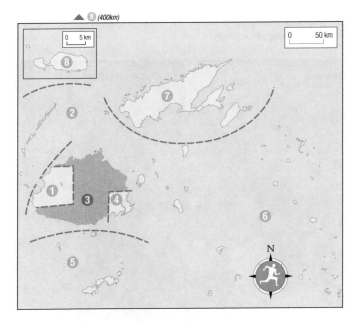

CHAPTER 3

Highlights

✱ **Sigatoka Sand Dunes**
Explore the wild beachfront
where ancient Fijians once
lived, and go surfing on the
waves. See p.124

✱ **River rafting** Journey along
the lush waterfall-lined rapids
of the Navua River either by
kayak, longboat or river raft.
See p.133

✱ **Navala Village** Fiji's sole-
surviving traditional thatch
village on the Ba River is truly
breathtaking. See p.135

✱ **Tavua** Charming Fiji-Indian
market town off the tourist
trail. See p.137

✱ **Mount Tomanivi** Climb Fiji's
highest peak for a spectacular
view of the surrounding
forests. See p.138

✱ **Tailevu Coast** Travel along
the remote and seldom-
visited east coast with
winding bays and delightfully
friendly Fijian villages.
See p.145

▲ Locals relaxing in Tavua

Rural Viti Levu

G iven that Fiji is renowned for its tiny coral islands, many visitors are struck by the sheer size of its main island, **Viti Levu** or "Big Fiji". Covering just over ten thousand square kilometres it's roughly half the size of Wales and offers a wide range of scenery from sunburnt yellow **sugarcane** fields along the dry north coast to the verdant blanket of **rainforest** spread over the eastern half of the island. With the exception of the Nadi to Lautoka corridor (see p.78) and the urban sprawl between Suva and Nausori (see p.151), Viti Levu is distinctly **rural** in character with only a handful of small market towns along the coastal road circling the island. Most such towns are found at the mouths of rivers which in turn connect the isolated and seldom visited **mountainous interior**.

Viti Levu can be hastily explored in two days, either by public bus or rental car, but a week is recommended to have a chance to meet some of the exceedingly hospitable characters who will welcome you along the way. More time will allow you to branch off the main roads to explore and **hike** amongst some of the most beautiful countryside in the South Pacific.

The Queens Road, the main artery connecting Nadi and Suva, travels along **South Viti Levu**, a relatively well developed tourist region. The first stop is the small town of Sigatoka, close to the absorbing Sigatoka Sand Dunes National Park. Further east are the beach resorts of the Coral Coast and the adventure sports capital of Pacific Harbour. By contrast, **North Viti Levu** appears rather barren, its scenery dominated by sugarcane farmland interspersed with the market towns of Ba, Tavua and Rakiraki. Inland, however, is Fiji's most attractive village, Navala, as well as the country's highest point, Mount Tomanivi; offshore are the budget resorts of Nananu-i-Ra island. **East Viti Levu** is the least developed area on the mainland, still mostly covered in rainforest; its main attraction is the picturesque Tailevu Coast, accessed by remote dirt road.

Climate

Viti Levu's **climate** splits into two zones. The area around Suva catches the brunt of the southeasterly trade winds, which roll in off the warm ocean and cause cloud build-up over the mountains. Consequently, everything east of a fairly distinct line extending from Rakiraki to Sigatoka lies in the **wet zone** with high rainfall, dense forests and often unbearable humidity. Once the clouds have blown over the mountain range, the highest point of which reaches 1,323m at Mount Tomanivi, they fall, cool and dissipate leaving the other half of the island with almost perpetual sunshine. This is the **dry zone** or "Burning West", as it is ridiculed by umbrella-clad Suva-ites.

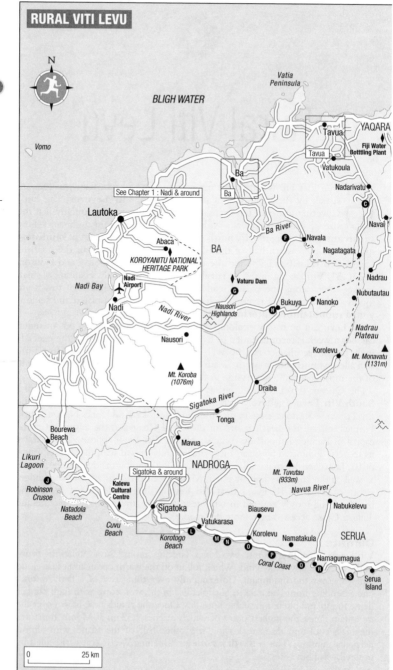

RURAL VITI LEVU

BLIGH WATER

Vatia Peninsula

Vomo

Tavua · YAQARA

Tavua

Fiji Water Botttling Plant

Vatukoula

Nadarivatu

Ba

Ba

Navai

See Chapter 1 : Nadi & around

Lautoka

Ba River

Ba River

Navala

C

F

BA

Abaca

KOROYANITU NATIONAL HERITAGE PARK

Nagatagata

Nadrau

Nadi Airport

Vaturu Dam

G

Bukuya

Nanoko

Nubutautau

Nadi Bay

Nadi

Nadi River

Nausori Highlands

H

Nadrau Plateau

Nausori

Korolevu

▲ *Mt. Monavatu (1131m)*

▲ *Mt. Koroba (1076m)*

Draiba

Sigatoka River

Tonga

Bourewa Beach

Mavua

NADROGA

Likuri Lagoon

▲ *Mt. Tuvutau (933m)*

J

Robinson Crusoe

Sigatoka & around

Navua River

Kalevu Cultural Centre

Natadola Beach

Sigatoka

Biausevu

Nabukelevu

Cuvu Beach

Vatukarasa

L

Korolevu

Namatakula

SERUA

Korotogo Beach

M **N**

O

P

Namagumagua

Coral Coast

Q

R

S

Serua Island

N

0 ——— 25 km

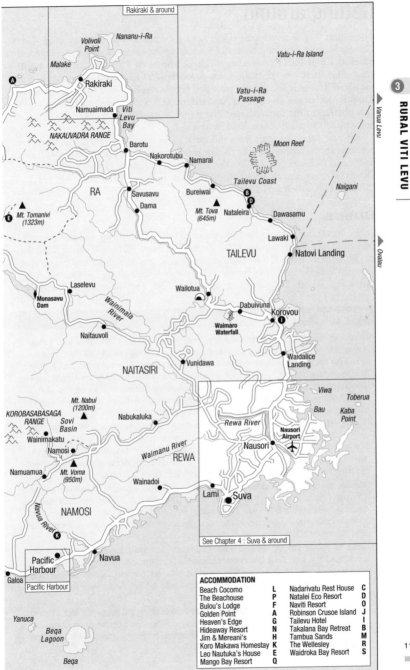

Rakiraki & around

Nananu-i-Ra

Volivoli Point

Malake

Vatu-i-Ra Island

Rakiraki

Namuaimada

Viti Levu Bay

NAKAUVADRA RANGE

Vatu-i-Ra Passage

▲ Vanua Levu

Barotu

Nakorotubu

Namarai

Moon Reef

RA

Savusavu

Dama

Bureiwai

Tailevu Coast

Naigani

Ⓔ ▲ *Mt. Tomanivi (1323m)*

▲ *Mt. Tova (645m)*

Nataleira Ⓑ
Ⓓ

Dawasamu

Lawaki

▲ *Ovalau*

TAILEVU

Natovi Landing

Laselevu

Wailotua ◉

Dabuivuna

Korovou Ⓘ

Monasavu Dam

Wainimala River

Waimaro Waterfall ✕

Naitauvoli

Vunidawa

Waidalice Landing

NAITASIRI

Viwa

Toberua

KOROBASABASAGA RANGE

Mt. Nabui (1200m) ▲

Nabukaluka

Sovi Basin

Wainimakatu

Namosi ●

▲ Mt. Voma (950m)

Waimanu River

Rewa River

Bau

Kaba Point

Nausori Airport ✈

Nausori

Namuamua

Wainadoi

REWA

NAMOSI

Lami ● Suva

Ⓚ

Navua River

See Chapter 4 : Suva & around

Pacific Harbour

Galoa

Navua

Pacific Harbour

Yanuca

Beqa Lagoon

Beqa

ACCOMMODATION			
Beach Cocomo	L	Nadarivatu Rest House	C
The Beachouse	P	Natalei Eco Resort	D
Bulou's Lodge	F	Naviti Resort	O
Golden Point	A	Robinson Crusoe Island	J
Heaven's Edge	G	Tailevu Hotel	I
Hideaway Resort	N	Takalana Bay Retreat	B
Jim & Mereani's	H	Tambua Sands	M
Koro Makawa Homestay	K	The Wellesley	R
Leo Nautuka's House	E	Waidroka Bay Resort	S
Mango Bay Resort	Q		

Getting around

The easiest way to travel around Viti Levu is by **road**, with the busy single-lane Queens Road connecting Nadi and Suva along the south coast (4hr), and the less travelled Kings Road connecting Nadi and Suva via Lautoka along the north coast (6hr). Between them the roads cover the 460-kilometre circumference of the island. The only section not yet sealed is between Korovou and Nyavu on the Kings Road but this should be completed by 2009. Stray cattle, especially at night, kids playing on the roadside, speeding minivans, over-laden trucks and deep pot holes make the roads somewhat hazardous.

There are no trains apart from industrial sugar train lines and no boat service between towns around Viti Levu. The only domestic **airports** are at Nadi (see p.60), and Nausori (see p.170), the latter thirty minutes' drive north of Suva. Flights between the two take thirty minutes and are operated by Air Fiji and Pacific Sun (6am–7pm; F$135 one way).

Buses

Public **buses** are the safest way to travel and offer lovely views of the country-side from the high windows. Sunbeam Transport (☎666 2086 in Lautoka, ☎338 2704 in Suva, ⓦwww.sunbeamfiji.com) operate regular express services between Lautoka and Suva running in both directions along the Queens Road and Kings Road. The southern route (F$13.50; 5hr) stops at Nadi Airport,

---

Exploring remote Viti Levu

Four less-travelled dirt roads provide a really genuine insight into **rural Virti Levu**. None of the routes below are served by buses and although all can be navigated by a regular car with good suspension in good weather, 4WD is recommended. Before you leave, check your tyres (including your spare) and take plenty of drinking water – *yaqona* roots are also good to carry as a *sevusevu* in case you decide to visit a village. Each of the following routes takes around five hours to drive but with overnight options in villages along the way it's worth taking longer to explore:

Nadi to Ba via Bukuya Start from the Nadi Back Road, climbing into the grassy hills of the Nausori Highlands. The scenery is barren and very remote, with panoramic views along most of the way. The route passes through two fascinating villages: Bukuya (see p.78); and Navala with over a hundred traditional thatch bures (see p.274). Overnight stopover: *Bukuya Homestay* and *Bulou's Lodge*.

Navua to Suva via Namosi Highlands Start from Namosi Road along the Queens Road, 11km east of Navua Town. The road meanders through dense tropical forest into the Namosi Highlands (see p.133), past traditional villages with stunning mountain views along the way. Overnight stopovers: *Namosi Homestay* and *Raintree Lodge*.

Suva to Tavua via Monasavu Dam This route journeys through the heart of Viti Levu, past the lush Sovi Basin and Monasavu Dam towards Mount Tomanivi, Fiji's highest mountain, before heading downhill into the farming valleys surrounding Tavua. Overnight stopovers: *Navai Homestay* (see p.139), *Nadarivatu Rest House* (see p.138).

Korovou to Rakiraki via the Tailevu Coast Travels along the secluded and winding coastline of Tailevu passing rivers, seldom-visited villages and scenic bays. Overnight stopovers: *Natalei Eco Lodge* (see p.146), *Takalana Bay Retreat* (see p.146), *Rainbow Lodge* (see p.145).

Nadi Town, Sigatoka, most Coral Coast hotels, Pacific Harbour and Navua; The northern route (F$15.50; 6hr) stops at Ba, Tavua, Rakiraki, Barotu, Nyavu, Korovou and Nausori. Pacific Transport (℡670 0044 in Nadi, ℡330 4366 in Suva) serve the Queens Road only (F$12.95, 5hr; departs Lautoka and Suva 6.30am & 5pm).

Coral Sun (℡672 3105, ⓦwww.coralsunfiji.com) provide a more comfortable and direct **tourist bus** service each way between Nadi Airport and Suva stopping at all Coral Coast hotels, Pacific Harbour and terminating at *Holiday Inn* Suva (departs Nadi Airport 7.30am & 1pm; Suva 7.30am & 4pm; F$19; 4hr).

Minivans and taxis

Minivans operate between all towns usually picking up passengers at bus stands. They are quicker than buses, cost approximately the same, but can be a hair-raising experience, especially at night when overtaking large vehicles, horn blaring and lights flashing. Open-backed **carrier vans** travel to all interior villages along dirt roads bringing produce to and from market – ask amongst the market vendors and you should be able to hitch a bumpy ride squashed in the back for F$2–5 depending on the distance. To hire a carrier van with driver costs around F$35 for a one-hour journey.

A **taxi** between Nadi Airport and Suva costs F$120 along the Queens Road, or F$180 along the Kings Road.

Organized tours

Round-island **bus tours** can be arranged with Feejee Experience (℡672 3311, ⓦwww.feejeeexperience.com; pass only F$396, departs Nadi Mon, Tues, Wed, Sat) which takes four days to travel around Viti Levu overnighting at the Coral Coast, Suva and Rakiraki. There are sightseeing and activity stops along the way including sand surfing down the Sigatoka Sand Dunes and tubing down the Navua River. Numerous **day tour** companies also explore inland Viti Levu from Nadi (see p.75).

South Viti Levu

The scenic Queens Road passes through countless fishing villages alongside the winding bays of **South Viti Levu**. Two fabulous beaches, **Natadola and Cuvu,** lie within an hour's drive south of Nadi. To the east is the region's main town, **Sigatoka**, a rather uninspiring market centre. However, in its immediate vicinity are several worthy attractions including the **Sigatoka Sand Dunes National Park** and **Tavuni Hill Fort**. Beyond Sigatoka the sunny climate and sugarcane fields give way to cloud-clad mountains which descend towards the picturesque lagoons of the **Coral Coast**. Graced by white sandy **beaches**, this was where tourism first began in Fiji and it's still home to a wide range of resorts from large family-friendly complexes to budget resorts tucked away in secluded bays. Further east is **Pacific Harbour**, with the fabulous Beqa Lagoon offshore for scuba diving and game fishing, and the oppressive virgin rainforest of the Namosi Highlands offering remote riverside villages, pristine waterfalls and **whitewater rafting**. From here, the bustling, rain-drenched capital city of Suva (see Chapter 4) is just forty minutes' drive along the coast.

Natadola and Cuvu beaches

Two of Viti Levu's most picturesque white sandy beaches, **Natadola and Cuvu**, are found hidden off the Queens Road less than an hour's drive south of Nadi. The initial journey from Nadi passes through flat featureless sugarcane fields for 17km before cutting inland through dense pine forests just after the Momi Bay turn-off. The longer, winding old coastal road from Momi Bay to Likuri Harbour is far more scenic. When the old coastal road rejoins the Queens Road, it's only another 4km to the Natadola turn-off.

The long sweeping crescent of **Natadola Beach**, blessed with regular waves, is one of the few **body surfing** beaches in Fiji. There's even a small surfing break on the south side close to the river mouth which is popular with local kids. Unfortunately, the massive *Natadola Beach Resort* (set to open in 2009) has begun to carve up the landscape around the beach and may prevent access in future. For the time being it remains an excellent day-trip, despite the persistent touts from the local village who will try to sell you handicrafts or a ride on a mangy horse. Also accessed down the beach road is the launch transfer to the lively *Robinson Crusoe Island* (T 651 0100, W www.robinsoncrusoeislandfiji.com, dorm F$85, bure ❹, lodge ❺, includes meals), a party-style **backpacker resort** featuring loads of organized activities and good snorkelling on the outer reef.

To reach the equally attractive deep sands and swimming lagoon of **Cuvu Beach**, turn right off the Queens Road at the Cuvu Village turn-off, 11km from Nadi. Two hundred metres further along, take another right down a dirt track signposted towards the Fiji Sugar Corporation rail depot where you can park your car. The area in front of Cuvu Beach was cleared for resort development but this is yet to materialize. Keep an eye out for broken bottles here as it's a popular drinking spot for the local villagers at weekends. At low tide you can wade across the channel to the narrow beachfront facing the *Shangri-La Fijian Resort* (T 652 0155, W www.shangri-la.com; ❽). *The Fijian*, as it's known locally, is the largest resort in Fiji. It's a rather superficial place full of lager-drinking Australians, kids engrossed in arcade games and a mini shopping centre.

Opposite the Queens Road turn-off for *The Fijian* is the **Kalevu Cultural Centre** (T 652 0200; 10am–2.30pm; F$15, 1hr guided tour). The wood-carving, matt-weaving and pottery-making demonstrations are informative and you do get a chance to have a go, but it's all rather lacklustre. Four kilometres along the Queens Road on the mountain side of the road is Pacific Green (T 650 0055, W www.pacific-green.com), a local company selling chic furniture made from coconut tree logs.

Sigatoka and around

Often incorporated into the tourist region of the Coral Coast, **SIGATOKA** marks the southern boundary of the dry leeward side of Viti Levu. The town itself is located 4km inland on the banks of the Sigatoka River and acts as a hub for the region. To the west is the **Sigatoka Sand Dunes National Park**.

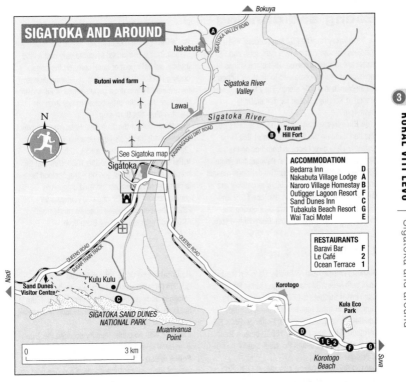

Inland, the Sigatoka River, the longest in Fiji, winds its way north for 120km eventually reaching Nadarivatu at the foothills of Mount Tomanivi (see p.138). The lower portion of the river valley makes for good exploring by car, but there are no designated walking trails other than the steep track weaving around **Tavuni Hill Fort**. Eight kilometres east of Sigatoka is **Korotogo Beach**, a pleasant resort area with a variety of accommodation, several restaurants and the **Kula Eco Park**.

The Town

Sigatoka is a busy **market centre** dominated by Indian traders and several restaurants specializing in hot curries. It's certainly not a place to stay but quite a few people visit either en route to somewhere else or whilst visiting nearby attractions. The **bus stand** and adjacent market is rather grimy. Belching bus fumes and the reek from an unhygienic public toilet linger in the air but the most irritating aspect is the market vendors who furiously push their souvenirs on tourists. By contrast, the smart air-conditioned **boutique shops** of Proud's, Jack's and Tappoo's found further along the Valley Road have fixed but somewhat inflated prices.

For **accommodation**, the pick of a dire bunch is the *True Blue Hotel* (☏650 1530, ✉ruebluehotel@connect.com.fj; dorm F$15, rooms ❷) on the roundabout beside the road bridge. The top floor en-suite rooms are adequately furnished with ceiling fans and some with air conditioning. On the middle floor are three dorm rooms whilst the *Sigatoka Club* graces the bottom floor.

Eating and drinking

Le Café Valley Rd. The F$7 fish burgers, F$10 boneless chicken curries with dahl soup and F$12 pizzas are all well prepared. This place shines in the hygiene stakes compared to its rivals although the ambience is a little sterile. They have a cosier branch at Korotogo Beach for dinner. Daily 9am–4pm.

True Blue Restaurant ☏ 650 1530 Queens Rd. Situated beneath the *True Blue Hotel*, this large restaurant has direct access from beside the Sigatoka bridge. Mostly Indian flavours but some Fijian and Chinese dishes too. The delicious masala crab will set you back F$31.50; alternatively the chicken biryani or vegetarian thali are F$12 and filling. There are tranquil views overlooking the river, plenty of tables and a bar. Daily 7am–11pm.

Raj's Curry House Queens Rd beside the Total Station. This is the locals' favourite, tiny and a little grubby, but with goat or duck curry on the bone costing F$14.40 and six simple vegetarian dishes for around F$7 you get a good sample of Fiji-Indian food here. Avoid the pre-cooked meals from the counter. Mon–Sat 8am–9pm.

Sigatoka Club at the *True Blue Hotel*. You can play snooker with the locals here on a full-sized table (20 cents a game) or enjoy a F$3.70 beer.

Vilisite's Lawaqa Creek ☏ 650 1030. Don't let the horribly naff interior put you off – the seafood here is pretty good, especially the fried octopus in coconut cream for F$27 and curry prawns for F$28. Cheaper blackboard specials range from F$10–F$20. Licensed. Daily 9am–9pm.

Listings

Banking Westpac and ANZ banks (Mon–Fri 9.30am–4pm) both have ATM machines on Market Rd.

Car rental Budget (☏ 650 0986), Queens Rd, 1km west of town just beyond the Mosque; Coastal Rental (☏ 652 0228), Korotogo Back Rd, Korotogo; Sharmas (☏ 650 1680), beside Total petrol station on Queens Rd, Nadi side of bridge.

Dentist Shortland Dental 46 Valley Rd (☏ 650 0300, Mon–Fri 8am–5pm).

Doctors Dr Dasi's corner of Valley and Mission Rds (☏ 650 0369 or after hours 652 0866)

Hospital ☏ 650 0455. On a side road off the Queens Rd, 1km west of town towards Nadi.

Internet access *Net Café* (Mon–Fri 9am–4.45pm, Sat 9am–12.45pm, 20 cents per minute) provides broadband Internet access.

Laundry With no public laundry services the *True Blue Hotel* is your best option.

Police ☏ 650 0222. The main station is at Lawaqa, west of the town centre but there's a police post on the Valley Rd opposite Morris Hedstrom.

Post office At Lawaqa, west of the main town centre (Mon–Fri 8am–4pm, Sat 8am–noon).

Sigatoka Sand Dunes National Park

Two kilometres east of Sigatoka Town, the **Sigatoka Sand Dunes National Park** makes for an inspiring day out. The dunes cover an area of 650 hectares, stretching for 3km and petering out to a sand spit at the mouth of the Sigatoka River. In places they rise to 80m with fantastic views of the crashing surf along the beach. The **visitor centre** (☏ 652 0243, daily 10am–4.30pm; F$8) has an informative display highlighting the fragile ecology and archeological importance of the region and can also provide guides. There are two designated **walking trails** from here: a fifteen minute hike to the ridge lookout and an hour's stroll through forest to the beach. Along the beachfront you'll find plenty of driftwood and if you look carefully you'll come across small sherds of **Lapita pottery**, evidence of human settlement from over two thousand years ago. There's good **surfing** around the Sigatoka River mouth at the southern end of the beach although the sea can be ferocious at times with strong currents – locals can advise the safest entry points for both surfers and swimmers. You can also arrange **horse riding** along the wild beach with Sand Dune Horse Riding (☏ 972 0386; daily 8am–5pm; F$25 per hour), perched on a hill at Yadua village 1km towards Nadi from the visitor centre; it's run by Arthur Ratuva, a member of the Fijian 2007 Rugby World Cup team.

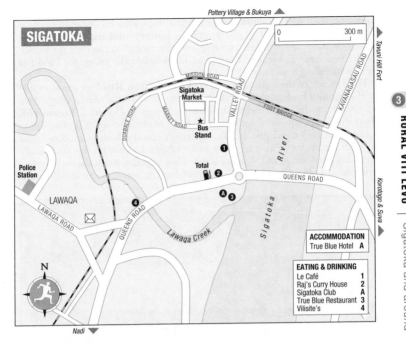

To explore the area fully you can **stay** at the budget *Sand Dunes Inn* (☎627 9064; dorm F$25, rooms ❷), which has direct access to the dunes and is only a ten-minute walk along the beach from the surfing break. The owners from adjacent Kulu Kulu village have four basic shared rooms in the main house and a large fourteen-bed dorm in a separate lodge; they will cook simple meals on request. Surf boards can be rented for F$25 a day, body boards or sand boards F$20 a day. It's a little tricky to find. Coming from Nadi on the Queens Road, turn right onto the dirt road immediately after passing under the railway bridge beyond the Sand Dunes visitor centre; keep right when the road divides after about 200m – the inn is 1.5km further on at the end of the track. Alternatively you can catch the Sunbeam bus from Sigatoka to Kulu Kulu, which departs at 7am, 7.30am, 8.30am, noon, 2pm, 3.30pm, 5pm and 6pm.

Sigatoka River Valley

Early morning mists rising from the **Sigatoka River** fill the surrounding valley giving it a surreal atmosphere. Along its banks is some of the most fertile farming land in Fiji with plantations of fruit, vegetables and sugarcane. A dirt road travels either side of the river from Sigatoka Town. The west side, known as the **Valley Road**, extends from Sigatoka Town all the way to Bukuya village (see p.78). Here the road branches off to Nadi, or continues across the centre of Viti Levu to Ba on the north coast. Valley Buses (☎650 0168) depart from Sigatoka Town at 9am, 12.30pm, 2.30pm, 5.30pm and 7pm and travel up the Valley Road for two hours to **Draiba** (F$4.10) before turning back around. The road makes an excellent **walking track** and passes many villages and viewpoints along the way. The initial 6km from Sigatoka Town is sealed, passing immediately through Sigatoka village and hugging close to the river. After 2km, just beyond Lawai, is the Butoni Wind Farm with 37 wind turbines lined on the hill ridge. A further kilometre leads to **Nakabuta** village (☎650 0929, tour by donation anytime from 8am–5pm) where a *yaqona* ceremony, **pottery-making** demonstrations and Fijian dance are performed for impromptu arrivals. You can even stay in one of the four basic and seldom-used guest bures beside the village for F$35 per person including breakfast.

The east side of the valley, accessed via **Kavanagasau Road** on the Suva side of the Sigatoka bridge, is less travelled and goes only as far as Mavua village. Five kilometres up the rough dirt road, beside the village of Naroro, is **Tavuni Hill Fort** (Mon–Fri 8am–5pm; Sat 8am–4pm F$10, guide additional $2) a fascinating example of Fiji's tribal past. In the eighteenth century, Tongan invaders began to push further into Fijian territory and established a base on this fantastically steep hill overlooking the Sigatoka River. They waged wars on the surrounding settlements until 1876 when they were subdued by native troops under British

▲ Sigatoka Sand Dunes National Park

control. What remains is a well excavated and easily accessible **hill fort** with stone foundations, rock barricades, ceremonial grounds and the chilling *vatu-ni-bokola*, or killing stone, where victims' heads were smashed with a war club. The views from the hilltop are worth the visit alone. You can also **stay** nearby with the Kuriviti family at *Naroro Village Homestay* (T623 1752; $20 per person, meals can be arranged for F$15).

To explore the Sigatoka River on an organized **tour** try Adventures in Paradise (T652 0833, Tues, Thurs & Sat; F$99 from Coral Coast, F$119 from Nadi; 5hr) who offer village visits, cave tours and the chance to float down river on a bamboo-made *bilibili* raft.

Korotogo Beach and Sunset Strip

Eight kilometres beyond Sigatoka Town, past the final stretch of sugarcane fields, is **Korotogo Beach**. The beach itself is ordinary and not great for swimming but the pleasant two-kilometre-long road towards it, known as the **Sunset Strip** has a few restaurants, budget motels and holiday homes and makes a convenient **base** for exploring the sights around Sigatoka. Just across the Queens Road from the strip is **Kula Eco Park** (T650 0505, Wwww.fijiwild.com; 10am–4pm daily; F$20) Fiji's largest collection of native wildlife. The park is nicely situated in a temperate forest with self-guided boardwalks meandering through aviary cages, reptile enclosures and a reef fish aquarium. The large crested iguanas (see box, p.224) are its highlight, endemic to Fiji, rarely seen and limited to only a couple of islands off Vanua Levu and Yasawa. At the end of the strip you can stock up on supplies at Johnny's Mini Mart (8am–9pm daily) although prices are quite inflated compared to Sigatoka.

Accommodation

Bedarra Inn Sunset Strip T650 0476, Wwww.bedarrafiji.com. Twenty spacious en-suite rooms in a two-storey block with views overlooking the pool and gardens with a bar, good restaurant and tour desk. Overall, excellent value for money. ❹

Outrigger on the Lagoon Queens Rd T650 0044, Wwww.outrigger.com/hotels-resorts/fiji. Five-star resort set in forty acres of beautifully landscaped grounds. The reception and most of the 207 rooms are perched on a hill overlooking the deluxe bures below – the latter all come with a butler to pamper you. Rooms have all the mod cons you could expect and there are three fabulous restaurants on site. The beach is not great, close to a swiftly flowing passage with rip tides – instead guests relax around a massive swimming pool. Rooms ❼, bures ❽.

Fijian pottery

The single most important item identifying the migration of people across the South Pacific is **pottery**. For Fijians, the trail commences with the introduction of **Lapita pottery**, a distinct form of geometric patterning impressed on clay pots by finely saw-toothed blades prior to firing. The oldest examples of Lapita, dating back to 1220 BC, were found at Bourewa Beach on the southeast coast of Viti Levu. The highest concentration of the pottery is found at Sigatoka Sand Dunes National Park (see p.124). In pre-European times, pottery formed the basis of Fijian homewares, with clay vessels used as water containers, *yaqona* bowls, and pots for baking, steaming and frying food. Today, potters around the islands retain traditional motifs, some using woven mats to create patterns, others using carved paddles or leaves. The potters, almost exclusively **women**, knead the clay with fine sand using the heels of the feet, beat it into shape using a wooden mallet, crudely fire the pots and then glaze them for waterproofing by rubbing over with the hot wax-like gum of the *dakua* tree which was also used as a candle in pre-European times.

Tubakula Beach Resort Queens Rd ☎ 650 0097, ⓦ www.fiji4less.com/tuba.html. Quiet retreat for backpackers looking to wind down. The 27 A-frame bungalows with kitchens, some set up as rooms and others as dorms, are neatly set in gardens alongside the beach and pool but the interiors show signs of age. Still, they are great value for money and the food here, though simple, is nourishing. Rooms ❷, bures ❸–❹.

Wai Taci Motel Sunset Strip ☎ 650 0278, ⓔ waitaci@scskydivers.com. Beachhouse style accommodation near a popular kite-surfing beach. The three green tin-roofed A-frame bungalows are a little tired on the inside with simple kitchens but they sleep up to seven making them a great choice for families. Two smaller self-contained units, also with kitchens, face the small swimming pool. ❷

Eating

Le Café Sunset Strip ☎ 652 0877. Cosy café-bar with a courtyard garden and happy hour lasting 5pm–8pm. Offers a varied menu with thin-crust pizzas, New York steak, fish curry and grilled catch of the day; mains around F$14 and lunch time specials F$6.95. The pancakes and ice cream are a winner. Licensed and BYO. 8am–10pm daily.

Baravi Bar at *The Outrigger* on Queens Rd ☎ 650 0044. The Mongolian Barbecue lunch around the pool is always lively with shrimp, chicken, beef or vegetarian options from F$16.50 to F$22.50. In the evening it's pasta and salads apart from Sat, Sun & Mon when it's Asian night, with wok stir fries around F$25. For more intimate evening dining, the *Ivi Restaurant* offers European cuisine starting from F$30 but children are not permitted.

Ocean Terrace at *Bedarra Inn* on Sunset Strip ☎ 650 0476. Good choice for a romantic night out, with candlelit dining upstairs on the terrace. The filling seafood curry and the rich *bulumakau* (local beef in a red wine mushroom sauce) are both divine costing F$21.95 and there's a daily chef's special. Licensed and BYO with F$5 corkage. Daily 6pm–9.30pm.

The Coral Coast

Driving along the **Coral Coast**, losely defined as the 60km section of the Queens Road between Korotogo Beach and Pacific Harbour, is perhaps the most pleasant drive in Fiji. The name, inspired by the exposed offshore reefs, was used to market Fiji's first collection of tourist resorts, which were set up here in the 1960s. The Coral Coast begins in the province of Baravi, passing through the small settlement of **Korolevu**, where Fiji's first tourist hotel once stood; along the coastline here are a dozen **beach resorts**. Beyond Korolevu, the scenery becomes more intense as the highway climbs inland over the mountains of **Serua**, which shield several deep bays with secluded budget retreats. There are few specific attractions on the Coral Coast apart from its scenery but, situated midway between the sites of Sigatoka and the activities of Pacific Harbour, it makes a good base from which to enjoy the two.

Korotogo Beach to Korolevu

Beyond Korotogo Beach, the Queens Road hugs the coastline for 30km all the way to Namatakula Village. One of the finest coastal views is found 15km beyond Sigatoka, past Malevu Village, overlooking the peaceful **Sovi Bay** with its pounding surf. There's plenty of roadside parking and you can scramble down the rocks to the grey sandy beach for a walk but with unpredictable currents, swimming is not advisable. On the far side of the bay is the pretty setting of **Vatukarasa**, once settled by Tongans and with several beautifully thatched bures surrounding the village green. There are two excellent **handicraft shops** here: tiny Kuki's Handicrafts (Mon–Sat 8am–5pm), on the Nadi side of the Queens Road, sources items mostly from Kuki's friends and relatives and also serves coffee, cake and cold drinks; Baravi (℡652 0588, Mon–Sat 7.30am–6pm, Sun 8.30am–5pm), on the Suva side of the village, is larger and more commercial with a wide range of wood carvings and jewellery made from all around Fiji.

The residents of **Namada**, a kilometre further on, have set up a walking tour (℡620 0355; departs Mon, Wed & Fri at 9.45am & 1.45pm; F$28; 2hr, although outside these times the tour guide, Lai, will likely take you anyway). The tour takes in the village plantations in the hills and offers the chance to learn about medicinal plants. At the end of the tour you will be offered souvenirs to buy at the village hall.

At **Korolevu**, 14km east of Namada, there's a BP petrol station with a small shop. Visible in the undergrowth behind is a small airport control tower, evidence of the old airstrip that served guests heading to the *Korotogo Beach Hotel*. The hotel was the pinnacle of tourism in the early 1970s before the Queens Road was tar-sealed. The hotel, the first tourist resort in Fiji, closed in 1983. A dirt road running parallel to the disused grass runway leads inland for 5km through lush tropical forest to **Biausevu** village. From the village, where you pay an F$10 entry fee, there's a thirty-minute relatively flat trail which crosses over a small stream half a dozen times and ends at the pretty **Savunamatelaya Waterfall** where you can swim in the natural pool.

Accommodation

Beach Cocomo Lodge ℡650 7333, ⓦwww.beachcocomo.com. Set on a small hill overlooking the ocean and with steps leading down to a secluded sandy beach, this little-known spot is a real gem for those seeking seclusion. The two wooden cottages with polished wooden floors are tastefully decorated and have hot-water en-suite bathrooms; the only downside is that they back onto the main road. Delicious meals are served in a breezy thatch bure overlooking the sea. ❸–❹

The Beachouse ℡0800 653 0530, ⓦwww.fijibeachouse.com. The location is pretty good with tall coconut palms and a white sandy beach but it's the efficiency that makes this place sparkle. You're made to feel instantly at home, there's a great swimming pool and bar, the food is fantastic and there's loads to do, from waterfall hikes to sea kayaking. The dorms and lodge rooms are squeaky clean and all share bathroom huts with hot-water showers. Camping F$22.50, mixed 6-bed dorm F$29.50, HenHouse dorm F$32.50, rooms ❸, includes breakfast.

Hideaway Resort ℡650 0177, ⓦwww.hideawayfiji.com. Once you're behind the prison-like walls which barricade this large resort from the highway, the atmosphere is rather quaint albeit cramped. The duplex and quad bures are prettily painted and set in landscaped grounds. Interiors are bright and airy, most with a/c and some with outdoor courtyard showers. The beach is adequate and there's good reef surfing in the passage one hour either side of high tide although there are no boards for rent. ❻–❽

Naviti Resort ℡653 0444, ⓦwww.navitiresort.com. Liveliest of the large hotels in Fiji, probably thanks to the excellent-value meals-and-drinks-inclusive packages which covers alcohol. The staff are very attentive especially with children, and within its 38 acres are 220 a/c rooms, five tennis courts, a nine-hole pitch and putt golf course, two swimming pools. Under-16s stay for free. ❻–❽

Tambua Sands ℡650 0399, ⓦwww.tambuasandsfiji.com. With just 25 bures, some interconnecting, this is the smallest of the Coral Coast resorts with a sedate but slightly dated atmosphere. The ocean and garden bures are comfortable with high roofs and ceiling fans and plenty of open spaces between them. If you're looking for something simple, with a small swimming pool and good restaurant, this pretty beachfront resort is great value. ❺–❻, includes continental breakfast.

Beyond Korolevu

Nine kilometres beyond Korolevu is the village of Namatakula in the province of **Serua**. Here the Queens Road cuts inland for 20km to climb over steep hills draped in thick **rainforest**. On the first ascent, a small dirt road leads to *Mango Bay Resort* with a beach backed by incredibly tall coconut palms. There's another pretty beach with good snorkelling at Namagumagua, accessed down a four-kilometre dirt road signposted to *The Wellesley Resort*, 10km further along the Queens Road. For a wonderful view of this **mountain scenery**, take yet another dirt road signposted towards *Waidroka Bay Resort* at the 69km roadside marker, and go past the Dogowale Radio Station track, turning left on Retreat Road. Walk up the first steep driveway on your left for a panoramic lookout – you can keep on walking for ten minutes up to the tower but the views at the top are sometimes obscured by long grass.

Accommodation

Mango Bay Resort ☏ 653 0069, ⓦ www .mangobayresortfiji.com. Marketed as a "flash-packer" resort, this is a fun place to party although it may be a little expensive for budget travellers. The four seven-bed dorms have individual bamboo screens and lockers whilst the smart safari tents, also set back a fair way from the beach, have polished timber floors and en-suite bathrooms. The ten beachfront bures are best suited to young couples and come with outdoor courtyard showers. There's a good restaurant, lively bar and nightclub and even an outdoor cinema. Game fishing and scuba diving are organized daily with PADI Open Water dive courses available for F$595. Dorm F$45, safari tents ❹, bures ❺, includes continental breakfast.

Waidroka Bay Resort ☏ 330 4605, ⓦ www .waidroka.com. This place is distinctly laid back, as you'd expect of a surfing and scuba diving retreat. It's tucked 4km down a dirt road, screened by thick

jungle but without a beach. The five simple terrace rooms are set on a hill with fine views, and six cosy bures and a swimming pool are scattered in gardens overlooking the sea. The Beqa Lagoon dive sites are 20–30min away by one of the five fully equipped fast boats, Frigates Passage surfing is a 45min trip while three local surf spots are within 10min of the resort. There's a handsome variety of boards to rent. Rooms ❹, bures ❺–❻.

Wellesley Resort ☏ 650 0807, ⓦ www .wellesleyresort.com.fj. One of the few chic yet affordable small resorts on Viti Levu. The fifteen suites are set some way back from the beach with heavy wood decor set off by colourful Gauguin prints. The restaurant serves excellent European-inspired cuisine, served overlooking the pool and beyond to the ocean. The beachfront is pretty with long strolls along the white sands in both directions and the snorkelling is pretty good for the mainland. ❻–❼

Pacific Harbour and around

Renowned as Fiji's adventure sports hub, **PACIFIC HARBOUR**'s suburban setting seems rather dull on first acquaintance but the surrounding environment is something quite special. The **Navua River**, some 10km to the east, offers stunning waterfall hikes and longboat excursions whilst further inland, the high mountains of the mysterious **Namosi Highlands** offer fantastic 4WD driving, whitewater rafting and remote village treks. Offshore is the phenomenal **Beqa Lagoon** (see p.177) with world-class scuba diving, including the raved about shark dives, and serious game fishing.

The Town

Pacific Harbour was purpose-built in the early 1970s, drained from swampland and laid out meticulously with suburban driveways and intermittent luxury villas. Today there are rather too many vacant lots with "For Sale" signs and Denarau and Momi in Western Viti Levu have taken over as the place for expats to invest. Apart from its offshore activities, Pacific Harbour's main attraction is the **Arts Village** on Hibiscus Drive (ⓦ www.artsvillage.com), an atmospheric colonial-style shopping centre with thirty boutique **shops and restaurants** including an ATM machine, Internet café and supermarket. Also here is the

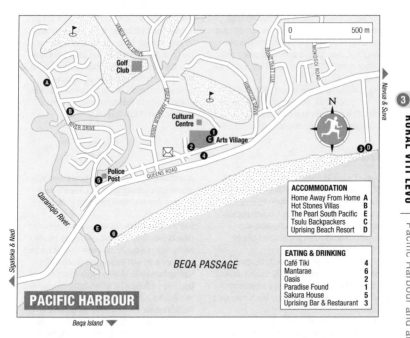

kitsch but fun **Cultural Centre** (☎345 0065; tours depart every thirty minutes between 9am and 4pm; day pass F$55, firewalking only F$35), a mock-traditional Fijian village with an artificial lake that you can be punted around in a canoe. You can also explore the replica *bure kalou*, or scared temple to hear about ancient customs and legends. The highlight, though, is the theatrical **firewalking** ceremony (Mon–Sat 11am) performed on an island in the middle of the lake.

The other star attraction of Pacific Harbour is its underutilized championship **golf course** (daily 7am–6pm; ☎345 0905; F$40 green fee; carts, caddies and rental equipment available) up on Great Harbour Road. The 18-hole mostly flat course has stunning views but the canal borders, bunkers and greens could do with a manicure.

Accommodation

Home Away from Home 47 River Drive ☎345 0102. This no-thrills one-bedroom open plan cottage with kitchen in a converted garage sits adjacent to the family-owned villa and at F$85 per night is superb value. Minimum three nights' stay. ❷

Hot Stones Villas 37 River Drive ☎345 0045, Ⓦ www.hotstones.com.fj. Two exclusive villas overlooking the canal and golf course with high ceilings, whitewashed walls and polished wooden floors. Both villas have private swimming pools, resident chef and nanny. The two-bedroom villa sleeps four adults with the slightly larger three-bedroom villa sleeping six. ❾

The Pearl South Pacific Queens Rd ☎345 0022, Ⓦ www.thepearlsouthpacific.com. The iconic Pacific Harbour resort was revamped in 2005 and given a fresh contemporary look – the box-like whitewashed rooms remain ordinary but the six lavish suites are something else, draped in exotic linens and with themes from India to Louisiana. There's an intricately designed pool and it's right on the beach with views of Beqa and breezes off the ocean. ❻–❾

Tsulu Backpackers Arts Centre ☎345 0065, Ⓦ www.tsulu.com. Located in the Arts Village, this resort resembles a children's nursery inside with colourful jungle and ocean murals, cheap furniture and plastic flowers. Rooms and apartments all have a/c, hot-water bathrooms, TVs with DVD and the family-style self-contained apartments can sleep four; there's also a communal games area. 24-bed dorm F$28, 10-bed dorm F$32, rooms ③, apartments ④.

🏃 **Uprising Beach Resort** off Queens Rd ☎ 345 2200, ⓦ www.uprisingbeachresort .com. This affordable beachside resort fits in seamlessly with Pacific Harbour's adventure label

offering plenty of activities. There's also a funky restaurant and the curved bar is a popular locals' hangout although it can get rowdy at weekends. The large 20-bed grand-looking dorm is set back from the beach with male/female showers and lockers. The twelve pine-panelled bures with polished wood floors vary in size sleeping between two and four with cute bathrooms and outdoor showers. Dorm F$35, bures ④.

Eating

🏃 **Café Tiki** Shop 16, Arts Village, opposite *Tsulu Backpackers*. With a variety of leaf teas and ground coffee, and delectable passion-fruit cheesecake for F$3, this is a neat place to while away the hours. They also have nice sourdough sandwiches and gourmet pies for F$3.50. 7am–7pm daily.

Mantarae The Pearl ☎ 345 0022. Soothing contemporary dishes around F$25 with European, Indian and Asian flavours. There's an extensive wine list with some pretty pricey labels here. Daily 6pm–10pm.

Oasis Shop 7, Arts Village ☎ 345 0617. Large airy dining restaurant serving hearty meals with a secondhand book exchange and Internet access for browsing. The ten Thai dishes are F$10–15, catch of the day is F$16 and a whopping T-bone steak costs F$28. Mon–Sat 6.30am–2pm & 6–9.30pm, Sun 10am–3pm & 6–9.30pm.

Paradise Found Shop 11a, Arts Village. This bright and bubbly place serves up thick shakes and

smoothies for F$4.75 and fresh local salads with papaya and passion fruit for F$8. There's also a tempting display of dried packaged fruits. Daily 8.30am–6pm.

Sakura House Corner of River Drive and Hibiscus Drive ☎ 345 0256. The plain uninspiring interior hardly depicts a quality Japanese joint but the food is reliably good with Teriyaki and Shabu Shabu starting from F$30. Mon–Sat 4pm–10pm.

Uprising off Queens Rd ☎ 345 2200. Located at the *Uprising Beach Resort* at the eastern end of Pacific Harbour, there's a funky atmosphere with light jazz playing in the background. The lunchtime quick snacks are filling and include handmade burgers, burritos and classic fish and chips, all around F$10. The dinner menu is Modern European but with some curries, mostly around F$12 and there are three 3-course blackboard specials usually with fish and local vegetables between F$18 & F$27. Daily 7am–9.30pm.

Activities

Jetski Tours Pacific Harbour ☎ 345 0933. Guided jet-ski tours circumnavigating Beqa island. The tour includes a picnic lunch on one of Beqa's deserted beaches and a snorkel on one of the stunning reefs. Solo ride F$400, dual ride F$430; daily 9am–1pm.

🏃 **Rivers Fiji** The Pearl, Pacific Harbour ☎ 345 0147, ⓦ www.riversfiji.com. American-run operator offering thrilling year-round whitewater rafting (Mon, Wed & Fri; departs 6.45am; F$275) on the Upper Navua River. The 4hr journey downstream passes over exciting Grade II-III rapids and through a stunning canyon with sheer rock walls overflowing with waterfalls. They also offer a more sedate inflatable kayak tour (Tues, Thurs & Sat; day tour departs 8am F$205, two-day camping tour F$540) heading down the Luva River. Pick-ups from Nadi hotels cost an additional F$50.

Xtasea ☎ 345 0280, ⓦ www.xtaseacharters .com. Game-fishing charters aboard a 20m well-equipped gamefishing boat (F$1,860 for full day; maximum of four anglers but up to eight people). Heads south of Beqa to the deep channels trawling for billfish and tuna. Includes breakfast and lunch.

Scuba diving

For more information about the Beqa shark dives, see p.177

🏃 **Aqua Trek Beqa** The Pearl ☎ 345 0324, ⓔ beqa@aquatrek.com. Professional dive operator with top-of-the-range gear and boats. Shark dives cost F$200 and depart 8.30am on Wed & Sat only with reef diving around Beqa Lagoon available on other days for F$180.

Beqa Adventure Divers Lagoon Resort ☎ 345 0911, ⓦ www.fiji-sharks.com; Local operator conducting staged shark dives departing 8.30am Mon, Wed, Fri & Sat only, two-tank dive F$200. **Dive Connections** 16 River Drive ℡ 345 0541, ℮ diveconn@connect.com.fj. Budget operator with two-tank dives costing F$155 and a maximum of sixteen divers departing daily at 9am. They don't offer the staged shark dives, but you'll likely encounter some sharks along the way.

Tropical Expeditions ℡ 345 0666 The 20-metre *Beqa Princess* acts as a live-aboard sleeping up to nine divers, heading south of Beqa to unchartered open reefs on various schedules – F$300 per night includes meals and diving. When it's not on an overnight trip, the boat heads out to Beqa for excellent-value day-trips, two-tank dive with lunch cost F$150.

Navua and the Namosi Highlands

NAVUA, 10km east of Pacific Harbour on the Suva side of the Navua River, is a dusty market centre with a mix of Fiji-Indian rice farmers from the delta and Fijian villagers from the highlands selling their produce. Most buses between Nadi and Suva call in at the bus stand for a fifteen-minute rest stop. The only reason to get off is to catch a boat to Beqa Island (see p.175) or to explore the Namosi Highlands which loom large above the river floodplain. Navua has an **ATM** machine behind the yellow Courts building, and a few supermarkets but no accommodation. The few restaurants sell only pre-cooked oily counter-food, the best being *Singh's* beside the bus stand.

At the north end of town, between the market and bridge, longboats line the riverbanks and journey up the murky **Navua River** to the villages of the **Namosi Highlands**. Guided **longboat trips** are available from Discover Fiji Tours (℡ 345 0180; ℗ www.discoverfijitours.com; F$169) an enterprising local operator with a base just before the market stalls when coming in off the Queens Road. If you fancy floating on a traditional *bilibili*, a raft of bamboo poles strapped together using vines, or tubing down the mild rapids, opt for the less commercial overnight tour (from F$130 per person per day) staying in a local village. Discover Fiji also has its own **accommodation** beside the Navua River at *Koro Makawa Homestay* (℡ 345 0180, ❸, including meals), 4km north of Navua.

With a 4WD vehicle, it's possible to drive from Navua along the Namosi Road, bearing right at the three-road junction and following the Waidina

▲ Bilibili raft, Navua River

River to Naqali through remote forests. From Naqali, the road heads south to Suva a journey which takes four hours from Navua, or north to Monasavu and eventually connecting through to Tavua on the north coast of Viti Levu. The most picturesque village along the road is **Namosi** village, sitting beneath the 950-metre sheer cliff peak of **Mount Voma**. You could present a *sevusevu* to the village headman and stay the night to explore the stunning environment with a village guide. Climbers can quite easily scale Mount Voma without ropes in around three hours and will be graced on a clear day with sweeping views of the surrounding mountains.

Rivers Fiji (see p.132) will take you through stunning remote scenery further inland towards Wainimakatu village for **whitewater rafting** through Grade II rapids. This remote region fronts the massive **Sovi Basin**, an amphitheatre of lowland rainforest surrounded by mountain ridges with an abundance of endemic birdlife – this is Fiji's largest and most important protected nature reserve.

Wainadoi

Leaving Navua, the main Queens Road continues east through the sparse flats of the river delta dotted with ancient pandanus trees and massive banyans whose roots descend from its branches like balls of rope. Beyond, on the mountain side of the highway, is **Wainadoi**, home to **Spices of Fiji** (T 336 1039; Mon–Fri 10am–4pm; F$10) which offers 45-minute walking tours around the gardens taking in various local spices in production. Alternatively you can zoom through the forest canopy 30m up on a zip line operated by **Zip Fiji** (T 930 0545, W www.zip-fiji.com; F$115 per person). They also offer the chance to spend a night high in the canopy sleeping on a **treehouse** platform (F$400 per person) From Wainadoi, it's a thirty-minute drive into Suva.

North Viti Levu

At first glance **North Viti Levu**, with its rolling sunburnt hills and succession of dusty inland towns might appear rather dreary. But delve a little deeper and you'll discover some charming unexpected sites. The raw **Ba hinterland** boasts Fiji's most spectacular traditional village, Navala, whilst further east and also inland is Fiji's highest mountain, Tomanivi, which can be conquered on a pleasant but arduous half-day hike. Off the undulating coast of **Rakiraki**, the tranquil island of **Nananu-i-Ra** has fabulous diving and is a popular retreat with budget travellers. Further east, the most scenic roadside views in Fiji are to be found around **Viti Levu Bay** with the high peaks of the Nakauvadra Range rising from the flat sugarcane fields.

Getting there and around

There is no airstrip along the north coast so the only **public transport** is by bus or minivan. Sunbeam Transport (see p.120) offers an express **bus** service along the Kings Road. Local buses from each town head along the dusty rural roads stopping frequently along the way – to hail one on the roadside simply put out your arm and flap your fingers. Otherwise, the best way to get around is by hiring a **carrier van** or taxi. Car rental is available from Ba (see p.136).

The Ba hinterland

The most scenic road from Nadi to North Viti Levu heads inland along a dirt track through the **Ba hinterland**. The road passes the remote village of **Navala** with its traditional thatch houses before rejoining the Kings Road five hours later at the dusty town of **Ba**. Further west, the charming one-street Indian-dominated town of **Tavua** is a wonderful place to soak up the region's friendly rural atmosphere. Inland is the high plateau around **Nadarivatu**, base camp for exploring the 1323-metre **Mount Tomanivi**.

Navala

Home to almost two hundred traditionally thatched bures, the village of **NAVALA** is an iconic symbol of Fiji. Back in 1950, the community decided to reject modern building materials and to encourage all school leavers to learn the art of traditional bure making. The result, sixty years on, is the last remaining **thatch village** in Fiji. The only cement structures are the church, school and a few generator huts. To visit the village, introduce yourself to the first person you come across on the roadside – they will take you to the village headman where you pay a F$20 village entry fee. The money represents a *sevusevu* and helps with the upkeep of the village. Strolling around is a delightful experience. The chiefly bures have elaborately designed rooftops and are set in a neat line facing the village green. The more disorganized clusters of bures on the lower slopes of the Ba River are where the ordinary people live. The village is surrounded by grass-covered mountains full of secret caves where the people once retreated in times of war.

You can **stay** at *Bulou's Lodge* (☎628 1224 or 666 6644 after beep dial 2116; dorm F$65, bure ❸, includes meals), perched on the banks of the Ba River five minutes' walk south of the village. The ten-bed dorm lodge forms part of Bulou's house and is a bit cramped, but you're likely have it to yourself. The two en-suite bures are set down a small trail on a hillside clearing overlooking the river. The lodge can arrange guided walks in the hills with the energetic Tui. The only way to reach Navala by **public transport** is from Ba town – Khan's bus (F$4.40; 1hr 30min) departs from the bus stand at 1.30pm and 5.15pm although the latter reaches Navala after dark – the bus heads back to Ba at 6am and 8am. A private carrier van from beside Ba market costs F$40 or you can visit on a day tour from Nadi (see p.75).

Pathways of the spirits

Viti Levu, particularly the grasslands between Ba and Rakiraki, is crisscrossed with **ancient pathways** known as *tualeita*. Dating back centuries before European contact, most of the paths run along the highest ridges allowing walkers to spot enemy war parties and to avoid being followed. The paths played an important role in the Fijian colonization of Viti Levu, linking pioneer settlements to the main chiefly villages. Before the widespread conversion to Christianity, *tualeita* also held a religious importance. It was believed that the spirits of the dead followed the trails on their journey back to their origins, and thence on to the afterlife. Most walking tracks today follow *tualeita*.

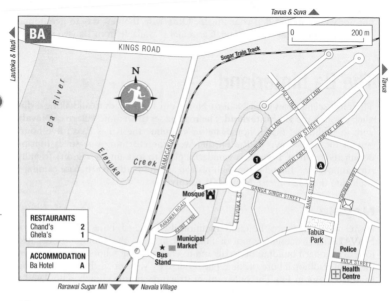

Tavua & Suva ▲

0 _____ 200 m

RESTAURANTS
Chand's — 2
Ghela's — 1

ACCOMMODATION
Ba Hotel — A

Rarawai Sugar Mill ▼▼ ▼ Navala Village

Ba

Located just south of the Kings Road and separated from the ocean by a huge mangrove estuary, **BA** can easily be missed. The town has a population of around 15,000 – mostly Indians – making it the fifth largest town in Fiji. Many of the residents are Muslim and the town **mosque** is a major landmark. The only other significant building is the large sugar mill south of the centre. Apart from stopping for a meal or visiting the market, few tourists pass this way. There is one quirky sight on the way out of town – a giant soccer ball sitting on the pavement at the western entrance of Main Street, a reference to the town's obsession with the beautiful game.

The bustling **market** and **bus stand** are on the south side of Ba off Rarawai Road which continues along a dirt track to Navala. The only **accommodation** is the slightly seedy *Ba Hotel* (☎ 667 4000; dorm F$20, rooms ❷) on Bank Street which doubles as a bar, nightclub and bottle shop; there are thirteen spartan rooms with bouncy beds, tiny bathrooms and air conditioning. The locals' favourite **restaurant** is *Chand's*, (Mon–Sat 7.30am–9.30pm, Sun noon–2.30pm) upstairs on Main Street near the roundabout, with excellent South Indian curries from F$10 to F$15. If you're interested in tasting colourful Indian sweets, try *Ghela's* (Mon–Sat 7am–6pm), across the road on Main Street.

Listings

Banking Westpac and ANZ banks (Mon–Fri 9.30am–4pm) both have ATM machines on Bank St.
Car rental Singh's Rental (☎ 667 4988) on Main St.
Internet access IT Intelligence Ganga Singh St (Mon–Fri 8am–5.30pm, Sat 8am–1pm, 50 cents for 10min) provides broadband Internet access.
Medical Family Clinic and Dental Lab, Tabua Park (☎ 667 0536, Mon–Sat 8.30am–5pm).

Ba Mission Hospital (☎ 667 4022) is on Yalalevu St, 1km west of Ba, over the bridge towards Lautoka.
Police ☎ 667 4222 on Koronubu St off Tabua Park.
Post office Nareba St (Mon–Fri 8am–4pm, Sat 8am–noon) but with a more convenient Post Shop on Main St.

Tavua

A forty-minute drive east from Ba brings you to **TAVUA**, a smaller, more intimate market centre set slightly inland from the coast. The Kings Road passes straight through town making it feel busier than it is. The roadside is lined with twenty or so tiny shops packed with all sorts of odds and ends while the cramped **town market** is found at the eastern end. You can easily spend an idle day here chatting with the locals without being pressured to buy anything. But what really gives this town an edge over its neighbours is the charming *Tavua Hotel* (T 668 0522, F 668 1225; dorm F$26, rooms ❸, cottages ❺) a five-minute stroll uphill on Nabuna Road. This whitewashed colonial-style **hotel** has eleven airy en-suite rooms with air conditioning, ceiling fans and TVs although the beds are rather uncomfortable. Around the swimming pool are three cottages sleeping five, each with a kitchen. The **restaurant** serves the best food in town, with a big breakfast costing F$7.50 and a lunch and dinner menu serving curry of the day for F$8 and a locally produced surf and turf for F$14.

There are few other good places to eat in Tavua, with a handful of canteens serving dubious pre-cooked counter food although *Fu Lee's* (Mon–Sat 7am–5pm), beside the market on Kings Road, has a blackboard menu offering decent-sized servings of chow meins and curries with dhal soup for F$4.50. To get to know the locals a little better over a beer, head to the *Tavua Farmers Club* on Kings Road at the western end of town, or across to the *Tavua Club* (daily 10am–10pm) on Nasivi Street, hangout for white-collar workers. Both places are likely to be predominantly patronized by men although tourists are always welcome.

Eight kilometres inland from Tavua on the Vatukoula Road is Fiji's largest **gold mine**. In 2006, the Australian-owned Emperor Mines Limited closed the mine claiming it was no longer profitable, having been mined continuously since 1935. The mine's ten thousand workers, mostly from Tavua and its sister town of Vatukoula, became instantly unemployed and many left the region altogether. A sliver of hope rests with the mine's new owners, Westech Mining, who took over operations in 2007. Public **tours** may be possible once the mine is working again. Vatukoula buses run a regular service to Vatukoula from Tavua.

Listings

Banking ANZ bank Vatukoula Rd (Mon–Fri 9.30am–4pm) and Westpac, eastern end of Kings Rd.
Internet access Internet Kona in H. Billmoria building, corner of Kings Rd and Nabukulu St (Mon–Sat 8am–1pm & 2pm–6pm, F$1.50 per hour for broadband).

Laundry The *Tavua Hotel* offers a laundry service.
Police T 668 0222 corner of Vatukoula Rd and Nasivi St.
Post office Nasivi St (Mon–Fri 8am–4pm, Sat 8am–noon).

Nadarivatu and Mount Tomanivi

Around 25km inland from Tavua is the old colonial settlement of **NADARI-VATU**, once the penal colony for Fiji and now the main access point for climbing Mount Tomanivi. It's a wonderfully cool and peaceful setting, located in a large depression surrounded by mountains and pine forests above the heat of the coast. The journey up here is quite spectacular, accessed 3km east of Tavua town via a dirt road. The trip can be done in fifty minutes but with wonderful views along the way, particularly on the steep ascent from pretty Waikubukubu village, it will probably take longer. Nadarivatu translates as "the stone bowl", which refers to a small black stone found beside the road close to the health centre – legend tells of water sprouting from the stone in times of drought and it being the source of the mighty Sigatoka River.

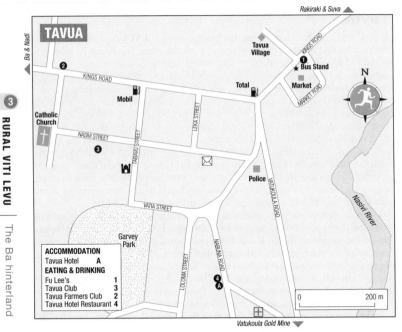

You can **stay** at *Nadarivatu Rest House* (☏ 628 0477; F$50 per cottage up to six people), two serene cottages with stone fireplaces, wooden floors and three bedrooms each with kitchen, cold-water showers and 24-hour electricity. The fireplaces are stocked with logs, which is a good thing as at almost 1000m, it gets pretty chilly up here at night, even in summer. The affable caretaker, Buli, can advise on a remote two-day **walking track** crossing the Nadrau Plateau to the south side of Viti Levu.

Climbing Mount Tomanivi

Mount Tomanivi, also known as Mount Victoria, is the highest point in Fiji standing at 1,323m. Unfortunately, at this high elevation, the mountain appears to be nothing more than a hill although the two-hour hike to the top is certainly strenuous. The trail starts from **Navai** village, 8km south of Nadarivatu. You'll need to hire a guide (F$20) and pay a F$20 admission fee which goes towards village projects. The walk is best attempted on a dry day, setting off from Navai around 8am – any later and the trail becomes swelteringly hot, any earlier and the summit is likely to be obscured by morning mist. The lower part of the trail is extremely muddy, passing plantations and crossing a couple of streams. About halfway up, it enters the government-leased **Tomanivi Nature Reserve** where you'll probably see masked shining parrots, long-legged warblers and hear whistling doves. From here on up the route follows an exceptionally steep ridge over boulders and contorted tree roots – it's quite a scramble but thankfully the trail is hemmed in by thick forest. There are a couple of clearings along the way with glimpses of the surrounding countryside, and the panorama from the top is exceptional. On a clear day you'll see the stark contrast between the dry valleys in the distant north and the rugged tropical mountains draped in rainforests to the south.

The only way to get to Navai Village, other than rental car, is by **carrier van** from beside the market in Tavua. Shared carriers cost F$5, usually heading out in the morning around 6.30am and in the afternoon at 1pm. If staying overnight in Nadarivatu, arrange for the Navai carrier van to pick you up for F$14 – otherwise it's a good two-hour walk south along the Monasavu Road. Two kilometres past Nadarivatu the road splits in two – the left-hand track goes to Navai and on to Monasavu; the right-hand track to Nagatagata (see p.139). For a true village experience, you can **stay** at Leo Nautuka's house in Navai (☎623 2154; F$30 per person includes meals but you should also gift a small *sevusevu* to the village). Leo is the caretaker for the track to the mountain.

Beyond Navai, the seldom used and very rough Monasavu Road cuts through virgin tropical forests for 25km to Monasavu Dam (see p.170) and thence on a slightly better dirt road to Suva (see p.151).

Nubutautau and the Nadrau Plateau

From Nadarivatu it's possible to head deeper into the Viti Levu interior on a two-day trail traversing the Nadrau Plateau and visiting the notorious village of **Nubutautau**. The trail starts from **Nagatagata** village, 15km south of Nadarivatu, at the end of a dirt track which branches off to the right from the Monasavu Road just south of Nadarivatu. Aim to arrive at Nagatagata in the morning and ask for a guide (expect to pay around F$40) to lead you on the three-hour trek to remote Nubutautau. It was here in 1867 that the Reverend Thomas Baker was killed and devoured by the villagers (see box below) – the steel axe used in the attack is still kept in the village. If you wish to continue along the trail you should present a *sevusevu* in order to stay a night. The next day a lad from the village will guide you along the difficult but scenic six-hour walk to the highlands village of Korolevu

---

Reverend Baker and the curse of Nubutautau

In 1867, having spent eight years in Fiji and speaking the language fluently, the English clergyman the **Reverend Thomas Baker** was appointed Missionary of the Interior. His job was to persuade the fierce hill people of Viti Levu to convert (or *lotu*) to the Christian faith. The odds were stacked against Baker as the hill people, or *Colo*, were great enemies of Cakobau, King of Fiji (see p.202) who had already converted to Christianity, making them suspicious of the new religion.

By 20 July, Baker had reached the village of **Nubutautau**. Wishing to cross over to western Viti Levu, he presented a *tabua* to the chief, Nawawabalavu, requesting safe passage. However, Nawawabalavu had already received a *tabua* from the people of Naitasiri village, lower down the valley, requesting him to kill the missionary. The following morning, whilst leaving the village, Baker and his party of nine men were ambushed by Nawawabalavu's warriors, clubbed to death and then eaten. Another version of the story maintains that the attack was in revenge for Baker insulting the chief by removing a comb from his hair although there is no evidence that this happened. News of the event reached the European stronghold of Levuka, and pressure was put on **Cakobau** to punish the murderers. Reluctantly, eight months after Baker's death, Cakobau led his forces towards Nubutautau but was ambushed, losing almost a hundred men including several influential chiefs.

The people of Nubutautau eventually succumbed to Christianity but for many years it was believed their land was **cursed** as drought consumed the hills. It wasn't until November 2003 that reconciliation was complete with the invitation of Reverend Baker's relatives to a formal *soro*, or forgiveness ceremony, conducted by the then Prime Minister, Laisania Qarase.

RURAL VITI LEVU | The Ba hinterland

③

(not to be confused with Korolevu on the Coral Coast), crossing the Sigatoka River a dozen times along the way – it's really only practical during the dry winter months from May to October, and then best in stable weather. Once at Korolevu, you can catch the daily early morning carrier van for the 75km journey down to Sigatoka on the south coast.

From Nagatagata it's also possible to head east across the interior to **Nanoko** village. The route takes six hours on foot or ninety minutes by 4WD vehicle and is only possible in dry weather – ask the Nadarivatu district officer (℡651 0756) about the state of the road before heading out. From Nanoko it's a short drive to Bukuya in the Nausori Highlands from where you can head down to Nadi.

A **bus** operated by Tavua General (℡668 0150; F$4) departs Tavua for Nagata-gata via Nadarivatu at 3.30pm on Monday, Tuesday, Thursday and Friday.

Tavua to Rakiraki

Back on the Kings Road, the journey east from Tavua to **Rakiraki** passes through the vast cattle farmland of Yaqara. The scenery here resembles a mini Wild West with cowboys rounding up the herds and the rugged mountain scenery of the **Nakauvadra Range** in the background. Further along the coast is the small market town of **Rakiraki**, also known as Vaileka Town. Nearby is the pretty coastal setting of Volivoli Point and the beautiful offshore island of **Nananu-i-Ra**, both featuring some lovely holiday cottages.

The Nakauvadra Range and around

Around 25km east of Tavua is the turn-off for the impeccably sterile bottling plant for **Fiji Water** (Ⓦwww.fijiwater.com), which since its inception in 1996 has become Fiji's most recognized global brand. The company was set up by Canadian billionaire David Gilmour and sold for a massive profit in 2004 to an American investor. Water is sourced from an artesian well fed from the legendery

▲ Mountain scenery, Nakauvadra Range

Degei, god of gods

Near the summit of Uluda, the northern peak of the Nakauvadra Mountains, is a cave. It is no ordinary cave, for it is said that **Degei**, the most important god in Fijian folklore, resides here. To the early Fijians, Degei was the creator of the world, creator of men and god of anger and war. He took the form of a **snake** and, when he moved, the earth shook. Noise irritated him so the bats were chased away from the cave, birds were ordered to sleep away from the summit and the waves crashing onto the nearby reef were silenced. Throughout Fiji, and particularly on Viti Levu, the snake god ruled supreme and was offered the first bowl of *yaqona* as a matter of respect. In the hills of Viti Levu you may still see the first bowl of grog poured outside in his honour.

Nakauvadra Range, said to be the home of Degei, the most powerful of Fijian gods (see box above). Seven kilometres before Rakiraki is a fabulous roadside view overlooking the rocky volcanic plug of **Navatu Hill** with an ancient fortification perched on its summit – there's a rough trail on the east side of the hill leading to the top with a panoramic view. The multi-unit **hill fort** was used as a defence from the fearsome **Udre Udre**, a chief from Rakiraki who folklore recalls ate nothing but human flesh. You can see Udre Udre's grave beside the Kings Road, 100m on the right before the Nadovi Police Post – the 872 stones placed here supposedly represent the number of people he ate. At the police post, the Kings Road continues on through Rakiraki village with a side road branching right into Vaileka Town. The sole **place to stay** before Rakiraki is *Golden Point* (T 620 5252, ❶) on the coast at Navilau Point, just past the Three Angels Mission Hospital. Accommodation is in six private air-conditioned rooms within a small wooden lodge overlooking a lagoon.

Rakiraki (Vaileka Town)

Vaileka Town, usually referred to as just **RAKIRAKI**, evolved from a tiny village site with the expansion of the **Penang Sugar Mill**, the oldest of Fiji's four working mills built in 1880. The town of around 1500 residents remains dominated by sugarcane farming and apart from a small market has little to entice tourists. For **eating**, try *Ady's Food Palace* (Mon–Sat 8am–9pm, Sun 1pm–9pm) down an alley off the main street beside Bank of Baroda, which has a peaceful courtyard and serves tasty F$6 curries with roti and dahl. The only **accommodation** is the *Rakiraki Hotel* (T 669 4101, W www.tanoahotels.com; dorms F$28, rooms ❷–❸) on the Kings Road in the original village of Rakiraki, 3km from the town centre. The hotel is surprisingly large, with 36 air-conditioned rooms with en-suite bathrooms, ten basic rooms with shower and a 16-bed dorm that is seldom used except for groups. There's a pleasant swimming pool and good restaurant but it's a bit out of the way if you don't have your own transport.

Listings

Banking ATM machines at both ANZ and Westpac banks on Rakiraki Rd opposite Vaiteka Market but tellers only open on Tues & Thurs, 9.30am–3pm.

Hospital T 669 4368, 2km beyond the town centre, over the bridge, turning left on Thompson Place.

Internet access *Lal's Net Cafe* next to Westpac bank on main street has slow broadband access for ten cents a minute.

Police T 669 4222 Corner of Market Rd and Main St.

Post office Market Square, opposite the bus stand (Mon–Fri 8am–4pm, Sat 8am–noon).

Volivoli

The placid hills of **Volivoli** mark the northern point of Viti Levu and look out on the offshore islands of Malake and Nananu-i-Ra. Taking advantage of this serene landscape are two small resorts, both with good scuba-diving operators. The budget *Volivoli Beach Resort* (℡669 4511, Ⓦ www.volivoli.com; dorm F$25; room ❸) is the newest of the two and has seven dorms with eight beds in each as well as five twin rooms. The large open-plan restaurant serves hearty and affordable European-style food. Feejee Experience (see p.121) overnight here four times a week (Mon, Wed, Fri & Sat) transforming the place from a quiet retreat to rowdy backpackers' hangout. The beach at high tide is non-existent but as the tide retreats, an eighty-metre **sand spit** emerges with a small area for sunbathing and bonfires. There are complimentary sea kayaks for in-house guests and full-day game-fishing charters available for F$750. The owners of *Volivoli* also operate Ra Divers (Ⓦ www.radivers.com; PADI Open Water course F$550, 2-tank dive F$160). Access to the resort is 5km east of Rakiraki village on the Kings Road and 4km along the extremely scenic Volivoli Road towards the coast.

Back on the Kings Road, and a further 1km from Rakiraki, is the turn-off to the more upmarket 🕮 *Wananavu Beach Resort* (℡669 4433, Ⓦ www.wananavu .com; bures ❺–❻, villas ❻–❼, includes buffet breakfast). The restaurant here takes pride of place with delightful views along the coast and serves excellent food. Accommodation is in one of 31 bures, mostly duplex lodges with pine-panelled interiors, or in the more luxurious Mediterranean-style villas in the hills. **Diving** at *Wananavu* is offered by Kai Viti Divers (℡669 3600, Ⓦ www .kaivitidivers.com; PADI Open Water Course F$595, 2-tank dive F$180). They run fast jet-boats out to the seldom visited but extremely impressive Vatu-i-Ra Passage in around 45 minutes. Kai Viti Divers also pick up from the resorts on Nananu-i-Ra (see opposite).

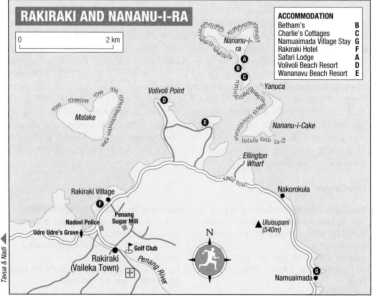

RAKIRAKI AND NANANU-I-RA

| 0 | 2 km |

ACCOMMODATION
Betham's	B
Charlie's Cottages	C
Namuaimada Village Stay	G
Rakiraki Hotel	F
Safari Lodge	A
Volivoli Beach Resort	D
Wananavu Beach Resort	E

Nananu-i-ra

Volivoli Point

Yanuca

Malake

Nananu-i-Cake

Ellington Wharf

KINGS ROAD

Rakiraki Village

Nakorokula

Penang Sugar Mill

Nadovi Police

Uluisupani (540m)

Udre Udre's Grave

Golf Club

N

Rakiraki (Vaileka Town)

Penang River

Namuaimada

▼ Barotu & Suva

Nananu-i-Ra

Fifteen minutes by boat across a choppy passage from Ellington Wharf (see below) takes you to delightful **Nananu-i-Ra**, a small hilly island surrounded by beautiful white sandy beaches. There are plans for luxury holiday homes and a *Hilton* resort development on the northern side of the island but until these appear it remains blissfully down to earth with just three family-owned **budget resorts**. *Betham's Beach Cottages* (T 669 4132, W www.bethams.com .fj; dorm F$25, room ➋, cottage ➌) is the pick of the bunch with five simply furnished beachfront cottages, a four-bed dorm and a few private rooms; the on-site *Anchor Restaurant* knocks up the usual mix of burgers, noodles and the like. At the eastern end of the beach, is *Charlie's* (T 669 4676, W www .charliescottages.com; dorm $25, cottage ➋–➌). The cottages here are spacious but rather sparsely furnished, with big windows and even bigger views overlooking frangipani trees and the ocean. There's no restaurant but Louisa will cook meals on request.

The long curving palm-fringed **Lomanisue Beach** fronting the east side of Nananu-i-Ra is accessible along a two-minute trail from behind *Charlie's*. Swimming on this side is much better and the sands deeper, but it's constantly buffeted by winds; while this may not suit sunbathers, it's probably the best spot in Fiji for **windsurfing**. *Safari Lodge* (T 669 3333, W www.safarilodge.com.fj; dorm F$30, room ➌, bure ➎, cottage ➐) along the beachfront, offers windsurfing lessons for F$110 per hour and a six-hour kite-surfing course for F$480.

From the north end of Lomanisue Beach, you can walk around the rocky headland at low tide to the secluded bay on the north side of the island – the centuries-old stone wall formations lining the shore here were built to catch fish on the outgoing tide. From the bay several walking tracks lead up the lightly wooded hills and head back to Sekoula Point.

Getting there: Ellington Wharf

Nananu-i-Ra is accessed from **Ellington Wharf**, 10km east of Rakiraki along the Kings Road. Sunbeam express buses between Lautoka and Suva will drop you at the junction for the wharf, as will Flying Prince (T 669 4346; 8 daily, F$2.50), a local bus service from Rakiraki which heads on to Namuaimada and Barotu. It's a two-kilometre walk from the junction to the wharf so if you have heavy luggage it's probably best to hire a taxi from Rakiraki (F$12). A small well-supplied shop and café beside the wharf run by *Safari Lodge* co-ordinates boat transfers to the island for F$15 one way.

East Viti Levu

The hilly, tropical countryside of **East Viti Levu** is the least visited part of the big island. Here you'll find some of the prettiest roadside landscapes in Fiji, particularly around **Viti Levu Bay** along the northeast coast. South of the bay, from the village of **Barotu**, the Kings Road cuts 20km inland through deep tropical rainforest alongside the Wainibuka River. An alternative track from Barotu heads over the high Nakorotubu Range to the undulating hills and bays of the remote **Tailevu Coast**. The two roads meet again at **Korovou** town from where the route descends into the fertile flat farming land of the mighty Rewa River, eventually rejoining the urban world at Nausori, just north of Suva.

Viti Levu Bay

Ten kilometers west of Rakiraki, the Kings Road loops south around the northeastern corner of Viti Levu. From here there are impressive views of the Nakauvadra Range tapering off into deep **Viti Levu Bay**. Thanks to volcanic activity, the coasts to the north and south of the bay are steep and irregular with numerous promontories.

Dwarfed by the high mountains and hugging the exposed northerly point of the bay, is the pretty beachside village of **Namuaimada**. Lodged between two bluffs the beach here bears the brunt of the trade winds and is a renowned **kite-surfing spot**. The village is a little rough around the edges but it's a friendly place with a pleasant mix of traditional thatch bures, wooden lodges and modern cement buildings surrounding the church. You can arrange to **stay** in one of the village houses through Anare Biciri (☏ 360 9141; F$35 with food); it's best to bring some snacks with you as the meals are basic Fijian fare. Guides from the village offer trekking in the mountains as well as hand-line **fishing** on the reef (both around F$10). The local Flying Prince bus from Rakiraki stops at Namuaimada; alternatively contact Api (☏ 921 4171; F$30) who comes from the village and drives a carrier van based at Rakiraki.

Eight kilometres south of Namuaimada at the base of the bay buffered by mangrove forests is **St Francis Xavier's Catholic Church** perched on a hilltop overlooking the school in Naiserelagi village. Inside are three beautiful **murals** painted by Jean Charlot in 1962. Challenging European colonization and superiority of the time, the centrepiece, a ten-metre-high fresco, depicts a crucified Black Christ wearing *masi* cloth, whilst two side altar panels, one with indigenous Fijians and the other with Fijian-Indian, show unique cultural scenes of *tabua* and *yaqona* offerings to Christ. There is also a mural of St Peter Chanel, Fiji's first martyred saint, holding a symbolic war club.

Barotu to Korovou via the Kings Road

The quickest and most commonly travelled route between Rakiraki and Suva follows the 72-kilometre **Kings Road** heading inland from Barotu to Korovou. From Savusavu village the road clings to a deep valley carved out by the Wainibuka River. Along the way you may see locals heading downstream on *bilibilis*, rafts made from bamboo poles, sometimes laden with market goods. At Wailotua, almost 50km south of Barotu is a large **cave** cut into the steep mountain abutting the village. Admission to the cave is F$5 and you'll be shown its star attraction, a bulky stalagmite said to resemble a six-headed **snake god**. In pre-European times chiefs would meet and consult here. Sadly, the ancient stone is now coarsely scribbled with the names of local tourists.

Eleven kilometres further along, past Dakuivuna village, is the scenic **Waimaro Waterfall** (F$2 admission). Steps lead down to a stream and picnic bench surrounded by forest. If you arrive on a weekend or during school holidays the local kids will show you the best spots for jumping into the pool below the falls.

▲ Black Christ mural, St Xavier's Catholic Church

From the waterfall, its 15km on to Korovou Town through rather tame dairy farming country.

The Tailevu Coast route

The most scenic route between Barotu and Korovou heads along an eighty-kilometre dirt track hugging the remote **Tailevu Coast**. With its lovely coastal scenery, secluded villages, hiking tracks and offshore dolphin-spotting, this seldom visited region is an exceptional place to explore. In the southern portion, 10km from Korovou Town, is **Natovi Landing**, departure point for ferries to Ovalau.

Access to the Tailevu Coast road is easy to miss if travelling along the Kings Road from Rakiraki – less than a kilometre south of Barotu, turn left onto the badly signposted **Nakorotubu Road**. Shortly afterwards turn left again at Luci's Shopping Centre, the last store you'll see until you reach Korovou. The tremendously scenic but steep road to the coast is best tackled by **4WD** although in dry weather can be comfortably driven in a car with good tyres and high clearance. Fifteen kilometres from the Nakorotubu Road turn-off is the tranquil *Rainbow Lodge* (☎651 3213; F$40 includes local-style meals), a private organic farm in a former coffee plantation. There are four traditional thatch bures here, all basic and a tad musty. The bathroom, shared with the family, has a bucket as a shower although there is a flush toilet.

Namarai to Nataleira

The Nakorotubu Road reaches the coast 5km on at **Namarai**, a neatly laid out village in a small bay. You'll be warmly received by the locals although note that this is a traditional, strongly Methodist area so try to dress appropriately. From Namarai, the most **scenic** section of the coastal road meanders south to Bureiwai around a series of beautiful bays covered in coconut palms. Two kilometres beyond Saioko village, keep an eye out for a small signpost for the Church of the Latter-day Saints. There's a small track on the opposite side of the road which heads out to a lovely **viewpoint** from a cliff overlooking the bay. Thirteen kilometres on is **Bureiwai**, where the daily bus from Suva terminates.

South of Bureiwai, the road cuts slightly inland for 10km passing over gently rolling hills interspersed with pine forests and grasslands towards Nataleira. Perched on a hill just before reaching the village is the delightful 🥘 *Takalana Bay Retreat* (☏991 6338, ✉takalana@gmail.com; ❹–❺, includes meals). There are just two bures here, connected by a communal sitting area where meals are served. Both bures are homely and well decorated with en-suite hot-water bathrooms and cooking stoves. The retreat is surrounded by 84 acres of private land descending to the coast with unobscured views towards Naigani and Ovalau islands. One of the great attractions here is **Moon Reef**, forty minutes away by boat. As well as offering fantastic snorkelling, the reef is one of only a couple of reliable places in Fiji to spot and swim with bottlenose **dolphins**. Other activities from the retreat include the two-hour hike through light forest to the summit of **Mount Tova** (645m), a volcanic plug looming above the resort with panoramic views.

Ten minutes' walk along the black-sand beach, or two minutes by road, is the pretty village of **Nataleira**. You can stay here at *Natalei Eco Lodge* (☏881 1168; dorm F$22, bure ❷–❸). The lodge has eight thatch bures alongside the beach, four of which are used as dorms, as well as two cottages with en-suite cold-water showers and flush toilets. Located right on the edge of the village, the lodge has little privacy but **cultural interaction** is without doubt the focus here. Activities include weaving lessons, *yaqona*-drinking, hiking and waterfall treks and, with larger groups, *meke* performances. A **restaurant** overlooks the beach – local-style meals are served at set times and cold drinks are sometimes available, but never alcohol.

You can reach Nataleira by **public transport** from Suva, but not from Rakiraki. Lodoni Transport (☏339 2888) have two buses departing Suva on weekdays at 1.30pm and 2.30pm, and one bus on Saturday at 1pm, heading to Korovou, Natovi Landing and beyond Nataleira as far as Bureiwai, where both buses spend the night before returning early in the morning to Suva. Otherwise, buses run regularly from Suva and Nausori to Korovou where you can hire a minivan to Nataleira or Takalana for F$40.

South to Natovi Landing

Heading south from Nataleira village the countryside becomes more densely vegetated, passing the scenic riverside setting of Dawasamu and Lawaki and eventually emerging to semi civilization at QVS boarding school, one of two prominent schools in the region set up in the early twentieth century for sons of Fijian chiefs. Ten kilometres south is **Natovi Landing** where passenger and car **ferries** operated by Patterson Brothers depart for Ovalau and Vanua Levu (7.30am to Naubouwalu, on Vanua Levu; 3pm to Ovalau, usually on Tues, Thurs, Fri & Sat although schedules change often).

Korovou

The grubby, one-street town of **KOROVOU** forms the intersection of the Tailevu Coast Road and Kings Road. The southern portion of the Kings Road heads 30km south to Nausori and on to Suva. The town is essentially a convenient stop for **buses** with a small market, a couple of stores, an Indian restaurant, and the *Tailevu Hotel* (☎343 0028; ❶–❷) with ten basic rooms. The hotel has a rowdy public bar used mostly by boys from the interior; the police station is conveniently located across the street on the Kings Road roundabout. Apart from the Sunbeam express bus, several local buses head inland to Vunidawa and on to Suva. Public minivans beside the road run north to Natovi Landing for F$2 and you should be able to persuade the driver to continue forty minutes on to *Natalei Eco Lodge* or *Takalana Bay Retreat* for another F$20.

Travel details

The only public transport serving rural Viti Levu is **buses**, mostly originating from either Lautoka or Suva, and travelling between the two cities on the Kings Road along the north coast, or on the Queens Road along the south coast, stopping at towns and most large hotels along the way. See "Getting around" (p.23) for more details.

Buses

Ba to: Lautoka (20 daily; 45min); Rakiraki (8 daily; 1 hr 45min); Suva (7 daily; 6hr 10min); Tavua (8 daily; 45min).

Bureiwai to: Suva ('2' Mon-Sat; 3hr).

Korovou to: Ba (7 daily; 4hr); Lautoka (8 daily; 4hr 45min); Suva (14 daily; 1hr 10min); Rakiraki (9 daily; 2hr 30min); Tavua (9 daily; 3hr 25min).

Navua to: Lautoka (14 daily; 4hr); Nadi (15 daily; 3hr 20min); Pacific Harbour (15 daily; 30min); Sigatoka (15 daily; 2hr); Suva (24 daily; 50min).

Pacific Harbour to: Lautoka (14 daily; 3hr 30min); Nadi (17 daily; 2hr 50min); Navua (24 daily; 30min); Sigatoka (15 daily; 1hr 30min); Suva (15 daily; 1hr 20min).

Rakiraki to: Ba (8 daily; 1hr 45min); Lautoka (8 daily; 2hr 10min); Suva (9 daily; 3hr 40min) Tavua (9 daily; 55min).

Sigatoka to: Lautoka (14 daily; 2hr); Nadi (15 daily; 1hr 20min); Navua (15 daily; 2hr); Pacific Harbour (15 daily; 1hr 30min); Suva (15 daily; 4hr 50min).

Tavua to: Ba (7 daily; 45min); Lautoka (8 daily; 1hr 20min); Rakiraki (9 daily; 1hr); Suva (9 daily; 4hr 40min).

Suva and around

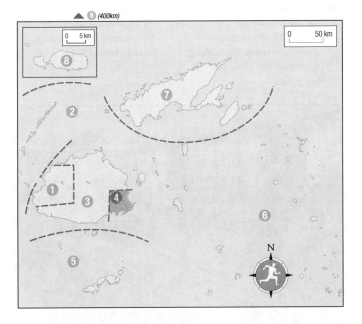

CHAPTER 4 # Highlights

✳ **Shopping in Mark Street**
Go bargain hunting for
colourful Indian saris and
other accessories along this
historical shopping parade.
See p.158

✳ **Fiji Museum** Come face to
face with Fiji's cannibal past,
including the half-chewed
shoe of the Rev Thomas
Baker. See p.160

✳ **Fire walking at Mariamma
Temple** Experience this
engrossing and hugely
passionate Hindu fire walking
ceremony held in August.
See p.163

✳ **Suva nightlife** Take a
bar crawl along Victoria
Parade to sample the best
nightlife in the South Pacific.
See p.165

✳ **Bamboo rafting** Take in the
lush rainforest scenery of
the Wagga Gorge on a sedate
bamboo raft adventure.
See p.170

✳ **Nausori Market** Absorb
the sounds and smells of
Fiji's friendliest and most
picturesque fresh produce
market. See p.170

▲ Traditional bamboo raft, Fiji Museum

Suva and around

iji's lively capital city, **SUVA**, sits on a five-kilometre-long peninsula in the southeast corner of Viti Levu, backed by steep mountains and fronted by a deep-water harbour. Visually it's one of the most attractive of all the South Sea ports with pretty colonial buildings in the centre and moody weather rolling in off the ocean, covering the surrounding rugged peaks in thundery clouds. Despite the often humid and rainy climate, Suva has a lot going for it. Shopping is good and the **nightlife** is excellent with trendy bars, lively restaurants and busy nightclubs. With a population of 86,000 there are also all the **facilities** you could hope for from banks to cinemas along with all government departments. The dark side of Suva, though, is equally visible: beggars and drunks roam the streets, the harbour and city centre are strewn with litter while the capital's murky **political history** gives the city a gritty atmosphere. Although it's perfectly safe during the day you should exercise caution after dark when taxis are the best way to get around.

Apart from the quaint **museum** and stately buildings there are few standout attractions in central Suva. However, spend some time here and you'll discover a vibrant **cosmopolitan** city with strong community bases from all corners of the Fijian archipelago and across the entire South Pacific. Organizations from throughout the region have their headquarters here and the University of the South Pacific attracts students from all over the world.

Beyond the five small suburbs that make up Suva City, and west along the Queens Road, is the seaside setting of **Lami Town** facing the attractive yachting anchorage of the Bay of Islands. Inland, the lush tropical rainforest of Naitasiri quickly takes hold – the peaceful **Colo-i-Suva Forest Park** is only twenty minutes' drive from downtown. Suva's poorer neighbourhoods sprawl north along the Kings Road in an almost constant parade of busy satellite towns to **Nausori**, an industrial and farming centre home to Suva's domestic airport along the banks of the imposing Rewa River. The river and its surrounding mangrove estuaries have long been Fiji's tribal power-base with both the Burebasaga Confederacy of **Rewa** and the Kubuna Confederacy of **Bau** based in the region.

Some history

The name **Suva** means "little hill" and refers to a mound in the Botanical Gardens where the temple of Ro Vonu stood in Suva village. In the 1840s the village became embroiled in a dispute which was to have far reaching consequences for the whole of Fiji. In 1841, **Qaraniqio**, a fearsome chief from Rewa visited Suva and stole a pig. Qaraniqio and his warriors were caught in the act and one of his men was killed. In retaliation the Rewans attacked the village, killing over three

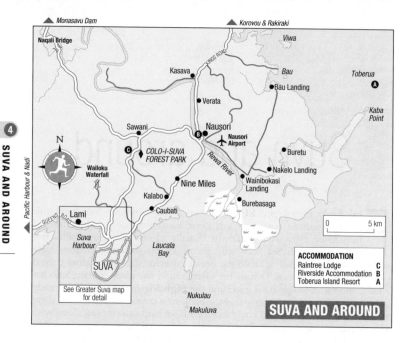

Naqali Bridge

Viwa

Kasava   Bau   Toberua

Bau Landing   **A**

Verata   Kaba Point

Sawani   Nausori   Buretu

N   Nausori Airport

COLO-I-SUVA FOREST PARK   **B**

Wailoku Waterfall   Nakelo Landing

Nine Miles   Wainibokasi Landing

Kalabo   Burebasaga

Lami   Caubati

Suva Harbour

Laucala Bay   0   5 km

SUVA

See Greater Suva map for detail

Nukulau   **ACCOMMODATION**
Raintree Lodge   **C**
Riverside Accommodation   **B**
Toberua Island Resort   **A**

Makuluva

SUVA AND AROUND

hundred men, women and children; the bodies were carried by canoe to Rewa for a celebratory feast. On hearing of the massacre, **Cakobau**, chief of **Bau** demanded retribution – Suva came under his protection as the chief of Suva village had married a woman from Bau twenty years earlier. His revenge attack on Rewa eventually sparked the eleven-year war which decided the fate of the islands.

Having achieved victory and crowned himself King of Fiji, Cakobau faced even greater problems. On July 4, 1849 at Nukulau island off Suva, the house of US commercial agent **John Williams** (see p.169) accidentally caught fire during Independence Day celebrations. Following Fijian custom, the locals looted everything inside. The US Government held Cakobau accountable and demanded US$42,000 in compensation. In 1868, when the first installment was due, the Australian-owned **Polynesian Company** offered to pay off the debt in exchange for 200,000 acres of land around Suva Point. Under threat of US naval attack, Cakobau had little choice but to accept and by 1870, 170 Australians had arrived to farm cotton in the area. However, they soon discovered the soil too thin and the climate too humid and sugar was planted instead. Fiji's first **sugar mill** was built to process the crop although this too failed to profit.

After Fiji was ceded to the **British Empire** in 1874, officials began to survey the islands to build a **new capital**. The Polynesian Company promised ample freehold land should they choose Suva and this, together with Suva's deep-water harbour, led the British to favour Suva over its nearest rival Nadi. By 1882 the move from the old capital of Levuka was completed. The dense jungle tumbling from the hills was cleared, the swamps were filled in and **Victoria Parade**, named after the monarch of the time, became the heart of the new town.

In its early days as capital, Suva was little more than a backwater trading port but gradually it grew, securing wealth and new impressive **colonial-style buildings**. In 1914, gracious living finally arrived with the completion of the *Grand Pacific Hotel* which boasted vintage champagne, haute cuisine and a manager from London's

Savoy. Not quite as swish were the merchant quarters around **Cumming Street**, fronted by *kava* saloons and brothels. Many a devout citizen had called on the street to be cleansed of its evil, and just that happened in February 1923 when a rampant **fire** spread through the area.

By 1952 Suva covered an area of fifteen square kilometres and was proclaimed Fiji's first official city. A year later, a tsunami caused by an offshore earthquake smashed into the shoreline causing damage to the city centre and eight deaths. In 1987 and again in 2000, Suva hit the world headlines after political **coups** threw the city into chaos with widespread looting. The most recent coup in 2006 was less fiery with the army quickly assuming control of the streets. For more background on Fiji's coups see p.268.

Arrival

The most pleasant way to arrive in Suva is **by sea**, cruising into the deep-water harbour surrounded by majestic mountains. The majority of visitors, though, arrive at the grimy **bus stand** in central Suva.

By air

Nausori Airport, 20km north of Suva, serves as the capital's airport and is often referred to as "Nausori Suva" (airline code SUV). Both Air Fiji and Pacific Sun operate regular flights from here to Nadi Airport but Air Fiji alone serves the regional routes to Ovalau, Labasa, Savusavu, Taveuni and Kadavu and to six islands in the Lau and Lomaiviti Group (see p.172 for travel details). There are few facilities and no lockers although the *Air Café* (5am–6.30pm) sells decent coffee, makes a good breakfast and sells F$1.50 roti parcels.

Taxis from Nausori Airport to Suva usually take thirty minutes and cost F$20. There's also a nine-seater public **minibus** operated by Nausori Taxis that runs to *Suva Holiday Inn* at 8.30am, 9.30am, 10.30am, 11.30am, 2.30pm, 5pm and 6.30pm (F$3 per person). To reach Suva by **local bus** from the airport you need to first head into Nausori town (every 30min 6am–6pm; 65 cents) and catch a Suva-bound bus from there (every 15min 6am–6pm; F$1.35). Note that traffic can be bad along the Suva–Nausori road and the journey may take an hour at peak times.

By road

There are two main roads into Suva. From Nadi, the southern **Queens Road** enters Suva via Lami Town, passing industrial Walu Bay, turning right at the roundabout and past the bus stand into the city centre. From Nausori, the **Kings Road** heads through the congested suburbs of Nine Miles, Nabua and Samabula before descending down Edinburgh Drive to the same roundabout at Walu Bay (keep left for the city centre).

Buses into Suva arrive at and depart from the hectic **Suva bus stand** beside the municipal market. The only exception is the comfortable tourist coach operated by Coral Sun (departs Nadi Airport 7.30am & 1pm, departs Suva 7.30am & 4pm; F$19; 4hr) which arrives and departs outside *Suva Holiday Inn* opposite the Old Parliament on Victoria Parade. Express bus services from Nadi (Queens Road) and Lautoka (Kings Road) are operated by Sunbeam Transport (12 daily each direction; F$13.50 to Nadi, 5hr; F$15.50 to Lautoka, 6hr) and Pacific Transport (℡330 4366; 5 daily each direction, F$12.95 via Queens Road, 5hr).

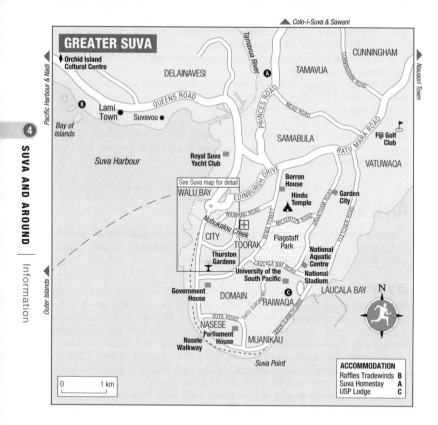

Minivans congregate around Stinson Parade behind the cinema or, if heading north to Nausori, behind New World opposite the bus stand.

By sea

All cargo boats and ferries dock at **Walu Bay**, west of the city centre. The more central **Kings Wharf** overlooking the Suva Municipal Market welcomes in overseas cruise liners and container ships. Passenger **ferries** operated by Consort Shipping (☎331 3344), Patterson Brothers (☎331 5644), Suilven Shipping (☎331 8247) and Venu Shipping (☎339 5000) ply the waters between Suva, Ovalau, Savusavu, Labasa and Taveuni, and also south to Kadavu, usually on a weekly run. **Cargo boats** (see p.25) serve the outer islands of Lau, Lomaiviti and Rotuma on an irregular monthly timetable – contact Fiji Shipping Corporation (☎331 9383) for the latest schedule.

Information

The **Fiji Islands Visitor Bureau** (☎330 2433; ⓦwww.bulafiji.com; Mon–Thurs 8am–4.30pm, Fri 8am–4pm, Sat 8am–noon) is housed in a quaint wooden building on the corner of Thomson and Scott streets. The staff are unable to make bookings for you and will simply dish out a few brochures of local tour companies and hotels. However, it is worth popping in to pick up the excellent *Kulcha Vulcha* (@www.kulchavulcha.com), a fortnightly **newsletter** listing local events and gatherings, as well as monthly tourist publications *Fiji Explore* or *Fiji Holidays*, both dominated by advertising but the latter with a comprehensive accommodation and tour directory.

Free **maps** are available at the visitor bureau but for more detail try the *Henna Fiji* map (F$10.50) available from the post office directly across the road or Bookmasters at 173 Victoria Parade. The **post office** also sells phone cards and has several public **telephones** to the rear. If you would like help with making bookings contact the long-standing **travel agent** Taina's (T 330 5889) at Shop 4 in the Epworth Building on Nina Street.

If you want to explore ecotourism opportunities, it's worth calling in on the **Ministry of Tourism** (T 331 2788) Level 3, Civic Tower on Victoria Parade who should have useful contacts and details of conservation projects.

Getting around

With a compact city centre and few attractions beyond, **walking** is the best way to get around by day. Thankfully, most streets have canopies to keep out the rain although the condition of the pavements is definitely not wheelchair- or pram-friendly. **Taxis** are exceptionally cheap and are the only really safe way to get around by night, even if it's a matter of going a few hundred metres down the street. City **buses** run frequently from Suva bus stand to the suburbs. There's nowhere to rent bicycles or mopeds but a dozen companies offer **car rental** – see "Listings" (p.167). Metered **parking** spaces are available along most streets (20 cents for 15min), or there's longer-stay parking (F$1 per hour) along the vacant foreshore behind Civic Hall, accessible from either Stinson Parade or Victoria Parade beside Civic Tower.

Buses

Local **buses** are exceptionally cheap – most inner city fares cost just 65 cents – and meander around Suva to all satellite towns on a frequent schedule between 6am and 6pm, with a more limited service running until 10pm. All buses congregate at the Suva bus stand, but if travelling to Suva Point in the suburb of Nasese or to the university or National Stadium at Laucala Bay, you can wait at the bus stop beside Vanua House on Victoria Parade which is more practical if you are in the city centre.

Taxis

Taxis are ubiquitous with a half a dozen taxi stands in the city centre alone – Carnarvon Taxis (T 331 5315) in Carnarvon Street behind Dolphin Plaza, Black Arrow Taxis (T 330 0139) in Central Street opposite Westpac Bank or Usher Taxis (T 331 2977) in Usher Street beside the market are the most convenient. Fares are calculated by a fixed-rate **meter** – the only place in Fiji that this law is observed – with a flagfall of F$1.50 (F$2 10pm–6am) plus ten cents for every 200m travelled. A journey across the city shouldn't cost more than F$2.50.

Guided tours

The only **guided tour** of the city is offered by Coral Sun (T 322 8099; Mon–Fri 9.30am, Sat 2pm; 3hr 30min; F$69). The small van tour visits the Fiji Museum for an hour and drives around the suburbs with photo stops at Parliament, the World War II tunnels and Suva Harbour lookout. Wilderness Ethnic Adventures (☎ 359 3230; F$119) run a trip along the banks of the **Navua River** where you'll have lunch, with tame rafting back from the village – pick-ups are available from all Suva hotels around 9.30am. The down-to-earth Rainforest Eco Tours (☎ 360 3061; day tour F$85 includes light lunch, overnight stay additional F$20) offer day and overnight village trips by minivan up into the high **rainforest** of Naitasiri.

Accommodation

As you'd expect, the capital has a decent variety of **accommodation** although it's the one place in Fiji you won't find palm-fringed resorts thanks to the lack of nearby beaches. The only time it is difficult to find a room is at Christmas or during the Hibiscus Festival (usually the school holidays in August). **Suva South** and **Central** are the best options for most visitors being close to the top restaurants and bars as well as the Fiji Museum. **Suva North** is distinctly seedier with several hotels offering rooms by the hour. Heading out of the centre the **suburbs** offer a few more characterful options. Note that most of the budget motels and inns are quite shabby and serve the local clientele only.

For **long-term rentals**, the classified pages of the *Fiji Times* or *Fiji Sun*, especially on Saturdays, are your best bet with a good selection of houses, apartments and rooms. When enquiring, try and get a local to call as they are more likely to get a discount. A room in a basic apartment in the city suburbs should cost around F$200 a month while furnished apartments will cost from F$2,000 a month, all of course depending on location. Otherwise, try Albert Flats (☎ 321 4567) or Quest (☎ 331 9119) for serviced apartments.

Suva North

Annandale Apartments 265 Waimanu Rd ☎ 331 1054. Despite its location in Suva North this is an excellent deal with clean rooms and harbour views. Accommodation for tourists is set aside from the locals' area and facilities include a/c, TV and hot-water bathrooms – deluxe rooms have kitchens and are ideal for long-term stays. ❷–❸

Colonial Lodge 19 Anand St ☎ 330 0655, ⓦ www.coloniallodge.com.fj. This charming wooden house on a quiet cul-de-sac is run as a bed-and-breakfast for backpackers. It feels small and homely with a chill-out gazebo outside, a quaint lounge area and wooden floors throughout. The dorm is open plan with three tiny single rooms running off it. Guests can use the family kitchen, there's Internet access and discounts for longer stays. Dorm F$30, rooms ❷, includes cooked breakfast.

Outrigger Motel 349 Waimanu Rd ☎ 331 4944, ⓔ sitasuva@connect.com.fj. Set on the hillside across the road from the CWM Hospital. The basic a/c rooms are located in a warren of alleyways and up a tight spiral staircase. The best views in town are from its rooftop. ❷

Suva Central

JJs on the Park Sukuna Park ☎ 330 5005, ⓦ www.jjsfiji.com.fj. Dowdy from the outside but with a contemporary interior, this one-time YWCA is set at the edge of Sukuna Park in the heart of the city. There are five floors with fine views of the ocean from the top two. Rooms are swish, catering to business travellers; with king-sized beds, a/c and broadband Internet access. ❻–❽

Southern Cross Hotel 63 Gordon St ☎ 331 4233, ⓔ southerncross1@connect .com.fj. Close to the city centre and nightlife and with 40 gleaming a/c rooms, a mock-marbled foyer and spacious lounge area, this six-storey hotel is the best value for money in the city. The pool is a bit claustrophobic, hemmed in by a courtyard on the ground floor. Up on the top floor is a Korean restaurant open till late. ❷–❸

Sunset Motel Corner of Gordon and Murray ☎ 330 1799, ⓔ townhouse@connect.com.fj. Great location close to bars and restaurants with simple en-suite rooms over four floors. Some rooms have interconnecting balconies, others come with small kitchens and the two-bedroom apartments are good for families. The same owners operate the rowdy *Town House Apartments* across the road and, on the same street, *Sarita Flats* suitable for longer stays. Dorm F$24, rooms ❷–❸.

Suva South

Holiday Inn Suva Victoria Parade ☏ 330 1600, Ⓔreservations@holidayinnsuva.com.fj. Its location is perfect for both tourists and business people, opposite the Old Parliament building and facing the ocean with beautiful harbour and mountain views. The 130 rooms are practical but uninspiring; sea-view rooms have small balconies. There's a swimming pool and a decent tapas bar although the café and restaurant are overpriced. ❺–❻

South Seas Private Hotel 6 Williamson Rd ☏ 331 2296, southseas@fiji4less.com. Cheapest accommodation in Suva in a pleasant colonial-style wooden house but a bit isolated down a side street north of Albert Park. Rooms all share bathrooms down poky corridors and are furnished with plastic bunk beds. There's a communal kitchen and lounge area with TV. Staff are a tad surly. Dorm F$18, rooms ❶.

Suva Motor Inn Corner of Mitchell and Gorrie sts ☏ 331 3973, Ⓔ suvamotorinn@connect.com.fj. Hidden at the end of Gorrie St, close to Albert Park, this is a good place for families with a fun swimming pool and water slide and two-bedroom apartments sleeping up to six people. The thirty studio rooms have a/c and kitchenettes and are popular with business people. Rooms ❹, apartments ❺.

Travel Inn 19 Gorrie St ☏ 330 4254, Ⓔtravelinn @fiji4less.com. Good location, quiet yet close to Victoria Parade in a comfortable courtyard setting. All rooms are split into apartments with a shared bathroom, lounge with kitchenette and lockable communal door. You can take both rooms as an apartment or else share the facilities with a stranger. Rooms ❶, apartment ❷.

Suburbs

Raffles Tradewinds Queens Rd, Lami ☏ 336 2450, Ⓦwww.rafflestradewinds.com. The prettiest setting of all accommodation in Suva but it's a 15min drive from the city centre. The 109 a/c rooms are adequately furnished but bathrooms are small and wearing thin. The ocean-view rooms are literally smack on the water's edge overlooking the Bay of Islands and are worth forking out the extra bucks for. The floating restaurant has superb views but the food is dull and overpriced. Trips to the islands can be organized from the tour desk. Rooms ❹–❺, suites ❻.

Suva Homestay 265 Princes Rd, Tamavua ☏ 337 0395, Ⓔhomestaysuva@connect .com.fj. If you don't mind being away from the city centre, this place is a real gem. The open-plan house acts as an art gallery for emerging Suva artists. The six rooms are all en-suite and tastefully decorated in unique designs, most with polished wooden floorboards and there are three cottages with private kitchens which can be taken as long-term rentals. There's a swimming pool with fine harbour views and hearty breakfast is included in the price. A few added touches include free tea, coffee, Internet, newspapers plus laundry service. ❹–❺

USP Lodges University Campus, Laucala Bay ☏ 323 2247, Ⓔtalouli_m@usp.ac.fj. Five studio flats on campus in two lodges, all with double bed, small kitchens and hot-water en-suite bathrooms. If you've come to study, or to immerse yourself into university life, this is a great base and there are plenty of buses into town, 10min away. ❷–❸

The City

The majority of Suva's shops, restaurants and sights are crammed into the area running south of Walu Bay alongside the harbour to Government House beside Ratu Sukuna Road. The bus stand and market lie north of Nubukalou Creek in distinctly seedy **Suva North** while south of here is **Suva Central** or "downtown", hosting the major banks and high-rise shopping arcades. Running down Victoria Parade are the government quarters of **Suva South** which has Suva's best nightlife and accommodation, along with several large parks and the Fiji Museum.

Suva North

The Suva **bus stand** on Rodwell Road typifies Suva's bustle. By day, Indian peanut sellers and Fijian barrow boys run around amongst the black exhaust fumes frenetically plying their trade. By night, the area becomes desolate, save for a few

Suva – a self-guided tour

The following **walking tour** (9km) should take three hours – a taxi ride covering the same ground will cost F$15 with waiting time. Start from the **Old Parliament** on Victoria Parade and head north into the city turning left at Sukuna Park along the harbour wall of Stinson Parade and into the **market**. From the market, walk along Usher Street bearing right at the traffic lights and into busy Cumming Street for shop browsing. At the end, walk uphill along Waimanu Road and at the fork, bear right up Toorak Road. Turn right on Amy Street past the Toorak mosque and continue along flame-tree-lined **Holland Street** with its fine city views and past the Laxmi Hindu Temple. At the roundabout, walk across Victoria Park to Pender Street and at the end, turn right and first left which takes you along winding Domain Road and past some expensive residences. When Domain Road eventually hits Ratu Sukuna Road, turn left and right again on Vuya Road off which lies **Parliament House** where you should make a detour. Carry on down Vuya Road to Suva Point and then head right on Queen Elizabeth Drive along the picturesque foreshore, past the grand **Government House** and through Thurston Gardens to finish your tour at the **Fiji Museum**, or back on Victoria Parade.

drunks and homeless people, who sleep on the benches and rummage amongst the rubbish. Opposite the north end of the bus stand is the **Flea Market** (Mon–Sat 8am–6pm), a great place to buy cheap clothes and souvenirs. This is where locals come to buy mats, *masi* and garlands for traditional ceremonies, and to get shirts and dresses tailor made. At the south end of Rodwell Road, towards the city centre, is the colourful **Municipal Market** (Mon–Sat 6am–6pm), the largest in Fiji with a huge variety of fruit and vegetables for sale. Upstairs are the *yaqona* and spice stalls, although note that *kava* drinking has been banned by the City Council. On Friday and Saturday mornings, Fijians from miles around visit the market, which spills out into the streets amongst the BBQ sellers and shoe-shine boys. Keep an eye out for pickpockets at these times. Behind Usher Street with the rowdy *Ritz* bar and nightclub on its corner are the **fish stalls** with amazingly fresh seafood supplied direct by Suva's fishing fleet.

Further south around Mark Street and Cumming Street is a cluster of Chinese and Indian **merchant shops**. Crammed with an unbelievable array of homewares and astoundingly colourful clothing, these are great places to poke around in. Inland, up Toorak Road, is the blossoming residential area of Toorak, home to the city mosque. At the end of Mark Street, Waimanau Road, with the raucous bars of the *Kings Hotel* on its corner, heads into the hills towards the Colonial War Memorial Hospital and beyond to grand Borron House, a government residence and ballroom used for ceremonial events.

Suva Central

The hub of the city, **Suva Central**, is not even half a square kilometre in size and runs south of Nubukalou Creek to Gordon Street. At its heart is **The Triangle** a tiny park where locals meet to gossip under an impressive *ivi* tree. Fijian history buffs will notice three of the four inscriptions on the concrete historical marker here are incorrect: Cross and Cargill, the first missionaries to land in Fiji, arrived on October 12, 1835, not October 14, 1835; the government approved the move from Levuka to Suva in 1877 not 1882; and the Public Land Sales of 1880 were not proclaimed under the current *ivi* tree, but one further down the street towards Morris Hedstrom. Heading north from the triangle, busy **Scott Street** is home to Village Six Cinemas (☎330 6006; 10am–11pm; F$5.50) showing the latest Hollywood and Bollywood flicks as well the Fiji Visitor Bureau (see p.53). Behind the post office, between Central and Edward streets facing Stinson Parade, is the dreary **Handicraft Market** with fifty stalls all selling pretty much the same stuff and each plying desperately for your attention. Prices here start ridiculously high so you'll have to bargain to get a fair deal.

Heading towards the sea from the triangle brings you to Stinson Parade, which runs parallel to the harbour walkway. At the southern end is **Ratu Sukuna Park**, venue for church meetings and pious preachers as well as being a hangout for drunks and prostitutes. Across the road on Victoria Parade is the **QBE Building**, with doctors and lawyers upstairs and the *Palm Court Café* (see p.164) and public phones in a quiet downstairs courtyard. Another place of solace open to the public is the **Catholic Cathedral** on Pratt Street, Fiji's only cathedral and one of fourteen in the South Pacific. Construction of the twin-towered

▲ Suva street scene

church commenced in 1895 with stone shipped in from the Hunter Valley in Australia and the timber flooring sourced from Quebec in Canada. The first mass was held in 1902 but the cathedral wasn't fully completed until 1935, 22 years after the death of its instigator, Bishop Julian Vidal from Australia. Services are held on weekdays at 6.30pm, Saturdays 1pm and on Sundays at 7am, 8.30am, 10am, 5pm and 7pm, although you're free to wander in at any time during the day. Along adjacent Renwick Road, towering above the colonial buildings including the pretty 1920s style *Garrick Hotel*, are three flash **shopping malls**: Morris Hedstrom, located on the same site since 1918 but burnt to cinders in 1997, was re-opened in 2008; Proud's built its twelve-storey centre in 2005; and Downtown Boulevard, with its pleasant food court, opened in 1995.

Suva South

Sitting on reclaimed land dug out from the hill surrounding Albert Park, **Victoria Parade** is the administrative centre of Fiji with modern high-rise office buildings lining the road. At the north end is the attractive whitewashed FINTEL Building built in 1922, which has public Internet access and sells phone cards. Behind, the modern 1970s style Civic Hall is the venue for occasional dance performances. Heading south on Victoria Parade is one of the prettiest buildings in Suva, the **Old Town Hall** with its cast iron columned veranda. The building is now a Chinese restaurant downstairs while upstairs is the headquarters for Fiji's branch of Greenpeace (☏ 331 2861). Next door is the imposing **Suva City Library**. You can borrow books here but the selection is pretty old and worn. For books on the Pacific Islands you're better off heading to the University, or try the **National Archives** (☏ 330 4144, Mon–Thurs 8am–4.30pm, Fri 8am–4pm; free) on parallel Carnarvon Street. The latter was once the print works for the *Fiji Times* and hosts a comprehensive collection of historical documents for public browsing including *Fiji Times* newspapers dating back to the first issue in 1869 and many old photographic albums.

Albert Park and Thurston Gardens

At the end of Carnarvon Street, facing Victoria Parade and Albert Park is the solemn-looking **Old Parliament**, built in 1939. It's now Fiji's judicial headquarters and houses various government departments. A block south is the muddy quagmire of **Albert Park**, used as a sports ground – there's usually a rugby game or cricket match going on. The park also hosts provincial *soli*, or fundraising events, with handicraft stalls and *meke* performances, and in the August school holidays is the main venue for the Hibiscus Festival. Overlooking the park on Victoria Parade is the doleful **Grand Pacific Hotel**, still derelict after many years of promises to revamp the old girl to her former glory. Facing the southern side of the park across Ratu Cakobau Road are **Thurston Gardens**, Suva's botanical gardens. Overgrown and littered, you'll have to search deep for the Latin name tags which label the various tropical plants. In its centre is a pretty clock tower, built in 1918 in memory of the first Mayor of Suva.

Fiji Museum

Within Thurston Gardens, accessible from Ratu Cakobau Road, is Suva's most rewarding attraction, the **Fiji Museum** (Mon–Sat 9am–4.30pm, Sun 12.30–4.30pm; F$7; ☏ 331 5944, ⊛ www.fijimuseum.org.fj). If you have even a slight interest in Fiji's history or want to see some of those wicked war clubs and **cannibal forks**, then it's worth the trip to Suva. The museum is neatly laid out with a grand hall displaying a double-hulled **war canoe**, some impressive oars twelve metres long and lots of intriguing daily items such as tattooing tools and

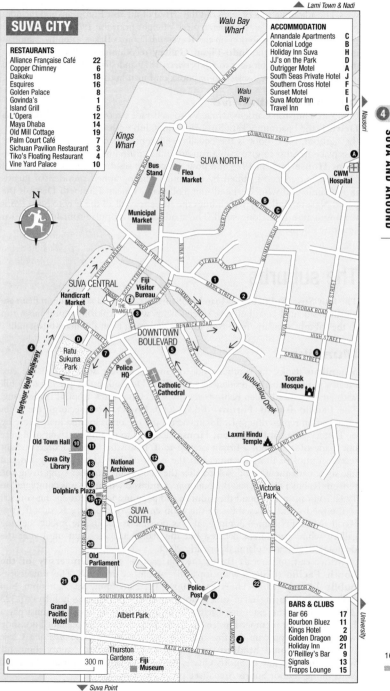

SUVA CITY

Lami Town & Nadi

RESTAURANTS
Alliance Française Café	22
Copper Chimney	6
Daikoku	18
Esquires	16
Golden Palace	8
Govinda's	1
Island Grill	5
L'Opera	12
Maya Dhaba	14
Old Mill Cottage	19
Palm Court Café	7
Sichuan Pavilion Restaurant	3
Tiko's Floating Restaurant	4
Vine Yard Palace	10

ACCOMMODATION
Annandale Apartments	C
Colonial Lodge	B
Holiday Inn Suva	H
JJ's on the Park	D
Outrigger Motel	A
South Seas Private Hotel	J
Southern Cross Hotel	F
Sunset Motel	E
Suva Motor Inn	I
Travel Inn	G

Walu Bay Wharf

Nausori

4

SUVA AND AROUND

Walu Bay

FOSTER ROAD

EDINBURGH DRIVE

Kings Wharf

SUVA NORTH

CWM Hospital

Bus Stand

Flea Market

HARRIS ROAD

RODWELL ROAD

ROBERTSON ROAD

ANAND STREET

WAIMANU ROAD

Municipal Market

USHER STREET

SCOTT STREET

NINA ST

STEWART STREET

MARK STREET

TOORAK ROAD

AMY STREET

SUVA CENTRAL

STINSON PARADE

Handicraft Market

Fiji Visitor Bureau

EDWARD STREET

THOMSON STREET

CUMMING STREET

THE TRIANGLE

DOWNTOWN BOULEVARD

RENWICK ROAD

SUVA STREET

HIGH STREET

SPRING STREET

CENTRAL STREET

VICTORIA PARADE

Ratu Sukuna Park

GREIG STREET

ELGIN STREET

Nubukalou Creek

Toorak Mosque

Harbour Wall Walkway

Police HQ

JOSKE'S STREET

PRATT STREET

BUTT STREET

FOSTER STREET

GORDON STREET

Catholic Cathedral

SELBOURNE STREET

Laxmi Hindu Temple

HOLLAND STREET

Old Town Hall

Suva City Library

Dolphin's Plaza

National Archives

CARNARVON STREET

SUVA SOUTH

GORDON STREET

Victoria Park

KNOLLY'S STREET

DISRAELI ROAD

FENDER'S STREET

VICTORIA PARADE

THURSTON STREET

GLADSTONE ROAD

LOFTUS STREET

Old Parliament

SOUTHERN CROSS ROAD

Police Post

MACGREGOR ROAD

University

Grand Pacific Hotel

Albert Park

WILLIAMSON RD

RATU CAKOBAU ROAD

Thurston Gardens

Fiji Museum

Suva Point

0 — 300 m

BARS & CLUBS
Bar 66	17
Bourbon Bluez	11
Kings Hotel	2
Golden Dragon	20
Holiday Inn	21
O'Reilley's Bar	9
Signals	13
Trapps Lounge	15

161

wigs. The adjoining gallery maps out the arrival of the first Europeans and includes part of the HMS *Bounty*'s rudder, a piece of eight from the *Eliza* shipwreck (see p.263), and a small exhibition on the Reverend Thomas Baker, eaten by cannibals in 1864. Upstairs is the **Indo-Fijian Gallery** recounting the history of Indian indentured labourers brought to Fiji between 1879 and 1916. The gift shop on the ground floor has a great selection of books on Fijian history and culture.

Queen Elizabeth Drive

Opposite Thurston Gardens, where Victoria Parade becomes **Queen Elizabeth Drive**, is the beautifully kept Suva Bowling Club with fine ocean views across the harbour. Next door is the equally well kept Umaria Children's Park, the best place in Suva to give kids a run around. A little further down is **Government House**, built in 1928 and now the private residence of the President of Fiji – its entrance is guarded by the much-photographed presidential guards in red tunic and white serrated *sulu*. Following Queen Elizabeth Drive is the paved **Nasele Walkway** which hugs the stone seawall all the way to Suva Point making a fine hour-long stroll. The roadside is a popular romantic spot for courting couples.

The suburbs

The four **Suva Suburbs** of Muanikau, Samabula, Tamavua and Cunningham are mostly residential areas but have several sights worth exploring. Local buses run to the suburbs regularly from 6am to 6pm departing from the main bus stand.

Muanikau

Muanikau flanks the southern side of Suva Peninsula, southeast of the city. Nearby is the upmarket residential area of The Domain, sitting prettily on a hill with large houses hidden behind security fences and thick tropical landscaping. The **Pacific Islands Forum** (☎331 2600, ⓦwww.forumsec.org), the main organization representing island states across the region, is located here. Close by, on Battery Road, is **Parliament House**, designed to resemble a traditional bure but made of steel with a bright orange roof. It was here that George Speight seized control of the government in the coup of 2000. The building has lain idle since parliament was dissolved after the 2006 coup. Another coup instigator, Sitiveni Rabuka (1987), had the building commissioned and it was completed in 1992. You can stroll around the grounds and peep inside by introducing yourself to the media officer based beside the main entrance on Battery Road off Vuya Road (Mon–Fri 8am–4.30pm) – it was possible to sit in the public viewing gallery whilst parliament debated but this won't happen again until after the democratic elections planned for early 2009.

Further east, in Laucala Bay, is the Fiji campus of the **University of the South Pacific** (USP; ⓦwww.usp.ac.fj) established in 1968. The university's **public library** (Mon–Thurs 8am–10pm, Fri 8am–6pm, Sat 9am–6pm, Sun 1.30pm–6pm during term time; Mon–Fri 8am–4pm during holidays; ☎323 2402) includes the extensive Pacific Collection, for which visitors must pay a F$20 temporary membership fee to access. There's also an excellent bookshop where you can pick up the free monthly student magazine, *Wansolwara*. Close by is the **National Stadium** with a capacity of close to twenty thousand, while across the way in Sports City is the new Olympic Swimming Pool and Vodaphone Indoor Sports Arena (see p.167 for details).

Tamavua, Samabula and Cunningham

Some of the most expensive residences in Suva are perched on the steep cliffs of **Tamavua** with fantastic views of the harbour. They also look down on industrial Walu Bay with its shipyards, oil storage tanks and car lots. At the far end of this gloom are the thick limestone walls of Suva Prison. Across the Queens Road is the **Royal Suva Yacht Club**, a pleasant spot to have a beer and enjoy the views across the harbour towards the Viti Levu highlands and the prominent volcanic plug of Joske's Thumb.

Samabula, east of Central, is divided between the middle-class homes along Rewa Street and the appalling estates around Raiwaqa further south. A short distance up Rewa Street is the **Mariamma Hindu Temple** which has spellbinding fire walking ceremonies in August. **Cunningham** is the newest municipality on Suva's northern and eastern boundary heading along the Kings Road towards Nausori. It includes the busy suburb of Nabua as well as Queen Elizabeth Barracks, headquarters of Fiji's army where four rebels were beaten to death after an attempted mutiny following the events of the 2000 coup.

Lami Town

Five kilometres west of the city centre along the Queens Road, is the pretty seaside residential area of **Lami Town**. There's a small market here and a row of shops including the reasonable *Castle Restaurant* (℡336 1223). Beyond is the tranquil setting of the **Bay of Islands** with yachts anchored offshore from the *Raffles Tradewinds Hotel* (see p.157). In the bay are the rocky islets of Drauni-bota ("cave island"), and Labiko ("snake island"). Another 2km west on the mountain side of the Queens Road is the **Orchid Island Cultural Centre** (℡336 1128; Mon–Sat 9am–4pm; F$10) a rather dated exhibition on Fijian culture set amongst landscaped gardens. You can enter a realistic *bure kalou* or temple or handle one of a dozen live pythons. A couple of giant leatherback turtles and several war clubs and other curios make up the other exhibits.

Eating

The most popular **restaurants** in Suva are **Chinese**, and many of these whip up over-the-counter meals for around F$6. However, with variable hygene standards, this kind of fast food is best avoided unless purchased from one of the two busy **food courts**: one at Dolphin's Plaza off Renwick Road; the other at Downtown Boulevard in Suva South on the corner of Victoria Parade and Loftus Street – both are open between 8am and 5pm but closed on Sundays. Otherwise, there's a good variety of cuisine on offer from European to Indian and prices seldom exceed F$20. **BBQ hawkers** set up on Victoria Parade beside Sukuna Park from 6pm every day selling large portions of chicken and sausage with *dalo* and salad for F$4 – make sure the food is cooked in front of you as it often sits around for a while.

Suva North

Copper Chimney 35 Amy St, corner of Spring St ☏ 331 5916. Tucked away in Toorak, this tiny Indian restaurant is often full. There's a good balance of North and South Indian dishes and prices are reasonable at around F$15 for mains. There are twenty vegetarian dishes in addition to an extensive meat selection, a few Chinese meals as well as pizzas with a spicy twist. Mon–Fri 11am–3pm & 6–10pm, Sat & Sun 6–10pm.

Govinda's 97 Mark St. Simple vegetarian café with a choice of twelve F$1 dishes with roti and ice creams. The most popular item is the great value "Combination Thali" which includes four curries, three vegetable dishes, chapati, samosa, three Indian sweets and juice for F$7.50. Mon–Sat 9am–5.45pm.

Suva Central

Island Grill Dolphin Plaza Food Court. One of five eateries in this busy food court and one of the few places in Suva you can buy Fijian food, albeit ready made. Try the delicious *palusami* and *dalo* for F$5.80 or rich octopus in coconut cream for F$7.20, the fatty meat dishes are best avoided. Mon–Sat 8am–5pm.

Palm Court Café QBE Courtyard off Victoria Parade. Convenient bistro in a quiet courtyard setting popular with the business crowd. The cooked breakfast costs F$8.20, steak or home-made fish burgers are just F$4.70 or you can simply sit and relax over a coffee, herbal tea or thick shake. Mon–Fri 7am–4.30pm, Sat 7am–2pm.

Sichuan Pavilion Restaurant Corner of Thomson and Pier sts ☏ 331 4865. Popular Chinese restaurant with an extensive numbered menu and food that's neither too spicy nor too salty. Make sure you bag a table on the veranda with views overlooking the busy Triangle. Mains F$12–14, licensed. Daily 11.30am–2.30pm & 5.30–10pm.

Tiko's Floating Restaurant Stinson Parade ☏ 331 3626. Not surprisingly, this floating restaurant is focused on freshly caught seafood including mud crabs, king prawns, octopus and lobster with a few steak and vegetarian dishes thrown in. Service is impeccable. There's a wide selection of wines and the serenading guitarists along with the creaking noises of the ship all add to the South Seas atmosphere. Mon–Fri noon–2pm & 5.30–10pm, Sat 5.30–10pm.

▲ Tiko's Floating Restaurant

Suva South

Alliance Française Café 14 McGregor Rd. If you fancy investigating Suva's artistic side, head to this small café adjacent to the Alliance Française library. You can browse photographic and art books over a good coffee and sandwich and find out about art-house screenings, mostly focusing on the South Pacific cultural scene but showing the occasional French language film with subtitles. Mon–Fri 8am–5pm.

Daikoku FNFP Place Victoria Parade, ☎330 8968. Cosiest of the three Japanese restaurants in town with five *teppanyaki* (griddle) tables, fresh sushi and reasonably priced *shabu-sabu* (hot pot). Mon–Sat noon–2pm & 5.45pm–10pm.

Esquires Dolphin Plaza Victoria Parade, ☎330 8968. Tiny corner café serving good coffee, cheese cake and quiche. There's a handy notice board here on Suva events and every Thursday 7pm–8.30pm the Socrates Club meet here for topical debates. Mon–Fri 7am–11pm, Sat 8am–11pm, Sun 8am–7pm.

Golden Palace 165 Victoria Parade. This upmarket Chinese restaurant decorated with colourful lanterns is a Suva institution. The food is good, albeit expensive, but the F$8 lunchtime specials are excellent value. Mains F$15–25, licensed. Mon–Sat 11.30am–2.30pm and 5.30pm–9.30pm, Sun 5.30pm–9.30pm.

L'Opera 59 Gordon St ☎331 8602. Tucked into an obscure building next to the *Southern Cross Hotel*, this Italian restaurant is definitely the swankiest spot in town. It's decorated in Renaissance prints and sculptures, with a cosy lounge area and candlelit dining. The food is delicious using only the best ingredients available in Fiji and the wine list is 160-strong including fifty Italian labels. Mains F$30–40. Mon–Fri noon–2.30pm & 6pm–10pm, Sat 6pm–10pm.

Old Mill Cottage 47 Carnarvon St. This unassuming-looking café with plastic tables is tremendously popular with Suva bigwigs – you may find yourself sitting next to an MP or top lawyer. The menu is broad, with several traditional Fijian favourites including *palusami*, either plain (F$6) or with tinned corned beef (F$5), as well as uninspiring but tasty Indian and Chinese dishes for around F$8. There's a pleasant wooden veranda where breakfast (F$7.50) and omelettes (F$4.50) are served and the home-made cassava chips are worth a try at F$1 a serve. Mon–Sat 6.30am–5.15pm.

Maya Dhaba 281 Victoria Parade ☎331 0045. Fine Indian dining in an open-plan contemporary setting. There are 28 main dishes which makes selection difficult – try the subtle North Indian goat masala, on the bone with whole spices; or the South Indian chicken *dora*, rolled in rice pancakes. Mains around F$15. Licensed and BYO with F$10 corkage. Daily 11am–2.30pm and 6pm–10.30pm.

Vine Yard Palace Old Town Hall, Victoria Parade. If you need a good feed on a budget, this all-you-can-eat lunchtime Chinese buffet (Mon–Fri 11.30am–2.30pm, F$11.90) is hard to beat. Hugely popular with a ravenous Fijian crowd. Otherwise, the à la carte menu is best avoided.

Drinking and nightlife

One of Suva's most enduring charms is its lively **nightlife**. Most of the bars and clubs are in one block around Victoria Parade and Carnarvon Street making it easy to hop from one to another and sample the different atmospheres. Fijians like to drink **communally**, as if drinking *yaqona* – if you buy a Fiji Bitter "long neck", which is more economical, it will be shared by passing round a small glass to down in one. It's a quick way of getting drunk and brawls occasionally break out in the wilder places. However, the locals are very protective of foreign visitors and on most occasions you'll be well looked after. Taxis are advisable for the ride back to your hotel, even if it's only a couple of streets away, and female travellers should avoid going out unaccompanied after dark. If you fancy sampling the edgier district of Suva North try the bar of the *Kings Hotel* on Waimanu Road – befriend one of the bouncers before heading inside.

Bars

Holiday Inn Victoria Parade. If you're after a quiet drink, the lounge bar at the *Holiday Inn* is the best choice although somewhat pricey. There's a pianist accompanied by light jazz musicians playing Tues–Thurs and a good R&B vocalist Fri nights. Daily 4pm–9.30pm, happy hour 5.30pm–6.30pm.

O'Reillys Bar 5 MacArthur St, corner of Victoria Parade ☏331 2322. Popular with tourists and USP students, the bouncers here keep a tight grip on proceedings. Loud music, it's the only place in Fiji you'll find Guinness on tap and there's a large-screen TV and pool table at the back. The bar is connected to the more pretentious *Bad Dog Café* on the corner, a wine bar serving overpriced but well-presented food. Mon–Sat 11am–12pm, Sun 5–11pm.

Royal Suva Yacht Club Queens Rd, Walu Bay ☏330 4201. A bit out of the way, 2km from the city centre in Walu Bay but with a lovely beer garden overlooking the sea, it's an ideal spot to watch the sunset over a F$2 draught beer. Mon–Thurs 8am–10pm, Fri–Sun 8am–12pm; happy hour Tues & Sat 6–7pm.

Traps Lounge 305 Victoria Parade ☏331 2922. The main bar at the front is the place to be seen for an after-work tipple. There's a pool bar at the back, a non-smoking chill-out lounge at the top and a buzzing dance floor with live music Tues & Thurs. Mon–Sat 5pm–1am. F$5 admission some weekends.

Clubs

Bar 66 Dolphin Plaza Victoria Parade, entrance on Loftus St. Hangout for the hip under-25s with DJs

playing pop and reggae and a small dance floor. Doesn't get going until after 11pm and it's usually the last place to close, picking up the crowds from *Traps* after midnight. Tues–Sat 9pm–late.

Bourbon Bluez Ratu Sukuna House, corner of Victoria Parade and MacArthur St. Best of the local Fijian hangouts with live bands most nights playing Fijian-style reggae to a packed dance floor; there's also a karaoke lounge at the back. Mon–Sat 6pm–1am, F$3 admission Fri & Sat.

Golden Dragon 379 Victoria Parade ☏331 1018. Long-standing favourite amongst the islanders with live music Wed & Thurs, mostly reggae-influenced, and lots of University students out for a laugh – you'll often see Polynesians dancing the hula here. Mon–Sat 7–12pm. Admission F$5 after 9pm Fri & Sat.

Signals 255 Victoria Parade ☏331 3590. Centrally located, this is the only club in Suva with any atmosphere before 10pm. You may wish to start your night here and then move on as it usually gets packed with drunken fishermen later in the evening. There's a long bar, dance floor and cheap drinks. Watch your pocket. Mon–Sat 6pm–1am.

Shopping

The best place for **handicrafts** is the small Government Handicraft Centre in the basement of Ratu Sukuna House on MacArthur Street (Mon–Fri 8am–4.30pm, Sat 8am–noon) – crafts here are made by local Lauan and Lomaiviti islanders and the prices are pretty much fixed. Otherwise there's a small selection of local crafts at Bulart, upstairs on 6 Ellery Street at the corner of Renwick Road, or try the upmarket Jack's boutique further up Renwick Road. Jack's has recruited the best wood sculptors in Fiji but their prices reflect this. For exotic jewellery try Aladdin's Cave in the QBE Building on Victoria Parade. Cumming Street (see p.158) has Suva's best selection of **clothes shops** – for fine Indian attire try Vastra at 20 Waimanu Road. Many stores sell fabric by the metre and you can get one of Suva's many tailors to sew you a suit or shirt – Jeff's at 76 Waimanu Road down a tiny side alley is worth a try. **Snorkelling gear** and fishing equipment is available from Bob's Hook Line & Sinker in the Harbour Centre on Scott Street. **Digital cameras** are best sourced from the large department stores, Proud's or Tappoo, or J. Maniklal & Sons (☏330 5384) at 68 Thomson Street. For other **electronics** and computer equipment, try Dick Smith Electonics (☏331 2808) at 35 Knolly Street, ten minutes' walk from the city centre, or Bondwell Computers (☏338 5530) on Moti Street in the suburb of Samabula.

For **fresh food**, the market (see p.158) has to be your first stop. Otherwise, Morris Hedstrom, located on Thomson Street, is the most central **supermarket**. Joe's Farm, on the roundabout at Flagstaff (Laucala Bay Rd and Rewa St) has a good selection of local produce and delicacies.

Sports and activities

The ocean around Suva is too polluted for swimming. The closest snorkelling reef is at Nukulau Island (see p.168) and a mediocre **surfing break** lies off Suva Point. For water activities it's best to head west to Pacific Harbour, thirty minutes along the Queens Road, or to the offshore islands of Toberua (see p.171) or Caqalai (see p.202), both popular weekend destinations for city dwellers. You may find overnight skippered **yacht charters** and crew work advertised at The Royal Suva Yacht Club at Walu Bay.

The most convenient **swimming pool** is the Suva Olympic Pool off Victoria Parade (☏330 5599; Apr–Sept Mon–Fri 10am–6pm, Sat–Sun 8am–6pm; Oct–Mar Mon–Fri 9am–7pm, Sat–Sun 7am–7pm) where you can swim all day for F$1.69. For **tennis**, Victoria Park on Pender Street (☏330 5599; daily 6am–6pm F$4 per hr, 6pm–9pm F$6 per hr) has five hard courts and offers ball and racket hire; the Suva Lawn Tennis Club (☏331 1726; 8am–6pm F$8 per hr, 6–10pm F$10 per hr, members only Wed 5–8pm & Sat 2–6pm), within Albert Park, has two hard courts but the four grass courts are in a terrible state. **Laucala Sports City** (☏331 2177) at Laucala Bay was built with Chinese money for the 2003 South Pacific Mini Games; there's an Olympic-sized indoor swimming pool at the National Aquatic Centre (daily 6am–7pm, F$3, no lockers) while the indoor Vodaphone Arena offers badminton, judo, volleyball and occasional music and cultural events.

For **cycling**, Wai Tui Cycles (☏337 2419) in Garden City, Muanikau, have a good selection of mountain bikes, crucial for Fiji's road conditions, and run weekly cycle meetings (Mon 5pm).

In north Samabula, beyond Vatuwaqa on Riffle Road is the flat eighteen-hole course of the **Fiji Golf Club** (☏338 1184, daily 7am–5pm; F$20, trolley, clubs and shoes extra), where non-members can play any day except Saturday. If you're after a pampering **massage**, try Sundara Spa (☏331 0288, daily 10am–10pm) at 59 Gordon St next to *Southern Cross Hotel* or Head to Toe (☏330 1211, by appointment only) at 25 McGregor Rd.

Listings

Airlines Air Fiji, 185 Victoria Parade ☏347 7160 Mon–Fri 8am–4.30pm, Sat 8am–noon; Air Nauru, Ratu Sukuna House, MacArthur St ☏331 2377, Mon–Fri 8am–4.30pm; Air Pacific/Pacific Sun, Corner of Victoria Parade and Central St ☏330 4237 Mon–Fri 8am–4.45pm; Air New Zealand, QBE Building Victoria Parade ☏331 3100 Mon–Fri 8.45am–4.45pm; Qantas Travel Centre, Colonial Building Victoria Parade ☏331 3888 Mon–Fri 9am–5pm.

Banking Westpac, corner of Scott and Central St, Mon–Thurs 9.30am–3pm, Fri 9.30am–4pm; ANZ Bank, 25 Victoria Parade Mon 9.30am–4pm, Tues–Fri 9am–4pm, also at Centrepoint and USP.

Bookshops Bookmasters, 173 Victoria Parade (☏331 8888 Mon–Fri 8.30am–6pm, Sat 8.30am–2pm) for general books including biographies and travel; Government Bookshop, Rodwell Rd for maps and stationery (Mon–Fri 8am-5pm, Sat

8am–2pm); Suva Bookshop, 5 Greig St for novels and overseas magazines (Mon–Fri 8am–5pm, Sat 8am–1pm); University Bookshop Laucala Bay (☏323 2500, ⓦ www.uspbookcentre.com; Mon–Fri 8am–5.30pm, Sat 8.30am–1pm) for Pacific titles; Fiji Museum gift shop, Thurston Gardens (☏331 5944) for historical titles and *Domodomo*, the museum's monthly journal.

Car rental The most convenient is Central Rental 295 Victoria Parade (☏331 1866; Mon–Sat 8am–5.30pm, Sun 8am–1pm); other reliable options include Budget, 123 Foster Rd, Walu Bay (☏338 1555); Carpenters 88 Foster Rd, Walu Bay (☏331 3644); and Khans, 157 Ratu Mara Rd, Samabula (☏338 5033). The cheapest cars are offered by Quality Rentals at 174 Ratu Mara Rd, Samabula (☏338 2877).

Cinema Village Six on Scott St for mainstream films and Bollywood; Some Pacific screenings at

USP Campus in Laucala Bay, Room NIII, SPAF Building (☏ 323 2402).

Dentist Shalom, First Floor Kadavu House, Renwick Rd ☏ 331 8477 Mon–Fri 8am–5pm, Sat 8am–1pm; on call 24hr.

Doctors Dr Fatiaki, First floor Epworth Arcade, Nina St ☏ 330 2421; Fiji Care Medical Centre, 123 Amy St ☏ 331 3355, Mon–Fri 8.30am–5pm, Sat 8.30–11.30am; Marie Stopes International, 157 Renwick Rd, ☏ 331 0101 Mon–Fri 10am–7pm, Sat 9am–1pm.

Embassies and high commissions Australia, Princess Rd ☏ 338 2211; France and EU Schengen States, Dominion House, Thomson St ☏ 331 2233; Federated States of Micronesia, Loftus Rd ☏ 330 4633; Indonesia, Gordon St ☏ 331 6697; Kiribati, McGregor Rd ☏ 330 2512; Nauru, Ratu Sukuna House, MacArthur St ☏ 331 3566; New Zealand, Pratt St ☏ 331 1422; Papua New Guinea, Gordon St ☏ 330 4244; Tuvalu, Gorrie St ☏ 330 1355; UK, Gladstone Rd ☏ 322 9108; USA Loftus St ☏ 330 6243.

Hospitals Bayview Medical, 361 Waimanu Rd ☏ 331 1361; CWM Hospital Waimanu Rd ☏ 331 3444; Suva Private Hospital, 120 Amy St (☏ 330 3404).

Immigration (☏ 331 2622) Civic Tower Victoria Parade, Mon–Fri 8.30am–12.30pm.

Internet access Connect Internet café in the post office on Scott St (Mon–Fri 8am–8.30pm Sat 9am–8pm, F$3 per hr); Skynet, Victoria Corner of

Building, Gordon St has forty terminals open 24hr (F$3.50 per hr).

Laundry Suva Electric Laundry, 31 Knolly St ☏ 330 1442, Mon–Fri 7.30am–5.45pm, Sat 8am–2pm; F$2.40 per kg same-day service.

Library 196 Victoria Parade ☏ 331 3433 Mon, Tues, Thurs & Fri 9.30am–6pm, Wed noon–6pm, Sat 9am–1pm; F$20 non-Suva resident membership fee. Also University Library, USP Campus Laucala Bay ☏ 323 2402, also F$20 temporary membership fee.

Optician Asgar Opticians and Hawley Eye Centre, QBE Arcade Victoria Parade ☏ 330 0433, Mon–Fri 8.30am–4.30pm, Sat 8.30am–12.30pm.

Pharmacy Superdrug Pharmacy, Central Building, Renwick Rd ☏ 331 8755, Mon–Fri 8am–6pm, Sat 8am–3pm; Nasese Pharmacy, Ratu Sukuna Rd, 2km from city centre, (☏ 331 4450) Mon–Sat 8am–5pm & 7–9pm, Sun 10am–1pm and 7–9pm.

Police Corner of Pratt and Joske sts ☏ 991 or ☏ 331 1222. There are 24hr manned police posts at Market (☏ 331 1122) and Gorrie St (330 9822) overlooking Albert Park.

Post office Scott St Mon–Fri 7.30am–5pm, Sat 8am–1pm.

Telephone Behind post office on Scott St, in QBE Building Victoria Parade. Phone cards available from post office.

Women's Crisis Centre 88 Gordon St, corner of Thurston St. Mon–Fri 8.30am–4.30pm, Sat 10am–noon; 24hr helpline ☏ 331 3300.

Around Suva

There are plenty of attractions around Suva worth exploring on day-trips or staying overnight. Off Suva Point is **Nukulau** island, which has the only sandy beach and snorkelling reef in the vicinity. Inland, the tranquil forest park of **Colo-i-Suva** forms a boundary between Suva and the hill people of **Naitasiri Province** part of the wet mountainous interior of Viti Levu. The mountains feed the impressive Rewa River which drains to the north of Suva through **Nausori** town and into the vast, mangrove-lined **Rewa Delta**. This region, and the coast to the north, remains the most influential power-base in Fiji with the chiefly villages of **Rewa** and **Bau**, the latter once home to Cakobau, the only King of Fiji.

Nukulau

Lying 8km west of Suva Point, and barely 1km from Laucala Point is **Nukulau**, a tiny coral cay with good snorkelling and a pretty sandy beach along its shore.

According to Fijian legend, the island is cursed by the devil god *Batidua*, who plagued the islanders for centuries. In 1846 the local Rewan people were only too happy to sell Nukulau to American **John Williams** (see p.264) who bought the island for US$30, paid in muskets and alcohol. The house he built here was burnt down and looted on July 4, 1849, an event which led to Fiji becoming a British colony (see p.264); there are no remnants of the house today. Recently the island was the location of the make-shift prison which held the 2000 coup perpetrator **George Speight** before he was transferred to Naboro Maximum Security Prison after the Bainimarama coup of 2006. There are plans to turn Nukulau into a tourist attraction and introduce a ferry service from Suva harbour. For now, the only way to visit is to charter a small boat from the Royal Suva Yacht Club.

Inland to Naitasiri

From Suva city centre it takes less than fifteen minutes to be amongst the lush tropical rainforest of **Naitasiri**, the huge inland province that covers most of the eastern half of Viti Levu. Just within the province, **Wailoku Waterfall** and **Colo-i-Suva Park** are popular weekend picnic spots for city dwellers, but few venture further north into the **Naitasiri Highlands**. Those that do will discover a lush, mountainous region with rushing rivers and remote villages.

Wailoku Waterfall

The **Wailoku Waterfall** enhances a rather dull residential area just beyond Suva's outskirts. To get there, follow the Princess Road alongside the Tamavua cliffs and, just beyond Tamavua village, take the first dirt road branching off left which leads steeply downhill to Wailoku. The natural swimming pool and waterfall lie just beyond the bridge; there's also a much larger waterfall two hours' walk through thick bush along the valley.

Colo-i-Suva Forest Park

Back on the Princess Road it's another 3km inland to **Colo-i-Suva Forest Park** (daily 8am–4pm; F$5; ☎332 0211), a pristine area of low-altitude rainforest. It's a pretty place, dominated by mahogany trees, their trunks thick with parasitical tree ferns. There's a good chance of spotting **wild orchids** in the park as well as endemic **birds**, including the Pink-billed Parrotfinch. An easy one-hour **nature trail** leads to a couple of small **waterfalls** with pools good for swimming and nearby picnic benches. Unfortunately, the park has a reputation for theft from cars and occasional muggings – the attendant at the park entrance can arrange a guide for F$5 and can look after valuables.

Just before the park entrance is the *Raintree Lodge* (☎332 0562, Ⓦwww.raintreelodge.com; dorm F$25, rooms ❷, cottages ❹), a pleasant **retreat** with three large dorm lodges with small rooms and kitchens and five quaint wooden cottages embedded in the surrounding forest. The lake here is over 50m deep, the relic of a disused quarry and now full of tilapia fish. The lodge has an excellent **restaurant**, which puts on a BBQ lunch every Sunday (F$17), popular with Suva residents. If you're just here for the day, stop in for morning coffee or afternoon tea. To reach Colo-i-Suva, take the Saweni or Serea **buses** from the Suva bus stand, which depart hourly costing F$1; a taxi will cost F$12.

Naitasiri Highlands

Beyond Colo-i-Suva, taking the Tamavua Road to Saweni, the road bears left and up through slash-and-burn farmland to the small settlement of Vunidawa, headquarters for **Naitasiri Province**. From Vunidawa a rough dirt road cuts through the rainforest to Naitauvoli village. From here you can raft down the **Wagga Gorge**, floating downstream on bamboo *bilibili* raft; there are no organized tours but rafting can be arranged at the village, usually involving an overnight stay. A rough, four-hour journey north takes you to the **Monasavu Hydroelectric Dam** from where the majority of Fiji's electricity is sourced. A dirt track continues north from Monasavu through splendid virgin forest to Nadarivatu (see p.137) and thence on to the north coast at Tavua, a full day's drive. From Suva, Tacirua Transport (℡332 1700) runs regular **buses** to Vunidawa, departing Suva at 6.30am, 10.30am, 1pm, 2pm, and 5.30pm. They also run a 1pm service (daily except Sun) to Laselevu Village, 12km south of Monasavu Dam. From Vunidawa you should be able to find a **carrier van** to take you on to Naitauvoli for F$30, or to Monasavu for F$70.

Nausori and around

Twenty kilometres north of Suva along the Kings Road is the farming town of **NAUSORI**. Between the two is the sprawling **Nausori Corridor**, a deprived area home to almost a hundred thousand people. Nausori itself has a population of 46,000 living along the Rewa River. The town grew up around the sugar industry but is now dominated by the Rewa Rice factory. Most tourists only visit the area on their way to and from **Nausori Airport** (see p.153), located on the region's sole stretch of flat land.

Nausori's main attraction is its **exotic market**, the best in Fiji for mingling and taking photos, especially on a Saturday when the streets overspill with stalls selling mud crabs, river prawns, mussels, asparagus and wild ferns alongside massive bundles of *dalo*, *kava* and coconuts. The town is also home to a notoriously wild **pub**, the *Whistling Duck* off Ross Street. As you enter, a sign reads "Precaution, beware of flying objects". When a drinker finishes a bottle of beer, it is simply tossed over the shoulder – the bar staff and live musicians playing there at weekends are protected behind a steel cage. Opposite is *KBs*, a night club with a more sedate white-collar clientele.

The only place to **stay** is *Riverside Accommodation* (℡347 6157; ❷) tucked away on O'Connor Lane opposite the *Nausori Club* on Lateef Street. The small wooden cottage occupied by a Fijian family has seven basic rooms sharing two bathrooms with cold-water shower. Two decent places to **eat** are *Chillies* (Mon–Sat 6am–6pm, Sat 7am–2.30pm), opposite the bus stand, which serves lamb *palau* for F$3.80, chilli fish for F$2.90 and hot masala tea for F$1 and *Gopala's* (Mon–Sat 7.15am–5.30pm), further down Patel Road selling vegetarian dishes for F$2 and classic Indian sweets.

Patel Road is the main street through Nausori with a Morris Hedstrom supermarket and the **bus stand** on one side, and ANZ and Westpac banks both with ATM machines opposite. **Minivans** for Korolevu depart further along Patel Road towards the Rewa Rice storage containers. The post office (Mon–Fri 8am–4pm, Sat 8am–noon) and police station (℡347 7222) are on Court Road, just beyond the market between the old and new bridges.

The Rewa River Delta

East of Nausori the landscape is dominated by the snaking tributaries and mangroves of the **Rewa River delta**, dotted with small fishing villages. The villages themselves hold little interest but the surrounding **mangrove estuaries** are fascinating environments, worth exploring by longboat. There are no organized tours of the delta but you should be able to arrange a longboat ride along the Wainibokasi River from Nakelo Landing, 9km east of Nausori beyond the airport. At the eastern end of the river is **Kaba Point**, where the great war between Rewa and Bau came to its bloody conclusion in 1855 with a battle involving five thousand warriors and a hundred war canoes (see p.263).

Bau Island

Seven kilometres north of Kaba Point or 12km by road from Nausori is Bau Landing, access point for the chiefly island of **Bau**. To visit the tiny island, reached by punt from here (F$6), you need to ask the *Turaga-ni-Koro* or village spokesman (T 362 4028) for permission. If you receive an invitation you should bring *yaqona* roots and dress respectably. The island is small in size but has over two hundred houses and a fascinating history (see box on p.172). The mound in the centre is where the chiefly families live; around the perimeter are sub clans: craftsmen from Lau, warriors from Botoni and fishermen from Kadavu. The island's Methodist **church**, dating from 1859, was the first to be built in Fiji. It was erected under the orders of King Cakobau, the fierce chief of the island who converted to Christianity in 1854. All the ancient temples on Bau were destroyed, their stone used in the construction of the church. The baptismal font beside the alter is reputed to be Cakobau's killing stone where the skulls of his captives were smashed before being eaten.

Toberua Island Resort

Three kilometres off Kaba Point is the delightful **Toberua Island Resort** (T 347 2777, W www.toberua.com; ●), one of Fiji's first boutique island resorts. The resort has built its reputation around its friendly staff, many of whom have worked here their entire lives, and guests often return year after year. The fifteen bures have spacious traditionally decorated interiors with outdoor airy showers but they are located rather too close to each other, some almost touching and sharing verandas. Only two face the beach which fronts the north side of the four-acre island. There are colourful coral formations and **reef sharks** at nearby Toberua Passage which is excellent for both snorkelling and scuba diving. The

▲ View of Bau Island

The rise of Bau island and King Cakobau

Despite its modest size **Bau island** played a key role in the history of Fiji. Up until the eighteenth century, Verata, 10km north of Nausori, and its rival **Rewa** had ruled the archipelago, the latter being the head of the aristocracy of Burebasaga, one of the three founding clans. In 1760, a tiny island named Ulu-ni-Vuaka ("the head of the pig"), barely 300m from the shore of Viti Levu, was settled by warriors of Verata lineage and in time became known as Bau. The island's first chief erected **sea walls** to protect it from invasion and built stone canoe docks making the island a powerful seafaring base. In 1808 a Swedish beachcomber named **Charlie Savage** visited Bau and brought with him **firearms**, until then never possessed by Fijians. Using these new, terrifying weapons, the ruling chief, Naulivou, fought a series of wars with Verata, 15km to the north. When Verata was weak Rewa grew in strength and between the two, they battled the upstarts from Bau for supremacy. Bau grew more powerful under the rule of the brutal cannibal chiefs of **Tanoa** and later **Cakobau**. The chiefs seized upon the right of *vasu* (see p.273) claiming wide support from villages throughout Fiji. At its peak, the island boasted three thousand inhabitants and twenty temples stood on its plateau.

By 1871, with the backing of the European merchants of Levuka, Cakobau had proclaimed himself **King of Fiji**. Three years later he ceded the islands to the British Empire (see p.265). Today, the chief of Bau remains one of the most powerful in political life. As for Rewa, the aristocrats managed to retain their hold over their far-flung subjects and the Burebasaga Confederacy remains the largest and most powerful of Fiji's three ancient confederacies.

PADI dive outfit based on the island runs trips to over fifty dive sites, all within a thirty-minute boat ride. The resort also organizes twice-weekly boat trips to **Mabualau**, a tiny limestone islet 5km to the east, dedicated as a nature reserve and packed with large white fluffy **boobies**. Toberua is accessed from **Nakelo Landing** along the Qaraniki River, 9km by road east of Nausori Town.

Travel details

Suva is the main access point for Fiji's **outer islands**. Walu Bay is the local shipping port for all outer island passenger ferries and cargo boats whilst Nausori Airport is the departure point for all **flights** to Lomaiviti, Lau and Rotuma, as well as serving Vanua Levu, Taveuni and Kadavu. Public **buses** depart from Suva for Lautoka, either along the north coast (Kings Road) or south coast (Queens Road), stopping at all towns en route.

Buses

Suva to: Ba (7 daily; 6hr 10min); Bureiwai (2 Mon-Sat; 3hr); Korovou (14 daily; 1hr 10min); Laselevu (daily; 3hr 30min); Nadi (13 daily; 5hr); Navua (24 daily; 50min); Pacific Harbour (15 daily; 1hr 20min); Rakiraki (9 daily; 3hr 40min); Sigatoka (13 daily; 4hr); Tavua (9 daily; 4hr 40min); Vunidawa (6 daily; 1hr 45min).

Ferries

Walu Bay to: Kadavu (weekly; 7hr 30min); Ovalau (5 weekly; 6hr); Koro (2 weekly; 8hr); Nabouwalu (5 weekly; 10hr); Savusavu (6 weekly; 10hr); Taveuni (6 weekly; 17hr); Northern Lau Group and Lakeba (weekly; 1-5 days); Southern Lau Group (monthly; 2-6 days); Rotuma (monthly, 2 days).

Flights

Nausori Airport to: Cicia (weekly; 1hr); Gau (weekly; 30min); Kadavu (daily; 30min); Koro (weekly; 35min); Labasa (4 daily; 35min); Lakeba (weekly; 1hr); Moala (weekly; 45min); Nadi Airport (12 daily; 30min); Ovalau (2 daily; 15min); Rotuma (weekly; 1hr 50min); Savusavu (2 daily; 45min); Taveuni (2 daily; 1hr); Vanua Balavu (weekly; 1hr).

Beqa, Vatulele and Kadavu

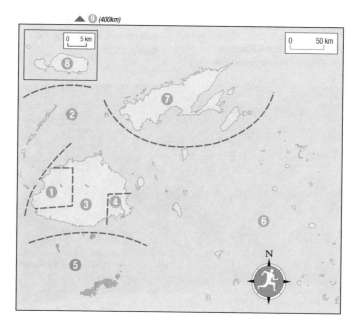

CHAPTER 5

Highlights

* **Shark diving, Beqa** Come face to face with tiger and bull sharks on this world-famous shark dive. See p.177

* **Beqa fire walkers** Watch the locals amble over white-hot stones in the village of Dakuibeqa. See p.178

* **Tapa cloth making, Vatulele** Try your hand at tapa cloth making with the women of Lomanikaya village on Vatulele. See p.181

* **Kayak around Kadavu** Explore the indented bays, mangrove forests and traditional villages along Kadavu's rugged coastline. See p.184

* **Bird watching, Kadavu** Spot one of Kadavu's four endemic bird species in the hills of the Muanakaka Bird Reserve near Vunisea. See p.185

* **Astrolabe Reef, Kadavu** One of the world's best dive sites, home to colourful soft corals, fast channels and large fish. See p.187

▲ Vatulele cliffs

Beqa, Vatulele and Kadavu

Beqa, **Vatulele** and **Kadavu**, the three main islands south of the Fijian mainland, present world-class scuba diving, hair-raising reef surfing and record-breaking game fishing. If that's not enough to entice you, several of Fiji's most beautiful beaches are located here, with shallow lagoons offering fabulous sea-kayaking and deep bays sheltering fishing villages.

The rugged island of **Beqa** is famed for its fire walkers and, just offshore in its huge lagoon, adrenaline pumping **shark dives**. West of Beqa is the delightful limestone island of **Vatulele**, a centre for **tapa cloth** making and home to several unusual attractions including ancient rock carvings and a cave full of bizarre red-coloured prawns. The farthest of the southern islands from Viti Levu and the largest of the three is **Kadavu**, barely a forty-minute flight from Nadi, and closer still from Suva, but a world away from the tourist trail. With its twisting **Astrolabe Reef** and dramatic mountain scenery, this is the place to visit for adventure on the water and to immerse yourself in Fijian culture.

Beqa and around

If not shrouded by clouds, the roughly contoured profile of **BEQA** (pronounced "Mbenga") can be seen clearly from Suva. It's closer still to Pacific Harbour, from where small boats bump across 12km of open sea to reach it. The island is roughly circular in shape with steep forest-clad mountains rising sharply from a meandering coastline. Its large lagoon, protected by a thirty-kilometre-long barrier reef, is renowned for **shark dives** and deep-sea game fishing as well as the famous **surfing break** of Frigates Passage opposite the small island of **Yanuca**. However, Beqa's most distinctive feature is its **fire walkers**. You can often see them perform on Viti Levu, especially at the Arts Village in Pacific Harbour, but nothing beats witnessing the real thing on

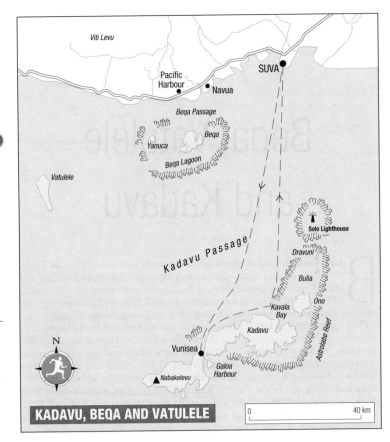

KADAVU, BEQA AND VATULELE

home soil – Rukua, Naceva and Dakuibeqa on the southeastern side are the main fire walking villages.

The island's 1400 inhabitants live in nine coastal villages. There are no roads on the island but several **walking tracks** between villages make for pleasant exploring. The easiest route runs from Waisomo on the northern tip of the island to Rukua along the west coast. You can also hike to one of the island's **three mountains** – Korolevu (439m), towering over Lalati village on the north coast, is the most challenging and highest. The best way to sample the coastline is from a kayak and *Lalati Resort* (see opposite) run a delightful kayaking trip to tranquil Malumu Bay, which bites deep into the west coast almost severing it from the main bulk of Beqa.

Practicalities

Most visitors reach Beqa on a pre-arranged **resort** transfer from Pacific Harbour although it's also possible to hitch a ride with one of the unlicensed

village boats which depart from Navua every day except Sunday sometime between noon and 2.30pm (30min; F$35 per person one way).

The only affordable **place to stay** is *Lawaki Beach House* (☎ 331 8817, ⓦ www .lawakibeachhouse.com; tent F$67.50, dorm F$75.50, bure ❹ includes all meals) on the west coast at the end of a long stretch of beach. The two bures have en-suite hot-water bathrooms, while the six-bed dorm lodge and pre-fabricated tents with mattresses share a cold-water bathroom. Diving can be arranged with local operator Saimoni who will happily take just two guests out for a two-tank dive for just F$180 or, for the same price, they will drop you off at the *Aqua Trek Beqa* dive site of the day, allowing you to link up with their twice-weekly shark dive. There's also a handful of upmarket **dive resorts** on Beqa catering mostly to the North American market, the pick being *Lalati Resort* (☎ 347 2033, ⓦ www.lalati-fiji.com; ❼–❾, includes meals) on the northwest coast hugging Malumu Bay with six spacious bures, swimming pool, spa and gourmet meals.

Beqa's shark dives

Beqa Lagoon is renowned for its **shark-feeding dives**, which attract divers from across the world. The best dive sites are on the western tip and north side of the lagoon which are equally accessible from Pacific Harbour (see p.130) where accommodation is more affordable and dining more diverse. Shark-feeding dives are available through Beqa Adventure Divers (☎ 345 0911, ⓦ www.fiji-sharks.com; departs Pacific Harbour 8.30am Mon, Wed, Fri & Sat, two-tank dive F$200) or Aqua Trek Beqa (☎ 345 0324, ⓔ beqa@aquatrek.com; departs Pacific Harbour 8.30am on Wed & Sat only, two-tank dive F$180). On a good day you may see up to a hundred sharks over the two dives, including reef sharks, silvertips, tawny nurse sharks, sicklefin lemon sharks, menacing-looking bull sharks and the occasional tiger shark, as well as schools of other large fish taking advantage of the free food (mostly tuna heads from a nearby factory). Despite one isolated incident of a diver being "nipped" by a tiger shark, both companies claim an excellent safety record. If you fancy a more sedate experience there are also soft coral and wreck dives available in the lagoon on the days that the sharks are not fed.

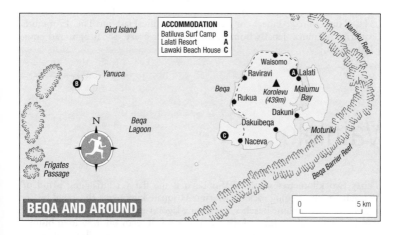

The legend of Beqa's fire walkers

Unlike Hindu fire walking (see p.163), **Beqa's fire walkers** perform purely for entertainment rather than religious purification. The legend of how the islanders obtained mastery over fire has been passed down through the generations:

Once there was a famous storyteller named **Dredre** who lived in the ancient mountain village of Navakeisese on Beqa. His tales would captivate the villagers throughout the night and it was customary to bring small gifts as a token of appreciation. One evening, Dredre requested all present to bring him the first thing they encountered when out hunting the next day. The following morning, a young warrior named **Tui** went fishing in a mountain stream and pulled out what he thought was an eel from the mud. To his surprise, the eel assumed the shape of a *Vu*, or spirit god, and Tui knew that Dredre would be most pleased with his gift. The spirit god pleaded for its life offering all sorts of tempting powers but only when Tui was promised the **power over fire** did he succumb. The spirit god dug a pit, lined it with stones and lit a huge fire upon it. When the stones were white hot, the spirit god leaped in showing no effect from the heat. Tui followed and to this day his descendants from the Sawau tribe re-enact the same performance of walking on white-hot stones.

Yanuca

By comparison with Beqa, **Yanuca**, 12km west, is a relatively low island with light forest, gentle hills and a solitary village on the east coast. The main reason to visit is the excellent **surfing** available at **Frigates Passage**, an extremely consistent and powerful left-hand break. Hemmed in on the west coast by the island's steepest hills is ⚐ *Batiluva Surf Camp* (☏ 345 0384, ⓦ www.batiluva .com; F$175 per person per night includes meals and surfing transfers). Run by a Hawaiian couple, there are two A-frame wooden lodges, one with two rooms for couples and the other with a four-bed dorm, all sharing two cold-water showers and four toilets. With kerosene lamps enhancing the secluded atmosphere, this is one of the most laid-back surfing destinations in the South Pacific. The coarse coral beach has lots of hammocks strung between coconut palms and a deep lagoon with good snorkelling. **Surf trips** depart every day at 8.30am and, depending on the group, return sometime in the afternoon. Dive trips can be also arranged with budget dive operator Dive Connections (☏ 345 0541, ⓔ diveconn@connect.com.fj) based at Pacific Harbour. The 45-minute boat trip to Yanuca departs from Pacific Harbour every day at 3pm and costs F$50 return.

Vatulele

Thirty two kilometres south of Viti Levu is the flat yet intriguing island of **Vatulele** or "the ringing rock". Covering 31 square kilometres, the island boasts ancient rock art, sublime beaches, a sparkling lagoon and four villages completely absorbed with making **tapa cloth**. Vatulele was first recorded in written history in 1799 when the American schooner *Anne and Hope* spotted villagers along its

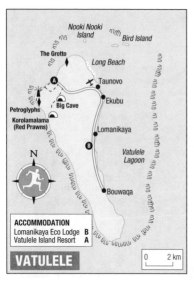

ACCOMMODATION
Lomanikaya Eco Lodge **B**
Vatulele Island Resort **A**

VATULELE

0   2 km

coastline. However, petroglyphs on the western tip of the island show evidence of human habitation for over 3000 years.

The four villages on Vatulele lie within a thirty-minute walk of each other along the flat east coast. The **health centre** and primary school are both in the chiefly village of **Ekubu**, sometimes referred to as "Village Number Two". This side of the island faces a bountiful fishing lagoon with a fringing reef 3km from shore and several small islets within. One of the islets, Vatulevu, was nicknamed "Bird Island", as it used to host thousands of nesting **red-footed boobies**. Unfortunately, when the landowner introduced goats in 2002 it took less than a year for them to strip the vegetation and leave the island barren. The birds now nest on the sharp limestone cliffs between **Long Beach** and the limestone passages of the **Grotto** along the northern tip of Vatulele. Guests staying at *Vatulele Island Resort* (see p.180) can kayak for twenty minutes along the coast to spot the boobies and their adorable fluffy offspring.

On the **west coast**, south of *Vatulele Island Resort*, are the island's famous **petroglyphs**, carved into the limestone cliffs at a height of ten metres. The designs include hands, faces and animals such as roosters. Just south of here is another island icon, the **sacred red prawns** in the tidal cave of Korolamalama. The prawns are known as *ura buta* or "cooked prawns" owing to their extraordinary deep red colour. Eating the prawns is strictly forbidden – the islanders believe anyone who harms them will be shipwrecked.

For a fabulous view of the lush green carpet of forest that covers Vatulele and for spotting eagles and swiftlets that thrive amongst the craggy cliffs, climb the ninety steps of the solar-powered **lighthouse**, perched on the cliff edge. The fifteen-minute trail to the lighthouse starts just beyond the gates of *Vatulele Island Resort*. Another inland trail, ten minutes' walk further along the bumpy road connecting the resort and the villages along the east coast, ends at **Big Cave** in the heart of the island. There's a cool freshwater swimming pool at the cave's entrance and, with a torch and guide, you can explore the network of tunnels which eventually connect through to the sea.

Practicalities

The grass **airstrip** on the east side of Vatulele is used exclusively to bring in guests staying at *Vatulele Island Resort*. The daily 25-minute flight from Nadi Airport departs at 11.30am, returning at 12.50pm and costs US$495 return. Anyone else visiting the island will need to rely on the small outboard **village boats** which leave from the site of the abandoned *Paradise Hotel* at Korolevu along the Coral Coast every Tuesday, Thursday and Saturday, generally around noon. The 45-minute boat journey costs F$25 one way.

▲ Vatulele petroglyphs

Vatulele's two **places to stay** couldn't be more contrasting. The exquisite *Vatulele Island Resort* (⊕672 0300, ⓦwww.vatulele.com; ◐) offers fine dining, private villas and a ratio of four staff to every guest. Straddling a beautiful white-sand beach and with its own tiny offshore island used as a picnic spot, the resort ranks as one of the finest in Fiji. The alternative is to stay in Lomanikaya village at the community-run *Lomanikaya Eco Lodge* (⊕949 1438; F$30 per person includes meals). Its two simple thatch bures have shared flush toilets, cold-water showers and overlook a sometimes littered and windswept beach just south of the village. Although basic in every respect, the lodge offers genuine hospitality and an authentic village experience – you should also be able to have a go at tapa cloth making during your stay.

Kadavu

KADAVU (pronounced "Kan-davu") is the fourth largest island in Fiji, snaking 57km from east to west with a rugged coastline littered with deep bays. The island is divided into three sections, each connected by a narrow isthmus. **West Kadavu** is dominated by the volcanic cone of Nabukelevu at its western end while to the east is Kadavu's only expanse of flat land, taken up by the small airstrip and the government centre of **Vunisea. Central Kadavu**, east of Vunisea, has the island's best **beaches** as well as the fantastic Namalata Reef off the north coast. **East Kadavu** overlooks part of the immense Astrolabe Reef and is home to a handful of **dive resorts** backed by steep tropical rainforest and a sprinkling of waterfalls.

There are just over ten thousand inhabitants on Kadavu, primarily engaged in subsistence farming and fishing, making it one of the best places to immerse yourself in **Fijian culture**. Most of the 75 coastal villages are hidden in bays or amongst mangrove estuaries and obscured from view when travelling along the coast by boat. Every third village has a primary school and all are connected by walking trails.

Some history

In 1792, on his second voyage to the South Pacific, William Bligh became the first European to chart Kadavu and its dangerous coral reefs which protrude 40km north towards Viti Levu. But for the next few decades the islanders had little contact with the outside world. This peaceful isolation was shattered in 1829 when the island was **conquered** by warriors from Rewa from southeastern Viti Levu. As such, Kadavu was brought under the influence of the powerful Burebasaga Confederacy and forced to assist Rewa in the 1840s war against Cakobau.

Thirty five years after Bligh's encounter, French commander Dumont d'Urville almost ran aground on the open-water reefs north of Ono and so named them after his ship, *L'Astolabe*. After publishing his journals which described the discovery of endless supplies of the Chinese delicacy **bêche-de-mer** (sea cucumber) in the southern waters, Kadavu began to attract overseas traders. Galoa Harbour, on the southern side of present-day Vunisea Town, became a busy port and it wasn't long before American **whalers** moved into Tavuki Bay on the north coast. Land was briskly traded with the locals for firearms and alcohol and Chinese and European merchants set up stores and began planting cotton. By the 1860s, mail and passenger steamers from New Zealand used Galoa Harbour as its port of entry to Fiji with local steamers transshipping on to other islands. Galoa reached its peak in 1871 but within a few years it had become a virtual ghost town when Levuka, backed by Cakobau, established itself as the main port for trade.

Many of the **Chinese** traders remained, eking out a living on their newly acquired freehold land and marrying into local Fijian families. Today, the

---

The making of tapa cloth

From sunrise to sunset, the deep resonating thump of wood beating against wood echoes around the villages of Vatulele. This is the sound of **tapa cloth** production, a fine paper made from the bark of the **mulberry tree**, or *masi* in Fijian. The cloth was traditionally used as clothing, wrapped around the waist and draped over the shoulder of people with chiefly status. It also represented a conductor between the spirit and living world, hung from the high ceiling of the *bure kalou*, or temple, and used by the priest to mediate with the gods. Today, it is used in decorative **artwork** and gift wrapping sold in boutique shops around Fiji.

The production of tapa is almost exclusively done by women. The first step is to slice and strip the long thin bark of the mulberry tree into single pieces which are then soaked in the sea for four nights. Once supple, the bark is beaten into a **pulp** using hardwood slabs and heavy wooden sticks and joined with other strips to make a single piece of cloth. Dried in the sun, the cloth is eventually **decorated** using patterned stencil designs depicting the origin of the artist and figurative icons relevant to a clan's totemic god – often a turtle or shark. Once stenciled, the cloth is known in Fijian as *masi*. Only two or three colours are used – brown dye is obtained from the bark of the mangrove tree; the black dye comes from charcoal; while a red dye is sometimes used, obtained from seeds. For the villagers on Vatulele, tapa is the main **cash crop** generating an average income of F$2,000 per household, although for some tapa artists this can reach F$6,000, equalling the basic salary of a Fijian civil servant.

182

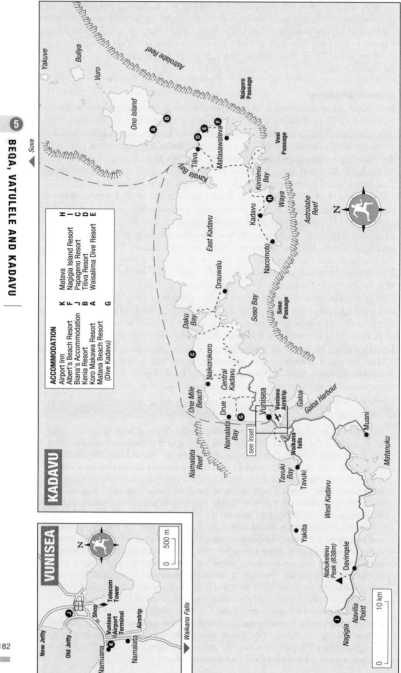

KADAVU

▶ Suva

ACCOMMODATION

Airport Inn	K
Albert's Beach Resort	F
Biana's Accommodation	J
Kenia Resort	B
Koro Makawa Resort	A
Matana Beach Resort (Dive Kadavu)	G
Matava	H
Nagigia Island Resort	I
Papageno Resort	C
Tiliva Resort	D
Waisalima Dive Resort	E

VUNISEA

▶ Waikana Falls

Chinese link remains strong with several recent shipping enterprises funded by the Chinese Government. Kadavu's largest export is **kava**, reputed as the finest and strongest in Fiji. The fourteen provincial chiefs on Kadavu remain relatively autonomous from the Burebasaga Confederacy and are amongst the most powerful local chiefs in Fiji.

Arrival

Vunisea has the island's only airport, connected by daily **flights** from both Nadi (45min) and Nausori (30min) operated by Pacific Sun and Air Fiji respectively. The weekly **cargo boat** to Kadavu departs from Walu Bay in Suva every Tuesday at 10.30pm and is operated by Venu Shipping (T 339 5000; F$45 one way, F$55 for a bed in a six-berth cabin), arriving at 6am on Wednesday at Vunisea where it unloads for a few hours before heading east to Kavala Bay for its second stop on Kadavu. The boat leaves Kavala Bay at 2pm on Wednesday back to Suva. You could also try Western Shipping (T 331 4467; lounge F$50 one way) which operates the *Cagi-Mai-Ba*, an aged cargo boat visiting Vunisea and various bays along the north east coast once or twice a month but to no fixed schedule.

Information and getting around

Apart from at the resorts, facilities are limited on Kadavu. There is no **tourist information**, no banks or restaurants and only a few basic shops selling mostly tinned food and kerosene. With few roads, **getting around** the island usually involves a journey by water, mostly within the reef. Each **resort** has its own fleet of boats and all meet pre-booked guests at Vunisea airport or one of the two ferry jetties. If want to explore, you should be able to pick up a **village boat** from Vunisea – go to Galoa Bay for boats heading along the south coast or alongside the airport for the north coast. Note that the seas can be rough, especially along the exposed south coast and the boats do not carry life jackets. It takes 35 minutes to reach the west point of Kadavu from Vunisea and an hour to reach the Astrolabe Reef in good weather, double if seas are rough.

The two winding roads on Kadavu are unsealed and used mostly by logging trucks making them impassable after heavy rains. There are **no buses** or rental cars, but several minivans and trucks shuttle around Vunisea between the airstrip and jetty and can be hired for exploring further. If planning to visit a village, it's essential to bring plenty of food and drink with you, as well as the customary *yaqona* roots as a means of introduction. A good place for meeting locals is at the Friday afternoon market in Vunisea.

Vunisea and west Kadavu

You're most likely to be swept in and out of the township of **VUNISEA** on your way to one of Kadavu's resorts. This would be a shame because it has quite a lot to offer. For one thing there's its pretty setting between Namalata Bay on the north coast of Kadavu and Galoa Harbour on the south coast. It also makes a convenient base for exploring the attractions of **west Kadavu**.

The **government station** is located on the hilly eastern isthmus between the north and south bay. In pre-European days, warriors would slide their war canoes on rollers over this isthmus to save themselves the long journey around the coast. Heading up the hill from the north coast, you first pass the imposing **hospital** (☎362 0788) on the right-hand side. Continuing up the hill and bearing left, the **post office** and police station (☎368 1268) are on the left side of the road. The **airstrip** covers the entire length of the flat western isthmus

Diving and water sports

Life on the water is such an integral part of Kadavu that it's little wonder water sports are the main attraction for visitors. **Scuba diving** tops the list thanks to the phenomenal one-hundred-kilometre **Astrolabe Reef**. The reef can be divided into two distinct sections: the 50km northern loop, forming a figure of eight shape, is all in open water, entwined with canyons, arches and other spectacular seascapes; while the section of reef hugging the east and south coast of Kadavu to Galoa Harbour has five rich current-fed passages all featuring a profusion of **soft corals**. There are strong drift dives at Naiqoro, shallow corals at Vesi, **sharks** at Nacomoto, **fans** at Soso and **manta rays** at Galoa.

Viti Water Sports (☎670 2413, ✉info@vitiwatersports.com; two-tank dive F$160, 4-day Open Water course F$600), offers PADI Open Water **dive courses** at the four resorts facing the Astrolabe: *Tiliva*, *Kenia*, *Waisalima* and *Matava* (not to be confused with *Matana Beach Resort* in central Kadavu). It also runs daily dive excursions for all but *Matava*, which operates its own fully certified dive boats. Dwarfed by the Astrolabe, the equally impressive and diverse **Namalata Reef** off the north coast of Vunisea is used by *Matana Beach Resort* and *Papageno Resort* which both operate their own private dive boats. Note that there are no independent dive operators for those staying in Vunisea.

Surfing

The passages at Soso and Vesi have unpredictable but sometimes massive **surfing breaks**, most easily accessible from *Matana Beach Resort* on the south east coast. The best spot for surfing, though, is from *Naigani Island Resort* (see p.201) off the western tip of Kadavu. Here you can watch the gnarly left at King Kong from your bure, or, if on the rare occasion it's blown out, head around the point to Daku Beach where there are both reef breaks and a beach break for beginners.

Kayaking

It's possible to **kayak** around Kadavu in nine days or Ono Island in seven days, camping on beaches, staying in villages or bedding down at a budget resort along the way. New Zealand outfit, *Tamarillo Tropical Expeditions* (☎360 3043, ⓦwww.tamarillo.co.nz/fiji; 7-day all-inclusive packages start from NZF$2,150 per person) have well organized itineraries and great contacts with the local villages, with guided two-person sea kayaks and support boats. It can be hard work, though, with a minimum of five hours of paddling in sometimes choppy seas working muscles you never knew existed but it's a great way to experience the island's remote coastlines and villages. Less strenuous overnight packages and day-trips exploring the mangrove estuaries run on demand from the base camp at Korolevu Bay on the southeastern corner of Kadavu.

Fishing

Game fishing charters are available from *Matava* on the southeast coast, and *Nagigia Island Resort* off the west tip of Kadavu. Both offer top of the range gear and cast in the surrounding reefs for Giant Trevalleys or trawl between one thousand and three thousand metres of water for marlin, tuna and sailfish. More casual hand-line fishing can also be organized from all resorts.

and the terminal building is the only place in Vunisea to buy **takeaway food**, but only with incoming flights around lunchtime.

Beside the airstrip and fronting the beach at Namalata Bay is pretty **Namuana village**, famous for its **turtle calling ceremony**, an event that now occurs only occasionally. The turtles, said to represent two maidens of the village lost to sea, are summoned to the surface by a chant sung by the women. If a turtle doesn't appear, it's said a person from its bitter rival village of Nabukelevu is present. A twenty-minute walk from the village leads up to the saddle of the hill where the ceremony takes place with great views of both bays. The trail continues to secluded **Waikana Falls** where you can swim in a shallow pool. Five minutes' walk further, the trail connects with the dirt road to Tavuki Bay. From here it's only 3km along the road to the **Muanakaka Bird Reserve** tucked into the hills on the east side of the bay. The reserve was established by the nearby village of Solodamu in 2008 with the assistance of the University of the South Pacific. It offers a one-hour hiking trail to bird hides from where you may spot one of Kadavu's four endemic bird species including the Kadavu Fantail and Kadavu Honeyeater. There's no official price for entry but a contribution of around F$20 per person is acceptable and a local guide can be arranged for F$5. To get back to Vunisea you could arrange for George's **carrier van** (☎ 934 9564) to pick you up from Solodamu for F$35, or hire a village boat for the ten-minute ride back to Vunisea for the same price.

Accommodation

You can **stay** in Namuana Village at the *Airport Inn* (☎ 944 2255, dorm F$25) but there's only one eight-bed dorm here housed in a tiny tin shack overlooking the beach. In the same fenced garden is a lovely unoccupied thatch bure and you could ask the owner to put a bed in for you if you plan staying for a while. A better option for shorter stays is *Biana Accommodation* (☎ 368 1270, ✉ bianaaccom @connect.com.fj; F$70 per person, includes breakfast and dinner) a bright blue cottage on the east side of Namata Bay overlooking the old jetty. The three rooms here are mostly used by government workers and you share a lounge, kitchen and cold-water bathroom. The owners cook and serve meals and also look after three decorated wooden cottages with private bathrooms on a secluded beachfront around the point but judging by the state of the interiors it doesn't look like they are often occupied. The beach here is sandy, though, and there's good snorkelling reefs in the bay but you'll need to bring your own snorkelling gear. **Homestays** can also be arranged at Solodamu village near the bird reserve – contact Isoa (☎ 362 3009). A contribution of at least $30 per person should be given to help pay your way.

The south coast road

A rough but scenic dirt road heads across the isthmus from Vunisea along the **south coast** of west Kadavu all the way to Nabukelevu-i-Ra village on the western tip of the island. Along the way it passes several beautiful bays and the towering peak of Nabukelevu, also known as Mount Washington. It's possible to climb to the 838-metre summit in a full day, starting out from Davinqele village on the south coast. From the top you'll see the dramatic north face of the peak tumbling down to the sea. Sitting in the lee of Nabukelevu, less than a kilometre from the western point of Kadavu is tiny *Nagigia Island Resort* (☎ 603 0454, ⓦ www.fijisurf.com; ❼). At the time of writing this surf resort was closed for refurbishment but it should open again in 2009. The sharp jagged island faces the fantastic King Kong **surfing break**, which is the main reason to visit.

Central Kadavu

East of Vunisea, a dirt road, better for walking than driving, meanders inland to the dense tropical rainforest of **central Kadavu**. Roughly 8km in, the road splits in two. The right-hand track heads north following an undulating valley to a series of five beautiful sandy **cove beaches** beside the picturesque village of Naikorokoro. Around the point, west of the village is the enviable location of *Matana Beach Resort* (☎368 3502, ⓦwww.matanabeachresort.com; ❻, includes meals). With the varied and protected **Namalata Reef** offshore, *Matana* is primarily a dive resort and the owners' dive business, Dive Kadavu, is often used as the resort name. Five airy A-frame cottages with polished timber floors and large windows are set back from the beach screened by thick vegetation.

Heading east from *Matana*, a ten-minute walk around the rocky point leads to **One Mile Beach**, a secluded beauty with deep sand and massive coconut palms leaning out over the lagoon. The beach marks the start of a ten-kilometre trail along the northern coastline, passing a couple of small rocky headlands and the village of Naivakarauniniu on the way and ending up at ⚐ *Papageno Resort* (☎600 3126, ⓦwww.papagenoresort.com; rooms ❼, bures ❽, includes meals). Set in 346 acres of serene tropical forests, this is a nature lover's paradise. The endemic **shining parrot**, with its red breast and vivid green and blue wings can usually be seen feeding in the cassava plantation behind the resort's seven colonial style bures. Higher up in the forest is a sweeping lookout over **Daku Bay** and, forty minutes' walk inland, a small waterfall with swimming pool. **Divers** have the option of either the Astrolabe or Namalata reefs and there are regular **snorkelling trips** to visit the manta rays at Vuro Island or game fishing off Nabukelevu. Food at the resort is outstanding, sourced from locally grown organic ingredients.

▲ Kadavu coastline

The battle of the octopus and the shark

The islanders of Kadavu are said to have no fear of sharks thanks to the protection of **Drakuwaqa**, a headstrong shark god from Taveuni. Drakuwaqa was the bully of the ocean. One morning he met **Masilaca**, another shark god protecting the reefs around Beqa. Masilaca despised and secretly feared the god guarding Kadavu to the south. Slyly, he challenged Drakuwaqa to go and meet him. Feeling particularly boisterous, Drakuwaqa sped off to investigate. At the entrance to the Kadavu passage a **giant octopus** loomed. Knowing this to be the god Masilaca had spoken of, Drakuwaqa attacked but soon found himself entangled by tentacles and his life being squeezed out of him. Like a true bully, he swiftly pleaded for mercy promising never to harm anyone from Kadavu. To this day fishermen from the island pour a bowl of *yaqona* into the sea in order to give thanks for his protection.

East Kadavu

Beyond Daku Bay is the heavily indented coastline of **east Kadavu**, difficult to access other than by sea. Kavala Bay, on the north coast and Korolevu Bay on the south coast form great basins surrounded by steep mountains. Their river estuaries are lined in **mangrove forests** and you can explore these incredibly peaceful environments by **kayak** (see p.184). However, it's the underwater spectacle of the **Astrolabe Reef** that attracts most visitors here, hugging the southeast side of Kadavu all the way to Galoa Harbour and extending 40km north in open sea.

Of the four **dive resorts** at the eastern end of Kadavu, the best for exploring the surrounding environment is ♁ *Matava* (☎333 6222, ⓦ www.matava.com; dorm F$120, bures ⑥–⑦, includes all meals and airport transfers) on the south coast, tucked into a small beachless bay enclosed by rocky Waya Island. *Matava* is fantastically well organized but retains a village-style atmosphere. The eleven bures are slightly rough around the edges but with welcoming hosts and a fine blend of European and Fijian cuisine, it's excellent value for money. Apart from its own dive operation, there's some of the finest **snorkelling** in Fiji just ten minutes away by boat at Vesi Passage with soft coral gardens and thousands of exotic reef fish.

A thirty-minute walk west from *Matava* along the rocky coastline leads to the village of **Kadavu**, hidden behind mangrove estuaries and hemmed in by steep mountains. At the back of the village, a high **waterfall** has carved and hollowed a russet-coloured rocky chamber into unusual shapes with a deep swimming pool below – when visitors arrive, energetic village kids swarm in to show off their courage by jumping from the twenty-metre-high rock faces surrounding it. From Kadavu you can hike for an hour meandering through rainforest to **Nacomoto** where village stays are organized through either *Matava* (see above) or *Tamarillo Expeditions* (see p.184). If you want to see grey **reef sharks** and large schools of barracuda, jacks and emperors, Nacomoto Passage is as good a bet as anywhere in Fiji, with dive boats from *Matava* (see above) diving the site frequently. In 2003 the village chief cast a traditional curse on anyone trying to fish in the passage, thus dedicating it as a marine sanctuary. A more strenuous full day hike from either Kadavu or Nacomoto crosses over to **Kavala Bay** on the north coast, passing several waterfalls along the way. The trail continues east along the coastline to **Tiliva** village and the adjacent *Tiliva Beach Resort* (☎333 7127, ⓦ www.tilivaresortfiji.com; ⑦–⑧, includes meals) a tiny unassuming retreat with just six bures and a small dive operation.

A pretty **coastal trail** heads east from *Tiliva* to *Waisalima Dive Resort* (☎603 0486, ⓦ www.waisalimafiji.com; tent F$10, dorm F$25, bures ❷–❸), the only backpacker dive resort on Kadavu with two four-bed dorms. The resort is just five minutes from **Naiqoro Passage**, the most varied scuba diving reef along the Astrolabe with brilliant corals and swift drift dives. *Waisalima* has 24-hour solar powered lighting and hot-water showers although there are reports that the food and hygiene standards have slipped recently.

Ono Island

Off the northeastern tip of Kadavu and surrounded by the Astrolabe Reef is **Ono Island**. There are two small villages here, several beautiful beaches and a dozen smaller islands including Vuro where **manta rays** congregate. Basic thatch bure **accommodation** with shared cold-water bathrooms is available on the southern tip of the island at *Kenia Resort* (☎603 0290, ⓦ www.keniafijiresort .com; tent F$10, dorm F$25, bures ❸), formerly *Jona's Paradise*. The beach here is picturesque, with soft sand and palm trees, but the new owners are struggling to attract guests and the atmosphere, like the food served here, is rather bland. By contrast, the private upmarket retreat of *Koro Makawa Resort* (☎603 0782, ⓦ www .koromakawa.com.fj; ❻, includes meals) offers a spectacular two-bedroom thatch roof **cottage** perched on a small hill with fabulous views overlooking the ocean. All inclusive packages are US$460 per night per couple (children US$86 extra) with hearty home-cooked meals included; there's also a fully certified PADI dive operation on site.

Travel details

Although relatively close to Viti Levu, the rugged nature of these islands and lack of roads makes exploring difficult and transport around them expensive. The only public airstrip is on Kadavu. Access to Beqa or Vatulele is by resort speed boat, charter plane or village fishing boat.

Ferries
Walu Bay to: Vunisea and Kavala Bay, Kadavu (weekly; 7hr 30min).

Cargo boat
Walu Bay to: Vunisea and Daku Bay, Kadavu (1–2 monthly; 9hr).

Outboard village boat
Korolevu to: Vatulele (3 weekly; 45min). **Navua Town** to: Beqa (daily ex Sun; 30min).

Flights
Nadi Airport to: Kadavu (daily; 45min) **Nausori Airport** to: Kadavu (daily; 1hr)

Lomaiviti and Lau

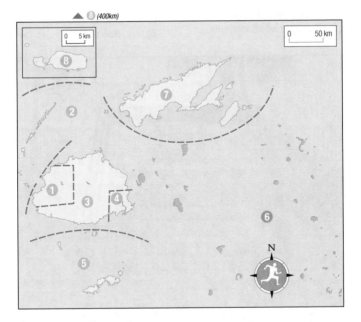

CHAPTER 6

Highlights

✳ **Historic Levuka** Soak up the colonial atmosphere of Fiji's old capital. See p.196

✳ **Bobo's Farm** Eco retreat on Ovalau with organic farm, waterfalls and fantastic hiking. See p.201

✳ **Lovoni** Hike your way up to to the historic village of Lovoni, dramatically sited in a volcanic crater. See p.202

✳ **Caqalai Island** Snorkel amongst reef sharks and take it easy at this tiny backpackers' resort. See p.202

✳ **Journey by cargo boat** Take a trip into the past aboard a cargo boat, mingling with locals and exploring the tiny remote islands of the Lau Group. See p.208

✳ **Bay of Islands** Marvel at the unusual limestone formations and explore caves at these remote islands off Vanua Balavu. See p.209

▲ Cession Site, Levuka

Lomaiviti and Lau

A world away from the beach resorts of the Mamanucas and Yasawa Islands, the historically fascinating **Lomaiviti** and **Lau** groups radiate from the east coast of Viti Levu, eventually dissipating before a massively deep ocean trench separating Fiji from Tonga. Those who visit these enchanting islands step into the Fiji of old, where islanders fish the lagoons as a matter of necessity and travel the open seas in small boats. As a tourist destination, the inner islands of the **Lomaiviti Group** are relatively developed, particularly Ovalau, home to Fiji's charming former capital, **Levuka**. In comparison, the Outer Lomaiviti and the entire expanse of the **Lau Group** offer few facilities but will captivate the minds of the most curious of travellers. The area has a rich **Tongan heritage** and is popular with visiting yachts drawn to its spectacular limestone islands and bays. With over sixty islands to visit across a wide expanse of ocean, virtually no accommodation and limited transport, time and patience are the main requisites for successfully exploring this region.

Some history

The Lomaiviti and Lau islands played a key role in the struggle for supremacy over the Fijian archipelago. By the mid-nineteenth century the ruthless **Ratu Seru Cakobau**, high chief of Bau, had brought much of Fiji under his control. However, the Tongans held a long association with the Lau Group which in most parts are closer to their islands than Viti Levu. In 1848, **Enele Ma'afu**, a Tongan prince, was sent to Lakeba in Lau under the guise of protecting the missionaries established there. By supporting Cakobau's enemies and plying his own brand of fierce warfare, Ma'afu soon began to dominate the region, even gaining control of Vanua Levu and Taveuni. By the 1870s, Cakobau concluded that Ma'afu had the upper hand. Fearful of a direct confrontation he decided to cede Fiji to Britain, which he believed would halt the Tongan's conquest. The British were reluctant to accept Cakobau's terms as he didn't represent the united people of Fiji. So, in 1871, Cakobau rallied a few white settlers in Levuka, and, with the backing of his allied chiefs, announced himself **King of Fiji**. After much debate and tension, **cession to Britain** was completed on October 10, 1874 and **Levuka** became the administrative capital of the new colony. Ma'afu, his aspirations of control of Fiji halted, reluctantly accepted administration over the Lau Group.

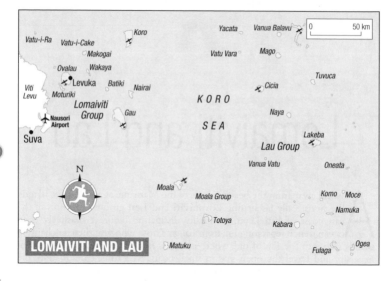

Lomaiviti Group

The sixteen islands of the **Lomaiviti Group** form a neat triangular cluster in the heart of the Fijian archipelago, 20km east of Viti Levu and 50km south of Vanua Levu. In the nineteenth century the island of **Ovalau** became the centre of European trade with whalers and merchants setting up camp beside the village of **Levuka**, eventually to become Fiji's first capital. Levuka remains the region's main tourist draw, yet visitor numbers are blissfully insignificant. Surrounding Ovalau, a handful of **small islands** lie within a fifteen-kilometre radius, entwined within stunning coral reefs and boasting secluded white sandy beaches and **hillforts**. Further east, the **Outer Lomaiviti** consist of half a dozen high volcanic islands but with virtually no tourist infrastructure.

Ovalau

From a distance, **OVALAU** resembles a giant meringue with its top bitten off. The missing top of the island is, in fact, a blown-out crater, 400m deep with three lakes and the proud village of **Lovoni** lying at the bottom. Just under eight thousand people live on the island, over half of them based in and around **Levuka**, hemmed in by sheer rainforest-covered mountains midway along the east coast. The drier coastline of **North Ovalau** has rolling grassy hills overlooking the island of **Naigani**, home to a small resort and several large hillforts. **South Ovalau** has few specific attractions although you are likely to pass through to access the island's airstrip and the road to Lovoni. Off the south coast are a handful of beautiful small islands with **backpacker resorts**.

Arrival

The small **airstrip** at Bureta on the southwest side of Ovalau is used only by Air Fiji for flights from Nausori (15min). A minibus meets all incoming flights and shuttles passengers to Levuka for F$5. Departing Levuka for the airport, minibuses leave at 6.15am and 3.45pm from outside the Air Fiji office on Beach Street or fifteen minutes later from the *Royal Hotel*.

Three **ferry services** connect Ovalau with Viti Levu. Of the two large passenger ferries, Venu Shipping (⊤ 339 5000; F$20 passenger one way, F$171 car plus driver one way; 6hr) is the most convenient, with two weekly departures from Walu Bay in **Suva** direct to Levuka although there is no fixed timetable (phone for details). Patterson Brothers (⊤ 331 6544; F$25 passenger one way, F$112 car one way; 5hr) have regular departures (usually Tues, Thurs, Fri & Sat) around 3pm from **Natovi Landing**, a rather isolated spot midway up the east coast of Viti Levu, to **Buresala** on the west coast of Ovalau from where there is a connecting bus into Levuka; the ferry returns to Natovi at 6am the following morning. A Patterson Brothers bus runs to Natovi Landing from Bay 6 at the Suva bus stand at 1.30pm (F$5). In addition, Turtle Island Transport (⊤ 337 3012; Tues, Thurs, Fri & Sat 8am; 5hr; F$18) offers a **bus-ferry-bus** service (Suva–Natovi–Buresala–Levuka) taking a maximum of thirty passengers – passengers meet at 8am at the carrier stand opposite the flea market in Suva (you can pre-order tickets from their office above the ANZ bank in Samabula, Suva).

If you're heading from Viti Levu direct to the small backpacker resorts on Caqalai or Leleuvia (see p.203), onward **small boat** passage from either island to Levuka costs F$30 and takes forty minutes. The boat journey can be done in either direction making a round trip a popular option with budget travellers.

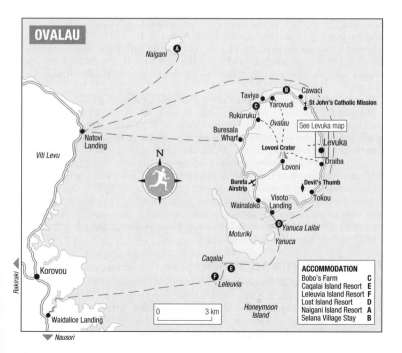

Getting around

The only **public bus** on Ovalau is the school service running from Bureta at 6am (daily except Sun; F$1) to St John's Catholic Mission via Levuka, returning along the same route around 3pm. Levuka itself is small enough to walk around, but to see the sights just north or south of town it's best to rent a **bicycle** (available from Ned Fisher behind Ovalau Watersports; F$15 per day). To explore further, **taxis** and **carrier vans** have a base beside the seawall opposite the Church of the Sacred Heart, but to reach the hilly north coast it's best to hire a driver with **4WD** through Ovalau Watersports (℡344 0166; F$120 for half-day round-island tour for up to four people).

Levuka

Once a wild whaling outpost, diminutive **LEVUKA** is now a charming seaside town with a laid-back atmosphere epitomized by its weathered yet colourful clapboard buildings. The town has a rich Fijian and colonial heritage and the best way to learn about it is by walking and talking with the genuinely hospitable locals, either on a guided tour or a home visit.

Some history

With a protected harbour and a welcoming chief, Levuka village hosted a small band of British and American **whalers** during the 1830s. In return for shelter, the whalers gave gifts of muskets which the villagers used to fend off the fierce hill people from Lovoni in the centre of the island. Soon to follow were a motley crew of fugitives, blackbirders and beachcombers with zealous Victorian **missionaries** hot on their heals. In the 1860s, following speculation that Fiji would soon become a British colony, Levuka grew rapidly with traders arriving from New Zealand and Australia. By 1871, when the great warrior Cakobau declared Levuka the **capital of Fiji**, there were over two thousand European residents and 52 hotels and bars. It was joked that ships would navigate into port by following the bobbing rum bottles drifting on the tide.

Levuka's short life as a South Pacific metropolis came to an abrupt end in 1881 when the British moved the capital to Suva, which offered more land for expansion. The town suffered a second blow in 1895 when the north side of town was flattened by a **hurricane**. After the collapse of the copra trade which briefly occupied Levuka in the 1920s, the town gained a new lease of life thanks to the PAFCO **tuna cannery** set up here in 1976. During the 1980s, with the emergence of **tourism**, Levuka found itself as a curio, a relic of Fiji's colonial past. It also realized its unique status as a town of Fijian firsts – the first Methodist church, the first hotel, the first bank, school and newspaper are but a few of its proud claims. The town's residents have tried unsuccessfully to protect its colonial architecture through UNESCO Heritage listing. Sadly four historic buildings have been lost to fire since 2000.

Information and tours

Dive-operator **Ovalau Watersports** (℡344 0166, ⓦwww.owlfiji.com; Mon–Fri 8.30am–4pm, Sat 8.30am–1pm) at the southern end of Beach Street opposite Westpac Bank acts as an unofficial **tourist information centre**. Run by an enthusiastic German couple, they can help book accommodation and arrange trips to the backpacker resorts off the south coast. The best source

Typical of the Levuka's friendly character, **home visits** involving tea and a chat with a local resident give a quirky insight into the town's past and present. Options include sprightly Scotsman Duncan Creighton (☎ 344 0481; Mon–Sat by arrangement; F$16), whose wooden house on top of Mission Hill has beautiful gardens, a talking parrot and a fine collection of rare iguanas. A more sedate affair and a better insight into the historical side of Levuka is offered by Bubu Kara in Nakuvukakuvu just south of town. Granny Kara chats effortlessly about the good old days at her ancestral home (☎ 344 0388; Mon–Sat 3.30pm or by appointment; F$15, minimum two people). Tours can be arranged through **Levuka Community Centre** or by calling direct for an appointment.

for historical information is the **Levuka Community Centre** (☎ 344 0356; Mon–Fri 8am–1pm & 2–4.30pm, Sat 8am–1pm) which organizes ninety-minute walking tours (F$8) on demand. A more impromptu **walking tour** is offered by the affable Nox (book via *Levuka Homestay*; F$15) who will guide you round the less-explored parts of town.

Accommodation

Small guesthouses make up the majority of Levuka's **accommodation** options. Although there are less than fifty rooms in total, the only time you will struggle to find a place to stay is during "Back to Levuka Week", the town's heritage festival (mid Oct) when booking is essential.

Levuka Holiday Cottage Vakaviti, North Levuka ☎ 344 0166, ⓦ www.owlfiji.com/holidaycottage .htm. This tiny one-bedroom bungalow located just over 1km north of Levuka is the only holiday home on Ovalau and sits in a spacious landscaped garden under the looming Gun Rock cliff. The lounge-cum-kitchen is well furnished but the hot-water bathroom and toilet is accessed from outside. Weekly rates of F$505.

🏃 **Levuka Homestay** Church St ☎ 344 0777, ⓦ www.levukahomestay.com. This delightful modern homestay ranks amongst the best in Fiji. Run by an Australian couple with just four a/c guest rooms staggered up the hillside with simple furnishings and cosy bathrooms. The complimentary breakfast is an event itself with banana pancakes, home-made muesli and fresh fruit followed by eggs, bacon and sausage. ❹

Mary's Holiday Home Beach St ☎ 344 0013. This quaint colonial style home with a cream-coloured picket fence is a little deceiving from the outside – this is by far the cheapest accommodation in town and it shows inside. The tiny rooms are musty and the windows lack screens; shared cold-water bathrooms are rather dingy. Dorms F$15 including breakfast, rooms. ❶

New Mavinda Lodge North Beach St ☎ 337 0995, ⓔ newmavindalodge@connect.com.fj. This mock-palatial modern building seems completely out of place in Levuka. The shiny ceramic floors give off an echo as you walk while the high ceilings come complete with glittering chandeliers. All eleven rooms have TV and air con and the clinical eight-bed dorm has its own his-and-hers hot-water en-suite bathrooms – not bad for the price; there's even a laundry service and Internet access. Dorms F$25, including breakfast, rooms. ❸

Ovalau Holiday Resort North Levuka ☎ 344 0329, ⓔ ohrfiji@connect.com.fj. Although this resort is not the most practical base, being 5km north of Levuka town, it does boast a small sandy beach with fair snorkelling across the road, a swimming pool and good restaurant. The five basic cottages sleep up to six people making them handy for families. Budget travellers can also camp in the landscaped gardens. Camping F$10, dorms F$12, rooms ❶, cottages ❷.

Royal Hotel Robbie's Lane ☎ 344 0024, ⓦ www .royallevuka.com. Originally constructed in the 1860s and rebuilt in 1916 after a devastating fire, the *Royal* is the oldest hotel in Fiji. The main building has plenty of colonial character – the fifteen rooms upstairs having slanted wooden floorboards, creaking four-poster beds and tiny bathrooms. The five modern cottages in front of the swimming pool overlooking Beach St are a lot more comfortable. The staff can appear rather aloof but with a full-sized billiard table, Internet café, bicycles and laundry there's a lot going for this place. Rooms ❶, cottages ❸.

The Town

The main thoroughfare of Levuka town, misleadingly named **Beach Street**, passes between the rocky seawall and the town's most historic buildings. It's a simple tar-sealed track where dogs roam and people wander back and forth unconcerned about the occasional carrier van that bundles along. At the southern end of Beach Street is the the large tuna cannery and **port**. There's a lovely view of the seafront from the port although the smell from the factory and the persistent noise of whirring generators from the power station spoil the atmosphere. At the junction of Beach Street and Queens Wharf is a drinking fountain on a small island in the road. Here once stood a pigeon loft used to send post between Levuka and Suva in less than thirty minutes. The modern **post office** is now located down Queens Wharf.

Beach Street is dominated by the **Morris Hedstrom building**, standing proudly at the southern end of town a hundred metres north of the power station. Opened in 1868 as a grocery store, Morris Hedstrom built up a trading empire which thrived during the colonial era, finding its way to every corner of the archipelago. You'll still find Morris Hedstrom supermarkets in most Fijian towns but this original store was dedicated to the National Trust in 1980 and today houses the **Levuka Community Centre**, as well as a tiny **museum** (℡344 0356; Mon–Fri 8am–1pm & 2pm–4.30pm, Sat 8am–1pm; F$2). The latter houses a rather sad collection of chemist's bottles, clay pipes and shells – a printing press and photographic equipment being the only tangible relics of the colonial era. There is a useful library, though, and its curators, Tabaki and Elizabeth are hugely knowledgeable about Levuka's history. Across the road from the museum is a colourful row of **clapboard wooden buildings** extending to the north. Most now function as Chinese or Indian-run **stores** and are so packed full of goods and groceries it's difficult to poke around without bumping into someone. Outside, the pillared pavement is where the town's residents meet for a gossip.

Midway along Beach Street is the **Church of the Sacred Heart**. This picturesque Catholic church with a domed roof was built in two stages. The main section for worship was crafted from local timber in 1858 with the arrival of the first Catholic missionaries, while the imposing **clock tower** was erected forty years later using thick limestone blocks baked from coral. The blue light on top of the tower acts as a beacon for ships together with another on top of the hill. The church is worth a peek inside for its gruesome yet humbling series of fourteen **paintings** depicting Christ's crucifixion. North of the church, beyond Hennings Street, are the newer and less intriguing quarters of Levuka, rebuilt after the devastating hurricane in 1895.

Nasau Park

Inland from Beach Street along Hennings Street are the playing fields of **Nasau Park**, once the venue of King Cakobau's headquarters on his visits to Levuka. Before you reach the park and beside the police station, a small bridge crosses Totoga Creek. Tucked away behind a delightful white picket fence and abutting the creek is the **Ovalau Club**, built in 1904 and now Fiji's oldest social club. Next door is the double-storey **Town Hall** built in 1898 to commemorate the silver jubilee of Queen Victoria. The neighbouring burnt-out neoclassical building is the old **Masonic Hall**, desecrated in 2000 by a mob of two hundred villagers from Lovoni. During the spiralling events of the Speight Coup, Lovoni's firebrand Methodist priest told his congregation that the hall was a centre for devil worship. It was also rumoured that secret tunnels under Nasau Park connected it to the *Royal Hotel*, Nasova House and, bizarrely, the Grand Lodge

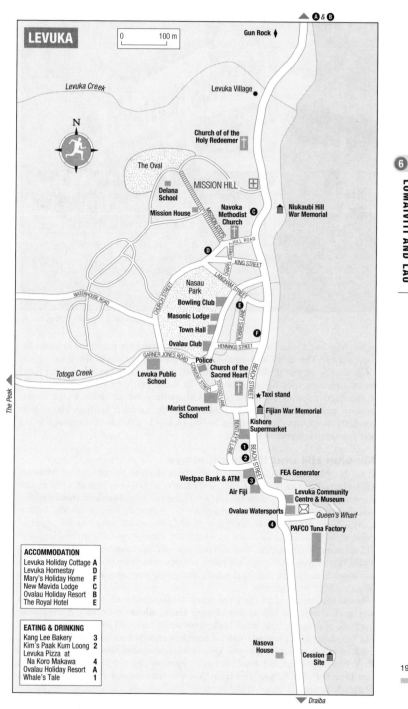

LEVUKA

0 — 100 m

▲ ● A & B

Gun Rock ◆

Levuka Creek

Levuka Village ●

Church of of the
Holy Redeemer ✝

The Oval

Delana
School

MISSION HILL ⊞

Mission House

Navoka
Methodist
Church ✝ ● C

Niukaubi Hill
War Memorial 🏛

● D

HILL ROAD

KING STREET

Nasau
Park

Bowling Club ■

Masonic Lodge ■

Town Hall ■

Ovalau Club ■

● E

● F

WATERHOUSE ROAD

CHURCH STREET

MISSION STREET

CHAPEL STREET

LANGHAM STREET

ROBBIES LANE

BEACH STREET

HENNINGS STREET

Totoga Creek

GARNER JONES ROAD

Police ■

Levuka Public
School

Church of the
Sacred Heart ✝

CONVENT STREET

TOTOGA LANE

★ Taxi stand

The Peak ◀

Marist Convent
School

Fijian War Memorial 🏛

Kishore
Supermarket

BENTLY'S LANE

● 1
● 2

Westpac Bank & ATM ● 3

Air Fiji

FEA Generator

Levuka Community
Centre & Museum

Ovalau Watersports

✉

Queen's Wharf

● 4

PAFCO Tuna Factory

ACCOMMODATION

Levuka Holiday Cottage	A
Levuka Homestay	D
Mary's Holiday Home	F
New Mavida Lodge	C
Ovalau Holiday Resort	B
The Royal Hotel	E

EATING & DRINKING

Kang Lee Bakery	3
Kim's Paak Kum Loong	2
Levuka Pizza at	
Na Koro Makawa	4
Ovalau Holiday Resort	A
Whale's Tale	1

Nasova
House

Cession
Site 🏛

▼ *Draiba*

▲ The original Morris Hedstrom Store, Levuka

of the Masonic Order in Scotland. The culprits were later pardoned in court for their naivety. The tunnels turned out to be drainage outlets to the sea.

Continuing on past the Bowling Club leads to the back of the colonial-era *Royal Hotel*, a pleasant spot for afternoon tea. To reach the hotel entrance turn right at the intersection of Langham Street. Otherwise, continue north to the quaint maroon and white **Navoka Methodist Church**, founded in 1862. The church conducts its services (Sun 10.15am & 4pm) solely in English to encourage Fijian and European communal worship.

Mission Hill and the back alleys

From Navoka Methodist Church, 199 steps lead up to the summit of **Mission Hill**. The hill was named after Fiji's first mission school built here in 1852 by the Reverend John Binner. From the top a path continues to **Mission House** where Cakobau was proclaimed King of Fiji in 1871. Beyond here is the flat hilltop known as the **Oval** where colonial residents gathered on Saturdays for a spot of horse racing. There's a fabulous unobstructed **view** from here overlooking the old quarters of Levuka and out towards the offshore islands of Makogai, Batiki and Wakaya. Keep an eye out for **pilot whales**, which are present year round in the Koro Sea – if you're exceptionally lucky you may spot a humpback whale between May and October.

At the southern end of the Oval you'll find a small bush track that winds its way back down the hill to the alluring **back alleys** of Levuka. A confusing network of pathways and small bridges meander back and forth connecting the old wooden houses where many of Levuka's residents live. There's no obvious track to follow but as long as you keep heading downhill you'll end up at Nasau Park. Alternatively, a dirt road continues on from the top of the Mission Hill, past Delana Public School and leads down to the Hospital at the northern end of Beach Street.

North to Levuka village and Gun Rock

Jutting out into the sea splitting Levuka town and Levuka village is **Niukaubi Hill,** a small bluff where the Supreme Court and parliament were located before the capital moved to Suva. In its place now stands a **war memorial** listing all Fijian soldiers who died fighting for Britain during World War I. The adjacent bay is where the *Leonadis* docked on March 3, 1879 bringing with it Fiji's first shipload of indentured Indian labourers. Three hundred metres north, beyond the hospital, is **Levuka** village where the first Europeans set up camp. The small village is backed by a large exposed rockface known as **Gun Rock**, used as target practice by the cannons of HMS *Havanah* to impress and intimidate Cakobau and other chiefs. Ask around the village for a guide to accompany you on the twenty-minute hike to the top.

Nasova House and the Cession Site

At the southern end of Levuka, beyond the tuna cannery, is the grand **Nasova House**, once the residence of the British Governor. Across the road is the ceremonial spot where King Cakobau signed the **Deed of Cession** on October 10, 1874, handing not only sovereignty to Great Britain but also his iconic warclub. A public re-enactment of this occasion is performed every year on the same date, coinciding with the week-long festival, "Back to Levuka" (see p.37). A stone embedded with a plaque was laid to mark the **Cession Site** in 1935, and two further stones accompanied this, one in 1970 to commemorate Independence and the second in 1974 to mark the centenary of the original deed.

Prince Charles presided over the 1970 Independence Ceremony and used the beautiful **thatch bure** across the road as his temporary home. The bure then became the Lomaiviti Provincial Headquarters until a new grander meeting house was built next door in time for the proposed Great Council of Chiefs gathering in December 2006. Unfortunately the Bainimarama coup put a stop to this inaugural event, and, with the Great Council of Chiefs since decreed as obsolete, the building has yet to be used.

Eating and drinking

Levuka has just enough **restaurants** to keep you happy on a short visit, but with only a trickle of tourists and few residents dining out, they lack panache. For **drinking**, the *Ovalau Club* is your best bet; alternatively, the courtyard in front of the *Royal Hotel* is a good choice for a quiet afternoon tipple.

Kang Lee Bakery Beach St. Quick takeaway snacks including sumptuous fifty-cent coconut rolls and F$1 meat pies. Mon–Sat 6am–7pm, Sun 6am–10am.

Kim's Paak Kum Loong Beach St, ☎ 344 0059. This place has a bit of everything: Chinese, Indian, European and Fijian. The best time to sample it all is at the F$15 Sun dinner buffet. Otherwise, meals are hearty and cheap, starting from F$8 for vegetarian stir fry and going up to $15 for lamb curry or fish in *lolo* sauce. There's outdoor dining on the wooden veranda with views of the waterfront but the drone from the town's electricity generators may irritate. Mon–Sat 7am–2pm & 6–9pm, Sun 6–9pm.

Levuka Pizza at Na Koro Makawa Beach St, ☎ 344 0429. Located almost opposite the tuna cannery, the specialty here is tuna pizza (F$8.30),

something of an acquired taste. Other popular toppings include prawn and lobster. Fish and chips and stir fry are also on the menu. Daily 7am–2pm & 6–9pm.

Ovalau Club Long-established social club where you can chat with the friendly regulars over a F$2 beer or play snooker on a full-sized table for twenty cents a game. Local bands sometimes play at weekends when it's at its liveliest; otherwise visit on a Tues for the weekly residents' get together (from 6pm). Mon–Thurs 4–10pm, Fri 2–11pm, Sat 10–1am, Sun 10am–9pm.

Ovalau Holiday Resort North Levuka, ☎ 344 0329. Run by an Indian family, the curry dishes are nicely authentic at this resort restaurant. They also offer tasty seafood including lobster and crab. It's 5km north of town, but if you call ahead they'll offer free pick-up and drop-off to your hotel. Daily noon–2pm & 6–9pm.

Whale's Tale Beach St, ☎344 0235. With a charming nautical ambience and delightful home cooking this is a top choice.

The lunchtime burgers are spot on and the three-course dinner special at F$16.90 is good value – try the fish fillet in lemon sauce or pasta with olives, capers and herbs. Lunch & dinner, closed Sun.

Activities

As well as the town history tours (see p.194), there are a couple of worthwhile **hikes** around Levuka. **The Peak trail** is an arduous two-hour hike through forest culminating in a panorama of the eastern coastline from the large hill which rears up behind Levuka. Less strenuous but equally rewarding is the serene **Waitovu Waterfall walk**, a fifteen-minute stroll through forest from Waitovu village, 2km north of town; you can swim at two pools at the falls. Both hikes are available with Nox who is best contacted through *Levuka Homestay* (☎344 0777; The Peak F$20, Waitovu Waterfall F$15). If visiting Waitovu on your own you should present a small *sevusevu* or F$5 to the village headman. For **diving**, Ovalau Watersports (see p.194) cruises in an eight-metre purpose-built dive boat to the wonderful and remote reef system between Wakaya and Makogai where sharks, dolphins and pilot whales are common (two-tank dive F$150, five-day PADI Open Water course F$650). Snorkellers can join in these trips for F$40. Otherwise, there's excellent **snorkelling** off Caqalai Island which can be visited as a day-trip.

Listings

Airlines Air Fiji, Beach St at the southern end of town next door to Kang Lee Bakery (☎344 0139, Mon–Sat 8am–4pm).

Banking Westpac Bank (Mon–Fri 9.30am–12.30pm & 1.30–4pm) at the southern end of Beach St has the town's only ATM machine.

Groceries Kishore Supermarket (Mon–Sat 6.30am–6.30pm, Sun 7–11am), in a blue and yellow building next to the *Whale's Tale* restaurant on Beach St.

Hospital (☎344 0164) Beach St, at the northern end of town.

Internet access Ovalau Watersports has one terminal with broadband costing twenty cents a minute. Cheaper access is available from M Narsey

& Sons in a cream building next door to the *Whale's Tale* restaurant.

Laundry Only available within guesthouses

Police (☎344 0222) on the corner of Totoya Lane and Garner Jones Rd; open 24hr.

Post office Located on Queens Wharf Lane leading down to the port and open 8am–1pm and 2–4pm weekdays.

Taxis Taxis and carrier vans are parked opposite the Church of the Sacred Heart. If you want to pre-book, try Bob's (☎344 0369) or Ovalau Watersports can arrange 4WD vehicles with a driver.

Telephones Outside the post office, in front of Kishore Supermarket on Beach St and at the *Royal Hotel*.

North Ovalau

North of Levuka, it's a pleasant seven-kilometre walk along the dirt road passing Vatukalo village to the large Catholic mission and boarding schools of **St John's College** at **Cawaci**. On the southern boundary of the mission, sitting on a bluff overlooking the sea, is the **Bishop's Tomb**, final resting place of Bishop Julien Vidal from France, Fiji's first bishop. From the tomb there's an impressive view north along the coast towards Cawaci's centerpiece, the French-inspired twin-towered **Church of St John the Baptist**, its thick whitewashed coral stone walls standing out against the green mountains.

At the northern point of Ovalau, 14km from Levuka, is a beautiful white sandy beach alongside **Arovudi** village. Between the beach and the village is an impressive rock foundation where once stood a *bure kalou* or priest's temple. At the western end of the beach is a large collection of jet-black volcanic stones used by the women of the village to make an unusual flavouring known as *kora*. Grated coconut is wrapped in banana leaves and placed under the heat-retaining stones where it ferments slowly for four days, a salty flavour being added with each incoming tide. The women are also renowned for catching **sardines**, which are chased by giant trevally into awaiting nets. When the trevally are jumping but sardines are not being caught, village tradition dictates that one of the village girls is hiding a pregnancy. You can easily visit Arovudi in an afternoon from Levuka but it's well worth **staying** nearby at ⚘ *Salana Village Stay* (☎992 1914, ✉sala_nagalu@yahoo.com; dorm F$25, cottage ❶) a few hundred metres up the beach. The accommodation is basic but clean with shared cold-water bathrooms and Fijian style food and there's a range of **activities** on offer including traditional mat weaving and a hike to a large **hillfort** on top of Tomuna Peak (F$35, minimum two people).

Four kilometres further along the coast, between Taviya village and the settlement of **Rukuruku**, is the turn-off to ⚘ *Bobo's Farm* (☎362 3873, bobosfarm@owlfiji .com; rooms ❷), a five-hundred-acre private farm run by energetic Bobo and his German wife Karin. The farm is accessed along a three-hundred-metre track leading down to the coast (a taxi from Levuka will drop you at the turn-off for F$30). It's a beautiful spot surrounded by **rainforest** and Bobo will talk passionately about the medicinal values of vines, roots and leaves. The single wooden A-frame **cottage** has two rooms, a shared lounge, solar power and a cold-water bathroom; delicious organic meals are served in the farmhouse. A five-minute trail alongside a stream leads to an unusual **black-sand beach** with good swimming and snorkelling, but you'll need to bring your own snorkel gear. Another trail heads inland to a series of small waterfalls linked by a natural water slide. Bobo can also organize fishing trips and a three-hour hike to Lovoni Crater (see p.202).

Naigani island

The history of **Naigani** island, 10km off the northwest coast of Ovalau, is typical of the region's volatility. The islanders trace their roots back to **Verata** on Viti Levu to which they remain politically aligned. Verata was one of the two traditional enemies of Bau, so when the island was invaded by Cakobau in 1860 a thousand of the islanders were killed and carried off to Bau to be eaten – only two people were left alive. A few years later, an Australian named **Riley** was given a portion of the island as a dowry, having married the daughter of a Verata chief. Today, Naigani has a population of around fifty, descendants of the two surviving islanders and Riley's offspring. They live in a village on the north coast, lodged between two volcanic peaks. The **original village** is found on the northernmost peak, protected by a rim with a killing stone at its entrance. A large **hillfort** higher up was used for additional security at times of war. Large amounts of Lapita pottery have been discovered around the island dating back more than two thousand years.

You can visit Naigani by **boat** from either *Bobo's Farm* or *Salana Village Stay* (see above) but the most practical way to explore the island is to **stay** at the intimate *Naigani Island Resort* (☎603 0613, 🌐www.naiganiisland.com; rooms ❹, cottages ❺, includes breakfast), built around Riley's old plantation house on the south coast. Popular with both families and scuba divers, the resort offers eleven two-bedroom plantation-style cottages, a swimming pool with water slide, three-hole golf course, good snorkelling off the beach and certified PADI scuba diving but no courses. The resort arranges **guest transfers** from Natovi Landing on Viti Levu or Taviya village on Ovalau, both around a thirty-minute journey.

Cakobau and the Lovoni tribe

During 1870 and 1871, **Cakobau** tried time after time to subdue the fierce **Lovoni tribe** who had been constantly menacing the European settlers around Levuka. Unable to break through the ring of defences protecting the village in Lovoni Crater, Cakobau sent a Methodist missionary to Lovoni, inviting the tribe to a **reconciliation** in Levuka. Tired of being pursued by Cakobau, the Lovoni chief consulted his priest and accepted the invitation. On June 29, 1871 the entire village came down to Levuka. A meal was prepared, but as soon as the tribe set down their weapons to eat, Cakobau's warriors surrounded and subdued them. In time the majority were sold off as **slaves** and dispersed throughout every corner of the archipelago. Those that remain are a stoutly proud group, believing their village to be the only one in Fiji not to have been conquered by Cakobau.

South Ovalau

The coast of **South Ovalau** is rugged and covered in thick tropical forest. Jutting out above Tokou village is the dramatic volcanic plug nicknamed the **Devil's Thumb**. At the southern end of the island, Visoto Landing offers boat transfers to *Lost Island Resort* on Yanuca Lailai (see opposite).

Heading up the west coast, flanked offshore by Moturiki island, you'll find the village of **Wainalako**, founded by freed Solomon Island slaves in the middle of the nineteenth century. A few kilometres beyond is the **Bureta airstrip**, from where a dirt track winds inland following the Bureta River to **Lovoni** village, one of the island's star attractions. The village was made infamous by the fierce tribe (see box above) who lived behind an impregnable hillfort in the centre of the volcanic crater here (they've since moved to a more practical location just to the side). The easiest way to visit is by road with Epi's Tours (Ⓣ923 6011; F$40 includes lunch) although note that this involves a bone-crunching ride from Levuka in the back of a carrier van followed by rambling two-hour lecture on the history of Lovoni. A more rewarding alternative is to take a **guided hike** with Nox (see p.200) starting from Draiba village, a few kilometres south of Levuka. This is the shortest trail from the coast but it still takes a tough couple of hours through thick rainforest before you reach the dramatic setting of the crater – arrange for a carrier van to bring you back by road. You can also approach Lovoni from *Bobo's Farm* or *Salana Village Stay* (see p.201) although these are full-day hikes.

The backpacker island resorts

Three small islands along Ovalau's south coast, **Caqalai**, **Leleuvia** and **Yanuca Lailai** all possess beach resorts and are becoming popular with **backpackers** keen to avoid the increasingly commercial Yasawa Islands trail. Each resort arranges **guest transfers** from Viti Levu (at Waidalice Landing north of Nausori) or from Levuka port. Costs from Waidalice are F$30 per person one way to Leleuvia or Caqalai, or F$45 to Yanuca Lailai, all with a minimum of two people. You can reach Waidalice by taxi from Suva (F$50) or by bus/minivan via Nausori (F$5). From Levuka, the forty-minute boat journey costs F$20 to Yanuca Lailai or F$30 to Caqalai or Leleuvia.

Caqalai Island Resort

The pick of the bunch is **Caqalai Island Resort** (Ⓣ343 0366, Ⓦwww.fijianholiday.com; tent F$35, dorm F$45, bure ❸, includes meals) run by the Methodist Church of nearby Moturiki island. The ten bures are beautifully thatched and hidden amongst palm trees on the edge of the beachfront, and the bathrooms, painted in colourful murals, have cold-water showers and flush toilets. At low tide you can wade out to nearby **Snake Island** which offers good **snorkelling** and the chance to spot black-and-white sea snakes. Although they are extremely venemous, the snakes are so timid and agile that you will have little chance of getting near them. Even better snorkelling is available at Honeymoon island, a sand spit 5km to the east where you'll likely spot small reef sharks hiding amongst the coral. The resort also offers **scuba diving** but at the time of writing the equipment had seen better days and there was no Dive Master on site. The only other drawback is that no **alcohol** is sold on the island, but it's fine to bring your own.

Leleuvia Island Resort

Two kilometres south of Caqalai is its close rival, **Leleuvia Island Resort** (☎368 0721, ⓦwww.leleuvia.com; dorm F$50, bures ❸, includes meals), slightly larger than Caqalai and with an equally stunning beach setting. The eight thatch bures have been recently rebuilt but the duplex rooms and dorm lodge remain shabby. There's one elaborate shared bathroom, built with thick spiral walls and thatch roofing but it's been plagued by drainage problems. The sand-floor **restaurant** is well positioned overlooking the beach and there's a fantastic Indian curry night on Friday and a "Cannibal night" with bonfire on Saturday when you can sample traditional Fijian food (minus the human flesh). Ovalau Watersports has a fully equipped **dive centre** on the island (☎344 0166; ⓦwww.leleuviadiving.com; 2-tank dive $150; PADI 5-day course $650).

Yanuca Lailai (Lost Island Resort)

Less than a kilometre from Visoto Landing is **Yanuca Lailai** home to *Lost Island Resort* (☎360 9404; tent F$35, dorm F$40, bure ❶, includes all meals). Of the three island resorts, this is undoubtedly the humblest with just two simple thatch bures at the back of the old family home. Each has a double bed with mosquito net and kerosene lamp hanging from the ceiling. There's a fabulous **view** from the top of Vatuviriki hill, a twenty-minute hike from the resort.

Outer Lomaiviti

Few travellers reach the six islands of **Outer Lomaiviti** other than to scuba dive the exceptional coral reefs around **Makogai** and **Wakaya**, accessible from live-aboard dive boats or on a day-trip from Levuka. Rising out of the Koro Sea some 50km east of Ovalau are the large volcanic islands of **Koro** and **Gau**, the fifth and sixth largest landmasses in Fiji respectively. Both are blessed with rich agricultural land and large indigenous populations, but they are difficult to get to, even harder to explore and seldom visited by foreigners except on organized working holidays.

Makogai and Wakaya

In 1911, the small hilly island of **Makogai** became a **leper colony** for sufferers of the disease from throughout the South Pacific. Under the care of Mother Mary Agnes, a community was built consisting of a large hospital, cinema, shops and a church, as well as a cemetery where 1241 leprosy sufferers now rest in peace. The colony closed in 1969, twenty years after an effective treatment for the disease was found. In 1986, Makogai was declared a **marine reserve** and is run by the Ministry of Fisheries as a research centre with a large hatchery breeding giant clams, trochus and sea turtles.

The figure-of-eight coral reef that wraps around both Makogai and the private island resort of **Wakaya** to the south offers phenomenal scuba diving. The area is visited by Ovalau Watersports from Levuka (see p.194) as well as the **live-aboard** dive boat, *Fiji Aggressor* (Ⓦwww.aggressor.com; seven-day package from US$2595) or the slightly more intimate *Nai'a* (Ⓣ345 0382, Ⓦwww.naia.com.fj; ten-day package US$4200 per person). If you fancy staying at the fabulously opulent *Wayaka Club* **resort** (Ⓣ344 8128, Ⓦwww.wakaya.com) you'll need to cough up US$2200 per night (includes meals, alcohol and scuba diving). The resort has its own small aircraft flying in guests from Nadi and Nausori airports (transfers US$960 per couple).

Koro

Seventy kilometres northeast of Ovalau and less than 50km south of Vanua Levu is the triangular-shaped island of **Koro**. Rising to a peak of 560m, this volcanic island has splendid views from its inland road with bush tracks, **water-falls** set among tropical forests and herds of wild horses in the grassy inland plains. The largest village is Nasau, midway along the east coast about 5km north of the airstrip, home to a hospital, post office and government headquarters. The women of Koro are renowned for their finely woven **handicrafts**, particularly mats and fans.

The only place to **stay** is *Koro Beach Resort* (Ⓣ368 3301; tent F$20, bure ❷, includes meals) in Dere Bay on the northwest coast. The six simply furnished bures have en-suite hot-water bathrooms facing a narrow beachfront or you can pitch a tent and cook your own meals on the cooking stove provided. The resort is adjacent to the upmarket *Dere Bay Resort*, which at the time of writing was closed having switched to selling private beachside real estate for wealthy investors.

Air Fiji fly to Koro from Nausori every Wednesday (F$149 one way). Consort Shipping (Ⓣ331 3266; F$46 one way) departs Walu Bay in Suva at 6pm on Monday and Friday, calling in at Muanivau Landing on the south point of Koro around 2am before heading off to Savusavu on Vanua Levu.

Gau

The substantial 140-square-kilometre island of **Gau** lies 60km south of Koro and is characterized by dense rainforest on its high ridges, grasslands in the lower hills, sandy beaches along the south coast and mangroves in the north. There is **no accommodation** but you can visit with the UK-based organization, *Frontier* (Ⓦwww.frontier.ac.uk; minimum four weeks £895) either working as a volunteer school teacher and staying in one of the eighteen local villages around the coast, or conducting research on the Reef Conservation Programme. The largest village is Qarani, home to internationally acclaimed rugby superstar **Waisale Serevi**. Qarani has the safest anchorage for yachts and the island's only doctor. The disused road around Gau has long been overgrown so travel between villages is by small boat or bush track. The village of Nawaikama on the west coast beside the island's jetty has a hot-water stream, fed by a thermal spring in the hills, where the village kids bathe.

A weekly Air Fiji **flight** departs to Gau from Nausori most Tuesdays (F$113 one way). An unscheduled monthly cargo boat from Suva is operated by the government-run *Fiji Shipping Corporation* (Ⓣ331 9383; Ⓔfscl@unwired.com.fj). The only other way to get here is by hitching a ride from Levuka with locals travelling by small outboard boat which takes around an hour.

Lau Group

Like the flick of a paint brush, sixty tiny dots in a canvas of deep blue make up the **LAU GROUP**, a widely dispersed collection of islands forming the distant eastern border of Fiji. Only half the islands are inhabited and the people who live here are almost completely reliant on the reef-strewn sea that surrounds them. Cargo boats from Suva bring in essential supplies and connect the islands with the outside world. Otherwise, they remain untouched, **undeveloped** and seldom visited by outsiders. For those that do venture here, a warm welcome awaits as well as the chance to sample a unique **culture** – a mixture of Polynesian **Tonga** and Melanesian Fiji.

The Lau Group can be split into three regions: Moala, Northern Lau and Southern Lau. The three high volcanic islands of the **Moala Group** are the closest to Viti Levu, the least influenced by Tongan culture and lie to the south of Lomaiviti. **Northern Lau** is the region most appealing to tourists thanks to the historic island of Vanua Balavu which has access to the spectacular Bay of Islands. **Southern Lau** is the most isolated part of the group, in places closer to Tonga than Suva. These islands hold the region's seat of power at the traditional village of Tubou on Lakeba.

Some history

Before **Captain James Cook** chartered the island of Vatoa in Southern Lau in 1774, the Lau Group was a little-known group of remote islands where Tongans and Fijians traded, occasionally fought and often intermarried. The Tongans came for the giant *vesi* trees that flourished around the islands of Fulaga and Lakeba. These were hollowed out to make large double-hulled canoes used for exploration, trade and war around the Tongan empire. In 1800, the *Argo*, one of the first Western merchant ships to enter Fijian waters, was **shipwrecked** on the Bukatatanoa Reef east of Lakeba. Its survivors were rescued in canoes by people from Lakeba and became the first white people to live amongst Fijians. Items from the ship, including ceramic plate and buttons moved briskly around the islands providing much curiosity. Sadly the ship also brought with it a strain of **cholera** which caused many deaths throughout the group.

In 1835, two Wesleyan Methodist **missionaries**, the Rev William Cross from England and Rev David Cargill from Scotland, landed at Tubou on Lakeba becoming the first missionaries to arrive in Fiji. The pair had already worked in Tonga for several years and were accompanied by several envoys of the **Taufa'ahau**, the Christian King of Tonga. During the great **wars** of the 1840s between Bau and Rewa, fierce Tongan warriors fought for both sides in different parts of the islands. By 1848, their reputation had begun to embarrass Taufa'ahau, so he sent the headstrong **Prince Ma'afu** to Lakeba to control his people. Ma'afu excelled at his task and soon began to dominate the Lau Group. He moved his seat of power to Lakeba and by 1869 had declared himself *Tui Lau* or "**King of Lau**". With a Christian ruler and the islands having being pacified, European planters moved in, purchasing the fertile islands of Northern Lau to grow cotton, and later for coconut oil production. When the entire Fijian archipelago was ceded to Britain in 1874, Ma'afu was granted control of the Lau Group and remained here until his death in 1881.

Today, Lauans walk tall amongst Fijians, retaining much power in political life. Two of Fiji's most revered figureheads hailed from Tubou on Lakeba: Ratu Sir

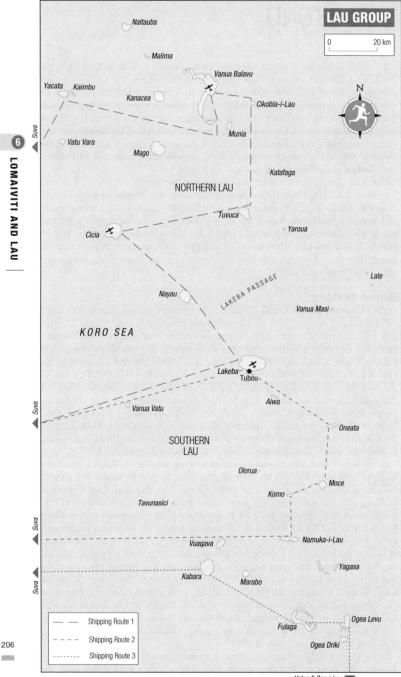

Naitauba

Malima

Vanua Balavu

Yacata Kaimbu

Kanacea

Cikobia-i-Lau

Vatu Vara

Munia

Mago

Katafaga

NORTHERN LAU

Tuvuca

Cicia

Yaroua

LAKEBA PASSAGE

Nayau

Vanua Masi

Late

KORO SEA

Lakeba
Tubou

Vanua Vatu

Aiwa

Oneata

SOUTHERN
LAU

Olorua

Moce

Tavunasici

Komo

Vuaqava

Namuka-i-Lau

Yagasa

Kabara

Marabo

Ogea Levu

Fulaga

Ogea Driki

Vatoa & Ono-i-Lau ▼

LAU GROUP

0   20 km

N

Suva ◄
Suva ◄
Suva ◄
Suva ◄

——— Shipping Route 1
- - - Shipping Route 2
········ Shipping Route 3

Lala Sukuna (1888–1958) who paved the way for the nation's independence and **Ratu Sir Kamisese Mara** (1920–2004), Fiji's first Prime Minister. The latter held the title of President from 1993 to 2000 before being unceremoniously disposed by the Speight coup (see p.269).

Arrival and accommodation

Air Fiji operates weekly **flights** from Nausori Airport direct to Moala (Tues; 45min; F$192), Lakeba (Mon; 1hr; F$210), Cicia (Thurs; 1hr; F$195) and Vanua Balavu (Sun; 1hr; F$206), but no flights between the islands. Flights are often booked out months in advance, especially around Christmas and other school holidays.

The only official **places to stay** are two budget guesthouses on the two main islands of Vanua Balavu and Lakeba. If you're interested in exploring the islands in depth, it's definitely worth contacting the Lau Provincial Council on Rodwell Street in Suva (☎331 6801) who should be able to assist in organizing **homestay** accommodation on some of the outer islands. Bring plenty of **cash** – there are no banks, only a handful of small village stores and food and fuel costs are inflated due to its isolation.

Moala Group

The three islands of the **Moala Group**, Moala, Totoya and Matuku, lie in a rather isolated part of the Fijian archipelago, south of Lomaiviti, east of Kadavu and west of the main portion of the Lauan islands. With infrequent sea traffic and no accommodation, they are seldom visited by travellers. Culturally linked to the Lomaiviti Group, all three islands were raided and seized by Ma'afu during the 1850s and have remained under the administrative control of the Lau Group ever since.

Covering 66 square kilometres, **Moala** is the largest and most populated of all islands in the Lau Group. It's an easy place to explore with eleven villages all linked by walking tracks crisscrossing the hills. The government station, airstrip and jetty are at Naroi on the northeast tip. Forty kilometres south of Moala, the stunning collapsed volcanic crater of **Totoya** has formed a steep rim shaped like a horseshoe and surrounded by a deep lagoon. From the air, the setting is spectacular but access into the horseshoe bay is difficult even with calm seas. There are four villages on the island, three of these are located on the bay. **Matuku**, the southernmost of the islands, is slightly smaller than Moala. Graced with lush tropical forests rising to a peak of 388m, the rich volcanic soil on its slopes is ideal for farming and some of the finest *dalo* is grown here. Three of the island's four villages sit alongside one of several long, white sand beaches which flank the south side of the island – you'll usually find the village women here engaged in basket weaving, finely crafted using spiky *voi voi* leaves (*Pandanus Thurstoni*).

Northern Lau

For an off-beat adventure, exploring **Northern Lau** is an unforgettable experience. The most appealing of all the Lauan destinations, **Vanua Balavu** lies in the heart of the region, surrounded by the dramatic, uplifted limestone islands of the **Bay of Islands** – a popular yachting destination. If you plan carefully, you can arrive by plane at Vanua Balavu, spend a few days exploring and then catch the **cargo boat** back to Suva via five other Lauan islands. Be warned, though, that boat schedules and sometimes even flights may change last minute or become delayed due to bad weather and both are overbooked during Christmas holidays.

Vanua Balavu

On a map, the long, thin curving island of **Vanua Balavu** looks uncannily like a sea horse with Masomo Bay as its eye and the small islets of Malata and Susui forming its hooked tail. Vanua Balavu is the secondmost populated island of the Lau Group, with 1800 people in fourteen coastal villages, farming copra or gathering bêche-de-mer from the lagoons as an income. In 1855, the Tongan prince Ma'afu invaded Vanua Balavu, the first of his Fijian conquests, and based his court in the village of **Lomaloma**, now the main village on the island. The island remains heavily influenced by **Tongan**

Cargo boats

Without doubt the best way to experience the islands of the Lau Group is to travel around the region by **cargo boat**. The round-trip journey from Suva on all routes takes between six and seven days, offering a wonderful opportunity to mingle with the locals and to get a feel for the vastness of the region. Although there is no fixed schedule, there's usually at least one departure a week to the islands from **Suva** with each boat visiting between three and eight islands before heading back to the capital. Three to six hours are spent at each port, giving you enough time to disembark and have a quick look around. It may be tempting to linger on an island a little longer but bear in mind it may be several weeks before the next boat turns up.

Conditions on board are basic. A few boats have **cabins**, each with five bunk beds, but these are often stuffy, stink of diesel fumes and come crammed with luggage. Instead you'll probably be sleeping under the stars on the open deck. It's wise to take at least a pillow for resting your head and preferably a mat to spread out on. Note that meals provided on board are basic and it's worth bringing plenty of drinks and snacks. Toilet paper is another necessity – and be prepared for the sometimes vile conditions of a cargo boat bathroom.

Operators and routes

Shipping companies come and go rather quickly in Fiji. If you find any of the following companies no longer in operation, it's worth contacting the Fiji Shipping Corporation (℡331 9383; ⓔfscl@unwired.com.fj) on Edinburgh Drive in Suva for the latest schedules.

Salia Basaga Shipping (℡331 7484; F$175 one way includes meals) operates the *Tunatuki II*, an ageing Russian fishing boat captured by the Fijian government for illegal fishing. The vessel departs from Walu Bay in Suva three times a month along the following routes: Suva–Vanua Vatu–Lakeba–Oneata–Moce–Komo–Namuka–Suva; Suva–Yacata–Vanua Balavu–Tuvuca–Lakeba–Cicia–Nayau–Susui–Cikobia–Suva; and Suva–Moala–Totoya–Matuku–Suva.

Western Shipping (℡331 4467; deck F$98, cabin F$125) operates the *Cagi-mai-Ba* which departs from Walu Bay in Suva three times a month, rotating along the following routes: Suva–VanuaVatu–Lakeba–Oneata–Moce–Komo–Namuka–Suva; and Suva–Yacata–Vanua Balavu–Tuvuca–Lakeba–Cicia–Nayau–Susui–Cikobia–Suva.

Seaview Shipping (℡330 9515; F$100–115) runs *The Sandy* travelling once a month from Narain Jetty in Suva to the remote small islands of Southern Lau along the following route: Suva–Kabara–Fulaga–Ogea–Vatoa–Ono-i-Lau–Suva.

customs, with the local dialect formed mostly of Tongan words and bures following the rounded Tongan style of architecture.

There are no public buses or taxis on Vanua Balavu but the guesthouse in Lomaloma (see p.208) can arrange a vehicle for **sightseeing** for F$50 for half a day. On foot you can hike the 5km from Lomaloma to the southern tip of the island, passing the cliffs flanking Nakama village. Ask around for a guide to show you the **hot springs** and burial caves in the hills. It's possible to wade across a sand spit from the southern tip of Vanua Balavu to explore Malata island. Hugging Malata's southeast tip is Susui island, a favourite picnic spot with locals. The island has an inland lake where turtles can be spotted and the protected Raviravi Lagoon off its northern shore.

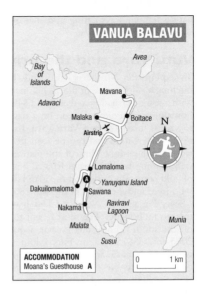

The **northern half** of Vanua Balavu beyond the grass airstrip is rocky with sharp limestone pinnacles along the coast and mostly inaccessible. The coastal road ends at Mavana village where the deposed prime minister, Laisania Qarase, comes from.

Practicalities

Vanua Balavu's **airstrip** and wharf are both located midway up the island. There's a weekly flight from Nausori (see p.207) and cargo boats stop here roughly three times a month. The only **official accommodation** is *Moana's Beach Bures* (☎889 5006; ✉moanas@connect.com.fj; standard bure F$65 per person, en-suite bure F$85 per person; includes meals) fifteen minutes' walk south of of Lomaloma on the southeast side of the island. The three simple beachside bures have mosquito nets, shared toilet, cold-water shower and solar power. You'll be well fed with local vegetables and fish although note there are also several small **stores** in Lomaloma village where you can buy snacks. *Moana's* can organize **village visits**, hiking trips and boat trips to both Raviravi Lagoon and the Bay of Islands (bring snorkelling gear).

The Bay of Islands

Off the northwestern tip of Vanua Balavu is the pretty **Bay of Islands**, known locally as Qilaqila, a collection of deep indented bays, islands and islets, secluded beaches and limestone caves with excellent snorkelling available in its brilliant turquoise lagoon. The bay makes an exceptional anchorage for visiting **yachts** between May and October (for permission to anchor, contact the government station in Lomaloma on VHF channel 16). The islands themselves are mostly impenetrable difficult to approach by boat and covered in a tangled mass of shrubs and ironwood trees. However, there are a couple of walking tracks worth exploring as well as easy access to **Vale ni Bose**, "the Meeting Place of the Gods". This huge cathedral cave, over forty metres high, is full of stalactites and has several windows letting in dashes of light – note that at high tide you'll be wading chest-high in water.

Vatu Vara and the private islands

To explore the Northern Lau islands **beyond Vanua Balavu,** you could try hitching a ride on one of the yachts anchored in the Bay of Islands. Alternatively, with a some persuasion and around F$400 in cash, you could ask a boatman from Lomaloma village to take you on a day-trip. One of the most dramatic islands to visit is forest-covered **Vatu Vara.** Its 305-metre plateau is the highest point in the Lau Group and can be seen from Vanua Balavu, 60km to the east. Up close, the limestone cliffs of the plateau cascade down to a coral terrace with rich farming land and palm-fringed beaches. It's rumoured that a treasure chest of gold coins was buried on the island by Joe Thompson, an American eccentric who lived and died here in the late 1800s.

Several islands in Northern Lau have been bought as **private islands** by foreign millionaires. The most recent to change hands is **Mago,** less than 20km off the south tip of Vanua Balavu, acquired by Hollywood star Mel Gibson in 2005 for US$15 million. Fifty kilometres west of Vanua Balavu are the twin islands of **Yacata** and **Kaimbu,** owned by Japanese investors. Kaimbu was once home to the most expensive resort in Fiji but it closed down shortly after the 2000 coup. Thirty kilometres northwest of Vanua Balavu, and a mere 60km from Taveuni (see Chapter 7) is **Naitauba,** once the island hideaway of 1970s actor Raymond Burr and now the "spiritual hermitage" of the Adi Dam religious cult.

Southern Lau

The diffuse islands of **Southern Lau** are the most remote in Fiji. The main island, **Lakeba,** administrative capital of the entire Lau Group, lies in its northern sphere leaving all islands to the south far removed from shipping and air services. The southernmost islands of Vatoa and Ono-i-Lau lie 200km south of Lakeba, a journey that can take several days by boat. The two most intriguing islands to

6

Lau crafts

The people of Southern Lau are renowned as fine **artisans**, with the women skilled makers of *tapa* cloth (see p.178) and the men, particularly from Kabara, well-known as the best **woodcarvers** in Fiji. You'll find examples of their work, mostly in the form of *tanoa* bowls, readily available in the handicraft markets around Suva or in the more expensive souvenir shops in Nadi. Unfortunately, most of the region's hardwood *vesi* trees – the best species for wood carving – have been cut down and the islanders are being encouraged to plant the faster-growing sandalwood, known locally as *yasi*, as an alternative.

As well as *tapa* cloth and woodcarving, Lau islanders produce the coarse twine known as **magimagi**. Commonly seen binding together bures, *magimagi* comes from the fibres of a coconut husk, baked in the sun, soaked in the sea and briskly rubbed together to make long threads. The threads are meticulously braided to form a strong twine, often several kilometres in length. *Magimagi* was once used to lash together the parts of a canoe, although today it is most often seen extending from a *tanoa* or *kava* bowl towards the person of highest rank; or attached to either end of a *tabua* or whale's tooth (see p.273).

visit are the Lakeba, rich in history and culture, and **Fulaga**, a rugged coral atoll with unusual limestone formations.

Lakeba

Lakeba, almost circular in shape with a diameter of 8km, has the region's only **airstrip** (connected by weekly flights from Nausori) and is the main link with the Fijian mainland. Before the Tongan conquest of Lau, Lakeba was the dominant power in the group, home to the *Tui Nayau* or "Lord of Nayau" which refers to a small island to the north. The most recent *Tui Nayau* was former prime minister Ratu Sir Kamisese Mara who also held the *Tui Lau* title created by Tongan prince Ma'afu.

The island's main village is **Tubou**, located on the southwest coast. With a population of around six hundred, it forms Lakeba's heartbeat and is home to the government and provincial headquarters, hospital, post office, several stores and jetty. The village has a strong Tongan influence with people living in rounded thatch bures and wearing *ta'avala* (woven mats) around the waist. The graveyard behind the provincial office has a small stepped platform where the Tongan prince and warrior **Ma'afu** lies buried.

A well-maintained dirt road hugs much of the flat **coastline** making it easy to get around by foot. Several impressive **caves** bearing stalagmites can be explored including Delaiono, south of Tubou on the southern tip, and Oso Nabukete along the uplifted west coast. Slightly inland, close to the airstrip, are more caves, originally used as refuges in times of war or for banishment. In the centre of the island is the largest **hillfort** in Fiji. Situated on top of the 360-metre Ketekete Peak, the fort was capable of sheltering over 2500 people, although today most of its stone walls lie buried in the undergrowth. Off the east coast is a myriad of tiny islands ideal for exploring by punt – you should be able to hire a boatman from the village of Nukunuku for around F$40 an hour.

You can **stay** on Lakeba at *Jeke Qica's Guesthouse* (☎820 1242; F$55 including local-style meals) in Tubou. Rooms within this family home are very basic and everyone shares the bathroom facilities. Alternatively, try the Lau Provincial Council in Tubou (☎822 0329) who will help arrange homestay accommodation – expect to pay F$50 per person per night for board and meals. You should present a *sevusevu* (see the *Visiting a Fijian village* colour section) when you arrive as your traditional request for assistance.

Fulaga

The crescent-shaped limestone island of **Fulaga** lies in the distant southern part of the group, 100km south of Lakeba. The low lying, three-tiered island has an unusual flooded basin in its centre which is littered with eroded mushroom-shaped rocks and cove beaches. There are three small villages on Fulaga but no accommodation. To visit from Lakeba, the Lau Provincial Council in Tubou can arrange a fibreglass boat to take you there for the day for around F$450. The journey across open sea takes ninety minutes. On the return leg you could ask to make a quick detour to the woodcarving centre of **Kabara**.

Travel details

With the exception of **Ovalau**, which is connected by regular flights and passenger ferries, transport in the Lomaiviti and Lau Groups is sporadic. **Flights** leave Nausori Airport on a weekly schedule and **cargo boats** depart from either Suva or the east coast of Viti Levu (see p.25 for full details on cargo boats).

Passenger ferries

Natovi Landing to: Buresala, Ovalau (4 weekly; 2hr 30min).
Waidalice Landing to: Caqalai (daily; 40min), Leleuvia (daily; 40min) and Yanuca Lailai (daily; 1hr).
Walu Bay, Suva to: Levuka, Ovalau (2 weekly; 6hr).

Cargo boats

Walu Bay, Suva to: Cicia, Northern Lau (2 monthly; 1–2 days); Fulaga, Southern Lau (monthly; 2 days); Lakeba, Southern Lau (3 monthly; 2-4 days); Moala, Moala Group (monthly; 1 day); Vanua Balavu, Northern Lau (2 monthly; 2 days).

Flights

Nausori Airport to: Cicia (weekly; 1hr); Gau (weekly; 30min); Koro (weekly; 35min); Lakeba (weekly; 1hr); Moala (weekly; 45min); Ovalau (2 daily; 15min); Vanua Balavu (weekly; 1hr).

Vanua Levu and Taveuni

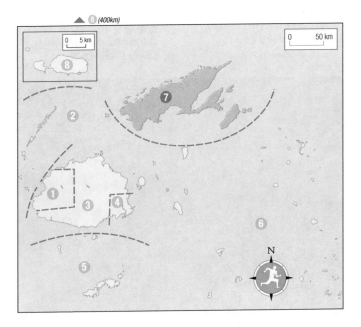

CHAPTER 7

Highlights

* **Labasa countryside** Mingle with the locals on an open-sided bus ride into the pretty Labasa hills. See p.222

* **Savusavu Yacht Club** Beautiful spot for a sundowner drink overlooking the bobbing yachts in Savusavu Bay. See p.224

* **Kioa and Rabi Islands** Sample two South Pacific cultures, one from Polynesia, the other from Micronesia, living on these adopted islands. See p.231

* **Rainbow Reef** Dive amongst world-renowned soft corals at this pristine section of reef between Vanua Levu and Taveuni. See p.231

* **Bouma National Heritage Park** Fiji's most varied national park offering walks, waterfalls, historical sites and a marine reserve. See p.240

* **Lake Tagimaucia** Spot the elusive orange dove or the even rarer Tagimaucia flower at this mountain lake on Taveuni. See p.246

▲ Suspension bridge, Buoma National Heritage Park

Vanua Levu and Taveuni

The northern islands of **Vanua Levu** and **Taveuni** are Fiji's forgotten frontier. Once the centre of European exploration and the ensuing copra (coconut oil) trade, they are far removed from mainstream tourism and offer a great opportunity for **adventure travel**. Vanua Levu, Fiji's second largest island at 5587 square kilometres, is dominated by rambling countryside and has just two towns, Labasa and Savusavu. **Labasa** has a hilly rural hinterland worth exploring by bus while the serene yachting anchorage of **Savusavu** boasts quaint drinking holes and restaurants as well as plenty of nearby hikes and snorkelling beaches. Off Vanua Levu's east coast is the rugged, forest-covered Taveuni, the third largest island in Fiji, yet not even a tenth the size of its neighbour. Dubbed the "Garden Island", Taveuni is dominated by the stunning **Bouma National Heritage Park**, a magnet for hikers and bird-watching enthusiasts.

Between the two islands is one of the world's best **dive sites**, the Rainbow Reef, while off Vanua Levu's north shore is the **Great Sea Reef**, the world's third largest coral reef system covering over two hundred thousand square kilometres.

Vanua Levu and Taveuni are often dubbed "The Friendly North" owing to the hospitality of the region's people, although the reality of life here is not quite so sweet. Battered by **hurricanes** and flooding in recent years and hit by the falling prices of both sugar and copra, the islands offer few opportunities for the younger generation, many of whom have moved to Viti Levu in search of work. **Tourism** is the region's greatest hope although it is hindered by the lack of infrastructure, particularly sealed roads and long runways capable of handling jets. A recent real-estate boom around Savusavu has given some local land-owning Fijians hope of riches but most profits from developments tend to end up abroad.

Arrival and inter-island transport

Vanua Levu and Taveuni are served by passenger ferries and flights from Viti Levu. It's relatively simple to combine a trip to **both islands** with most ferry routes calling in at both Vanua Levu and Taveuni. Ten days should give plenty of time to get a feel for the islands; one itinerary would be to arrive by plane in Labasa, travel by bus to Savusavu and then over to Taveuni by boat. For those on

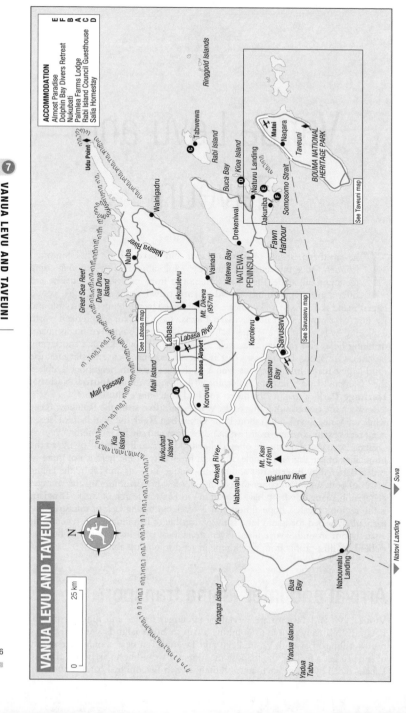

VANUA LEVU AND TAVEUNI

ACCOMMODATION	
Almost Paradise	E
Dolphin Bay Divers Retreat	F
Nukubati	B
Palmlea Farms Lodge	A
Rabi Island Council Guesthouse	C
Salia Homestay	D

N

0 — 25 km

Ringgold Islands

Udu Point

Tabwewa C

Rabi Island

Wainigadru

NASEVA RIVER

Nuba

Great Sea Reef

Drua Drua Island

Lekutulevu

Labasa

Labasa River

See Labasa map

Mali Island

Mali Passage

Kia Island

Nukubati Island

Korovuli

A

B

Dreketi River

Nabavalu

Mt. Kasi (416m)

Wainunu River

Yaqaga Island

Yadua Island

Yadua Tabu

Bua Bay

Nabouwalu Landing

Natovi Landing ▶

Suva ▶

Mt. Dikeva (957m)

Vainadi

Natewa Bay

NATEWA PENINSULA

Drekeniwai

Buca Bay

Koa Island

Natuvu Landing D

Dakuniba E F

Somosomo Strait

Fawn Harbour

Korolevu

Savusavu

Savusavu Bay

See Savusavu map

Labasa Airport

Matei

Naqara

Taveuni

BOUMA NATIONAL HERITAGE PARK

See Taveuni map

a tighter schedule, Air Fiji has direct daily flights between Savusavu and Matei on Taveuni (see below).

Ferries

Passenger ferries to the islands depart from Lautoka, Suva and Natovi Landing (on the east coast of Viti Levu). Ferries from Natovi Landing offer the fastest journey time (3hr 30min) although they arrive at the remote Nabouwalu Landing on the west coast of Vanua Levu. Most travellers prefer to head direct to Savusavu. Seas are often rough, particularly across the perpetually choppy Bligh Waters – ferries from Suva or Natovi miss the worst of this section. Two small **inter-island ferries** connect the islands across Buca Bay with services starting in Taveuni, crossing over to Vanua Levu where they pick up passengers from Savusavu and Labasa for the return leg.

Bligh Water Shipping ☎ 666 8229 in Lautoka; ☎ 885 3191 in Savusavu. Operates two aged vessels: the *MV Suilven* departs Lautoka twice a week for Savusavu via Natovi Landing (Wed 7pm, Sun 11pm; 11hr 30min; F$63); and the *MV Westerland* departs Suva three times a week for Savusavu and Taveuni (Mon & Wed 6pm, Fri 4pm; Savusavu F$63, Taveuni F$73). Travel between Savusavu and Taveuni costs F$42 one way and takes four and a half hours.

Consort Shipping ☎ 331 3266 in Suva, ☎ 881 1454 in Labasa; ☎ 885 0279 in Savusavu. Operates the comfortable two-hundred-passenger *MV SOFI* departing Suva for Savusavu (12hr; F$55, cabin bunk F$82) on Mon & Fri at 6pm, and Wed at 1pm, stopping on the way at Koro island on the Wed & Fri runs and connecting on to Taveuni (16hr; F$64, cabin bunk F$92) on the Mon & Fri runs. Charter buses meet passengers arriving at Savusavu Wharf for connections to Labasa Town. Travel between Savusavu and Taveuni costs F$37 one way and takes 4hr 30min.

Patterson Brothers ☎ 666 1173 in Lautoka, ☎ 881 2444 in Labasa. Daily ferry departing 7am from Natovi Landing, 60km north of Suva and crossing Bligh Water to Nabouwalu (3hr 30min;

F$45) on the southwest tip of Vanua Levu. A charter bus connects between Nabouwalu and Labasa (2hr 30min; F$10).

Inter-island ferries

Grace Shipping ☎ 885 0320. Departs from the Korean Wharf at Lovonivonu on Taveuni at 8.45am (daily except Sat) crossing over Buca Bay to Natuvu Landing on the eastern tip of Vanua Levu (1hr 30min; F$10). A bus departing Savusavu at 7.15am reaches Natuvu Landing at 10.15am in time for passengers to catch the ferry back to Taveuni; the bus also picks up passengers from Taveuni and drops them into Savusavu (3hr; F$10) or Labasa (5hr; F$15).

Venu Shipping ☎ 885 0466 in Savusavu, ☎ 820 3391 in Taveuni. Departs from Wairiki Wharf in Taveuni at 9am on Mon, Wed, Fri and Sat crossing to Natuvu Landing on the eastern tip of Vanua Levu (1hr 30min; F$14). A bus from Savusavu (departing at 7.30am) arrives at Natuvu Landing at 10.30am in time for passengers to catch the ferry back to Taveuni; the same bus picks up passengers alighting from Taveuni and drops them into Savusavu (3hr; F$10).

Flights

Flights to the islands are in small propeller planes from either Nadi or Suva. Note that seats often fill up quickly, especially when dive groups and their equipment take over the entire plane so book as far in advance as possible. The baggage allowance is twenty kilos per person so call ahead if you are bringing your own scuba gear.

Air Fiji ☎ 331 3666 in Suva, ☎ 881 1188 in Labasa, ☎ 885 0538 in Savusavu, ⓦ www.airfiji .com.fj. Operate fifteen-seater planes with four flights to Labasa from Nausori (35min; F$238) and another four into Savusavu, two from Nadi Airport (1hr; F$233) and two from Nausori (45min; F$171).

The two flights from Nadi continue on to Taveuni (1hr 30min; F$281) and fly back again to Savusavu providing the only direct flights between Vanua Levu and Taveuni (20min; F$128). There are also two daily flights direct to Taveuni from Nausori (45min; F$210).

Pacific Sun ☎672 3555, ⓦwww.pacificsun .com.fj. Offers three daily flights to Labasa in a 44-seater ATR, one from Nadi Airport (1hr 5min; F$178–250) and two from Suva (45min; F$152– $210); or three daily flights to Savusavu (1hr; F$165–245) and two daily flights to Taveuni (1hr 20min; F$199) in small 9-seater twin-propeller Twin Otters from Nadi Airport.

Tui Tai Adventure Cruise

One of the best ways to explore Vanua Levu and Taveuni is on the luxurious ⚓**Tui Tai Adventure Cruise** (☎885 3032, ⓦwww.tuitai.com; five nights from US$2500 per person, seven nights from US$3250 per person, includes meals and activities). The cruise takes place on a 42-metre, three-masted schooner with air-conditioned cabins, en-suite bathrooms, spa treatments and on-deck daybeds. Along the way you can **dolphin-watch** off Vanua Levu, snorkel or dive the **Great Sea Reef** and kayak up the mangrove-lined Nasavu River to a remote village. Probably the only time you'll run into other travellers is on the visit to Bouma National Heritage Park on Taveuni. The cruise also calls in at the gloriously remote **Ringgold Islands** and the fascinating cultural enclaves of Kioa and Rabi (see p.231). Pre-booked guests are picked up from both Savusavu on Vanua Levu and Matei on Taveuni.

Vanua Levu

VANUA LEVU is about half the size of its big brother Viti Levu but in terms of tourist facilities it pales by comparison. There are few white sandy beaches and little accommodation outside of Labasa and Savusavu, which are connected by the island's only sealed road. However, the lack of other tourists makes it a joy to explore, especially on an inland bus ride, and the spectacular setting of Savusavu Bay is worth the trip alone.

As with Viti Levu there are distinct leeward and windward sides to the island. The dry north coast is strewn with sugarcane farms, pine forests and mangroves with the Fiji-Indian dominated **Labasa Town** as its focal point while the hillier south is dominated by tropical rainforest and huge coastal coconut plantations. Midway along the south coast is **Savusavu**, a picturesque sailing town which makes a lovely base for a few days.

Three remarkable islands lie off Vanua Levu's coast – **Yadua Taba** to the west, home to the endemic crested iguana, while to the east, facing Taveuni, are the two culturally unique islands of **Rabi** and **Kioa**, each home to a displaced South Pacific community.

Some history

Vanua Levu was the site of the initial European rush into Fiji in the early nineteenth century fuelled by the discovery of **sandalwood** in Bua Bay on the southwestern coast of the island. Opportunist merchants from Port Jackson (Sydney) and London first began arriving in 1804, loading up with sandalwood before sailing on to the ports of Asia, where it was sold at a great profit. In return the Fijian landowners received muskets, pans, mirrors and other trinkets until every tract of the prized resource had been cut down.

During the 1860s more Europeans began to arrive, this time in search of land for the **cotton trade**. The chief of Vanua Levu and Taveuni, Tui Cakau, sold fifty thousand acres of fertile land on Vanua Levu to European traders at just two shillings per acre. The balance was paid in the form of credit to buy liquor and luxury goods from the new landowners. After the collapse of cotton prices at the end of the 1860s, the Europeans switched to the **copra trade** which flourished until the 1940s. Huge areas of coconut plantations still stand tall amongst the coastal landscape and a few die-hard *kai loma* planters, mixed-blood descendents of the original Europeans, continue to eke out a living from the crop. Recently some of the old European and *kai loma* families have begun to carve up their huge plantations, selling them off in small chunks to **expat investors**. The most popular properties are located around Savusavu which has seen prices rise to as much as F$200,000 (US$133,000) an acre.

Labasa and around

The hot and dusty market centre of **LABASA** on Vanua Levu's north coast is the largest town outside of Viti Levu but receives virtually no tourists. On the outskirts is the town's lifeline, the Labasa Sugar Mill, which perpetually hisses, creaks and bellows out smoke during the sugar crushing season between May and December. Labasa's surrounding hilly **countryside** is the main attraction for visitors and exploring this area by open-sided bus offers great mountain vistas. Also nearby are two resorts with diving access to the fabulous, unchartered **Great Sea Reef**.

Arrival, orientation and transport

Labasa Airport, which features the only tarmac runway outside Viti Levu, is located 10km southwest of town. Taxis into the centre of Labasa cost F$10; minivans (every 30min; 5.45am–5pm) pass along the main road near the terminal and cost 95 cents to Labasa. Labasa's port at Malau is 8km east of town and generally open only for container ships. **Ferry passengers** arriving at Nabouwalu are met by a connecting bus to Labasa. All public **buses** pull in at the Labasa bus stand, adjacent to the Municipal Market at the eastern end of town.

Labasa is a small town and most places are within walking distance. **Taxis** cost twenty cents per 200m within the town area plus a flag fall of F$1. There is no **tourist information** and hotel staff are pretty clueless about onward transport

Moving on from Labasa

From Labasa there are regular buses to **Savusavu** (6 daily; F$6.75; 2hr 30min) heading west along the Seaqaqa Highway. You can also reach Savusavu the long way round via **Natewa Bay**. This route follows the sealed Wainikoro–Dama Road east of Labasa and then switches to dirt roads through the mountains to Wainigadru village. From Wainigadru another dirt road heads south along the coast to Savusavu. A daily service run by Waiqele Buses covers the route, leaving Labasa at 9am and arriving in Savusavu at around 4.30pm (7hr 30min). Heading from Labasa to the Patterson Brothers ferry terminal at **Nabouwalu** takes around five hours by bus (departures 6.30am, 10.30am, 1pm & 2pm; F$8.30).

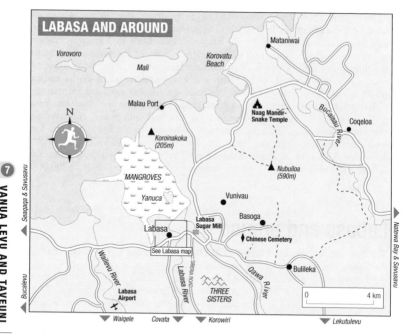

LABASA AND AROUND

Vorovoro

Mali

Mataniwai

Korovatu Beach

Malau Port

N

Naag Mandir-
Snake Temple

Coqeloa

Bucaisau River

Koroinakoka
(205m)

MANGROVES

Yanuca

Nubuiloa
(590m)

Vunivau

Basoga

Labasa
Sugar Mill

Labasa

See Labasa map

Chinese Cemetery

Wailevu River

Labasa River

SIBERIA ROAD

Qawa River

Bulileka

Labasa
Airport

THREE
SISTERS

0   4 km

Waiqele   Covata   Korowiri   Lekutulevu

Seaqaqa & Savusavu

VANUA LEVU AND TAVEUNI | Labasa and around

Bucalevu

Natewa Bay & Savusavu

and attractions. The best bet for exploring the surrounding rural area is to take
a **bus journey** (see p.223) or rent a car if you are on Vanua Levu for a while
(see "Listings"). If hiring a taxi to tour the countryside, you should negotiate a
price before departing – try the friendly Anthony John on ☎938 5387. Expect
to pay F$15–20 for an hour's tour or F$80 to Savusavu (5hr).

Accommodation

Labasa's five **hotels** are mostly aimed at Fijians travelling on business. You shouldn't
have a problem finding a room and discounted rates are usually available at
weekends. If you're looking for a quieter base, consider *Palmlea Farm Lodge* (see
p.223), 14km west of town, overlooking the ocean.

Centrepoint 24 Nasekula Rd ☎881 1057,
ⓔ centerp@connect.com.fj. Small budget hotel
located upstairs at the busy east end of Nasekula
Rd. The twelve a/c rooms with en-suite hot-water
showers are pretty basic with lumpy beds but are
cheap for its central location. ❷
Friendly North Inn Siberia Rd ☎881 1555,
ⓔ fni@connect.com.fj. Not quite as far out of
town as its address suggests, but still a 20min
walk. This is the best option if you're staying
awhile as most of the sixteen duplex cottage
rooms have kitchenettes. There's a pleasant
garden, bar and restaurant and the Labasa
swimming pool is a short walk along the road
past the hospital. ❷

Grand Eastern Hotel Gibson St ☎881 1022,
ⓔ grest@connect.com.fj. Labasa's smartest hotel,
popular with business people – you should get
walk-in rates at weekends or quiet periods. The 24
rooms are a little tired but the setting is lovely, in a
quiet cul-de-sac close to the busy bus stand. The
hotel has a swimming pool and slightly expensive
restaurant and bar. 24hr reception. ❸–❹
Riverview Private Hotel Nadawa St ☎881 1367.
Pleasant house overlooking the river a 15min walk
north of town past the police station. The spacious
dorm room has five single beds and a private
balcony but the private rooms are a bit poky with
dingy bathrooms and no hot water. Dorm F$20,
rooms ❷

The Town

Labasa is the administrative centre of Vanua Levu and has a purposeful bustle during the day. By sundown, though, with the departure of the last local bus, the streets become deserted. The town centre is flanked on its west side by the flood-prone Labasa River, which flows 5km north to the coast through mangrove forest. Beside the Labasa bridge is the delightful **Municipal Market** (Mon–Fri 7.30am–4.45pm, Sat 7am–1pm) a good place to mingle with the locals. In the small park overlooking the river are six small open-sided huts where locals gather to drink *yaqona* – you can join in by offering a F$1 donation towards the grog bowl.

Heading east from the bridge is Labasa's main street, **Nasekula Road**, lined by colourful Fiji-Indian shops. The busiest spot along the street is Dragon Entertainment, a pool hall with blaring reggae music where Fijians and Fiji-Indians congregate. Two shops down is the Elite Cinema, which shows Indian films only. South of the bus stand, a pleasant **riverside walk** leads from Reddy Place to Guru Nanak School beside Nacula village. From the village you can head back to Nasekula Road via Vunimoli Road.

Eating and drinking

Colonial Arms Grand Eastern Hotel, Gibson St. If you're after decent European cuisine, this is the only place to go with salads and beef burgers at lunch and a full mixed grill, steaks and pizzas for dinner. Mains F$20–30. Daily 7–9.30am, 11.30am–2pm & 4–10pm.

Oriental Bar and Restaurant Upstairs, Jaduram St. Labasa's best place to eat out, this a/c Chinese restaurant has pleasant decor and background music and serves over two hundred dishes from *chilli taufu* (F$7) to pizzas (F$9). It's also a popular bar with beer served by the jug. Come early at lunchtime to get one of the window tables overlooking the bus stand. Mon–Sat 10am–3pm & 6.30–10pm, Sun 6.30–10pm.

PPK Punjabi Foods Upstairs in Ali Arcade, Nasekula Rd. Pakistani restaurant in a simple café setting serving goat *khada-he-ghosh*, a pungent creamy curry, for F$6, *shahi dahl* for F$4.50 and *zarda palau*, a sweet orange flavoured rice with chicken and chick peas, for F$3. Mon–Sat 8am–7pm.

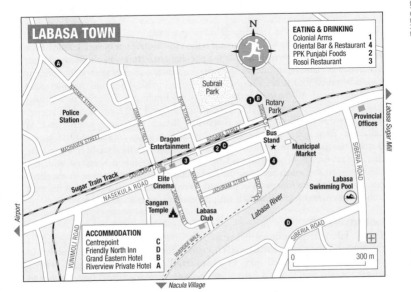

Rosoi Restaurant 30 Nasekula Rd. Pick of the many cheap Indian restaurants serving curries and chow meins. This one has pleasant wooden tables and serves well-made curries with dhal with huge plates of rice. Also makes refreshing milkshakes and cakes. Mon–Sat 6.30am–6.30pm.

Listings

Airlines Air Fiji, Corner of Nasekula Rd and Nanuku St ☎881 1188, Mon–Fri 8am–4.30pm, Sat 8am–noon; Pacific Sun Corner of Nasekula Rd and Damann St, ☎881 1454, Mon–Fri 8am–5pm, Sat 8am–noon, also agents for Air New Zealand and Air Pacific.

Banking ANZ, Corner of Nasekula Rd and Gibson St, Mon 9.30am–4pm, Tue–Fri 9am–4pm; Westpac, Corner of Nasekula Rd and Sangam Ave, Mon–Thurs 9.30am–3pm, Fri 9.30am–4pm; both with ATMs.

Car rental Carpenters Motors ☎881 1522 on Rosawa St has the cheapest 4WD Jeeps at F$200 per day (limited selection). At Vanua Rentals ☎881 3512 in the Mobil station (Corner of Nanuku and Jadaram sts) starting from F$240 per day; or Budget ☎881 1999 at Vakamaisuasua Industrial, a few kilometres west of town.

Doctors Singh's Medical Centre, Reddy Lane ☎881 3824, Mon–Fri 8am–4pm and Sat 8am–noon.

Hospital Northern District Hospital off Siberia Rd on the east side of the river ☎881 1444. Open 24hr.

Internet access Govinda's, Nasekula Rd next to Pacific Sun has twelve terminals and serves coffee, Mon–Sat 8am–7pm, Sun 5–7pm.

Pharmacy My Chemist, 5 Nasekula Rd ☎881 4611, Mon–Thurs 8am–6pm, Fri 8am–7pm, Sat 8am–3pm, Sun 9.30–11am.

Police ☎881 1222, Nadawa St, open 24hr.

Post office Nasekula Rd, Mon–Fri 7.30am–4.30pm, Sat 8am–noon.

Telephone plenty outside the post office, although you'll need a calling card. Skype calls are available from Govinda's.

Around Labasa

Some of the most attractive countryside around Labasa lies to the east of the sugar mill across the Qawa River. Past the river, the main Wainikoro–Dama road turns north towards the coast. Five kilometres along is the turn-off for **Malau Port**, protected by the large offshore island of Mali. Hugging the eastern tip of Mali is the island of **Vorovoro**, home to the *Tribe Wanted* (Ⓦ www.tribewanted.com) community tourism project. The brainchild of English Web entrepreneurs, the project has successfully blended an online and real-life community by building an eco-friendly village that aspiring tribe members can visit by buying time slots (seven nights £180/US$350, not including transfers).

Six kilometres past the Malau turn-off is the Hindu shrine of Naag Mandir, better known as the **snake temple**. Inside is a peculiar attraction – a cobra-shaped rock that devotees claim has grown by 3m over the space of seventy years – the roof has had to be raised four times. Visitors are welcome to visit the shrine (remove shoes before entering). All Parmod buses from Labasa heading to Coqeloa or Matawai pass the temple (30min; F$1.15); a taxi should cost F$10. Two hundred metres past the temple is the turn-off to **Korovatu Beach**, the nearest sandy beach to Labasa. It's 3km from the main road to the beach and cars are charged F$5 access. Beyond the turn-off, the main road continues in a perfectly straight line for 3km, the longest stretch of straight road in Fiji. The surrounding **scenery** with big mountains to the south and unusual rocky outcrops to the north is an excellent place to **explore** by foot, with opportunities to wander along dusty roads through Indian settlements and climb hills for panoramic views.

Lekutulevu

Twelve kilometres south from Labasa, accessible along the Bulileka Road, is the remote village of **Lekutulevu**. The village has a simple bamboo church and offers a delightful guided hike to a **waterfall** (one hour; local guide F$10). Along the way you'll pass a natural stone *tanoa* (drinking bowl) three metres in

Hopping on and off Labasa's charming **open-sided buses** is a great way to see the countryside and meet the locals The following routes are highly recommended, each departing hourly from Labasa bus stand from 6am to 6pm with increased services during peak hours:

Labasa to Basoga or **Vunivau** (Northern Buses; 20min; 85 cents). After passing the sugar mill and turning left up Valebasoga Road, get off the bus at the brow of the hill before the Chinese Cemetery. Walk towards the telecommunication tower (15min), following the ridge for stunning mountain views. Head back down via the tower access road, past Indian houses to Bulileka Road (20min). From here, frequent buses head back into Labasa.

Labasa to Coqeloa (Parmod Buses; 50min; F$1.35). This route passes the sugar mill, snake temple and travels through Indian sugarcane settlements around the Bucaisau River Valley. Plenty of dirt roads branch out from the valley making tempting walking diversions amongst beautiful mountain scenery.

diameter which is reputed to be used by the ancient god Dakuwaqa. A thirty-minute detour from the waterfall leads to the summit of **Mount Uluinamolo** from where you can see Taveuni on a clear day. The road to Lekutulevu is extremely rough – regular **buses** run to the village from Labasa (daily except Sun; 7am, 10am & 2.45pm; F$3.20) taking over an hour – if the road is bad, the bus stops at Dreketilialia and you'll need to walk the remaining 4km.

West of Labasa: The Great Sea Reef

Fourteen kilometres west of Labasa the tar-sealed Wainikoro–Dama Road branches towards the coast at Tabia to the remote *Palmlea Farm Lodge* **eco-resort** (T 828 2220, W www.palmleafarms.com; ⑤–⑦, includes breakfast). The resort grows its own organic fruit and vegetables and has three spacious bures, all overlooking the ocean. Although there is no dive operator on site, scuba diving can be arranged to explore the **Great Sea Reef** which boasts 44 percent of Fiji's endemic marine life. Better access to this massive reef system is available from the private island retreat of *Nukubati Island* (T 881 3901, W www.nukubati.com; ⑨), accessed from a jetty further along the coast. This upmarket resort is aimed at honeymooners and divers and offers seven luxury bures. Currently, this is the only place that provides access to the recently discovered **surfing breaks** around Kia Island, forty minutes by boat to the north in the far reaches of the Great Sea Reef.

Savusavu and around

SAVUSAVU, Vanua Levu's main tourist centre, is a small one-street town squeezed between rolling hills and a silvery ocean. Sitting alongside a bay that was once a giant volcano and protected by three small islands entwined in mangroves, Savusavu is Fiji's most popular anchorage for visiting **yachts**. With several excellent **restaurants** and bars, splendid walks in the hills and fabulous nearby snorkelling at Lesiaceva Point, the town makes for a pleasant short stay. For many, a brief visit has turned into a lifelong obsession. Charmed by the relaxed and slightly eccentric atmosphere, many expats have bought land here and built their dream home in the hills.

From Savusavu, the sedate **Hibiscus Highway** passes old coconut plantations, hugging the south coast of Vanua Levu while to the west are two picturesque waterfalls hidden amongst tropical rainforests, one at the village of Vuadomo, the other at the **Waisali Nature Reserve**.

Arrival, information and transport

Flying in to **Savusavu Airport** involves a dramatic descent over the hills to land at a short runway fronting the ocean. Both Air Fiji and Pacific Sun fly in daily from Nadi and Suva. It's a five-minute ride from the airport to town; buses run hourly (85 cents) otherwise a taxi will cost F$3. Passenger and car **ferries** arrive at Savusavu Wharf a five-minute walk west of the town centre. If you are arriving by **private yacht** you should contact Customs House (☎885 0727, VHF16; Mon–Fri 8am–1pm & 2–5pm) on the west side of Main Street. There are three privately run **marinas** running east–west: Waitui Marina (☎885 0536, ⓔwaituimarina@connect.com.fj), The Copra Shed (☎885 0457, ⓔcoprashed @connect.com.fj) and Bosun's Locker (☎885 0122, ⓔcurly@connect.com.fj). All offer moorings costing from F$8 to F$12 per day depending on the season with weekly and monthly rates available.

There is no official tourist information centre in Savusavu but the **Savusavu Tourism Association** (ⓦwww.fiji-savusavu.com) distributes a brochure on the town which you can pick up from **Trip N Tour** (☎885 3154; Mon–Fri 9am–4.30pm, Sat 9am–noon) in the Copra Shed Marina. The helpful staff here can book the few organized tours available (see p.228). There's also a useful information board at *Seaview Café* on the west end of Main Street.

A good time to visit is during **Savusavu Festival Week** in November when local arts, music and culture are promoted. Other annual events include the Hindu Krishna Lele Festival, which features fire walking and is held at the Khemendra School just before Christmas, and the Savusavu Triathlon held in September/October (contact Sharon at *Naveria Heights Lodge* for details).

Transport

Walking is practical around town but to visit Lesiaceva Point it's best to hire a **taxi** (F$2 to *Daku Resort* or F$6 to *Cousteau Resort*) or take the Vishnu bus (7.15am, noon & 4pm; 20min; 65 cents). All buses depart from the Savusavu **bus stand** on Main Street. The best way to explore the Hibiscus Highway and Natewa Peninsula is by **renting a car**. Trip N Tour (☎885 3154) are agents for

---

Fijian crested iguanas

The seldom seen **Fijian crested iguana** (*brachylopphus vitiensis*) is one of the few large reptiles living in the South Pacific and found only on a handful of islands in Fiji. Averaging forty centimetres in length (split evenly between body and tail), they are distinguished from the more common and slightly smaller banded iguana by three thin white stripes around the body and a mohican style head-dress. If aroused, their skin turns from a pale green colour to jet black. These fascinating creatures were first discovered by Australian zoologist John Gibbons in 1979 on the tiny island of **Yadua Taba** which nuzzles its larger sister Yadua 20km off the western tip of Vanua Levu. The 170-acre uninhabited island, declared as Fiji's first wildlife reserve in 1981, is home to around twelve thousand crested iguanas who eat the leaves and flowers of the island's wild hibiscus trees. Other habitats include Monuriki in the Mamanucas and several small islands in the Yasawas, although populations at these locations are small. The only way to **visit** Yadua Taba is on a scientific research project, but you can view the iguanas without disturbing their natural habitat at Kula Eco Park on the Coral Coast (see p.128). For more information see ⓦwww.icffci.com.

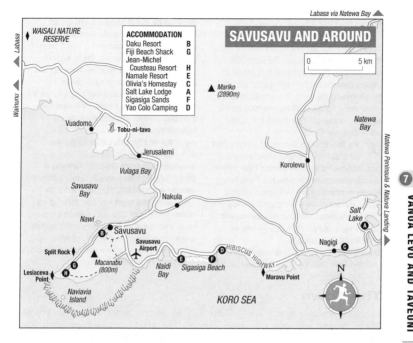

SAVUSAVU AND AROUND

ACCOMMODATION
Daku Resort	**B**
Fiji Beach Shack	**G**
Jean-Michel Cousteau Resort	**H**
Namale Resort	**E**
Olivia's Homestay	**C**
Salt Lake Lodge	**A**
Sigasiga Sands	**F**
Yao Colo Camping	**D**

0   5 km

WAISALI NATURE RESERVE

Labasa

Wainunu

Vuadomo

Tobu-ni-tavo

Jerusalemi

Vulaga Bay

Savusavu Bay

Nakula

Nawi

Savusavu

Savusavu Airport

Split Rock

Lesiaceva Point

Naviavia Island

Macanabu (800m)

Naidi Bay

Sigasiga Beach

Mariko (2890m)

Natewa Bay

Korolevu

Salt Lake

Nagigi

HIBISCUS HIGHWAY

Maravu Point

KORO SEA

N

Natewa Peninsula & Natuva Landing

7

VANUA LEVU AND TAVEUNI | Savusavu and around

Carpenters Motors and rent out small 4WD vehicles for F$110 per day. They also offer scooters (F$50 per day) although these are suitable only for driving along the sealed section of road which extends for the first 20km. Otherwise try Budget Rentals (☎881 1999, Mon–Fri 8am–4.30pm, Sat 8am–1pm) in the *Bula Re Café* at the east side of town.

Accommodation

Accommodation in Savusavu ranges from basic guesthouses in town to the lavish *Cousteau Resort* out on the point. Hotels in **Savusavu town** are dull but adequate for exploring the restaurants and sometimes rowdy bars. Staying in the **hills** or along the **point** is a lot more interesting and only a few dollars' taxi ride away.

Savusavu town

Hidden Paradise West Main St ☎885 0106. Just west of the Copra Shed, this guesthouse has a handy location and is the only place with a backpacker atmosphere. Unfortunately the six shared-facility rooms are tiny and mostly window-less and the dorm opens directly into the lounge. Dorm F$25, rooms ❷, includes breakfast.

Hot Springs Hotel off Kabana Rd ☎885 0195, ⓦ www.savusavufiji.com. This four-storey cement block hotel isn't the most attractive building in town but the views from the top two floors are great. Rooms are uninspiring but there's a pool, restaurant and 24hr reception. Heavily discounted walk-in rates are often available and a few of the rooms have been converted into four-bed dorms. Dorm F$36, rooms. ❸–❺

Savusavu Budget Lodge West Main St ☎885 3127, ⓔssvbudgetlodge@connect.com.fj. Located at the quiet west end of town and above the owners' tiny Indian restaurant, this affordable lodge has simple rooms, most with air con, tiny TV and small en-suite hot-water shower rooms. ❶–❷

Waterfront Apartment East Main St ☎885 0307, ⓔcafebulare2001@connect.com.fj. Open-plan self-contained apartment above the *Bula Re Café* with air con, kitchen, hot-water bathroom and a view over the veranda roof to the bay. Great spot for long stays, and discounted rates are given. ❸

Savusavu Hills and Lesiaceva Point

Daku Resort 1km along Lesiaceva Point Rd ☏ 885 0046, ⓦ www.dakuresort.com. Excellent-value lodge rooms, cottages and bures built around a swimming pool in spacious landscaped gardens and overlooking the ocean. This versatile resort specializes in holiday study courses featuring bird watching, singing, poetry and local craft. Lodge rooms ❷, bures ❹–❺

Fiji Beach Shack 6km along Lesiaceva Point Rd ☏ 885 1002, ⓦ www.fijibeachshacks .com. Boutique holiday home blending Fijian architecture with contemporary furnishings and with two en-suite bedrooms on split levels, one boasting a Jacuzzi with ocean views. The house is perched on a steep hill one hundred steps up from the road with fabulous views overlooking the bay – handy for snorkelling at Split Rock. ❻

Jean–Michel Cousteau Fiji Islands Resort Lesiaceva Point ☏ 885 0188, ⓦ www.fijiresort.com.

Owned by the son of Jacques Cousteau, this luxurious and environmentally sensitive resort boasts 25 beautifully hand-crafted thatch bures plus a fabulously opulent villa. The beach isn't great, but there's fine snorkelling off the pier and kids are spoilt with their own play centre, swimming pool and personalized carers. As you'd expect, scuba diving is brilliantly managed and there also are well-organized kayaking and waterfall trips. ❾

Naveria Heights Lodge Council Ave, Savusavu Hills ☏ 885 0348, ⓦ www .naveriaheightsfiji.com. Delightful homestay in the hills offering two rooms with a view featuring polished wooden floors. It's a steep and puffy 15min walk uphill to get here from town but the owners happily pick up guests. A healthy, homemade breakfast is served on the wooden veranda which has serene views over the bay and a hammock to relax in; other meals can be cooked on request. ❸, includes breakfast.

The Town

Savusavu town is strung along Ratu Suliano Street, better known simply as **Main Street** and split into two sections. The commercial centre with the bus stand, municipal market, post office, banks and shops lies to the east; this area springs to life on Fridays and Saturdays with an influx of visitors from the countryside. To the west is the **Copra Shed Marina** which marks the beginning of the town's quieter quarters where Main Street hugs the foreshore. Here you'll find the **Yacht Club** which has beautiful views overlooking the bay across to distant blue-tinted mountains. You can sip a drink at the water's edge here, eat at one of two lovely waterfront restaurants or shop for local arts in the posh boutiques nearby. Two hundred metres further on, turning up Nakama Road and across from the playing field on the left, are Savusavu's **hot springs**. The three small bubbling pools are too hot to bathe in and are often full of sacks of *dalo* being slowly cooked. The boiling water trickles into a small stream below the pools where it cools sufficiently to dip a toe in. A little further west along the gritty beachfront is the jetty for the **pearl farm** at Nawi Island. To visit the underwater farm and learn about the unique multi-hued pearl production in Savusavu Bay, contact J Hunter Pearls

Moving on from Savusavu

From Savusavu there are regular **buses** (6 daily; F$6.75; 2hr 30min) to **Labasa** heading north via Waisali Nature Reserve and Seaqaqa. You can also reach Labasa via Natewa Bay, a rough journey with Waiqele Buses departing Savusavu at 9am and reaching Labasa around 4.30pm. For those heading east along the **Hibiscus Highway**, Vishnu Buses depart Savusavu bus stand for Nabuka on Buca Bay (3 daily; F$6.65; 4hr). Those travelling to **Taveuni** by small passenger **ferry** with either Grace Shipping (daily except Sat) or Venu Shipping (Mon, Wed, Fri & Sat) can catch a charter bus departing Savusavu bus stand at 7.15am to Natuvu Landing where the ferry departs for its 1hr 30min journey across the Somosomo Straits to the west coast of Taveuni.

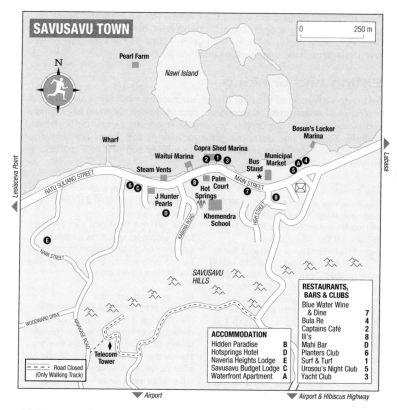

SAVUSAVU TOWN

0 — 250 m

N

Pearl Farm

Nawi Island

Bosun's Locker Marina

Wharf

Copra Shed Marina

Waitui Marina ❷ ❶ ❸

Municipal Market ❹ ❹

Steam Vents

Bus Stand ❺

Leslaceva Point

RATU SULIANO STREET

MAIN STREET

Labasa

❻ ❼

❼ Palm Court

Hot Springs

J Hunter Pearls ❹

Khemendra School

HIGH STREET

❽

NAWI STREET

SAVUSAVU HILLS

RESTAURANTS, BARS & CLUBS
Blue Water Wine
& Dine   **7**
Bula Re   **4**
Captains Café   **2**
Ili's   **8**
Mahi Bar   **D**
Planters Club   **6**
Surf & Turf   **1**
Urosou's Night Club   **5**
Yacht Club   **3**

WOODWARD DRIVE

NAWASE ROAD

Telecom Tower

- - - - Road Closed
(Only Walking Track)

ACCOMMODATION
Hidden Paradise   **B**
Hotsprings Hotel   **D**
Naveria Heights Lodge   **E**
Savusavu Budget Lodge   **C**
Waterfront Apartment   **A**

▼ Airport

▼ Airport & Hibiscus Highway

(☎885 0821, ⓦwww.pearlsfiji.com; farm tours Mon–Fri 9.30am & 1.30pm; F$25; 1hr 30min). Tours take place on a glass-bottomed boat and there's usually time for a quick snorkel (bring you own gear). If you're visiting between September and October or February and March you'll get to see the harvesting of the pearls by hand.

Savusavu Hills and Lesiaceva Point

To marvel at the fine views over Savusavu Bay, take a walk around **Savusavu Hills**. The best route starts from the eastern end of town, turning right up Buca Bay Road towards the airport. After a steep fifteen-minute walk, turn right again up the imaginatively named "Access Road" and follow the ridge westwards which features nice **views** overlooking the town and Nawi Island. There are three routes back into town. The shortest trail, which takes around thirty minutes, diverts off the road to the telecoms tower perched on the hilltop. From the far end of the clearing above the tower, a small grassy track leads down to a dirt road within five minutes. Follow this road and take the second turning on the left, heading uphill again on Nawi Street. From here, the ridge walk has views over the southern end of the bay and winds its way through light forest, past corrugated iron lean-tos back into town. The other two options continue along Access Road for thirty minutes south towards the airport. From here you can either catch a bus or taxi back into town or continue for thirty minutes along the south coast via Nukubalavu village to **Lesiaceva Point**.

Near the point, on the north side of the *Cousteau Resort*, is a **public beach** with excellent snorkelling at Split Rock, 500m offshore. Buses head back into town from *Cousteau Resort* at 7.45am, 12.30pm & 4.30pm, a taxi costs F$6 or it's a seven-kilometre walk along the coastline.

Eating and drinking

Savusavu is a wonderful place for dining out, rivalling Nadi for choice and with several good **restaurants** on the water's edge. Although the town has a genteel feel by day, don't be surprised to see drunks staggering around on Friday and Saturday nights – one notorious place to avoid is the *Tavern Bar* next door to the *Planters Club*. After around 8pm it's probably best to take a taxi back to your accommodation.

Restaurants

Blue Water Wine & Dine East Main St. Good-value cafeteria-style restaurant with a large menu with mostly Indian and Chinese dishes for around F$6. Mon–Sat 8am–10pm, Sun 5–10pm.

Bula Re East Main St ☎ 885 0307. Trendy café-restaurant with a cute wooden veranda on the foreshore. It serves excellent coffee and cooked breakfasts (F$6.50) as well as offering a heartier lunch and dinner menu of European and Fijian mains (around F$10). Be sure to try the Wednesday night *lovo* buffet (6.30pm; F$15). The location is a little hard to find, tucked at the back of the Waterfront Building at the east end of town. Mon–Sat 9am–9pm, Sun 4.30–9pm.

Captains Café Copra Shed Marina ☎ 885 0511. Shakes, cakes and coffees with views over the water. Light meals include caesar salad and curry of the day for F$8 or pizzas from F$15. Daily 8am–9pm.

Cousteau Resort Restaurant Lesiaceva Point ☎ 885 0188. Exquisitely presented food served in the elaborate setting of a twenty-metre-high thatch bure. The set lunch (F$53) and dinner (F$70) menus offer two courses with a choice of around three mains. Daily lunch and dinner only.

Ili's East Main St. Popular with local Fijians, *Ili's* is the cheapest restaurant in town serving fish in *lolo*, curry on the bone and sausage with cassava, all for

under F$5. It's a bit stuffy inside but there are two wooden tables on the front veranda overlooking the st. Mon–Sat 7am–5pm.

Surf & Turf Copra Shed Marina. A tad expensive, but the seafood and meat dishes are superbly cooked and the F$8 lunch specials are great value. The view on the water's edge is outstanding. Daily 11am–2.30pm & 5–9.30pm.

Bars and clubs

Mahi Bar at the *Hot Springs* Hotel ☎ 885 0195. Sweeping views of the bay from the veranda but drinks are pricey. There's live music and (usually drunken) dancing on Fri and Sat night from 7pm.

Planters Club West Main St. Old boys' hangout where you can sit in peace with a draught beer and watch the sunset. The main lounge displays interesting memorabilia recounting the bygone copra days. Mon–Sat 10am–10pm, Sun 10am–8pm.

Urosou's Night Club East Main St. Savusavu's only modern nightclub popular with Savusavu's young crowd at weekends, but only after 10.30pm. Wed is karaoke night with DJs Thurs–Sat. 7am–1pm; F$5.

Yacht Club Copra Shed Marina. Refined watering hole with cheap beer on draught, great sunset views and live reggae music on Sat at 5pm. Happy hour 5pm–7pm. Daily 10am–10pm.

Activities

For **kayaking** around Savusavu Bay or **scuba diving** in its sheltered waters, contact Rock N Downunder (☎ 885 3447, ✉ rockndownunder@connect.com .fj; kayak hire F$25 half day; two-tank dive F$160, PADI Open Water Course F$550; half-day snorkel trip F$70). Long-established dive operator Koro Sun Divers (☎ 885 2452; ⊛ www.korosundive.com; two-tank dive F$240) offer daily pick-ups from Savusavu area and dive the reefs in the Koro Sea off the south coast as well as the Rainbow Reef. Once a week they run trips to the remote reefs of Namena Island. The best place to **snorkel** around Savusavu is at Split Rock close to *Cousteau Resort*. You can get public bus from town at 7.15am, noon or 4pm (get off when you see the signboard: "Aunty Bui's Place"), or a taxi will cost F$6 – snorkel out towards the pearl buoys for the best coral patches. For **game fishing** contact Ika Levu (☏944 8506, ⓔikalevucharters@connect.com.fj; half-day boat charter F$1,012) based at The Copra Shed. In the busy sailing season between May and October one of the visiting yachts may offer day or overnight **sailing charters** – check at the Copra Shed or Waitui marinas. **Tui Tai Adventure Cruise** (see p.218) have their head offices in Savusavu, between the *Planters Club* and the J Hunter Pearl Office on Main Street.

Fitness enthusiast Sharon from *Naveria Heights Lodge* organizes **guided hikes** around the Savusavu Hills (2–5hr, F$45–65, min 2 people) as well as **mountain bike tours** for experienced cyclists (F$65 including lunch); you can also rent a mountain bike from *Naveria Heights* for F$30 a day.

Listings

Airlines Air Fiji ☏885 0538, Mon–Fri 8.30am–4.30pm, Sat 8.30am–12.30pm; Pacific Sun ☏885 2214, Mon–Fri 8am–1pm & 2pm–5pm, Sat 9am–noon; both in the Copra Shed Marina.
Banking ANZ and Westpac are both on Main St, opposite and either side of the bus stand.
Doctors Dr Taoi, Palm Court, West Main St ☏885 0721, Mon–Fri 8.30am–1pm & 2–4.30pm.
Hospital Savusavu District Hospital ☏885 0444 is 2km east of Savusavu on the road to Labasa, Mon–Fri 8am–1pm & 2–4.30pm; outside these times on-call for emergencies only.
Internet access Savusavu Computers, Waterfront Building at east end of town, Mon–Fri 8.30am–5pm, Sat 8.30am–1pm, F$4 per hr.

Laundry Waitui Marina, Mon–Sat 7.30am–5pm, F$8 a load.
Pharmacy Siloah Chemist, Palm Court, West Main St ☏925 0062, 8.30am–1pm & 2–4.30pm.
Police ☏855 0222. There's a multi-coloured painted Tourist Police Unit inconveniently located 2km east of town on the road to Labasa.
Post office East Main St, almost on the corner of Buca Bay Rd, Mon–Fri 8am–4pm, Sat 8am–noon.
Telephone Opposite Copra Shed Marina and in front of post office.

▲ Yacht, Savusavu Bay

Vuadomo and Waisali Nature Reserve

The road north of Savusavu, leading eventually to Labasa, offers a couple of pleasant day trips. Past the pretty village of Jersualemi, keep an eye out for Vuadomo Road on the left, 16km from Savusavu. A steep two-kilometre dirt track leads down to coastal **Vuadomo** village where you can pay a F$2 entrance fee to visit the attractive **Tobu-ni-tavo Waterfall**, an easy twenty-minute hike up the valley. Fifteen kilometres north of Vuadomo is **Waisali Nature Reserve** (Mon–Sat 9am–3pm; F$5) administered by the National Trust but in a rather neglected state. Waisali also has a waterfall trail (30min), leading down from the car park through lush tropical rainforest. Buses heading to Labasa can drop you at the Vuadomo turn-off and Waisali Nature Reserve car park. A taxi to Waisali costs F$40.

The Hibiscus Highway

Heading south from Savusavu, past the airport, the Buca Bay Road turns eastwards hugging the southern coastline of Vanua Levu to the eastern tip of the island at Buca Bay. The first 20km of road out of Savusavu is tar sealed and nicknamed the **Hibiscus Highway**. It passes through old copra plantations and colonial style homesteads and has several quiet **resorts** along the coast but no restaurants or shops. There is generally good **snorkelling** off the coast, especially around the mushroom islets of Maravu Point but you'll have to walk out some way from shore over a raised platform of dead exposed coral to get to the reefs. A decent public **sandy beach** backed by rows of massively tall coconut palms is accessed through a gate at *Sigasiga Sands* (the landowners charge F$5 for parking).

Accommodation

Namale Resort ☎ 885 0435, ⓦ www.namalefiji .com. Exclusive retreat with luxury bures (over US$1000 per night) and a spa centre overlooking a beautiful beach. Owned by American life coach Tony Robbins, "life mastery" courses are taught here Jan–April. ⑨

Olivia's Homestay Nagigi Village ☎ 885 3099. Suitable as a village stay experience with the energetic Olivia encouraging interaction with her relatives. Rooms are basic and cold-water showers are shared by all. Dorm F$18, rooms ①

Sigasiga Sands ☎ 885 0413, ⓔ geeda-sands @connect.com.fj. Private plantation resort set among coconut palms and a huge lawned area

beside a beach. There's a pretty thatch roof cottage available for short stays plus a two-bedroom holiday villa for long-term rent. Both come with kitchen facilities. Cottage ③, villa ⑥

Yao Kolo Camping ☎ 885 3089, ⓔ yaukolo @yahoo.com. Basic dorm lodge with ample room in the spacious gardens to pitch a tent although no kitchen facilities – home-cooked meals can be arranged. There's fair snorkelling and a narrow beach across the road and a 15min trail leads to a small waterfall. Camping F$12, four-bed dorm F$20 includes breakfast; sometimes closed around Christmas.

The Natewa Peninsula

The **Natewa Peninsula** is almost severed from the main chunk of Vanua Levu, connected only by a kilometre-wide sliver of land east of Savusavu. To the north of the peninsula is Natewa Bay, while to the south is the Somosomo Strait separating Vanua Levu from Taveuni. At the eastern end of the peninsula is **Buca Bay** from where there are ferries to Taveuni as well as the two smaller islands of **Kioa** and **Rabi**.

Salt Lake and Natewa Bay

Twenty seven kilometres east of Savusavu, at the narrowest part of the peninsula, is the turn-off to **Salt Lake**, a brackish lake with excellent **fishing**. You can stay and explore the lake at *Salt Lake Lodge* (☏828 3005, ⓦwww.saltlakelodge .com; ❷–❹) which sits overlooking the mangrove-lined Qaloqalo River. There are just two lodges here, with a communal kitchen and lounge area. As well as fishing from the pontoon, kayaks are available for drifting up and down the river. Being in the mangroves, it's also a reliable spot for bird-watching.

Thirty kilometres east of the Salt Lake turn-off, the Buca Bay Road heads inland to a deep protected bay known as Fawn Harbour. Here, the Natewa Peninsula broadens and features increasingly dense rainforest teeming with endemic birdlife – it's one of the few places in Fiji to spot the rare **silktail**, a tiny black bird with a speckled blue head. A 4WD vehicle is needed to explore the region as the roads here are terrible, especially during the rainy season. Two side roads branch off to the fishing villages of Drekeniwai and Vuasivo on **Natewa Bay**; ask around at either village to hire a boat and guide to search for **spinner dolphins**, commonly sighted in the bay – expect to pay F$100 for an hour.

Buca Bay and the offshore islands

The Buca Bay Road finally hits **Buca Bay** at Loa village from where dirt roads branch off north and south along the coast. The road north heads through a dozen fishing villages to Napuka at the tip of Natewa Bay, facing Rabi Island – boats for Rabi leave from Karoko village, 2km to the south of Napuka. Boats for Kioa and Taveuni (see p.231) depart 2km south of Loa on the southern road at **Natuvu Landing**. Twelve kilometres south of Natuva is Dakuniba village where you can see **petroglyphs** etched into stone boulders alongside the creek bed (ask at the village to see them).

Two **dive resorts** are hidden in the heavily indented southeastern tip of the peninsula, which has the closest access to the stunning **Rainbow Reef**. *Almost Paradise* (☏828 3000, ⓦwww.almostparadisefiji.com; ❹, includes meals) has three simple wooden cottages with fans and en-suite bathrooms. *Dolphin Bay Divers Retreat* (☏888 0531, ⓦwww.dolphinbaydivers.com; camping F$8, safari tents ❷, bure ❸) has two bamboo bures and safari tents beside the beach. Both resorts are in remote bays, inaccessible by road, and pick up guests across the straits from Taveuni.

Kioa Island

Just offshore from Buca Bay is the small, hilly island of **Kioa**, home to four hundred Tuvaluans. Back in the 1940s the people of Vaitupu, the largest of the nine coral atolls in Tuvalu, were faced with a stark choice: cling on as rising sea levels began to erode their tiny island or look for a new home. In 1947, the freehold island of Kioa, 1000km to the south in Fiji, was purchased by the people of Vaitupu for £3,000. The first migrants arrived almost immediately and a steady trickle has continued ever since. The islanders live in the solitary village of **Salia** on the south coast. In 2005, they were formally granted Fijian citizenship.

The fair-skinned Polynesian Tuvaluans have a lifestyle and language quite different to the Fijians. They are known as skilled fishermen and are often seen handline fishing from outrigger canoes way out to sea. One gastronomic treat from Tuvalu is **toddy**, a syrup obtained from the sap of the dwarf coconut tree. Toddy can be made into a sweet jam or a strong naturally fermented alcoholic drink, which is consumed on the island in large quantities on Friday and Saturday nights.

There is no official accommodation on Kioa but you can arrange a **homestay** visit through Paula Kaisamy (☎994 1327; F$20). To get to the island ask the captain of Grace Ferry (see p.217) to drop you off on its run between Buca Bay and Taveuni, or catch the Nabuka bus departing Savusavu at 10.30am to Vatuvonu village where you can charter a boat for the fifteen-minute journey to Kioa for F$40.

Rabi island

Rabi, 15km to the north of Kioa, shares a similar history. The island, 66 square kilometres in size, is home to the displaced **Banaban Islanders** from faraway Kiribati in Micronesia. Their tiny five-square-kilometre original homeland, Banaba Island, was systematically stripped of its **phosphate** deposits by British mining interests between 1902 and 1942. Soon after, during World War II, the island was captured by the Japanese who slaughtered many of the islanders. At the end of the war the British Government relocated the remaining Banabans to Rabi Island in Fiji which it had purchased shortly before the Japanese occupation. The first arrivals landed on December 15, 1945 and today, almost five thousand Banabans live on Rabi in four villages along the coast. As on Kioa, the islanders received formal Fijian Citizenship in 2005.

Tabwewa, halfway along the north coast, is the largest village and adjacent to Nuku Government Station where you'll find the *Rabi Island Council Guesthouse* (☎330 3653 in Suva), used mostly for visiting government workers but it also accepts tourists by prior arrangement. The seldom used **airstrip** and secondary school are at Tabiang village on the southern tip of the island. To get to Rabi, catch the daily Nabuka bus departing Savusavu at 10.30am and get off at Karoko village where you should be able to charter a boat over to the island for F$80.

Taveuni

Across the strait from Vanua Levu, the smaller island of **TAVEUNI** is a stunning combination of luxuriant forest, soaring mountains and colourful coral reefs. Much of the island's pristine rainforest is protected by the Bouma National Heritage Park and tourism is handled sensitively, making it one of the best places to sample Fiji's varied **wildlife**. Geologically, Taveuni is one of Fiji's youngest islands and its dramatic volcanic scenery, wild flowers and laid-back atmosphere bring to mind Hawaii as much as Fiji.

Most visitors arrive at the small settlement of **Matei** on the north coast, home to the airstrip, plenty of accommodation and a series of pretty beaches. South of here, along the rugged east coast is the access point to the huge **Bouma National Heritage Park** which features world-class bird-watching and hikes through a series of waterfalls. Just offshore are the thriving coral reefs of the **Waitabu Marine Park**. Across the knife-edge ridge splitting the 42-kilometre-long island is the smoothly sloping **west coast** where most of the island's eleven thousand inhabitants live. Here, **Somosomo**, head village of the powerful Cakaudrove Province, merges into the modern trade centre of **Naqara**. To the south is the peaceful Catholic Mission at Wairiki with **De Voeux Peak**, accessible by 4WD

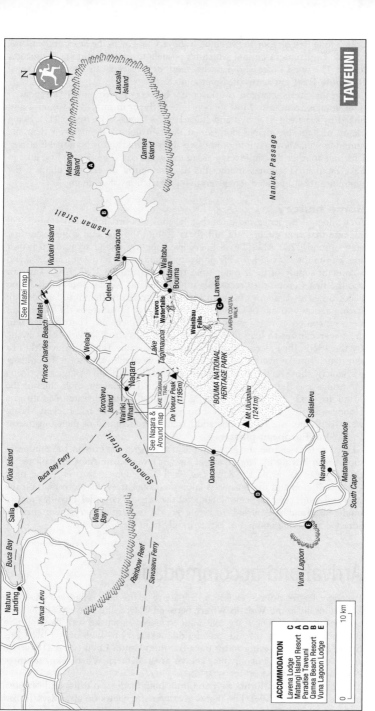

TAVEUNI

ACCOMMODATION
Lavena Lodge   C
Matangi Island Resort   A
Paradise Taveuni   D
Qamea Beach Resort   B
Vuna Lagoon Lodge   E

0   10 km

233

or by a long trek on foot, towering high above. Close by, in the heart of the island, is **Lake Tagimaucia** around which it's possible to find the unique Tagimaucia flower. The west coast also has the most direct access to the phenomenal **Rainbow Reef** just across the Somosomo Straits.

By far the cheapest way to visit Taveuni is **by ferry** but this involves a sixteen-hour voyage from Suva. Most tourists instead **fly** in from Nadi. Taveuni is also linked by sea from Savusavu and Buca Bay on Vanua Levu (see p.217). Bring plenty of light, breathable clothes – if the rain doesn't drench you then the humidity will. Allow a minimum of **two days** in the Bouma National Heritage Park and another day sightseeing along the west coast. The demanding hike to Lake Tagimaucia requires another full day. For **scuba divers**, five nights is the minimum recommended stay given flying restrictions after diving.

Some history

Archeological evidence indicates that Taveuni was first inhabited around 250 BC and that ring ditches and **hill forts** around the volcanic cones were first built around 1200 AD. The islanders lived slightly inland to protect against attack from the sea and led a life of plenty thanks to the fertile volcanic soil and a constant supply of fresh water from the mountains. In 1643 **Abel Tasman** was the first European to record sighting the island. Hit by poor weather and negotiating the dangerous Nanuku Passage, he made no attempt to land despite having almost run out of supplies. This is probably fortunate as the Taveunians were renowned as fierce warriors. In the early nineteenth century they sent great **war canoes** to help the alliance of Bau in its struggle with the Rewans. By the 1840s, they faced a battle on home turf as the Tongan Prince **Ma'afu** threatened to take over the island. Allegiances were split with some Taveunians, particularly those on the small offshore islands of Laucala and Matagi, supporting the prince and the remainder sticking with the **Tui Cakau**, high chief of the island. In 1862, after much wrangling, Tui Cakau's army defeated Ma'afu in a bloody sea battle off the coast near Somosomo. Those that had backed Ma'afu were hastily punished – Laucala and Matagi were stripped of their inhabitants and sold to **European planters**.

Lured by the rich soils and gentle slopes ideal for growing **cotton**, the Europeans soon began buying up large tracts of Taveuni's west coast. After the collapse in cotton prices following the American Civil War, copra took over as the most viable cash crop and the organized lines of coconut trees still loom high on the west and south coast plantations. Some of the original **colonial families** remain on the island and have moved tentatively into the tourism industry; this in turn has attracted a growing number of expats, mostly from the US.

Arrival and accommodation

Passenger ferries from Suva (see p.151) arrive at the new wharf at Nayalayala, known locally as the **Wairiki Wharf**, between Wairiki and Waiyevo on the west coast of the island. The ferry calls in at Savusavu along the way allowing you the option of getting off and catching the next ferry to Taveuni at a later date. **Small ferries** journeying across Buca Bay from **Vanua Levu** (see p.218) arrive at the old wharf in Lovonivonu, known as the Korean Wharf, 3km south of Naqara town and also on the west coast.

There are **regular flights** to Matei from both Nadi (two daily) and Nausori, outside Suva (two daily). The flights give awesome views on clear days. In bad weather, turbulence can be a problem, especially with the frequent crosswinds at Matei. Most Air Fiji flights stop over at Savusavu in both directions.

Accommodation

Taveuni is one of the few places in Fiji where you can rent a self-catering **holiday home** or cottage with self catering. There are also several excellent small **boutique resorts** around Matei and on the offshore islands. For budget travellers, there are two **campsites**, one in Matei, the other near Naqara, a basic **lodge** within Bouma National Heritage Park but no backpacker hostels.

Transport

Once on Taveuni, getting around can prove a little unpredictable. You won't get lost as there's only one **road** following the coast, but heavy downpours cause frequent **flooding**, particularly at the bridge at Qeleni which separates the two tourist hubs of Matei and the Bouma National Heritage Park. Floods generally subside in a few hours and seldom last for more than a day, although landslides along the steep and muddy roadside may cause longer delays. The only section of sealed road extends for 20km along the northwest coast from Matei to Wairiki; potholes and fallen coconuts on the dirt coastal road are notorious hazards.

By car

With few taxis on the island, the most convenient way to get around is by **minivan** or **carrier van**. These can be found at Matei Airport, Naqara or, with a bit of luck, waved down on the roadside. Alternatively, arrange a pick-up with Patrick (☏ 921 5434) or Vikram (☏ 888 0716 or 921 0447). The fare from Matei to Bouma costs around F$40 one way. For F$120 you can hire a local driver and van for the day which generally works out cheaper than renting a car. Unfortunately van drivers are reluctant to venture off the coastal highway and into the bush. If you plan on scaling De Voeux Peak, you'll certainly need a 4WD vehicle. Budget Car Rental in Naqara (☏ 888 0291, Mon–Fri 8am–5pm; 4WD only, F$145–185 per day) is the only **car rental** company on island.

By bus

Pacific Transport (☏ 888 0278), based at Naqara run the island's limited **bus service**. Buses run to Navakawau in the south (Mon–Fri 9am, 11.30am & 4.40pm, 2hr, F$4.15) and between Wairiki and Lavena on the northeast coast via Matei and Bouma (Mon–Sat 8.45am, 12.05pm & 4.40pm, Sun 11.05am & 4.05pm, 1hr 45min; F$3.60). The last bus from Wairiki spends the night at Lavena and departs the next morning at 5.45am – useful for those wanting to spend a lazy afternoon on the beautiful Lavena Walk and overnight in the village.

Organized tours

Most hotels and resorts on Taveuni offer private **sightseeing tours** (usually with a minimum of four guests). Otherwise, try Taveuni Adventures (☏ 888 1700, Mon–Fri 8am–5pm, Sat 8am–noon) in Naqara (see p.244). They have good contacts with local communities and can find knowledgeable guides or organize specialist tours.

Matei and around

MATEI, jutting out on the northernmost tip of Taveuni, is the ideal base for exploring the island, lying midway between the Bouma National Heritage Park and Rainbow Reef. This modern settlement of around five hundred people is a mix of old colonial families, Indian entrepreneurs and a new wave of foreigners living the dream in luxury oceanfront villas. The settlement stretches along the main coastal road either side of the small bluff known as Naselesele Point. Matei has plenty of water-based **activities** (see p.238) including access to the Rainbow Reef, pleasant **beaches** and a good selection of **restaurants**.

Off the north side of Matei, four tiny uninhabited islands lie in the sheltered **lagoon** while across the Tasman Strait to the west are the larger **offshore islands** of Qamea, Matangi and Laucala, each home to a luxury resort.

Arrival and information

A small, much photographed wooden hut welcomes visitors to **Matei Airport**. There is usually a taxi waiting for incoming flights. If none are available, call Sukhlal Taxis (☎888 0517) from the public telephone outside the terminal – the fare to Matei is F$2. Most guests with pre-booked accommodation are met by their hosts. There is no tourist information centre – hotels and resorts organize tours and can advise on activities.

Accommodation

Resorts

Maravu Plantation Resort West Matei ☎888 0555, ⓦwww.maravu.net. If eco-tourism is your thing, this environmentally conscious luxury resort is a great choice. It's set on a 90-acre coconut plantation on the mountain side of the coastal road and offers horse riding, spa treatments and snorkelling off the beach which is a short walk down the hill and across the road. The 21 bures

have a warm, colonial feel with dark wood furnishings, mosquito nets and thatch roofs; most have air con. ❼–❾, includes breakfast.

Taveuni Island Resort West Matei ☎888 0441, ⓦwww.taveuniislandresort.com. Exclusive resort set on a landscaped hilltop with perfect ocean views across the straits to Vanua Levu. The thirteen villas, which start from US$450 per night, are rather box-like from the outside but interiors are spacious

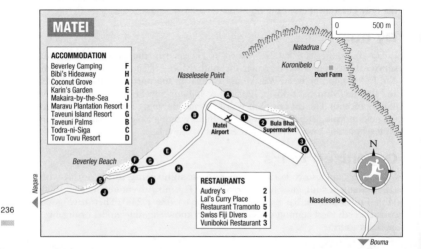

MATEI

ACCOMMODATION	
Beverley Camping	F
Bibi's Hideaway	H
Coconut Grove	A
Karin's Garden	E
Makaira-by-the-Sea	J
Maravu Plantation Resort	I
Taveuni Island Resort	G
Taveuni Palms	B
Todra-ni-Siga	C
Tovu Tovu Resort	D

Natadrua
Koronibelo
Pearl Farm
Naselesele Point
Beverley Beach
Matei Airport
Bula Bhai Supermarket
Naselesele
Naqara
Bouma
N

RESTAURANTS	
Audrey's	2
Lal's Curry Place	1
Restaurant Tramonto	5
Swiss Fiji Divers	4
Vunibokoi Restaurant	3

0   500 m

and come with luxury fittings, fine white linen and private rainforest showers. Steps from an infinity pool lead down to a delightful sandy beach. ⑨, includes meals.

Taveuni Palms West Matei ☎ 888 0032, ⓦ www.taveunipalms.com. At US$1150 a night, this is one of the most expensive resorts in Fiji. At this price, you may be left wondering why the two-bedroom villas are located smack opposite the airstrip. However, each comes with its own swimming pool, seven personal staff and a private cove beach. ⑨, includes meals.

Tovu Tovu Resort East Matei ☎ 888 0560, ⓦ www.tovutovu.com. This locally owned budget retreat with an excellent-value restaurant and dive operation is just beyond Bula Bhai supermarket at the eastern end of Matei. The seven bamboo cottages come with old-fashioned furniture and tiny bathrooms but are clean and comfortable. There's no beach, although the lagoon across the road is good for kayaking. ②–③

Holiday homes, cottages and camping

🏃 **Beverley Camping** West Matei ☎ 888 0326. The cheapest place to stay with the best location in Matei, right beside the beach. There's a basic kitchen with cooking facilities and fridge, two flush toilets, 24hr electricity and also a simple thatch bure with two tiny rooms and private cold-water shower. F$10 for own tent, F$15 for pre-erected tent, room ①

Bibi Hideaway West Matei ☎ 888 0443. Five cottages, very reasonably priced but a little untidy, set in a large hillside plantation full of flowering shrubs and fruit trees (the fruit is free to guests).

The "million dollar ocean view", as the owner Jim Bibi describes it, is mostly obscured by massive coconut tree; the beach is just a 3min walk away. Electricity runs only at night. ②–③

🏃 **Coconut Grove** East Matei ☎ 888 0000, ⓦ www.coconutgrovefiji.com. Three well-kept cottages set on a hillside overlooking Matei Beach, with exceptional views over the lagoon. The restaurant serves some of the best food on Taveuni and the staff are very welcoming. ⑥, includes continental breakfast.

Karin's Garden West Matei ☎ 888 0511, ⓦ www .karinsgardenfiji.com. Owned by German couple Karin and Peter, this two-bedroom wooden cottage makes an affordable base for exploring. If you don't feel like cooking in the small kitchen, Karin will knock up mostly organic meals on the covered gazebo at the cliff's edge for an extra charge. ⑤

Makaira by the Sea West Matei ☎ 888 0680, ⓦ www.fijibeachfrontatmakaira.com. Owned by a lovely Hawaiian couple with a passion for deep-sea fishing, this two-acre hilltop property has two bungalows with stunning sea views plus access to Beverley Beach across the road. Both cottages have quality furnishings with decorative art work. There's a massage bure and sundeck and Roberta, the owner, puts on a delicious seafood buffet every Tuesday. ⑤–⑥

Todra-ni-Siga West Matei ☎ 925 9893, ⓔ todrafj@yahoo.com. Two airy wooden cottages with en-suite hot-water bathrooms perched on the cliff face overlooking the ocean with a small cove beach beneath, although you'll have to walk 10min along the coast to get down to it. ④, includes continental breakfast.

Eating and drinking

There are several grocery stores along the roadside in East Matei, the most comprehensive being Bula Bhai & Sons (☎ 888 0039, Mon–Sat 7am–6pm, Sun 8–11am), just beyond *Audrey's*, but none sell alcohol. There are a couple of good independent **restaurants**, which on the outer islands is something of a rarity.

Audrey's East Matei ☎ 888 0039. Long-established café dishing out real coffee and irresistible banana cake. Mon–Fri 10am–6pm, closed Jan.

Lal's Curry Place ☎ 888 0705. Tiny Indian restaurant with home-style cooking served from the wooden veranda of Mrs Lal's house. It's a bit hard to find, tucked down a driveway three houses down from the Satish Kumar supermarket, but the chatty Mrs Lal cooks the finest curries in the north. She will also offer deliveries if you call a few hours in advance. Mon–Sat dinner only.

🏃 **Restaurant Tramonto** ☎ 888 2224. Perched on a hilltop at the southernmost point of Matei, this pizza restaurant offers the most spectacular waterside dining in Fiji from a wooden veranda overlooking the placid waters of the Somosomo Straits. The pizzas are thin crusted and delicious.(from F$25) and there's a bar serving cocktails. Daily 10am–9pm.

🏃 **Vunibokoi Restaurant** at *Tovu Tovu Resort* ☎ 888 0560. Resort restaurant specializing in delicious Fijian food. The creamy *rourou*

(vegetable leaf) soup is divine, there's usually fresh
qari (crab) and *kari* (prawns) cooked in *lolo*

(coconut cream) and they offer home-made
burgers for the less adventurous. Daily 7am–9pm.

Activities

Two kilometres west of Naselesele Point is **Beverley Beach**, a deep sandy gem
backed by lush hardwood trees. The coral reef here lies close to shore and offers
great **snorkelling** along a thirty-metre-deep drop-off, with reef sharks occasionally paying a visit. Confident swimmers can also reach the snorkelling reef off
Natadrua island, in the sheltered lagoon 700m off the north side of Matei, but
it's best to paddle out on a **kayak** which can be rented at *Beverley Camping* (F$10
an hour).

From Matei it takes roughly forty minutes by boat to reach the superb
dive sites along the **Rainbow Reef** off the south coast of Vanua Levu. Jewel
Bubble Divers (T 888 2080, W www.jeweldivers.com; two-tank dive F$170,
snorkel rental F$5 per day) and the long-established Swiss Fiji Divers (T 888
2070, W www.swissfijidivers.com; two-tank dive F$160) both offer trips to the
reef and have bases at Beverley Beach. The rich current-fed waters off Matei
are also fantastic for big **game fishing** with marlin, swordfish and yellowfin
tuna plentiful. Contact John at *Makaira by the Sea* who offers game-fishing
trips (F$595 per half day) aboard his 24-foot aluminium boat.

For something less energetic try the two-hour **tea plantation** walk with Bill
from *Beverley Camping* (F$10 per person, min two people) which winds through
light forest and small plantations to an old tea farm planted in the early 1900s.
You can also take a **pearl farm tour** operated by Peckham Pearl Farm (T 888
2789, Mon–Fri; F$25 per person, minimum two people; 1hr 30min) based out
in the lagoon. Tours depart from the beach by *Audrey's* café, normally at high
tide, and include a brief introduction to pearl farming and a chance to snorkel
in the lagoon.

The offshore islands

The three offshore islands of **Qamea**, **Matangi** and **Laucala**, scattered across
the deep Tasman Straits from Matei, possess some of the best private island
resorts in Fiji. Boats for the islands leave from the unusual black sand beach
at **Navakacoa** village, 12km south of Matei. Almost 30km north of Taveuni,
the remote **Ringgold Islands** pop out of the horizon just about visible from
Matei on a clear day.

Qamea

Just over 2km offshore, **Qamea** is the closest and largest of the islands with a
meandering and rugged coastline and hilly peaks thick with tropical forest. Much
of the island is freehold land and there are no roads. Facing Taveuni, *Qamea Beach
Resort* (T 888 0220, W www.qamea.com; ●) has a picturesque deep sand beach
although note that it's exposed to the strong southeasterly trade winds between
May and October. The central grand bure restaurant is very impressive, replicating
a traditional Fijian temple, but the bungalow-style accommodation is rather
claustrophobic, albeit air-conditioned.

Matangi

Matangi was purchased in 1853 by the Mitchell family, planters from England,
who farmed copra here for over a century. The Mitchells' fifth-generation descendants have turned the island into the private ⚑ *Matangi Island Resort* (T 888 0260,
W www.matangiisland.com; ●, includes meals and boat transfers from Navakacoa),

▲ Matangi island

one of the finest in Fiji. The horseshoe-shaped island has the usual sandy beach and snorkelling lagoon but what really sets it apart are the beautiful treehouse bures set in forest that is home to orange doves, silktails and parrots. Bures, both treehouse and beachside, are spacious with high ceilings, en-suite bathrooms plus outdoor rainforest showers. There's a new swimming pool and delightful restaurant and the scuba diving nearby is first class.

Laucala

Laucala, another freehold island at the northern tip of Qamea, was once owned by publishing tycoon Malcolm Forbes who created an idealistic model plantation on the island in the 1970s. A small luxury resort was built along with an airstrip and staff village complete with a church. After his death, the island became neglected and was eventually sold for US$11 million in 2003 to Dietrich Mateschitz, founder of Red Bull energy drinks. The old resort and staff village have been bulldozed to make way for a new multi–million-dollar **private resort** which, at the time of writing, was yet to be completed. The island boasts pristine beaches and the thirty-kilometre-long Heemskerck Reef lying off its north coast is a great spot for fishing.

The Ringgold Islands

Almost 30km northwest from Taveuni, the remote **Ringgold Islands** are a collection of small islands supporting thousands of breeding **seabirds** including the red-footed booby and black noddy on Vetaua island. The only inhabitants live on rolling Yanuca island where farming is viable. To visit these enchanting islands you need to join the Tui Tai Adventure Cruise (see p.218) which spends a day exploring the sunken crater of Cobia island with hiking and snorkelling in the lagoon. **Nuku**, an atoll surrounded by tiny coral islets, has some of the finest white sand in Fiji where hundreds of sea turtles lay their eggs between September and January.

Bouma National Heritage Park

Fifteen kilometres south of Matei is the northern boundary of the **Bouma National Heritage Park** (⊛ www.bnhp.org), an important wildlife reserve, protecting 40,000 acres of ancient rainforest laced with waterfalls and home to rare birds and plants. The park was established in 1990 by the people of Bouma District, with assistance from the Fijian and New Zealand governments.

Within the park are four villages, each running a specific eco-attraction: **Waitabu**, the first of the villages encountered along the road from Matei, has a protected **marine park**; 4km further into the park, **Vidawa** offers a rewarding rainforest hike to ancient ruins in the hills; neighbouring **Korovou** maintains the spectacular Tavoro Waterfall Trail through three sets of falls; and the last of the four villages, **Lavena**, 15km to the south and at the end of the road, has a beautiful coastal walk with kayaking and another refreshing waterfall at its end. Also within the park are **Lake Tagimaucia** and **De Vouex Peak**, although these are best accessed from the west coast (see p.246).

Practicalities

The only road **access** to the park's four main attractions is from the north, along the winding dirt coastal road from Matei via Navakacoa. The majority of people visit on a **day-trip** organized by their accommodation. Alternatively you can get here by **public bus** on the Pacific Transport service (see p.235) running from Naqara via Matei. There's no fancy sign to welcome you to the park and general access is **free**. However, to participate in the four village enterprises, a small fee is paid at each village visitor centre. The only **accommodation** in the park is *Lavena Lodge* (see opposite) on the beachfront at Lavena village.

Waitabu Marine Park

Waitabu Marine Park, set in a secluded bay off the main road, is the first attraction you'll come to. There's no sign indicating the village – keep an eye out for the access road heading towards the coast from the brow of a steep hill, about fifteen minutes' drive south of Navakacoa. Waitabu translates as "sacred waters" and in 1998, the seven Fijian communities here signed an agreement to neither fish nor anchor in a one-kilometre stretch of coastline up to the fringing reef. Consequently, the coral and fish here are thriving and can be visited on a **guided snorkelling trip** (F$20). The **visitor centre** (☏ 888 0451) at the end of the access road beside the beach, has cold-water showers and an extensive selection of snorkelling equipment. If you turn up unannounced it may take a while before someone from the village wanders down to help out so it's worth calling in advance; hotels will arrange this if you are visiting on an organized day-trip.

Vidawa Rainforest Hike

A kilometre beyond the Waitabu turn-off, the road passes through the smallest of the four villages, Vidawa. Here, the community has organized the **Vidawa Rainforest Hike**, a full-day trek to the pristine upper forests. The guided hike (F$40, bookings essential; 6–7hr) departs from the small **visitor centre** (☏ 920 5833) in the village. The earlier you start, the more chance you have of spotting the **native birds** which forage in the fruit trees of the lower slopes before heading back to the cover of the high forest – golden whistlers, silktails, red shining parrots and blue-crested broadbills are commonly sighted. Once you

Visiting a Fijian village

Visiting a traditional village is one of the highlights of a trip to Fiji. As soon as you arrive at a village, excitable kids call out "bula!", elders take the time to shake your hand and you'll invariably receive offers to stay for a meal or longer. To do so will provide a unique insight into Fijian culture.

Village elder on horseback, Navala ▲

Many villages rely on fishing as a source of food ▼

Tours and homestays

Most resorts offer **village tours**, often including a trip to a craft market and a simple *yaqona* ceremony (see overleaf). While these can be a good option for those short on time, you may end up with a rather sanitized experience, as resorts tend to visit nearby villages which have become over commercialized. The best tours visit the more remote, traditional villages and are often combined with adventure activities such as rafting or kayaking. Look out for tours running to the Namosi Highlands and Naitasiri (see p.75) on Viti Levu or try a trip to Kadavu (see p.183).

There's nothing to stop you visiting a village **unaccompanied**, providing you follow the tips given below. For a fuller immersion into Fijian life consider staying overnight at a village **homestay**, which involves staying with a family, usually in a traditional bure. Homestay accommodation is listed throughout the guide.

Village etiquette

When visiting a village there is a certain amount of **etiquette** to be aware of. As an outsider, locals won't expect you to follow all the rules but the more you pick up the more you'll be respected. The following are a few useful pointers:

▶▶ Dress conservatively – men and particularly women should cover shoulders and knees, and preferably wear a **sulu** (Fijian sarong) around the waist.

▶▶ Avoid visiting a village on a **Sunday**, which is a special day for religion, family and rest.

▶▶ Before entering a village, remove your hat and sunglasses and carry any backpacks in front of you – don't hide them as this arouses suspicion.

▲ Women making pottery, Nakabuta

▼ Dried and powdered yaqona roots

▶▶ On arrival, ask to see the **turanga ni koro** (village headman) to whom you should present a **sevusevu** or introductory gift. *Yaqona* is the most appropriate form of *sevusevu* and can be bought at all town markets, either in root form or ready prepared as *waqa* (powder) – about half a kilo or F$30 worth of roots is appropriate.

▶▶ Other appreciated **gifts** include books and magazines; food (if staying overnight); school stationery for children or toys such as balloons or balls.

▶▶ On entering a home, remove your shoes, crouch when passing through the door and sit cross-legged with your head a little stooped as a sign of respect. It is polite to shake hands with anyone already present and introduce yourself simply by name, town and country.

▶▶ Taking **photos** is acceptable in almost all instances except the initial *yaqona* ceremony. Fijians take pride in being photographed and will often ask you to take their picture and to see it afterwards. Sending printed photographs is a nice follow-up gesture.

▶▶ If invited to **eat**, sit cross-legged and wait until everybody has sat down. The head of the house will say grace (*masu*) after which you can start eating, normally using your hands. You may find yourself the only person eating, with someone fanning the food for you – don't be put-off, this is a common gesture reserved for guests.

▼ Village volleyball

Trying yaqona – an essential Fiji experience ▲

Village boys, Navala ▼

Yaqona

Also known as kava or more simply "grog", **yaqona** is Fiji's national drink. Made from the pounded roots of the pepper plant (*piper methysticum*), it has an earthy, rather bitter taste and resembles muddy water. Although it takes some getting used to, *yaqona* (pronounced "yan-go-na") is thoroughly refreshing and has a relaxing effect upon the body. Drunk socially by Fijians and Fiji-Indians, it is also used in formal situations and will be offered as part of a **ceremony** to welcome you to a village. The ritual begins with the presentation of your *sevusevu* (see previous page) accompanied by a speech by the village herald. After this, the *yaqona* roots are mixed with water in a carved bowl (*tanoa*) while all participants sit in a circle on the floor. Once ready, the drink is served in a half coconut shell known as a *bilo*. It is presented first to the chief and then to any guests. When it's your turn to drink, cup your hands, clap once and say "**bula**" (cheers); you then take the cup and down the contents in one go. Return the cup to the bearer and clap your hands again three times, proclaiming "**maca**", a signal of gratification. The formal ceremony ends when the *tanoa* bowl is empty, indicated by a round of clapping. Throughout the ceremony it's considered bad manners to talk, turn your back on the chief or to point your feet towards the *tanoa* bowl.

> After a few cups of *yaqona* you may notice your tongue and lips become numb, a temporary effect caused by the active ingredients in the root. Consuming *yaqona* in large quantities can cause **drowsiness** so avoid driving or going swimming immediately after drinking it.

start ascending the hills into the forest, the foliage becomes thick with tangled vines and there are only fleeting views of the surrounding mountains. It was in the deep jungle, away from the exposed coasts, that Taveuni's first inhabitants used to live, protected from warring tribes and cannibalism. Today the only evidence of their existence is a series of **stone platforms** hidden in the undergrowth. After trudging through the sweaty and often muddy rainforest, the hike emerges in the lower forests at the first Tavoro Waterfall (see below) where you can take a refreshing swim.

Tavoro Waterfall Trail

The most popular of the four adventures in the park is the **Tavoro Waterfall Trail**. The self-guided walk starts from the **Tavoro visitor centre** (℡888 0390, daily 8am–5pm; F$8) in Korovou village, often referred to as Bouma village; the centre has toilets and sells souvenirs and cold drinks. From here, an easy ten-minute stroll through gardens leads to the first of the three **waterfalls**. The first falls are arguably the most picturesque and have the best pool for swimming. Boulders on the left side of the pool lead to a five-metre-high rock ledge which cuts in behind the cascading water – if you summon up the courage, you can throw yourself through the falls and into the deep pool beneath. You could easily spend a few hours splashing around here (changing huts are provided) or cooking yourself a **barbecue** on the grills provided. However, most visitors generally push on for the more adventurous trail to the second and third falls, returning to the first falls for a swim at the end of the hike.

The section of trail to the **second falls** is the prettiest, starting with a steep ten-minute climb up, helped along by wooden steps and a crushed coral path to the ridge above the first set of falls. From the top there's a view over Thurston Point towards Qamea island. The track then heads into light forest, passing a delightful grove of palm ferns and crosses the Tavoro River, where there are large boulders to hop across and a rope for hanging onto. Another ten minutes on through increasingly dense forest brings you to the photogenic thirty-metre-high second falls, which cascade over numerous ledges into a natural pool.

The trail to the **third falls** offers the most demanding hiking and can be very slippery after heavy rain. It's worth the effort, though, as most day-trippers only visit the first and second falls leaving the third blissfully uncrowded. The trail starts 30m downstream from the second falls, and climbs a steep bank on the far side of the stream into thick forest. It takes another thirty minutes to reach the falls. At only ten metres high, they are the smallest of the three but the wide pool below is great for swimming and deep enough to jump into. It's possible to climb up the slippery rock ledges of the falls and continue upstream, following the river (you'll need sturdy shoes for walking along the river bed) to reach a succession of smaller falls. Allow yourself an hour to return from the third falls to the roadside.

Lavena Coastal Walk

The pretty beach at **Lavena**, 6km south of Tavoro, marks the start of a scenic **coastal walk** to another set of waterfalls hidden in forest. **Accommodation** is available at *Lavena Lodge* (℡820 3639; dorm F$20, room ❶) at the entrance to the village where the coastal road from Matei ends. The lodge's three twin rooms are screened and have mosquito nets but are otherwise very basic and the shared bathroom is rather dingy. However, it's worth staying here in order to make an early morning start on the walk. Meals can be arranged with one of the villagers or you can use the lodge's kitchen facilities.

▲ Waterfall, Bouma National Heritage Park

The lodge doubles as the **visitor centre** where you pay the F$12 entrance fee for the coastal trail (3hr return). The first forty-minute section is a flat amble with wonderful views along the coast, passing a black-sand beach and a lagoon littered with rocky pedestals resembling giant mushrooms. About halfway you'll reach the tiny settlement of **Naba**. It's respectful not to wander through so follow the path down to the beach to the small stream at the far end of Naba from where the trail continues. After meandering around several cliffs and over a suspension bridge, the trail gradually ascends inland under a light forest canopy to a rocky stream. The two waterfalls, known as **Wainibau Falls**, are obscured from view by a ten-metre rock face on either side. To get to the falls you'll need to swim through the passage – keep to the left side, there's a small ridge just under the waterline to follow. You can jump from the top of the smaller waterfall into the pool, which is deep and full of prawns.

Another way to explore this section of the park is on a **guided kayak tour** (F$50, includes lunch; 4hr). Experienced guides from the village will accompany you on a one-hour paddle south from Lavena before trekking inland to the falls for lunch. The guides will tow your kayak back to the village allowing you to return along the coastal walk. Avid kayakers can hire a guide for the day and paddle further down the coast where the cliffs become steeper and several water-falls tumble directly into the sea – it's a gruelling six-hour trip across open sea to view this spectacle and conditions can be rough.

The west coast

The **west coast** of Taveuni, protected from the trade winds, overlooks the Somosomo Straits towards Buca Bay on Vanua Levu. Most of the coastline is rocky with few beaches and no fringing reef. The land was cleared of its hardwood trees by colonial farmers and planted instead with neat rows of **coconut palms**. Today, the six-kilometre stretch of road between the chiefly coastal village of **Somosomo** and the Catholic mission at **Wairiki** is the population centre of the island, home to the only town, **Naqara** and the hospital and police headquarters at Waiyevo. The bulk of travellers visit the region solely for its close access to the **Rainbow Reef**. However there are also a few land-based attractions nearby including the hair-raising **natural waterslide** at Waitavala and the **180 Degree Meridian** line which passes through Taveuni here. Also nearby is the access road to **De Voeux Peak**, the island's second-highest mountain and **Lake Tagimaucia**.

Cakobau's war canoe

Ra Marama, the last great double-hulled **Fijian war canoe** to grace the South Seas, was built at Somosomo during the 1830s to 1840s. The canoe, measuring thirty metres long and six metres wide, took seven years to complete and could carry over 130 warriors. At the keel-laying ceremony, several young warriors were clubbed to death to increase the canoe's *mana*, or spiritual power; missionaries intervened at the canoe's launch when more warriors were due to be sacrificed. The canoe was presented as a gift to **Cakobau** of Bau who used it as a powerful symbol of strength in his wars against Rewa which eventually crowned him King of Fiji. After Cakobau's death in 1882, the canoe was returned to Somosomo where, beached, it perished to the wind and sea – no trace of it remains.

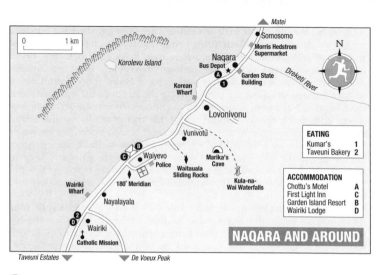

Somosomo

Eighteen kilometres south of Matei along the west coast is the village of **SOMOSOMO**, home to the **Tui Cakau**, high chief of an area encompassing all of Taveuni and much of Vanua Levu. Compared to the surrounding homes along the roadside, the **chief's house** with its adjacent meeting hall (*bure bose*) looks imposing but elsewhere it would appear rather ordinary. This disregard of monetary wealth yet strict observation of stately rank is found throughout Fijian villages and is at the very core of Fijian tradition. There's no accommodation at Somosomo and little reason to stop except for shopping at the new Morris Hedstrom store, the largest **supermarket** on Taveuni (Mon–Fri 8am–6pm, Sat 8am–noon).

Naqara and around

Across the bridge from Somosomo is **NAQARA**, a rather disorganized collection of wooden shacks and corrugated-iron buildings that passes for the island's main town. Looking completely out of place in the centre of town is the three-storey Garden State building. On the ground floor is a branch of Colonial Bank (Mon 9.30am–4pm, Tues–Fri 9am–4pm) with an **ATM** machine, while upstairs is a pool hall and Budget car rental. Taveuni Adventures (☎888 1700) on the next floor up offers **4WD guided tours** around the island costing F$100 for half a day.

If you're peckish try *Kumar's Restaurant* (☎820 4082, Mon–Sat 7am–7pm), in a small red hut next to the primary school. The long-standing *Chottu's Motel* (☎888 0034, ⓔchottus@connect.com.fj, ❶–❷) has the cheapest **rooms** on Taveuni with cold-water shared bathrooms. Larger self-contained units are equally affordable and have basic kitchen facilities, fridge and en-suite hot-water bathrooms. Next door, in the bright mauve building, David Reynolds offers broadband **Internet access** (F$3 for 15min) from his home on the second floor.

A kilometre south of Naqara is Taveuni's old wharf at Lovonivonu village, now known as the **Korean Wharf** and used only by small boats including small ferries crossing to and from Buca Bay on Vanua Levu (see p.231). Two minutes walk south of the wharf is the secluded *Waimakare Camping Ground* (☎993 0319; F$8 for own tent), set in light forest within the grounds of a Fijian family home. A further ten minutes' walk south is **Vuniuto** village where you can hire a guide to visit the **Kula-na-Wai Waterfall**, a one-hour walk inland (ask for landowner Fa, F$10 per person, minimum two people; 2hr return from village).

Waiyevo and the 180 Degree Meridian

Three kilometres south of Naqara, the hillside settlement of **WAIYEVO** makes up the island's administrative centre and could easily be missed if it wasn't for the large satellite dish and the island's supply of oil kept in drums beside the main road. Sandwiched between the two is the rather ordinary looking *Garden Island Resort* (T 888 0286, E garden@connect.com.fj; dorm bed F$40, rooms ●, includes breakfast). There's no beach here, but the oceanfront setting is pleasant enough once inside the landscaped gardens. A large sea almond tree (*tavola*) at the north end of the resort hosts hundreds of **fruit bats** which tend to make a large amount of noise at dusk and dawn. The main reason to stay is for the **diving** provided by ⌁ *Aqua Trek* (T 888 0286, W www.aquatrek.com; two-tank dive F$165, PADI Open Water course F$690), who have the best dive gear on the island and run well-organized trips. Access to Rainbow Reef is only ten minutes away by boat; non-divers can snorkel at **Korolevu Island**, a five-minute paddle by kayak from the resort.

Next door to the resort is a two-storey building with a **post office** and general store downstairs and the *First Light Inn* (T 888 0339; ●) upstairs. The five pastel-coloured motel rooms are clean and simple with air conditioning, satellite TV and telephone and there's a restaurant next door.

Opposite *First Light Inn*, obscured by thick trees, is the unsignposted road to the **hospital** and **police station**, which sit on a small hill 200m from the main road. On the corner, hidden at the far end of the playing field as you head up the hill towards the hospital, is Taveuni's quirkiest attraction, a small information board covered by a tin roof marking the exact spot of the **180 Degree Meridian**. Fiji is one of only two places in the world where this line of longitude passes through land, the other being at the far eastern tip of Russia. The meridian theoretically marks the beginning and end of each day although for the sake of convenience, the International Date Line kinks eastwards to avoid splitting Fiji into two time zones and two different days. In colonial times, several unscrupulous planters justified the working of labourers on Sunday by claiming they were actually working on Monday's side of the dateline.

Waitavala Sliding Rocks

The most popular attraction along the west coast is **Waitavala Sliding Rocks**, a fun two-hundred-metre natural waterslide where you chute down the rapids of a narrow stream on your backside. Old clothes are recommended, and if the water is foaming in the lower pool at the bottom it means the currents are fast – in these conditions it's wise to watch a local slide down before giving it a go yourself. The water slide is a little tricky to find lying south of Vuniuto: walk north from *Garden Island Resort* for five minutes and turn into the hills at Sand Road beside a wooden bus shelter. From here it's a twenty-minute walk to the bottom of the waterslide – when you see a large metal shed on your right, take the path on the left and you'll soon hit the stream. Don't cross here – take the path on the right, walk uphill to the concrete steps and cross the stream at the top. A path leads alongside the left side of the stream and turns in at the large waterfall where you begin the slide.

Wairiki

The new **wharf** of Nayalayala, where all large ships dock on Taveuni, marks the division between Waiyevo and **WAIRIKI**, which otherwise seamlessly merge. The pretty settlement revolves around the imposing **Catholic Mission** where a two-hour Mass is celebrated every Sunday at 7am – it's said that the congregation sing with such enthusiasm that cracks have appeared in the windows. Located on a hill, the mission overlooks the ocean where the island's warriors fought thousands of invading Tongans in a **sea battle**, fighting with clubs from their canoes. The Taveunians won the day, promptly ate their adversaries and halted the Tongan invasion of Fiji.

If that hasn't affected your appetite, head to the ✕ *Taveuni Bakery Restaurant* (daily 8am–8pm) on the roadside 100m towards Waiyevo. The huge English breakfast here costs just F\$9, there's fabulous coffee and smoothies and the menu includes local organic beef served as steaks and beefburgers; Internet access costs F\$10 an hour. The owners are redeveloping the back of the building as a **backpacker hostel** (☏ 888 1211; rooms ❶–❷). At the time of writing it was a burrow of corridors with rather claustrophobic bathrooms, although the two guest rooms at the back overlooking the ocean are airy and spacious. Next door is the base for Taveuni Divers (☏888 0063; two-tank dive F\$160, full day snorkelling with lunch and gear F\$100, minimum two people) which runs **diving** and **snorkelling** trips to the Great White Wall on Rainbow Reef, a ten-minute boat ride away

De Voeux Peak and Lake Tagimaucia

From Wairiki, a dirt road heads to the telecoms station at **De Voeux Peak** (1195m). You can take a five-hour guided 4WD tour here with Taveuni Adventure (see p.244) for F\$150 (minimum two people). If you feel fit, it's not difficult to walk but will take a couple of hours from the turn-off just before the Catholic Mission. Once at the **summit**, the view overlooking Taveuni, Vanua Levu and south to Gau and Koro is incredible on a fine day. Be warned, though, clouds often obscure the peak and whilst it may be sunny by the coast, rain could easily be falling on the mountain. The **bird-watching** up here is excellent with regular sightings of silktails and orange doves, especially in the nesting season during August and September.

From the summit, it's possible to continue for another two hours, hacking through bush along the northern ridge to **Lake Tagimaucia**, a crater lake 823 metres above sea level where the endemic **Tagimaucia flower** blooms in profusion between September and January. The beautiful flower has two red waxy outer petals and four white inner petals resembling a bell. It grows only at high altitude near water and, apart from at a few isolated locations on Vanua Levu, this is the only place in the world you can see it. A relatively well-maintained but arduous trail leads to the lake from Waiyevo (7hr return) – a guide is essential and can be arranged through most west coast resorts or Taveuni Paradise.

Southern Taveuni

Southern Taveuni is dominated by rows of coconut palms growing on the rich volcanic soil. Inland, a series of volcanic cones pop out from the gently slanting slopes rising to the island's highest point, the inaccessible Mount Uluiqalau (1241m). Offshore there are deep drop-offs which offer great opportunities to see sharks and other marine life. Right at the southern end of Taveuni is the rocky **South Cape** and, just up the east coast, the **Matamaiqi Blowhole**.

Nabogi Ono Farm and Vuna Lagoon

Ten minutes' drive south of Waiyevo the road unexpectedly becomes tar-sealed for a few kilometres as it passes through the luxury residential area known as **Taveuni Estates**, now looking rather forlorn with an unkempt nine-hole golf course and tennis courts. The main reason to head this way is to visit **Nabogi Ono Farm** (☎888 0246, ⓦwww.taveuniconservation.com), a hundred-acre fruit farm run as an ecological reserve. This is the most accessible place on the island for regular **bird-spotting** and the only place outside Bouma National Heritage Park where the native forest almost reaches the coast. Offshore is a pristine section of reef which you can visit on a guided **snorkel safari** (F$35 for half day, minimum two people).

Three kilometres further south and an hour and a half by road from Matei is *Paradise Taveuni* (☎888 0125, ⓦwww.paradiseinfiji.com, ❼), the main resort in the area. The beautiful hand-crafted bures here are made from coconut palms and the restaurant serves local cuisine blended with European flavours. There's no beach but the resort operates an extremely efficient **dive operation** visiting both the Rainbow Reef and the rarely explored dive sites off **Vuna Lagoon**. The lagoon is a good site for novice divers with lots of coral heads and reef fish but without the steep drop-offs or strong currents found at Rainbow Reef. Facing the lagoon further south is *Vuna Lagoon Lodge* (☎888 0627; dorm F$20, rooms ❷), a family-owned **guesthouse** in a peaceful location with three rooms, one with private bathroom and a larger occasionally used dormitory. The picturesque **Namoli beach** is fifteen minutes' walk north and you can also reach the blowhole at Matamaiqi in about ninety minutes.

The South Cape and Matamaiqi Blowhole

South of Vuna village and the lagoon, jet black rocks litter a premonitory known as the **South Cape** where Taveuni's last volcanic eruption spilled into the sea around 500 years ago. The highlight of the region is the **Matamaiqi Blowhole**, an unpredictable beast which occasionally spouts jets of sea water 15m or more into the air – it's most likely to perform on the turn of the low tide. The coast here is brutally rugged and exposed to the sometimes forbidding trade winds – watch to see what the seas are doing for at least five minutes before getting too close to the blowhole. Buses from Naqara heading to Navakawau village pass the blowhole but head back to Naqara via the inland road. Alternatively you can walk from the *Vuna Lagoon Lodge*.

Travel details

Buses on Vanua Levu

Labasa to: Basoga (8 daily; 20min); Coqeloa (10 daily; 45min); Dreketilialia (6 daily; 45min); Lekutulevu (3 daily; 1hr 20min); Nabouwalu (4 daily; 5hr); Savusavu (6 daily; 2hr 30min).
Nabouwalu to: Labasa (4 daily; 5hr).
Natuvu Landing to: Savusavu (3 daily; 4hr).

Savusavu to: Labasa (6 daily; 2hr 30min); Natuvu Landing (3 daily; 4hr).

Buses on Taveuni

Naqara to: Lavena (3 daily; 1hr 45min); Matei (3 daily; 30min); Navakawau (3 daily except Sun; 2hr).
Navakawau to: Naqara (3 daily except Sun; 2hr).

Lavena to: Matei (3 daily; 1hr 15min); Naqara
(3 daily; 1hr 45min).
Matei to: Lavena (3 daily; 1hr 15min); Naqara
(3 daily; 30min).

Ferries

Nabouwalu, Vanua Levu to: Natovi Landing, Viti
Levu (daily; 3hr 30min); Savusavu, Vanua Levu
(2 weekly; 7hr).
Natuvu Landing, Vanua Levu to: Taveuni (daily;
1hr 30min).
Savusavu, Vanua Levu to: Natovi Landing, Viti
Levu (2 weekly; 7hr); Lautoka, Viti Levu (2 weekly;
11hr 30min); Suva, Viti Levu (6 weekly; 12hr);
Wairiki Wharf, Taveuni (5 weekly; 4hr 30min).

Wairiki Wharf, Taveuni to: Natuvu Landing,
Vanua Levu (daily; 1hr 30min); Savusavu, Vanua
Levu (5 weekly; 4hr 30min); Suva, Viti Levu
(5 weekly; 12hr).

Flights

Labasa, Vanua Levu to: Nadi Airport (daily;
1hr 5min); Nausori, Suva (6 daily; 40min).
Savusavu, Vanua Levu to: Nadi Airport (5 daily;
1hr); Nausori, Suva (2 daily; 45min); Taveuni
(2 daily; 20min).
Taveuni (Matei) to: Nadi Airport (4 daily;
1hr 20min); Nausori, Suva (2 daily; 45min);
Savusavu (2 daily; 20min).

Rotuma

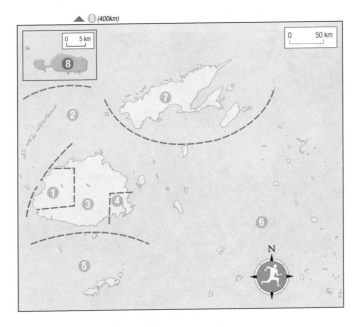

CHAPTER 8

Highlights

* **Fara festivities** Dance the night away under the stars to the island beat. See p.253

* **Circle-island tour** Explore the island by walking along the scenic coastal road, sampling Rotuman life and hospitality along the way. See p.254

* **Vai'oa Beach** One of the prettiest in the South Pacific, with towering palm trees, fabulous snorkelling and usually deserted. See p.255

* **Sisilo Hill** Journey back in time on a hike to the burial grounds of the Rotuman kings. See p.255

* **Split Rock island** Check out this scenic wonder off Rotuma's east coast – an island seemingly sliced in half. See p.256

▲ Coastal sand road, Rotuma

Rotuma

The most remote of the Fijian islands, **Rotuma** lies over 600km north of Suva in a lonely stretch of ocean south of Tuvalu. The island is only part of Fiji thanks to an accident of history and its **Polynesian culture** and language (see p.291) are significantly different from that of the Micronesian Fijians. If you have the time it's well worth a visit. The fertile 43-square-kilometre island is enclosed by a lagoon fringed by a reef and is almost completely surrounded by stunning white **sandy beaches** set off by jet-black volcanic rock. A handful of impressive **archeological sites** can be found inland as well as over a dozen volcanic cones. The highest of these rises to 256m, protruding from the gently rolling hills, which are extensively planted with *taro*, yams, *kava* and numerous varieties of fruit trees, particularly **oranges**. Naturally fermented orange wine is consumed in vast quantities over Christmas, a period noted for the singing and dancing festivities of **Fara** (see p.253), without doubt the liveliest time to visit. Above all else, it's the laid-back lifestyle of its people that makes Rotuma so enticing to discerning travellers.

Some history

According to legend, Rotuma was created by **Raho**, a chief from Samoa who, while searching for a new home found two rocks in the open ocean. He poured a basket of soil between them, creating the fertile island seen today. Raho is acknowledged as the first of 106 *Sau* or **kings of Rotuma**; the last title bearer died in 1870. Neither hereditary nor particularly powerful, the kings were elected by Rotuma's chiefs on a rotational basis and served for only short periods, usually between six months and six years – the length depending on the prosperity of the island during each reign.

In 1791 Captain Edwards of the **HMS Pandora** became the first European to record sighting the island and landed in hope of tracking down the mutineers of the *Bounty* (see p.262). Finding none, he sailed on having named it "Grenville Island". In 1841, Wesleyan **missionaries** landed at Oinafa on the east side of the island followed six years later by Marist Catholics who established themselves in Fag'uta to the south, bitter rivals of the Oinafa people. Over the years the numbers of Catholic islanders began to grow significantly and one of the Wesleyan missionaries, Rev Thomas Moore, despaired at their success. He encouraged rival chiefs to wage war on Riamkau, Chief of Fag'uta, in the hope of wiping the Catholic religion off the island. The task was taken up in 1878 and the fighting lasted several months before Riamkau was killed. Upon defeat, the district of Fag'uta was divided in two to lessen its power but the Catholics stayed on.

In 1881, tired of the continued religious friction, the seven chiefs of Rotuma decided it was in their best interests to cede their island to **Britain**, following

ROTUMA

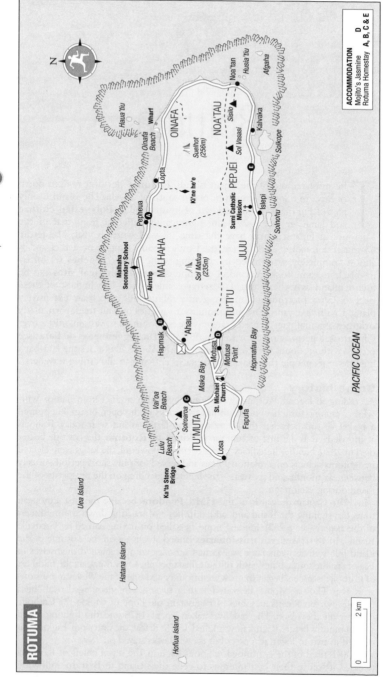

N

PACIFIC OCEAN

Haua 'itu
Oinafa Beach
Wharf
OINAFA
Noa'tan
Husia 'itu
Afgaha
Lopta
Suelhot (256m)
NOA'TAU
Sisilo
Sol Vasasi
Kalvaka
Soikope
Solnohu
Ki'ne he'e
PEP JEI
Pepheua
MALHAHA
Islepi
Sumi Catholic Mission
JUJU
Malhaha Secondary School
Airstrip
Sol Matua (235m)
ITU'TI'U
Ahau
Hapmak
Motusa
Motusa Point
Hopmafau Bay
Maka Bay
Val'oa Beach
St. Michael Church
Solraaroa
Lulu Beach
ITU'MUTA
Fapufa
Ka'ta Stone Bridge
Losa

Uea Island
Hatana Island
Hofliua Island

0   2 km

ACCOMMODATION
Mojito's Jasmine   D
Rotuma Homestay   A, B, C & E

the example of the Fijians. Unfortunately for the Rotumans, the island was deemed too isolated to justify its own governor. Instead it was decided that Rotuma should politically become part of Fiji, its remote neighbour to the south. On May 13, 1881, at a spot in Motusa marked by a stone wall embedded with a brass plaque, Rotuma relinquished its sovereignty to Fiji.

Movements for **independence from Fiji** have been mooted since Fiji's independence from Britain in 1970. The most notable claim came in 1987 when the radical Mölmahua clan declared Rotuma a republic, taking advantage of the uncertainty caused by the Fijian coup of the same year. The clan's leader, **Henry Gibson** claimed to be the rightful king of Rotuma and even drew up a new flag for the country. He and his supporters were swiftly arrested by the Fijian authorities and charged with sedition. Today, with over five thousand Rotumans based in Suva, many employed as doctors, lawyers, teachers and other prominent professionals, Rotuma's independence movement has little support.

Arrival

The grass **airstrip** at Malhaha on the north coast of Rotuma is served exclusively by Air Fiji from Nausori Airport (☎889 1044 in Rotuma; F$439 one way, departs Wed; 2hr 20min). Note that flights are often delayed by poor weather, even just persistent rain. There are always plenty of small trucks meeting incoming flights at the airstrip and you should be able to negotiate a ride to 'Ahau or Motusa.

Western Shipping runs the *Cagi-mai-Ba* **cargo boat** (deck F$98, cabin F$125) once a month (usually a Saturday) between Suva and Oinafa wharf on the northeast coast of Rotuma. On occasions, usually at Christmas, other cargo boats head up to Rotuma – to find out if any are visiting contact the Fiji Shipping Corporation (☎331 9383, ✉fscl@unwired.com.fj) on Edinburgh Drive in Suva.

There's no bank on Rotuma, and no credit card facilities – everything operates by **cash** so bring plenty with you. In an emergency you can have money wired to you through Western Union operated by the post office (☎889 1003) in 'Ahau.

Accommodation

Mojito's Jasmine (☎889 1288; ❷, includes meals) is the only **official accommodation** on Rotuma and is used mostly by Fijian civil servants. It's located across the road from Motusa Primary School, 3km southeast of the airstrip. There are two

Fara – the passion of Christmas

Fara is the joyful epitome of the Rotuman spirit and combines **music and dance** with long treks around the island. The festival predates the introduction of Christianity but now incorporates Christmas as its focus. The party begins on December 1 (Dec 24 for Juju and Pepjei districts) and lasts until mid January. Each evening children wander around their villages singing *fara* songs and clapping their hands for a beat. When the kids stop at a house, the family comes out to watch, rewarding them with the traditional gifts of perfume, talc and fruit, usually watermelon. If the singing is poor, water is thrown to chase the group away. As the evening progresses, the rest of the villagers join in, grabbing guitars, ukuleles, one-string drums and perhaps a bucket of orange wine. The group either walks or piles into the back of a van moving from house to house, village to village, visiting friends and relatives along the way until the early hours. If you visit Rotuma during fara you will certainly be invited to take part. Make sure you book **flights** in advance as it's the most popular time for Rotumans to visit family on the island. To listen to fara songs online check out ⊛www.rotuma.net, an excellent resource on the island.

thatch bures here, each with two rooms sharing a cold-water bathroom, plus a small **bar** which can be lively on weekends. To stay with a **local family**, contact Nadi-based *Rotuma Homestay* (℡672 2600, Ⓦwww.rotumahomestay.com; ❸, includes meals) which has contacts at various villages around the island. You'll have your own room within a family house sharing a cold-water bathroom eating with the family at mealtimes. Supplies on the island are limited so it's wise to take some snacks and drinks with you.

Transport

With a quiet sandy coastal road and an interior crisscrossed with forest tracks, exploring the island is easy on **foot**. Alternatively, you can rent a truck and driver in most villages for around F$100 for half a day. The only **bus** is the school service which circles the island Monday to Friday, shuttling children between their villages and Malhaha secondary school.

Exploring the island

Rotuma measures only 14km from east to west and is divided into seven districts. A narrow isthmus connects the main western "body" of the island to the small eastern "head". The largest section, **eastern Rotuma**, has several historic tombs inland and a handful of lagoon islets off its sandy beaches. On its western side, overlooking Maka Bay, is **'Ahau**, government centre for the island. **Western Rotuma** is more sparsely populated and features a couple of stunning cove beaches. Beyond the lagoon, between three and five kilometres off the western coast, are three intriguing **offshore islands** including the dramatically shaped Split Rock.

'Ahau and around

The government headquarters for Rotuma have been stationed at **'Ahau** in Itu'ti'u district since 1902. Colonial-style buildings house the hospital, police and judiciary as well as a small cement jail with two tiny cells. The island's **post office** is also located here and has an impressive satellite dish and public telephones linking Rotuma to the outside world. A well-stocked **shop** on the south side of 'Ahau is the best place to buy supplies and on Friday mornings the road alongside the playing field is used as a **market**. If you're lucky, you may be able to find one of three local delicacies on sale: *porasam*, wrapped *taro* leaf cooked in thick coconut cream; *fekei* a sticky, starchy sweet; and *tähroro,* a fermented coconut sauce flavoured with chilli. The playing field is the focus for the island's main **festivals** including: Cession Day (May 13); the Methodist Conference (Aug, date varies); and Fiji Independence Day (Oct 10), all featuring traditional dancing and feasting.

Heading south from 'Ahau, down the hill, takes you into the village of **Motusa** which straddles the narrow isthmus. The south side of the isthmus, accessed via a small track beside the Motusa primary school, leads to Motusa Point, a secluded spot for picnics with a beautiful beach and good snorkelling in the bay.

Eastern Rotuma

The best beach on eastern Rotuma is at **Oinafa** beside the island's wharf on the northeastern point of the island. As well as having fine white sand, the beach is a good spot for **body surfing** and boasts excellent snorkelling in

Pre-Christian Rotumans believed in the **'atua**, or spirits of the deceased who would haunt enemies and give advice and warnings to loved ones in their dreams. Some people, referred to as *ape'aitu*, could communicate willingly with the *'atua* by summoning them in the form of an animal. In this manner, various clans around Rotuma have affiliations with turtles, sharks and sting rays. The only deity the Rotumans believed in was the powerful *Tagaroa Siria*. By praying to him hurricanes could be diverted, droughts ended and epidemics driven away.

Deep inland lived a lineage of Rotumans believed to be much larger in size than the coastal dwellers and giving rise to the present-day myth of **giants** or *toa*. At Lopta village ask for a guide to show you the huge **stone platform** of Ki'ne he'e, thirty minutes' walk inland, believed to be home of the giant Faumi.

the turquoise lagoon around the twin islands of Haua. From the wharf, the prettiest stretch of coastal road runs south to Noa'tau district, shaded by tall coconut trees and hugging the ocean. Inland from the village of **Noa'tau**, considered the most important clan village on Rotuma, is the ancient **burial site** of the kings of Rotuma on top of **Sisilo Hill**. The site was established to mark the death of the seventh king, Tafaki, whose tomb is marked by a large smooth stone shaped like a saddle. The last king to be buried at Sisilo was Marafu who died in a war with Riamkau in 1837. Marafu's tomb is marked by his prized possession, a cannon, which terrified his enemies but jammed during his final battle.

Three kilometres along the south coast is the tiny district of Pepjei, which features the imposing **Sumi Catholic Mission** at its western end, built between 1868 and 1881. In the 1950s, one of the French Catholic priests here supposedly introduced the making of **orange wine** to the island by fermenting sweet oranges for over a month producing a potent brew. Orange wine is still made on Rotuma but it's usually achieved by the addition of processed yeast which leaves a sickly taste and thumping hangover. A lovely walking track heads inland from beside the Catholic school. It meanders through garden plantations, passing the base of several scalable volcanic craters and eventually leads to the north coast close to Pepehua village.

East of the mission near Islepi village is a small hill with an ancient **stone tomb** at the top. It is believed that the stones were carried all the way from Motusa by giants. The beach in front of Islepi has a deep channel suitable for a refreshing swim. It's possible to wade over to the crescent-shaped island of Solnoho which features dramatic rock ledges on the south side facing the waves of the Pacific.

Western Rotuma

Beyond Motusa and the isthmus is the rugged landscape of **Western Rotuma**. Isolated **Vai'oa Beach**, accessed via a bush track just beyond Lopo village, is one of the most striking beaches in Fiji with huge coconut palms leaning over the sea. The bay offers fantastic snorkelling among large formations of coral, home to many small reef sharks. Around the southern point of Vai'oa is another secluded beach, Lulu, and from here a small trail leads to **Ka'ta**, an impressive natural **stone bridge** linking the island with two sea arches. On the north side of Vai'oa is the towering 219-metre peak of **Solroaroa** which you can climb with a guide from Itu'muta village.

The offshore islands

From the top of Solroaroa is a fabulous view of Rotuma's three **offshore islands**. The largest and closest of these is **Uea**, a collapsed caldera roughly 3km from the Itu'muta coast. Just southeast is the sacred coral island of **Hatana**, where Rotuma's founding ruler, Raho, retreated in his waning years – his grave is identified by two small upright rocks in the centre of the island. A kilometre further south, you should be able to make out the narrow vertical slice of **Split Rock**, or Hofliua. A local tale recalls that the split was the result of a mighty swordfish striking the rock during a race from Tonga. It's possible to take a small boat right through the split, where you can see a rock precariously lodged between the two halves; you should be able to persuade a local boatman to take you out although this will depend entirely on sea conditions.

8

ROTUMA | Travel details

Travel details

Cargo boat

Walu Bay, Suva to: Rotuma (monthly; 2 days).

Flights

Nausori Airport to: Rotuma (weekly; 2hr).

256

Contexts

Contexts

A brief history of Fiji

Feared for its **cannibal** tendencies and avoided by mariners for its treacherous **reefs**, Fiji was one of the last island groups in the world to be encroached upon by the West. When the *kaivalagi*, the men from far away, finally arrived in 1803 they found a deeply hierarchical tribal culture characterized by allegience to village chiefs, fierce warfare and pagan religion. **Europeans** exploited the Fijians' natural resources, particularly sandalwood, coconuts and bêche de mer (sea slugs), and brought with them firearms and alcohol with which to pay off the local chiefs. The arrival of firearms sparked several bloody wars between tribes, particularly the powerful clans of Rewa and Bau on eastern Viti Levu. This turbulent state of affairs eased in 1874 after **Cakobau**, the self-proclaimed "King of Fiji" converted to Christianity and renounced cannibalism, events which lead to Fiji becoming a **British colony**. The Fijians, however, proved a reluctant workforce for the new authorities and so indentured **labourers from India** were shipped in to toil the land and make profitable this curious outpost of the empire. This situation continued for almost a hundred years until the country secured its **independence** in 1970 and was faced with the challenging task of forming a harmonious national identity, a struggle that continues today.

The first Fijians

With no written record, the movement and lifestyles of the first Fijian peoples have been revealed only with the advent of accurate archeological research, particularly the discovery of **Lapita pottery**. Many Fijians, however, give credence to the legend of **Lutunasobasoba** as the first settler of the islands.

Lapita migration

Scientific findings place **Bourewa**, north of Natadola Beach on the west coast of Viti Levu, as the earliest site of human habitation in Fiji, dating back to 1220 BC. Distinctive **Lapita pottery** (see box, p.127) found all around the Melanesian archipelago, suggests that the settlers originated from Southeast Asia, most probably Taiwan or the Philippines. Thought to be lighter skinned than modern Fijians, they inhabited Papua New Guinea, then the Solomon Islands before settling on Vanuatu, New Caledonia, Fiji and Tonga. This migration was followed by a more dynamic flow of people, likely to be darker-skinned Melanesians who reached Fiji between 1000 and 500 BC. The Melanesians continued east to Tonga, the remote islands of Rarotonga and Tahiti, before eventually reaching Aotearoa (New Zealand) and Hawaii around 800 AD, all part of present-day Polynesia.

Lutunasobasoba

The majority of Fijians recognize **Lutunasobasoba** as the first person to settle the islands and as founder of the tribal system. However, the story of his discovery of Fiji only entered the national consciousness in 1892 after a competition in a local newspaper to find the best explanation for Fijian evolution. Supposedly, the great chief Lutunasobasoba landed on the west coast of Viti Levu at Vuda, arriving by canoe from Tanzania in East Africa. Either his spirit or one of his clan moved north to Ra where he was immortalized as **Degei**, the supreme god of Fiji who is said to have lived in a cave in the form of a **snake**. Today, it's common for Fijians to claim an impressive genealogical network of around twelve generations tracing their tribe (*yavusa*) back to either Lutunasobasoba or Degei.

Tribal culture

Very little is known about the Fijian islanders in the centuries before European contact, although it's clear that they built extensive hill fortifications and stone fish traps around the coastline. They also created beautiful **wood carvings** including war clubs, *yaqona* bowls and head rests, wove *tapa* cloth to adorn the body and made jewellery. **Tattooing** or *qai* was commonplace, often around the mouth and conducted with a chipped *kai* shell to form a raised scar.

Tribes seldom ventured beyond their territorial boundaries unless to hunt or pay homage to their superior neighbouring chiefs. Consequently, a variety of distinct tribes evolved in relative isolation, each with their identifying customs, gods and dialects.

Early religion

Two tiers of **gods** ruled the living: the highest-ranked gods, the *kalou-vu*, were universally venerated immortals. For everyday affairs, the people sought blessings from a collection of localized gods known as the *kalou-yalo*. These were ancestral spirits who in the living world had been respected chiefs or triumphant warriors. These gods commanded the weather, had powers over war and sickness and were called upon to bless the people with abundant fish and fruits, but were otherwise not invoked. Contact with these gods was conducted through the **high priest** (*bete*), a member of the priestly clan or *bete mataqali*. The *bete* sat in a high-roofed temple known as the *bure kalou* and, possessed with *yaqona*, would call the spirits to descend down the *tapa* cloth hanging from the temple roof and speak through his body.

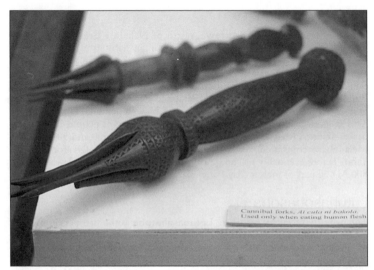

Cannibal forks. *Ai cula ni bokola.* Used only when eating human flesh

▲ Cannibal forks, Fiji Museum

And now the drums beat pat, pat, pat, pat, pat. What is the signal? It means that a man is about to be cut up and prepared for food, as is a bullock in our own country. See the commotion! The majority of the population, old and young, run to gaze upon the intended victim. He is stripped naked, struck down with the club, his body ignominiously dashed against a stone in front of a temple, and then cut up and divided amongst a chosen few, ere the vital spark is extinct.

Rev Joseph Waterhouse, *The King and People of Fiji*, Pasifika Press, 1886

Cannibalism in Fiji wasn't something that happened every so often, it was a routine part of life. In crudely pragmatic terms, human flesh served as a much-needed source of protein, especially amongst the hill people, for Fiji was almost devoid of meat-bearing animals. But its real power lay in **intimidation** – by eating the flesh of an enemy, a Fijian was consuming the *mana* or strength of their foe. **Warfare** was usually a tit-for-tat process. Small bands of marauding warriors would prowl the countryside looking for easy prey. If a stand-off between two warring parties ensued, taunts would be cast but seldom was there a full confrontation – securing just one victim was enough for a wild orgy back home.

With the procurement of a **bokola**, or uncooked human, men performed a *cibi* or war dance and unmarried girls responded in an erotic *wate* dance around the captive. The humiliation of the victim didn't usually end there. Young boys were given sharpened sticks and encouraged to taunt and torture the captives, a practice echoed today when a pig is brought down from the plantation for eating. In some severe accounts recorded by missionaries living amongst the Fijians in the 1800s, the tongue was cut out while the victim was still alive and eaten whilst his blood was drained and drunk. Eventually, the *bokola* was placed at the **killing stone** and the head smashed using a war club. The bodies were cleaned and cooked. The heart and tongue were considered the choicest parts and given to the chief, who would consume the flesh using a specially carved cannibal fork with four prongs whilst other body parts were distributed amongst the villagers.

Understandably, in the early days of encounter, Europeans were afraid of the "Cannibal Isles" although most often, visitors, however strange looking, were treated gracefully and generously. A few did end up in the pot: Charlie Savage (see p.172), met his end on the island of Vanua Levu in 1813. It is said his bones were later made into sail needles. The most notorious case of cannibalism in the islands, though, rests with the unfortunate **Reverend Thomas Baker** who was killed and eaten by the Colo hill people of Viti Levu (see p.139) in 1867.

By the mid-1800s, with the introduction of firearms and the ensuing power struggle of Cakobau over his Rewan enemies, cannibalism hit its peak. Some first-hand accounts of missionaries stationed at Bau claimed that as many as three hundred people were brought back as the spoils of a single war and body parts hung off every house waiting for consumption. By the 1870s, Cakobau had converted to **Christianity** and ceased to practise cannibalism; following his lead, so did the majority of the Fiji islanders.

C

Customs

Blood spilling was an integral part of Fijian custom and imbued items with what was known as **mana**, or spirituality. *Mana* was especially important for warriors and chiefs; their personal war clubs were anointed in human blood in order to bring them mystical powers. War canoes were launched over the bodies of sacrificial victims and the building of temples and chiefly houses required people to be buried alive with the foundations. **Cannibalism** (see above) was the apotheosis of such blood lust with war parties constantly scouting for unsuspecting victims. Direct tribal confrontations were less frequent, though when they occurred they tended to take the form of the sacking of entire villages by uprooting crops and burning houses, usually once the survivors had surrendered and moved on to new land.

Polygamy was commonplace among the early Fijians. On a man's **death**, his spirit was believed to linger in the village for four days to haunt his enemies, during which period it was also customary for the widows to be strangled to death in order to accompany the husband's spirit to the afterlife or *Bulu*. Witchcraft and superstition were similarly deeply ingrained in the Fijian culture. Certain people had the power to invoke the spirits to taunt their enemies, most notably through illness, in which case the village **sorcerer** would perform an elaborate *yaqona* ceremony (see p.34) to chase the spirit away and reveal the perpetrator.

European encounters

Bypassed by the early Spanish explorers who had headed north to the Philippines, Fiji had to wait until the seventeenth century before European ships reached Fijian waters. In 1643, Dutch navigator **Abel Tasman**, who had discovered New Zealand and Tasmania the previous year, sailed past the Fijian island of Taveuni on his way back to Jakarta in Indonesia. He narrowly avoided shipwreck off the Nanuku Reef east of Vanua Levu and quickly made a northward passage away from the islands. Another 130 years were to pass before European explorers returned.

William Bligh and the Bounty, 1789

During his celebrated voyage of 1774, **Captain James Cook** made a note of the remote Vatoa Island in the southern Lau Group. Although he didn't explore the region further he later met Fijians while in Tonga. Greater recognition goes to **William Bligh**, who in 1789 found himself passing through the heart of the Fijian archipelago aboard a small wooden launch along with seventeen men and just six rowing oars. Having captained his ship, the **HMS Bounty**, to Tahiti, Bligh was famously the victim of a mutiny led by Fletcher Christian on April 28 just off Tofua in Tonga. Mindful of the dreadful stories of the warlike, cannibalistic people from Tonga, Bligh and his small crew anxiously paddled for five days past Gau and between Vanua Levu and Viti Levu. On the sixth day, in the Yasawas, two war canoes set out in pursuit of their vessel but, thanks to a timely squall, Bligh escaped and eventually made it to the Dutch settlement at Coupang on Timor forty days later. Bligh had managed to successfully chart 39 Fijian islands and the section of sea where he made good his escape is known as Bligh Waters.

The Argo and the arrival of beachcombers 1800–1810

The first white people to land on Fijian soil were probably the crew of the schooner **Argo** (see p.205), who were shipwrecked off Lakeba in Lau in 1803. They brought with them Asian cholera which promptly annihilated much of the local population. A few years later, a steady stream of merchant ships from Sydney Harbour began to arrive, attracted by the fragrant **sandalwood** newly discovered at Bua Bay on the remote southwestern coast of Vanua Levu.

A few Europeans, mostly escaped convicts or mercenaries, chose to settle on the islands. Known as **"beachcombers"** they aligned themselves with local chiefs and acted as go-betweens for the merchants and Fijians. One particular beachcomber, a Swede named **Charlie Savage** (see p.172) had a strong influence on the tribal balance of power in Fiji. Shipwrecked aboard the *Eliza* in 1808, he was presented as a hostage to the chief of **Bau**, a tiny island off the east coast of Viti Levu. Over the following years his knowledge of muskets and unscrupulous demeanour soon saw the island's opportunist chief, Naulivou and later Cakobau (see p.202), with whom Savage had aligned himself, begin to dominate the region. The possession of **firearms** soon became a matter of survival for rival villages. With gun in hand and mercenaries by their sides, they turned the previous petty marauding style of warfare into full-blown genocidal campaigns with entire villages being laid waste and their inhabitants shot, cooked and eaten.

The arrival of the missionaries, 1835

In 1835, after a lull in visiting European merchant ships, Cross and Cargill of the Wesleyan London Missionary Society arrived on Lakeba in the Lau Group and established the first mission in Fiji. Though they found little resistance to their efforts they managed to convert only a few Tongans living on the island. Other **missionaries** soon followed and set up base around **Levuka** where a few hardened European merchants had huddled together in a small trading outpost. Appalled at the entrenched traditions of cannibalism and widow strangulation, the missionaries soon realized that the spread of Christianity would depend on the powerful pagan chief of Bau.

Cakobau's war with Rewa

Bau's ruling chief, **Cakobau**, was a particularly ruthless warrior and received homage from many islands in Fiji, from Kadavu in the south to Taveuni in the north. But having waged an unsuccessful war with Qaraniqio, chief of bitter neighbour **Rewa** since 1840, Cakobau had overstretched his domain and accrued too many dangerous enemies. He had also lost the support of the white traders of Levuka and had to endure a trade and ammunition blockade.

In 1853, several disaffected chiefs and five hundred warriors rebelled at Kaba Point, a few kilometres south of Bau, and stole the sails of Cakobau's prized 72-ton **gunboat** which he'd recently acquired from the Americans. In retaliation Cakobau led a raid on Kaba but the heavily fortified stronghold proved resilient. In March the following year Cakobau's status was further eroded by a devastating fire which destroyed many houses on Bau as well as his sacred war temple – the chief took this as a sign that his gods had abandoned him.

On April 30, Cakobau received a letter of from his old adversary, King George of Tonga, encouraging him to accept **Christianity**. After a long conversation with Joseph Waterhouse, the resident Methodist missionary on Bau, he decided to *lotu*, or convert. There were so many subsequent conversions throughout the islands that there were not enough missionaries to baptize all the newly faithful, let alone instruct them in the scriptures. Such mass conversion was a seismic social shift, necessitating not just the widespread acceptance of the Christian God and the rejection of all other gods, but also the destruction of the temples and the cessation of cannibalism and widow strangulation.

In early 1855, Qaraniqio, chief of Rewa, died. Weary of war, the Rewans sued for peace. But hearing of his abandonment of Fijian traditions, Cakobau's other enemies now rallied at **Kaba Point** to wage war not only on Bau, but on

Christianity. King George of Tonga came to Cakobau's assistance with two thousand Tongan warriors led in part by **Ma'afu** (see p.205), ruler over the Lau Group. Their intervention proved decisive with the Tongans leading the main assault and Bauan warriors holding back any retreat. After victory was assured, Cakobau, keeping faith with his new religion, forbade celebratory feasting on his enemies. With Rewa and Verata finally subdued, he arrogantly declared himself *Tui Viti* or **King of Fiji** although it was to be years before the title was formally recognized.

The path to colonialism

It soon became apparent that King George's assistance in the Kaba victory had come at a price – the control of northern Fiji. The Tongan prince **Ma'afu** had already established his seat of power on Vanua Balavu in the Lau Group and was making steady inroads into the province of Cakaudrove, hitherto home of Cakobau's strongest allies. Ma'afu, full of confidence after his leading role in the assault on Kaba, now became a serious threat to Cakobau's kingdom and over the nineteen years leading up to cession, the two chiefs **battled** indirectly for absolute control over Fiji with Ma'afu steadily gaining the upper hand.

The American claims

While dealing with the Tongans, Cakobau faced a new problem – a **debt** to the US Government. Back in 1849 on Nukulau island off Suva, the house of **John Williams**, the US commercial agent, had accidentally burned to the ground during US Independence Day celebrations. What remained of his stockpile of supplies was subsequently ransacked by locals. Ever since the fire, Williams had been pressing the US government to claim compensation from the Fijians. In 1851 he had asked the captain of a US warship to demand US$5000 but the claim was dismissed as unfounded. However, the next time a US Navy ship visited in 1855, Williams was successful in gaining the support of its captain for his and a number of other American claims for compensation. Cakobau, now the most powerful local chief, was held accountable to the impossible tune of US$42,000. Taken aboard the warship, he was bullied into signing acceptance of these claims and forced to promise payment within a year. Afraid of being taken prisoner to the US, Cakobau appealed to Pritchard, the British consul in Levuka, and promised **sovereignty of Fiji** to the British along with thousands of acres of land if the debt to the US was paid off and Ma'afu could be persuaded to relinquish his pursuit of power. Pritchard, hopeful of cession, managed to stall the American demands, and at a gathering of chiefs in Levuka in 1859, he persuaded Ma'afu to cease his war with Bau. Despite his efforts, cession was initially rejected by Britain in 1862 on the grounds that Cakobau, despite claiming kingly *s*tatus, did not represent the united peoples of the islands. There were also concerns that the colony would prove unprofitable and a hindrance in times of war.

The second wave of European migration

Although Britain had rejected taking on Fiji as a colony, the following decade saw a new **rush** of Europeans to the islands, fuelled by rumours of imminent

Blackbirding, the recruitment of slave labourers through trickery, flourished in Fiji during the 1860s driven by labour shortages in the cotton plantations. European merchants would drop anchor at remote islands, particularly Vanuatu and the Solomon Islands, and persuade the illiterate locals into signing papers which legitimized a work contract to take them off to far away islands as labourers. The locals usually knew nothing of what they had signed and were lured onto the merchant ships by trinkets and locked in the hold to prevent them jumping overboard. As trade in this "black ivory" flourished, merchants became more unscrupulous, succumbing to blatant kidnapping, rape and murder along the way before selling their human cargo in Levuka for £10 per head. By 1872, when the trade was put to a stop by the presence of British warships, roughly four thousand overseas labourers were working in Fiji's plantations, each man being paid £6 a year under a three-year contract. Most of the labourers were eventually **freed**, some returning to their homelands, but many stayed on establishing new settlements on Ovalau and Viti Levu, or being adopted into nearby Fijian villages.

cession. A further hundred thousand acres of land were sold to white traders by rogue chiefs eager to obtain firearms and alcohol. Plantations of **cotton** were established on Taveuni, Vanua Levu and the Lau Group and with a shortage of labour, **blackbirding ships** (see box above) began to bring in captives from the Melanesian Islands. As more traders arrived, the small whaling outpost of Levuka began to take on the role of Fiji's capital. Beyond the control of Imperial authorities it soon developed into a debauched frontier-like town characterized by vice and alcoholism.

Meanwhile, Ma'afu continued his advances on Bau and the Americans again pursued their claim with Cakobau. In 1867, with an American warship threatening to bombard Levuka, Cakobau turned to the newly formed Australian-owned **Polynesian Company** which guaranteed payment of the claim by instalments in return for land around Suva (see p.152).

The deed of cession, October 10, 1874

With the Americans off his back, Cakobau declared the formation of a **government** in Levuka in 1871 with the backing of a few chiefs and gained formal recognition of his claim to be **king**. Of the many bills passed, most concerned regulations in the sale of land, alcohol and firearms, and a poll and land tax was introduced to raise funds. These laws didn't go down well with some parts of the lawless society in Levuka who immediately incited riots. Meanwhile, the local Fijians, unable to pay their taxes, were coerced to work on plantations as their penalty. After two years of government, Cakobau had lost the trust of his people, divided the Levuka traders and accrued a **financial deficit** of £87,000. If that wasn't enough, Ma'afu and his allies in the north had refused to pay their taxes and the wild Colo hill people of Viti Levu had begun to attack Christian villages.

With the situation looking bleak, Cakobau once again offered to cede Fiji to Britain. This time, the new consul, James Goodenough, reported favourably and with other foreign powers, notably the Americans, Prussians and French keen to annex the islands, the British government agreed. On **October 10, 1874**, in a pompous ceremony in Levuka, Cakobau, Ma'afu, other high chiefs and representatives of Queen Victoria signed the deed ceding sovereignty to Britain.

One of the first and most significant acts to be passed by the first Governor General, Sir Arthur Gordon, was the indefinite **suspension of land sales** in order to protect the Fijian system of *vanua* or tribal land ownership. The British were keen to preserve the Fijian tribal system in order to rule more efficiently. In 1876 the **Great Council of Chiefs** or *Bose Levu Vakaturaga* was established to advise the colonial government on Fijian matters with Queen Victoria recognized as the most powerful chief.

Indenture and development

Immediately after cession Cakobau and his two sons made a stately visit to Sydney. They returned carrying **measles**, and swiftly passed it on to chiefs from all around Fiji who had come to learn about their adventures overseas. Within two months almost a third of the Fijian population had died from the outbreak. Faced with this crisis, those opposed to cession and Christianity reverted to their heathen ways. A longer-lasting effect of the outbreak was a decimated workforce, and one unwilling to toil in the plantations to add to the coffers of empire. In response Sir Arthur Gordon proposed to bring in **indentured labourers** from India; a move that would have lasting consequences for the evolution of Fijian society.

The first shipment of Indian labourers arrived aboard the *Leonadis* in Levuka in 1879. Between then and 1916 when the scheme was abolished, 60,553 Indians, mostly men, arrived in Fiji. Their working contract or "**girmit**" was to last for five years, after which time the labourer could return home. Life was harsh on the sugar and copra plantations but having endured five years of serfdom, the majority preferred to stay on in Fiji working as farm hands or clerks and eventually setting up trading stores or leasing small tracts of farmland with the savings they had made. Word of these new opportunities soon reached India and by 1904, **Indian merchants**, mostly Gujarats and Punjabis of all castes and religions, began to arrive.

The largest employer and backbone of the Fijian economy was the Australian-owned **Colonial Sugar Refining Company** (CSR) established in 1880. But once the indenture programme ceased in 1920, a series of strikes for better living and working conditions of the existing Indian labourers eventually forced CSR to transform its huge plantations into small-holdings, leased by aspirational Indians. By the 1930s indigenous Fijians were becoming resentful of the wealth and status accrued by the Indians and began to refuse to renew their leases. Pressure was exerted by CSR but it was **Ratu Sir Lala Sukuna**, high chief and Oxford graduate, who persuaded his people to work with the Indians. To protect indigenous interests, the Native Land Trust Ordinance (later to become the present-day Native Land Trust Board) was established to negotiate land tenure leases on the behalf of Fijian landowners.

World War II

During World War II, Fiji's strategic position saw it being used as a base by Allied forces. With the British occupied in Singapore and Burma, Fiji's defence was initially placed under the control of **New Zealand**. Three airfields were built at Nadi and a series of gun batteries were erected overlooking Nadi Bay and Suva Harbour. After the Japanese attack on Pearl Harbor in 1942, the **US Navy** was given control of Nadi Bay.

With the Japanese encroaching into Papua New Guinea and the Solomans, Fijian soldiers volunteered for combat duty. The Americans immediately recognized their aptitude for **jungle warfare** and sent Fijians to assist in the Solomans, notably at Guadalcanal and Bourganville where they served with distinction. Fiji-Indians were not encouraged to enlist under the orders of the British who were fearful of giving them military training in light of the independence movement in India.

Independence

As the war ended, politics in Fiji split along ethnic lines. The majority of **indigenous Fijians** remained content with the colonial administration, ruled in essence by their village chiefs and with both their land and chiefly system protected. **Fiji-Indians** had always wielded economic clout, as demonstrated through sporadic trade union strikes against the CSR, but as their population increased, so too did their political power. Disenchanted with low sugar pay-outs, their inability to buy freehold land, and growing antagonism fuelled by India's independence from Britain in 1947, they became more vocal and determined to oust the colonial government. The British, too, wanted to move on from their control of the islands, but were reluctant to let the Fiji-Indians take their place. An initial move towards **self-government** occurred in 1953 with the expansion of powers of the Legislative Council. Half its members were elected, a third of which were Fijian, a third European and a third Fijian-Indian. By 1963, the Legislative Council became an entirely elected council, except for two members appointed by the Great Council of Chiefs to ensure Fijian political dominance. But this was not enough for dissident Fiji-Indians. At the forefront of this group was A.D. Patel, founder of the National Federation Party. He demanded independence for Fiji with a government elected by universal suffrage.

The Fijians became increasingly wary of the Fiji-Indian influence and fearing loss of land lobbied Britain for support. As a compromise, the British introduced a form of self-government in 1967 with **Ratu Kamisese Mara** appointed the first Chief Minister and seats allocated ethnically. In April 1970, the Legislative Council was replaced by a parliament with a 52-member House of Representatives. Indigenous Fijians and Fiji-Indians would each be allocated 22 seats, the rest were elected by "general voters", European, Rotumans and other minority groups. The general voters tended to vote for indigenous Fijian candidates so Fiji-Indian dominance was held in check.

Full independence from Britain was granted on October 10, 1970 ending 96 years of colonial rule. The Alliance Party, headed by **Ratu Sir Kamisese Mara** of the Lau Group, ruled the nation for the first seventeen years of independence and set in motion policies to prioritize **Fijian affairs** over those of the Indian population. The most contentious policy of the era was to restrict land leases to a maximum thirty-year tenure.

The four coups

Simmering ethnic tension, a large, well-funded military and a relatively recent transition to democracy have seen Fiji experience **four coups** since independence. Although all were relatively peaceful in nature, they have permanently altered the political landscape and caused immense damage to Fiji's international reputation.

Rabuka and the first two coups, 1987

Ratu Mara's Alliance Party dominated Fijian politics in the post-independence years. However, in 1987 a **coalition** of the Fiji-Indian-supported Labour Party and the Fijian breakaway National Federation Party won a historic victory in the April elections. Headed by **Dr Timoci Bavadra**, a chief from the west of Viti Levu, this new-look government seemed to promise a bright and harmonious future. Unfortunately, this hope proved premature, and the government was dogged by the insecurities of the Fijian chiefly system which opposed the political power of both Indians and the western chiefs. Influenced by the fascist Taukei Movement, which sanctioned a "Fiji for Fijians only" policy, and encouraged by the authoritarian Methodist Church, **Sitiveni Rabuka**, a little-known colonel from the military, stormed parliament on May 14, 1987, and took over the country in a **bloodless coup**. He handed power to the Governor General, **Ratu Penaia Ganilau**, high chief of Cakaudrove.

To Rabuka's surprise, Ratu Ganilau, a strong supporter of parliamentary democracy, ruled the military takeover unconstitutional and attempted to form a government of national unity comprising both parties. In response Rabuka staged a **second coup** on September 23, 1987. He proclaimed Fiji a **republic**, with the intention to serve only the interests of the Fijian people and to sever all links with the Commonwealth. Under a new **constitution** legalized in 1990 government

Coup cast list

Ratu Sir Kamisese Mara Lauan high chief and leader of the Alliance Party which ruled Fiji from 1970 to 1987. Accused of being behind the first coup of 1987.

Dr Timoci Bavadra Ethnic Fijian from western Viti Levu and founder of the multiracial Fiji Labour Party. Served as prime minister for one month before being ousted by the Rabuka coup.

Sitiveni Rabuka Ethnic Fijian and colonel in the Fiji Military Forces. Carried out Fiji's first military-led coup in May 1987 and was suspiciously silent during the 2000 coup events.

Mahendra Chaudhry Ethnic Indian leader of the Fiji Labour Party which defeated Rabuka in the 1999 general elections. Appointed as minister of finance in 2007.

George Speight Fijian businessman who stormed parliament with rebel militants on May 19, 2000, holding Chaudhry and 35 government officials hostage for almost two months.

Laisenia Qarase Ethnic Fijian banker appointed by Bainimarama as interim prime minister in 2000. Introduced contentious ethnically biased parliamentary bills favouring ethnic Fijians. Removed from power in a coup led by Bainimarama on Dec 5, 2006 after a year of continuous political tension.

Commodore Frank Bainimarama Commander of the Fiji Military Force (FMF) and currently interim prime minister following his coup of 2006.

seats were allocated solely along racial lines and heavily weighted towards Fijians. Rabuka won the nominally democratic elections which followed in 1992. Flushed with victory, he now set himself above the chiefly hierarchal system that he had initially intended to uphold. Internal conflict led to Josefata Kamikamica walking out of Rabuka's government with his five seats, causing Rabuka to lose his majority. Elections were forced in 1994 and this time, failing to homogenize the Fijian voters, Rabuka made a coalition with the independent General Voters Party promising a new constitution removing the ethnically biased voting system. Subsequently, Fiji was **readmitted to the Commonwealth** in 1997.

Speight and the third coup, 2000

Whilst Fijian politicians bickered over provincial power struggles, **Mahendra Chaudhry**, the grandson of an indentured labourer, rallied the Indians into a combined force under the Fiji Labour Party and won a resounding victory in the 1999 elections. Aware of the ethnic tension that could result, Chaudhry appointed eleven of the eighteen cabinet posts to indigenous Fijians. Unfortunately, even this was not enough to appease the extreme right.

On May 19, 2000, **George Speight**, a failed Fijian businessman, stormed parliament with a gang of armed thugs and took Chaudhry and his government hostage. Whether Speight worked alone in the coup remains uncertain but unlikely. Ratu Mara, at that time president, tried to assume control over the country in a coup within a coup, but was removed by the army commander, **Frank Bainimarama**, on the advice of his colleague and 1987 coup perpetrator Sitiveni Rabuka. Rabuka claimed that it was Ratu Mara who had instigated the Speight coup in the first place. Ratu Mara in turn accused Rabuka of being behind Speight. Bainimarama, caught in the middle, declared martial law and appointed **Laisenia Qarase**, an ethnic Fijian, as the interim prime minister.

On July 12, 2000, 56 days after storming the parliament, Speight released the hostages having been assured sanctuary by Bainimarama. However, he was later arrested and found guilty of treason – he remains locked up in a high-security prison. On September 2, 2000, an attempted **mutiny** of the army was quashed by Bainimarama with the loss of eight lives – again Rabuka was accused of being its instigator. Ten days later, a High Court ruling officially found the interim government illegal and returned power to Chaudhry. The decision was challenged by the ousted prime minister, Laisenia Qarase, and in March 2001 the ruling was overturned. Afraid it wouldn't hold, Qarase immediately resigned as prime minister to ensure the dissolution of parliament and to force a general election. Five months later, campaigning under a newly formed SDL party, **Qarase** was returned legally as prime minister. The country regained economic stability but the government introduced several extremely controversial policies, including the **Reconciliation, Tolerance and Unity Bill** (2005) which would pardon all preceding coup perpetrators, and the **Qoliqoli Bill** (2006) which entrusted all beaches, lagoons and reefs to indigenous land owners with strong implications for the tourist industry.

Bainimarama and the fourth coup, 2006

Commodore Frank Bainimarama, head of Fiji's oversized military forces, had publicly disapproved of Qarase's contention of the 2001 elections, claiming that it had been a condition of his appointment as interim prime minister after the 2000 coup that he would not stand for re-election. Bainimarama was hell-bent on prosecuting all those involved in the previous coups, regardless of chiefly status, and on undertaking the even greater task of weeding out the **corruption** and

▲ Soldier outside the Fiji parliament building during the 2006 coup

nepotism rife amongst Qarase's highly paid and bumbling senior civil servants. Despite a very public war of words between the two, Qarase and his SDL party were returned to power in the general elections of May 2006.

By October, Bainimarama had issued a number of demands to the Qarase government relating to corruption and bringing the 2000 coup perpetrators to justice. A three-month deadline was set and when it came and went he announced that the Fijian military was taking control of the country in a televised address on **December 5, 2006**. Qarase was flown to his home island of Vanua Balavu. The coup, Fiji's fourth, had been widely expected and there was little disruption to daily life apart from army roadblocks. Foreign governments, particularly **Australia** and **New Zealand**, condemned the coup as illegal and issued stern advisories against all travel to Fiji, paralyzing the country's tourist industry.

In order to appease the international community, Bainimarama promised **democratic elections** for March 2009 and established a multiracial interim government including Mahendra Chaudhry as minister of finance with Bainimarama acting as interim prime minister. A comprehensive enquiry into corruption and an ostensibly transparent investigation to bring the perpetrators of the 2000 coup to prosecution was announced.

The current outlook

Ironically, Bainimarama's coup was an attempt to put an end to Fiji's coup culture and to reduce the power of the archaic chiefdoms. He certainly can't be accused of lack of ambition although he faces an uphill battle to prove his point that justice can be achieved through military intervention. Recently his government introduced a **People's Charter** which aims to "rebuild Fiji into a non-racial, culturally vibrant and united, well-governed, truly democratic nation that seeks progress and prosperity through merit-based equality of opportunity and peace." At the time of writing a forty-member council was undertaking discussions in every town and village with the aim of forming a new constitution. Unfortunately, its progress has been plagued by politics with the majority of provincial high chiefs banning its representatives from entering their villages. With this attitude, the country's future may be decided upon without the guidance of the indigenous population.

Tourism and the economy

Fiji's great economic hope lies in **tourism** and, fickle though the industry can be, visitor numbers have bounced back after each coup. However, with the proliferation of overseas investors in the industry it is increasingly difficult to ensure that tourist profits are reinvested in Fiji. One solution seems to be the development of community ecotourism as seen at Bouma National Heritage Park (see p.240). Tourism aside, the future of industry on the islands looks bleak. The country's dependence on imported produce has crippled Fiji's balance of trade. **Sugar**, once the mainstay of foreign income and the exclusive domain of Indian commerce, has slipped so desperately in price that the country no longer earns a profit from its largest trade, despite obtaining preferential price agreements from the EU. The threat of a total abandonment of the industry, as happened in Hawaii, is very real. **Fishing** rights within Fiji's huge Exclusive Economic Zone (EEZ) offers some hope for sustained development, but with many of the fishing permits being sold to Taiwanese fishing boats, and without a policing unit to rid its waters of illegal longline fishing vessels, there is great fear of rapid depletion of fish stocks. Fiji's greatest success in recent years has been the export of bottled drinking **water**. Several brands now compete succesfully on global markets including Fiji Water, Aqua Blue and VTY, and have brought the country close to F$100 million in export value, ranked third behind sugar and fish.

Society and culture

Fijian society is essentially split into two groups: indigenous or ethnic Fijians and the large Indian or "Fiji-Indian" minority. Ethnic Fijian culture is a unique blend of Melanesian and Polynesian tradition influenced by rigid Methodist Christianity introduced in the nineteenth century. Fiji-Indians maintain Hindu, Sikh and Muslim customs that were brought to the islands by indentured labourers from the Indian subcontinent. Other smaller minority groups include the Chinese as well as other Pacific Islanders such as the Rotumans and Banabans.

Indigenous Fijians

C

Indigenous Fijians are bound in a strict hierarchal order based on a loyalty to their home village and tribe, an attachment which connects them in a broader sense to the land or *vanua*. At the pinnacle of ethnic Fijian hierarchy sit the **chiefs** or *ratu* whose titles are inherited through the paternal lineage.

The tribal structure

Fiji is split into three **confederacies** or tribal unions: Burebasaga (southern Viti Levu and Kadavu), Tovata (northern Fiji and the Lau Group) and Kubuna (eastern Viti Levu and Lomaiviti). Kubuna is traditionally considered the most powerful as it was once ruled by Ratu Seru Cakobau (see p.263), who became King of Fiji in 1871. Tovata is the smallest but has been the most politically successful contributing two post-independence prime ministers (Ratu Sir Kamisese Mara and Laisenia Qarase), while Burebasaga is the largest,

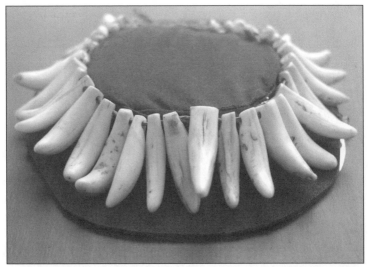

▲ Whales' teeth necklace

incorporating Suva, Lautoka and Nadi and is the only one permitting a woman to be its paramount chief.

Each confederacy is made up of a collection of **yavusa** or tribes. Each tribe usually lives in one village and is sub-divided into **mataqali** or clans. There are usually between three and six *mataqali* in a tribe. Each has a prescribed role within the village – the chiefly *mataqali* is known as the *turaga* and it is from here that the *yavusa*'s high chief is selected. The final order in the hierarchy is the **tokatoka**, or extended household, which binds closely related families. Within the *tokatoka* are individual households known as *vuvale*, and these are presided over by the senior male. All ethnic Fijians can thus define their position in society by declaring their family name, *tokatoka*, *mataqali* and *yavusa*.

Vasu and tauvu

Two important concepts can influence the tribal hierarchy: *vasu* and *tauva*. **Vasu** is a special Melanesian privilege held by a nephew over his uncles on the mother's side. The extent of this privilege is limited by the rank of those concerned but a son born to both a chiefly mother and father can expect rights over the property of his uncles on the mother's side. Cakobau famously used this privilege to extend his powerbase from Bau.

The term **tauvu** literally means "sprung from the same spirit" and is the special relationship between two tribes sharing the same totemic god, usually an animal such as a turtle or shark. Every tribe knows its corresponding *tauvu* around the country even though the actual *vu*, or spirit, may well have been forgotten by the younger generation. The relationship of the *tauvu* enables free access to food and hospitality between the respective tribes and once meant allegiance in times of war.

Administration and village law

For administrative purposes, the colonial government divided Fiji into four geographic areas – Western, Central, Eastern and Northern – made up of fourteen **provinces**, or *yasana*. These divisions still apply today. Within each province are a number of districts known as *tikina* which share a common pool of amenities such as health centres and schools. Villages are each expected to elect an administrator or **turaga ni koro** to enforce government rules. It is the *turaga ni koro* whom visitors should address when first entering a village (also see the *Visiting a Fijian village* colour section), and not the chief, who is considered above such matters.

In most instances, **village law** takes precedence over the law of the land. For example, if a theft takes place, the suspect's family is advised and expected to punish the wrongdoer and seek forgiveness for the crime, usually by presenting food to the victim. Should this fail to resolve the matter, the *tokatoka* are gathered at a formal *yaqona* ceremony at which the individual is shamed and held accountable. Persistent offenders are dealt with by the leader of the *mataqali* who in extreme cases may insist on a public flogging. For serious crimes, for example drug dealing, murder or rape, the *turaga ni koro* steps in to enforce government law.

Land rights

The issue of **land rights** is central to ethnic Fijian culture and identity. The vast majority (87 percent) of Fiji's land is owned by indigenous Fijians and classed as "native land" under a tenure system introduced by the British. Clan chiefs distribute land among their members for building homes or planting gardens for personal use. Should an individual wish to make a profit from the land, an official **government lease** must be obtained through the Native Lands Trust Board (NLTB). It is from these land leases that the majority of rural Fijians receive an income to support their traditional lifestyles.

Traditional customs

One of Fiji's great achievements has been the retention of **traditional customs** in everyday life, not only within the village community but also throughout the business and political world. The most visible of these traditions is **yaqona drinking** (see p.31). The drink, known as *kava* across the rest of the South Pacific, is obtained by pouring water through pounded roots of the *piper methysticum* plant. It was once a tradition reserved only for high priests and chiefs as a means of communicating with the ancient spirits. In times gone by, the *yaqona* roots were chewed by young maidens to make them soft and then grated and squeezed through hibiscus fibres into a wooden or clay bowl known as the *tanoa*. By the late 1800s, *yaqona* drinking had become the social event it is today and it remains very much at the heart of traditional Fijian culture. Ceremonial *yaqona* gatherings are usually followed by **feasting** and a **meke** (see opposite).

Yaqona is always drunk to mark the most important **celebrations**: the first birthday of the first-born child, puberty, marriage and death. Each features elaborate feasts and gift presentations, which all *mataqali* members should attend and contribute towards. Money for village necessities is usually raised by a **soli**, a community fundraising event, which takes place in the nearest city or town and involves a *meke* dance performance or the selling of handicrafts.

Bure building

Traditional Fijian homes or **bures** are usually built communally by members of the same *mataqali*. The main wooden structure is made from a hardwood tree, often *vesi*. Bure shapes vary slightly between regions: most are broadly rectangular although in Lau they have rounded ends similar to those found in Tonga. The wooden posts are joined together with *magimagi* (see p.210), a fibrous coconut string, rather than nails or bolts. There is no central post, ensuring a large open-plan living area and a high ceiling for ventilation. The walls are usually made from bamboo, sliced and woven together. A raised platform makes up the floor, and this is laid with straw as a cushion and woven mats for decoration. The roof is thatched using a reed called *sina* and lasts for around five years before being replaced. Across the top of the roof, or piercing either side, is a black post known as the *balabala*. This is the trunk of a fern tree and is decorated with white cowrie shells to indicate various forms of chiefly status. Roofs of lesser huts or kitchens are made from the leaf of the coconut tree and will last from three to ten years depending on the skill in weaving.

Bures are usually laid out around a central *rara*, or **village green**, used for ceremonial events and daily rugby practice.

Meke

One element of Fijian life that seems to have changed little since the 1800s is the **meke**, a performing art of dance and song. Legends and tales have been passed down the generations through *meke* and it remains Fiji's most prominent form of artistic expression. Traditionally, music was created only by chanting and rhythmic clapping often with the addition of a *lali* (hollowed wood) drum hit with bamboo sticks. More recently the guitar and ukelele have been introduced. *Mekes* are generally performed by male-only or female-only groups, although a modern introduction, the *vakamalolo*, combines the two. At formal *mekes*, men may perform club and spear dances and the women perform fan dances.

In village *mekes*, the practice of *fakawela* involves presenting the dancers with a gift in appreciation of their performance, often fine cloth or fabric. At times of weddings or other celebrations bringing two parties together, this usually involves encircling the dancers with long rolls of cloth. Otherwise money is collected as they perform.

Fiji-Indians

First brought to Fiji as indentured labourers, **Fiji-Indians** today make up 38 percent of the population. Indian influence can be seen throughout the islands, especially in the towns and cities of Viti Levu and Vanua Levu where small shops and businesses are almost exclusively run by Fiji-Indians. You'll also find Indian food is extremely popular in Fiji with almost every small town boasting a curry house. However, despite repeated campaigns for equal rights, Fiji-Indians cannot buy freehold land or even call themselves "Fijian" (see box, below). Given these circumstances, this large minority tends to operate as a society within a society and today many Fiji-Indians are looking for new opportunities overseas.

A key factor separating Fiji-Indians and Indians from the subcontinent is the more relaxed social structure seen in Fiji. When Indian labourers first arrived from the subcontinent under the *girmit* contract (see p.266), the **caste system** which regulated life back home was instantly shed. Those of different castes were forced to live and work together and inter-caste marriage was common owing to the lack of female immigrants. In time, a form of pidgin Hindi became the universal language of both Hindus and Muslims, with words, phrases and accents borrowed from both English and Fijian. The resulting language, now known as **Fiji-Hindi**, is today almost unintelligible to Indians from the subcontinent.

What's in a name?

Under the Fijian constitution anyone who can trace their ancestry back to the Indian subcontinent is classed as "**Indian**" rather than "Fijian". Alternative names such as "Indian Fijian", "Indo-Fijian" and "Fiji-born Indian" have all been proposed but all have proved too controversial to be accepted by nationalist politicians. This is often due to the issue of property whereby only "Fijians", ie ethnic Fijian tribal members, can claim rights to native land. One of the more widely accepted terms is **Fiji-Indian** and we have used this name to refer to Fijians of Indian descent throughout this guide.

Fiji's Hindu and Muslim populations share the same **religion** as their forefathers and celebrate all the major festivals. There are noisy celebrations at *Diwali* (October), face-painting at *Holi* (March) and enthralling fire-walking ceremonies regularly held at temples (April and September). The most notable Muslim celebrations are Ramadan and Eid.

During much of the postwar period Fiji-Indians outnumbered native Fijians although the reverse is now true owing to mass emigration and a higher ethnic Fijian birthrate. Many well-educated Fiji-Indians have moved to Canada, Australia and New Zealand in response to Fiji's repeated political instability. The remainder struggle to get by on the **sugarcane farms**, hit by falling prices and the expiry of land leases. The continuing lure of life abroad was dramatically highlighted in 2002 when 220,000 Fijians, most of them Fiji-Indians, applied for the USA "Green Card" lottery.

Women in Fij

Unless born of chiefly status, **women in Fiji** hold few positions of authority and the general attitude amongst both indigenous Fijians and Fiji-Indians is that a woman's place is at home or as a menial worker. Women received the right to vote in 1963 but appreciation of women's rights and equal opportunities is mostly overlooked by politicians. The non-governmental Fiji Women's Rights Movement (⊛www.fwrm.org.fj) has aimed to redress this balance since its establishment in 1986 and has set up programmes to encourage women in leadership. By far the greatest concern to women of Fiji is **domestic violence**, accounting for sixty percent of cases reported to the Fiji Women's Crisis Centre (⊛www.fijiwomen.com).

Modern culture

Modern Fijian culture preserves aspects of traditional Fijian and Indian life whilst being strongly influenced by globalization. Brought up with the Internet and satellite TV, young Fijians, both ethnic Fijian and Fiji-Indian, tend to mimic the trends in modern music and fashion of the West, especially Australia and New Zealand. In addition, interaction with tourists has lead some Fijians to question their strictly religious and hierarchical culture.

A few **Fijian musicians** have established themselves over the past two decades, including female singer Laisa Vulakoro, who blends Fijian folk with R&B in a style of music known locally as *vude*; and Lautoka-born Daniel Rae Costello, who has released over thirty albums and created a fusion style of calypso, latin and reggae known as "Aqualypso". The most successful Fijian band of recent years are Black Rose who started out performing covers at tourist resorts in Nadi and now sell out gigs across the South Pacific. Their biggest hit, *Raude*, a blend of traditional *meke* music mixed with high-tempo dance beats, can be heard on their debut album *Voices of Nature* (2000). The current music trend in Fiji is hip-hop, gentler than the US urban version and with a definite reggae influence. Local MC Dave Lavaki from Suva is at the forefront of Fijian hip-hop while upcoming acts include Red Child, BSQ and Lautoka's New Money.

Fiji's first and most celebrated native **film**, *The Land Has Eyes*, premiered at the Sundance Film Festival in 2004. Directed by Vilsoni Hereniko and filmed mostly on Rotuma, the film is a fabulous low-budget depiction of the islanders' conflicting attitudes to change. Focusing on the struggle of a young Rotuman girl caught between two worlds – the traditional life on Rotuma and a possible scholarship to the Fijian mainland – the film shares parallels with the internationally successful Maori film *Whale Rider*. Fiji has also proved a popular location for Hollywood films including the *Blue Lagoon* (1979), *Return to the Blue Lagoon* (1991), *Castaway* (2001), as well as the forgettable sequel to snake horror *Anaconda* (2004).

Contemporary Fijian **art and craft** reflects tradition, with paintings made upon *tapa* cloth and the wooden designs of war clubs, priest dishes and *tanoa* bowls providing inspiration. The Western Arts and Craft Society (☎672 0717) organizes intermittent **craft fairs** at various venues around Nadi and you can view displays and sometimes performing arts at the Oceania Centre for Arts and Culture (☎323 1000), part of the University of the South Pacific in Suva.

Sport

For a tiny nation, Fiji has had a significant impact in the world of **sport**. **Rugby union** is a particular obsession and fills the back (and often front) pages of all the daily newspapers. The Fijian team won the Rugby World Cup Sevens in 1997 and 2005. The full fifteen-a-side team has also excelled but never quite matches the high expectations of the people – the national team reached the last eight of the 2007 Rugby World Cup, beaten by the eventual champions South Africa. Several **Fiji-born players**, Lote Tuqiri and Sitiveni Sivivatu to name a couple, have been poached to play for Australia and New Zealand although they still remain local heroes in their homeland. Another international star is golfer **Vijay Singh** who claimed the world number one title from Tiger Woods between 2004 and 2005. Singh has won over US$56 million in prize money – not bad considering that he used to practise with coconuts on the beach as a child in Nadi. Other sports Fiji has excelled at on the world stage include netball, lawn bowls and judo.

Wildlife

The most obvious natural wonders of Fiji are to be found in its vast ocean habitats, littered with diverse **coral reefs** and bursting with over four thousand species of fish. Equally fascinating are the islands' steamy **rainforests** and **mangroves**, thick in vegetation and home to an elusive and vivid collection of native **birds**, though, with the exception of bats, devoid of any native mammals.

As with many isolated island groups, Fiji's terrestrial and freshwater ecosystems are particularly rich in **endemic species** (unique occurrences of species within a limited geographic area). Almost a thousand have been documented and over half of the country's plant species are unique to the islands.

Threats and conservation

Fiji's wildlife faces many **threats**, most notably: unregulated fishing, badly planned resort developments, terrestrial habitat destruction through logging and sugarcane farming and rising sea temperatures causing coral bleaching. Despite its globally important marine and terrestrial biodiversity, **conservation** efforts are in their infancy. There is only one fully protected national park (Sigatoka Sand Dunes) and the country's two national heritage parks, Bouma and Koroyanitu, are largely community-led initiatives. Twelve Fijian species, including the Fiji tree frog, Fiji snake and Fiji goshawk are listed on the IUCN Red List as **critically endangered** although only the Fiji crested iguana on Yadua Taba (see p.224) has any form of active protection. Additionally, large parts of the country, especially the marine ecosystem, have not been fully surveyed or researched.

Fijian conservation received a boost in 2007 with the establishment of Nature Fiji (℡338 3189, ⓦwww.naturefiji.org), the first locally based non-governmental conservation organization. Based in Suva, Nature Fiji has begun to work with schools, resorts and landowners in order to promote Fijian wildlife and increase awareness through education programmes. Their website provides a handy photographic guide to fifty endangered Fijian species.

Coral reefs and marine life

Fiji has some of the most accessible **coral reefs** in the world, often starting just metres from the beach and extending along veins or passages to the steep drop-offs of the fringing reefs where **reef sharks** or spinner dolphins can often be spotted. Deep, rich currents support large pelagic fish including tuna and trevally as well as bull, tiger and hammerhead sharks. Humpback **whales**, once frequent visitors between May and October, are now seldom encountered, with only a handful of sightings each year mostly around Lomaiviti, though smaller **pilot whales** can be seen year-round.

For more background on coral reefs and **fish species** see the *Underwater Fiji* colour section.

This fascinating annual natural event occurs at various locations around the Pacific, but most prolifically in Fiji. The **balolo** (*Eunice viridis*) is a long spaghetti worm that lives deep in the coral reef. On two nights each year the male and female worms release their tails, containing sperm or eggs, to the surface in perfectly synchronized spawning event. Amongst Fijians the worm's tail is a delicacy. Villagers head out to the reefs to gather the tails before the sun rises when they melt into a gooey mess. The worm is eaten raw or fried and said to taste like caviar. The larger of the two risings is known as the *Vula i Balolo Levu*, and occurs at high tide at the last quarter of the moon in either October or November.

On Vanua Levu, the appearance of the *balolo* coincides with the arrival of a deep-water fish called *deu* which swims up the mangrove estuaries to lay its eggs. Fijian women from villages along the southeast coast gather in the rivers to catch the *deu* with nets – if a lady doesn't catch one she's believed to have committed adultery and may be banished from the village for a year.

Extensive **barrier reefs** flank most of the larger volcanic islands. The longest is the Great Sea Reef off Vanua Levu, which has been ranked as globally significant owing to its unique diversity and exceptional level of endemic species. Other globally important **reef system**s include the Lomaiviti Triangle in the Koro Sea as well as the isolated reefs of Rotuma which support unique coral species. Smaller **patch reefs** can be found within the huge lagoon system of the Mamanuca Group and make popular snorkelling and diving spots. In the shallow lagoons of Viti Levu, those reefs not damaged by fishing are increasingly becoming bleached as a result of rising sea temperatures.

Four species of **sea turtle** – loggerhead, leatherback, green and hawksbill – lay their eggs deep in the sand of Fiji's coral cays. Hawksbill turtles are the most common, and can be found in Fiji's oceans year-round while greens and leatherbacks only visit during the nesting season (Nov–Feb) – the latter is the largest type of sea turtle and is sadly becoming a rare sight. The islands' seagrass beds and coral reefs also provide habitats for three species of **sea snakes** including the distinctive black and white banded sea snake. **Hermit crabs** in stolen shells can be seen crawling around most beaches leaving curious trails in their wake, while massive **coconut crabs**, whose claws are so powerful that they can rip through the husk of a coconut, make a tasty meal if caught – a tin strip is often wrapped around the trunk of coconut trees to stop the crab from climbing up to scavenge the nuts.

Sea birds

Nineteen species of endemic **sea birds** are found in Fiji's lagoons, most nesting on tiny coral and limestone islands or on cliff edges along the larger islands. The stately **frigate bird** is the largest of this group and its distinctive split tail outline is often seen high in the sky and near the coastline when stormy weather is approaching. Strikingly white **tropicbirds** with long tail feathers and clumsy-looking oversized **boobies** are also prolific, along with the smaller terns and noddies which follow each other around on fishing expeditions and dive bomb the lagoons in spectacular fashion. Shearwaters and **reef herons** can be spotted island-wide, cautiously prancing along the beach edge in search of fish.

Mangrove forest

Fiji's eighteen thousand hectares of **mangrove forest** buffer much of the coastline along Viti Levu and Vanua Levu and provide important breeding grounds for many of Fiji's reef fish. They also perform an invaluable role in protecting the coastline from hurricanes and wave erosion. With thick tentacle roots draping from the forest canopy and stumps thrusting upwards from the murky blend of fresh and salt water, these forests are unforgiving environments but incredibly productive. **Bird life** abounds with mangrove herons, kingfishers, lorries and orange-breasted honey-eaters the most commonly found species. For the Fijians living around the river deltas, the *tiri* (mangrove) offer a plethora of foodstuffs, with an abundance of **small fish** caught in reed traps, shrimps and, most delicious of all, **mud crabs** scooped up in fishing nets.

Rainforests and terrestrial wildlife

Fiji's tropical **rainforests** are incredibly dense with tall, thin trees entangled with vines and creepers crowding upwards towards the elusive light. Below the canopy, impressive prehistoric-looking **tree ferns** grow in profusion while several beautiful species of **wild orchids** can be found on the forest floor. Of the 1,600 known plants found in Fiji, 56 percent are endemic, most found only within the rainforest.

More than forty percent of the forest cover of the islands remains intact, and some islands, such as Taveuni, still have contiguous forest stretching from the high-altitude cloud forest all the way to the coast. The largest tract of virgin primary

---

Coconut – a lifeline

The **coconut palm** (*Cocos nucifera*) is a symbol of paradise and lines the shores of most Fijian beaches. For the islanders, it's a symbol of life and once accompanied the early Polynesians on their epic journeys across the Pacific. Its practical uses are considerable: the **leaves** are woven to make hats and baskets and used to thatch roofs; whilst the rigid discarded midrib of the leaf is gathered to make *sasa* brooms. **Milk** from the young nuts is drunk while the meaty **flesh** is eaten or scraped to make coconut cream. The mature nut has a hard flesh which is dried and cut to make **copra** from which commercial grade coconut oil is produced. The hard inner **shell** of the coconut makes a handy bowl traditionally used for *yaqona* drinking (see the *Visiting a Fijian village* colour section) and to make earrings and other jewellery. The dry stringy fibres of the outer husk are rolled to make *magimagi* (see p.210), a coil used for binding bures and for decorative art. Coconut fibres are also perfect for use as kindling and the husks often fuel the village kitchen stove.

Coconut palms often reach 30m in height and you'll frequently hear the dull thud of a nut falling to the ground. In fact, the threat of **death by falling coconut** has become something of an urban myth with a figure of 150 fatalities per year often reported by journalists (often used in comparison to, say, shark attacks or plane crash statistics). This story can be traced back to an article in the *Journal of Trauma* which focused on coconut injuries in Papua New Guinea. Although there were four reported injuries and two deaths, these included people who had died whilst climbing the trees. Given deaths caused by falling coconuts are not recorded, the 150 figure is likely to have been plucked out of thin air.

forest is the Sovi Basin on Viti Levu, which has become an important area for sustaining birdlife. The remainder of Fiji's rainforest has usually been influenced by people, either through logging or farming. On the wet **windward** sides of the islands, Fijian hardwood species such as *kauvula* and *kadamu* are common as well as *dakua*, a softer conifer from the kauri family used locally for furniture making. The heavier hardwoods of *damanu*, *vesi* and *rosawa* have been cut extensively for timber export and craft. Perhaps the most beautiful of trees found in the forest is the **banyan**, a member of the fig family. The banyan initially grows as a vine on a host tree before its aerial prop roots descend and embed themselves in the ground, creating huge buttress roots which meander along the forest floor.

The dry **leeward** sides of Fiji's islands were once home to large tracts of casuarinas, ironwood and sandalwood forests. Most of the land is now covered in **grassland** or planted with imported Caribbean pine. The most fertile soil is found along the river valleys, particularly on the larger islands, and this is almost always converted to **sugarcane farmland**.

Several rogue species are beginning to dominate Fiji's native forests, notably the soft-wooded and fast-growing **African Tulip** found along riverbeds and the **mahogany tree** introduced over forty years ago. Over forty thousand acres of mahogany plantation are now ready for cultivation, the largest supply of the lucrative hardwood outside of Brazil.

Terrestrial birds and animals

Most impressive of the 57 native breeding terrestrial **birds** is the crimson **Kadavu shining parrot**, unique to the islands of the Kadavu Group. Other large parrots can be found on Taveuni, Gau and Koro. Most common of the smaller forest species are fruit doves, fantails and white-eyes, with the fabulously vivid **orange dove** and golden dove being the most striking. The velvet-black silktail and dusky coloured long-legged warbler are the most elusive of Fiji's birds and listed as critically endangered. The dry grasslands are the preferred hunting grounds for Fiji's **birds of prey** which include the Fiji goshawk, Pacific harrier and peregrine falcon. Collared lorries, parrot finches and honey-eaters can be spotted in urban gardens.

The only terrestrial **mammals** native to Fiji are **bats** of which there are two endemic species – the Fijian flying fox and the small Fiji blossom bat. Otherwise the islands' largest land-based species are comprised solely of reptiles and amphibians. These include the crested iguana (see p.224), two snakes, the Pacific boa and the mildly poisonous but seldom seen Fijian burrowing snake, two frogs and a variety of tiny geckos or skinks. Fiji's forests support a huge range of **insects** including 44 recorded varieties of **butterflies**; most have simple brown and black colourings in order to blend in with the dark foliage. Much more vivid are the **dragonflies** which are commonly seen at streams within the forest.

The **mongoose**, often seen scuttling across roads between cane fields, was introduced from India in the 1880s to control rats that were damaging sugar plantations. Without a natural predator they thrived and along with the **mynah**, an aggressive and chatty black and white bird introduced at the same time, they have been responsible for chasing much of Fiji's native bird life away from the coastal areas and into the deep forest. The best islands for **bird-watching** are Kadavu and Taveuni which remain free of the mongoose. The introduction of the exceptionally ugly **cane toad** from South America in the 1930s to check the spread of cane beetles was similarly shortsighted. When threatened, the cane toad and its tadpoles excrete a milky poison from glands on the back which can kill native wildlife. Unfortunately, the toad is now prolific around Fiji's countryside.

Books

Fijian literature has focused mostly on political analysis with numerous critical writings confronting the country's ethnic problems and military coups. Fiction makes for slim pickings and Fijian books can be hard to find outside of the country. The most reliable source is the University Books Centre at the University of the South Pacific (☎321 2500, ⓦwww.uspbookcentre.com) which will ship books internationally. Other bookshops are listed in the Guide.

History

R. A. Derrick *A History of Fiji* (Government Press, Fiji). Originally written in 1942, this classic of early Fijian history up to cession in 1874 is arranged thematically which makes it much more interesting than the usual trawl through dates.

Kim Gravelle *Fiji's Heritage – A History of Fiji* (Tiara Enterprises, Fiji). Thoroughly readable history highlighting fifty important events that have shaped the destiny of the country.

Rajendra Prasad *Tears in Paradise* (Glade, New Zealand). Documenting the Indian struggle for acceptance and identity, this book is the best of a collection of contemporary writings giving the Indian perspective on the last 125 years.

Baron Anatole von Hügel *Fiji Journals 1875–1877* (Fiji Museum Press). Wonderful diary of a young half British, half Austrian rogue who tramped around Fiji in the late nineteenth century. Von Hugel made several expeditions into the interior of Viti Levu, collecting many artefacts and drinking vast quantities of *yaqona* along the way. A lively insight into Fijian life during early colonial times.

David Routledge *The struggle for power in early Fiji* (Institute of Pacific Studies, Fiji). An academic perspective tracing events from early Fijian history to independence in 1970 – historical photos and engravings keep things lively.

Culture and society

Mensah Adinkrah *Crime, Deviance and Delinquency in Fiji* (Fiji Council of Social Services). If you can't quite believe Fiji has a dark side, this thought-provoking collection of essays, balanced with sociological reasoning, makes for essential reading.

Solomoni Biturogoiwasa *My Village, My World; Everyday Life in Nadoria, Fiji* (University of the South Pacific). Refreshingly simple insight into everyday village life, packed with colourful detail.

Winston Halapua *Tradition, Lotu & Militarism in Fiji*. An insider's view of local politics and ethnicity revealing the deceptive world of self-interest and fascism amongst Fiji's elite.

Asesela Ravuvu *The Facade of Democracy: Fijian Struggles for Political Control* (Reader Publishing, Fiji). An insight into the mind of a Fijian nationalist, critical of both European and Indian involvement in Fijian society.

Sir Vijay R. Singh *Speaking Out* (Knightsbrook, Australia). Not to be confused with the golfer of the same name, the author of this bold collection of thought-provoking articles is one of Fiji's most prominent Fiji-Indian politicians. Focuses on the events of the 1987 and 2000 coups and ruffled quite a few feathers prompting several nationalist politicians to call for it to be banned.

Peter Thomson *Kava in the Blood* (Tandem Press, UK). A recollection of life growing up in Fiji, of serving in the government administration and of confronting and ultimately accepting the hard realities of the coups.

Nature and the environment

Clare Morrison *Herpetofauna of Fiji* (University of the South Pacific). A little book covering a pretty slim subject in scientific detail, with colour photos of Fiji's reptiles and amphibians.

Ian Osborn *Beautiful Fiji* (Pacific Travel Guides, Fiji). Photographic journey through Fiji's pristine environment.

Dick Watling *A Guide to the Birds of Fiji & Western Polynesia* (Environmental Consultants, Fiji, ⓦ www.pacificbirds .com). The birdies' bible with colour plates and detailed accounts of 173 species found throughout the region.

Dr Michael A. Weiner *Secrets of Fijian Medicine* (University of California Press, US). Records some of Fiji's dying knowledge of traditional medicine. Arranged by type of illness and listing Fijian and English plant names.

Travellers' tales

Kim Gravelle *Romancing the Islands* (Graphics Pacific, Fiji). Written by one of the South Pacific's leading photojournalists, Gravelle recounts forty-four of his liveliest tales of adventure all featuring a refreshing hint of humour.

Paul Theroux *Happy Isles of Oceania* (Penguin, US & UK). A good read from one of the few big-name travel writers to have written about the South Pacific. His account of Fiji, one of several island nations covered, portrays some of the less-than-democratic aspects of Fijian society and was felt by many to have cut a little too close to the bone.

J. Maarten Troost *Getting Stoned with Savages* (Broadway Books, US). A witty tale of misadventure that begins in Vanuatu and ends with a candid view of Fiji in the modern world.

Fiction

Robert Campbell *Tradewinds & Treachery* (Steele Roberts, New Zealand). A clash of cultures and ideologies haunt this tale of love in the turbulent years leading up to colonial rule.

Allan Carson *Pacific Intrigue* (Durban House, US). A fast-paced American detective story of Islamic terrorist activity set between Seattle and Suva, touching on the simmering tensions between Fijians and Indians.

Daryl Tarte *Fiji: a Bloody and Lustful Story of Fiji's History* (Pascoe Publishing, Australia). Renowned local writer Tarte permits himself a little bit of fantasy entwined with the facts to produce this fine tale of intrigue in grand Michener-style proportions.

Joseph C. Veramu *Moving through the Streets* (Mana Publications, Fiji).

This Suva-set novel by a lecturer at the University of the South Pacific provides a realistic account of the pressures and temptations facing Fiji's urban youth.

Language

Language

Introduction

English is the official language of Fiji, taught and spoken in schools and used in parliament and in business. Throughout the upper strata of Fijian society the language is spoken with great fluency, with an accent not dissimilar to British Received Pronunciation or "Queen's English". Young people speak their own casual blend of English, spoken with a hint of a South African accent, and with words and phrases borrowed from both Fijian and Fiji Hindi.

At home, indigenous Fijians speak **Fijian**, Rotumans speak **Rotuman** and Fiji-Indians speak **Fiji Hindi,** a unique form of Hindustani. Some Fiji-Indians, especially in the rural areas around north Viti Levu, Vanua Levu and Taveuni, speak Fijian as a third language and a few Fijians speak Fiji Hindi but the two ethnic groups tend to converse in English. Learning a few basic phrases in either language will raise a smile among the locals and prove especially useful for travellers staying in rural areas.

Fijian

Fijian is part of the Malayo-Polynesian branch of the huge Austronesian family of languages, which stretches from Madagascar to Easter Island, and from Taiwan and Hawaii to New Zealand. Within Fiji, regional isolation has led to the formation of nine distinct dialects. For example, the commonly used word "*vinaka*", which in its simplest form means "good" has many variations: "*vinaduriki*" in the Yasawas, "*vina'a*" in Taveuni and "*malo*" in Lau. In the 1840s, the dialect known as **Bauan** was the first version of Fijian to be transcribed into the roman alphabet (by Scottish missionary David Cargill). This has lead Bauan to become the most universally accepted type of Fijian and is the version taught in schools and used at formal occasions.

The two most difficult aspects of Fijian to a foreign ear are the pronunciation of consonants and the difficulty in differentiating words. Fijian sentences sound as if they are spoken as one long jumbled word with syllables rolling into each other. It is common for Fijians to speak in a **monotone**, with one person talking uninterrupted before the second person speaks – bouncing conversations back and forth is considered impolite.

Bula!

Bula literally means "life" in Fijian. You'll hear it everywhere and from everyone. It is used as a greeting, and in its simplest form translates as "hello". "*Ni sa bula*" is a more polite form of greeting, with the reply being "*bula vinaka*".

Further reading

A. Capell *The Fijian Dictionary*. Comprehensive dictionary with Fijian/English and English/Fijian.

A.J. Schütz *Say it in Fijian*. Well-written guide to Fijian; includes a small dictionary

G.B. Milner *Fijian Grammar*. Detailed text covering all grammatical aspects.

Pronunciation

The majority of letters are pronounced as in spoken English, although the first **vowel** in a word is usually emphasized. Some vowels are drawn out, in which case they are marked with a macron (ā). More awkward to pronounce are the **consonants**:

b is pronounced "mb" with a soft m as in number

c is pronounced as a "th" sound as in mother

d sounds like the "nd" in sandy

g has a soft "ng" sound as in singer

q has a harder "ngg" as in finger

r is usually rolled

Once the above system is mastered, **place names** begin to make sense. For example, Lakeba is pronounced "Lakemba", Nadi becomes "Nandi" and Beqa is pronounced "Mbengga".

Basic phrases

hello (polite)	(nī sā) bula	what?	cawa?
yes	io	when?	naica?
no	sega	how many?	vica?
please	yalo vinaka, mada	it's ok	sa vinaka
thank you (very much)	vinaka (vakalevu)	no problem	sega na leqa
		excuse me	tulou
good morning (polite)	(nī sā) yadra	I'm sorry	lomana
what is your name? (polite)	o cei na yacamu (nī)?	go away	lako tani
		stop!	kua!
my name is ...	na yacaqu o ...	slow down!	malua!
where are you from?	o nī lako mai vei?	one more	dua tale
I'm from ...	au lako mai ...	see you again	sota tale
who?	cei?	see you tomorrow	sota ni mataka
where?	vei?	good bye (polite)	(nī sā) moce

Numbers

1	dua	10	tini
2	rua	11	tini ka dua
3	tolu	12	tini ka rua
4	vā	13	tini ka tolu
5	lima	14	tini ka vā
6	ono	15	tini ka lima
7	vitu	16	tini ka ono
8	walu	17	tini ka vitu
9	ciwa	18	tini ka walu

19	tini ka ciwa	30	tolusagavulu
20	ruasagavulu	100	dua na drau
21	ruasagavulu ka dua	1000	dua na udolu

Getting around

where is the …?	e vai (beka) na …?	farm, garden	teitei
where are you going? (also used as how are you?)	o lai vei?	forest	veikau
		house	vale
		island	yanuyanu
nowhere particular (general response)	sega, gāde gā	mountain	qulunivanua
		road, path	sala
near	vōleka	school	koronivuli
far	yawa	shop	sitoa
let's go	daru lako	sleeping house	bure
I am going to …	au lai na …	village	koro
beach	matāsawa		

Timings

today	ni kua	late	bera
tomorrow	ni mataka	night	bogi
yesterday	nanoa	ready	vaka rau

Useful vocabulary

beautiful	totoka	possible	rawa
big, many	levu	rain	uca
busy, full	osooso	request	kerekere
clean	savata	sanitary towel	qamuqamu
cold	batabatā	shark	qio
cup	bilo	single, alone	taudua
delicious	maleka	small, little	lailai
diarrhoea	coka	strong	kaukaua
difficult	drēdrē	sunny	siga
dirty	duka	swim	qalo
fishing	siwa	tired	oca
hot	katakata	toilet	vale lailai
knife	isele	too much	rui
money	ilavo	turtle	vonu
old	makawa	walk	gādē
perhaps	beka	wind	cagi
photo	taba		

Food and drink

bele	green vegetable	qari	cooked crab
bulumakau	beef	rourou	spinach
dalo	taro, a root crop	saqa	boiled
ika	fish (general)	tapioca	cassava, root crop
jaina	banana	ura	cooked prawn
kokoda	fish marinated in lime juice	uvi	yam
lolo	coconut cream	vakalolo	pudding made from *dalo* and coconut cream
lovo	underground oven		
mai kana!	come and eat!	vua	fruit
niu	coconut	wai	water
ota	seaweed	weleti	papaya/pawpaw

Fiji Hindi

Fiji Hindi, spoken by all Fiji-Indians, is a unique blend of several Hindustani dialects with a smattering of Arabic, English and Fijian words and phrases thrown in. In religious worship, classical Sanskrit written in Devanagari is used and Devanagari is taught in Indian schools. Gujaratis and Sikhs retain closer ties with their traditional languages when speaking amongst each other.

Basics

hello (casual)	ram ram	please	thoraa
hello (polite)	namaste	thank you, goodbye	dhanyewaad
hello (Muslim)	salaam walekum	good, I see	achaa
how are you?	kaise?	bad	kharab
fine	theek	ok	ha or rite
what is your name?	kon naam tumhar?	come and eat	aao khana khao
my name is …	hamar naam hai …	drink, smoke	pio
what's this?	honchi he?	tea	cha
how much?	kitna?	warm, hot	garam
yes	ha	wait	sabur karo
no	nahi or na	sit	baitho
too much	bahut	perhaps	shayad
I don't want it	nahi magta	photograph	tasveer
excuse me, sorry	maaf karna	see you again	phir milenge

Numbers

1	ek	7	saat
2	do	8	aat
3	teen	9	no
4	chaar	10	das
5	paanch	100	sao
6	cha	1000	hazaar

Fiji-Indian food

archaar	pickles	pilau	rice, gently fried with spices
baigan	eggplant		
bhaath	cooked rice	puri	puffed up bread, deep-fried and crispy
bhindii	okra		
biryani	rice dish of meat or vegetables baked with turmeric and whole spices	roti	round unleavened flat-bread, cooked on a hot plate
		samosa	stuffed pastry cooked in oil
chapatti	unleavened flat-bread	thali	combination of vegetarian and sometimes meat dishes with chutney, pickles, rice, roti and dhal; served as a single meal
dhal	lentils, often cooked in soup		
ghee	clarified butter		
gulgula	pancake		
halwa	Indian sweet		
korma	meat braised in yoghurt sauce (mild)		
		vindaloo	meat, usually pork, seasoned in vinegar (hot)
masala	curry powder		
murga	chicken		
naan	white leavened bread baked in a tandoor oven		

Rotuman

Rotuman is spoken exclusively by the people of Rotuma, a Polynesian island in the far north of Fiji. It has a distinctive word structure featuring metathesis (two vowels following each other but creating two separate quite abrupt sounds) and an extensive use of diphthongs (vowel clusters). To confuse matters further, many words have been borrowed or adapted from Samoan and Tongan. The apostrophe is used between vowels to indicate a glottal stop while the macron (ā) indicates extended vowels as in Fijian. The use of diaeresis (ä) means that a vowel should be pronounced apart from the letter which precedes it.

If you're interested in **studying Rotuman** it's worth getting hold of Elizabeth Inia's *A New Rotuman Dictionary* available from ⓦwww.pacificislandbooks.com. Alternatively, the excellent Rotuman website ⓦwww.rotuma.net has links to sound files of spoken Rotuman.

Basics

hello	faiäksia noa'ia	please	figalelei
where are you going?	'äe la'se tei?	thank you	faiäksia
		yes	'i
what is your name?	sei ta 'ou asa?	no	'igka
my name is ...	'otou asa le ...	goodbye	nonoam
what's this?	ka tese te?		

Useful words

dance	mak	rest	au'ua se
drink	īom	sea	sasi
eat	äte	sit down	päe se lopo
fishing	hagoat	sleep	mös
hurry up	rue la mij	slow down	ariri'se
plantation	vekaogta	swim, shower	kakou

Rotuman dishes

fekei	sticky, starchy sweet	porasam	*taro* leaf cooked in coconut cream
tähroro	fermented coconut milk flavoured with chili		

Glossary

Adi female chiefly title

balabala the trunk of a tree fern, used decoratively in villages and gardens

balolo marine worm living in coral reefs and considered a delicacy

bati warrior

bete priest

bilibili bamboo raft, affectionately known as "HMS *No Return*"

bilo coconut shell used for drinking *yaqona*

boso slang for "boss"

bure bose meeting hall

bure kalou traditional Fijian temple

chautaal traditional songs sung at the Hindu Holi festival

cobo clapping with cupped hands

copra the dried, oil-yielding kernel of the coconut

dakua popular wood for carving

Daquwaqa Fijian shark god

Degei most revered of the Fijian gods

Diwali Hindu celebration, festival of lights

drua war canoe

Eid Muslim holiday marking the end of Ramadan

Fara Rotuman Christmas festival

girmit labour contract given to Indian indentured labourers

Holi Hindu celebration, festival of colours

ivi Tahitian chestnut tree believed to have spiritual connotations and found in ancient villages

kai colo hill people from the interior of Viti Levu

kai loma people of part Fijian, part European descent

kai viti people of Fiji

kai vulagi people from overseas

kava Polynesian word for *yaqona*

kerekere communal borrowing

lali slit drum hollowed from a hardwood tree

Lapita ancient Pacific Ocean culture named after their distinct style of pottery

loloma affectionate greeting

lotu in broad terms, Christianity or the Church

lovo traditional food cooked in an underground oven

magimagi plaited coconut fibre

mana spiritual power

manumanu the three totems of a clan, usually a fish, an animal and a fruit or tree

masi tapa cloth decorated with stencilled designs

masu prayer said before meal

mataqali land-owning clan

meke traditional song and dance performance

qai tattoo

qoliqoli area from high tide mark to the reef edge, perceived by some as public access and others as mataqali-owned

Ramadan the Islamic holy month of fasting

rara village green

Ratu male chiefly title

reguregu sniff to the cheeks, used as a greeting between clan members

Ro chiefly title of Rewa, Naitasiri, Namosi and Serua provinces

Roko chiefly title of the Lau Group

salwar kameez traditional dress worn by Muslims

sari traditional Indian dress

sere chant at a *yaqona* ceremony

sevusevu ceremonial offering of *yaqona*

solevu large ceremonial gathering

soli fundraising event

sulu Fijian sarong

suluka home-made, rolled tobacco leaf

tabu forbidden, sacred

tabua traditional gift, usually a whale's tooth, given in return for a favour or to ask for atonement

tanoa wooden bowl with four or more legs used for preparing *yaqona*

tapa paper cloth made from the mulberry plant, used as traditional dress

taukei original inhabitant; movement for indigenous rights

tauvu tribes sharing the same totemic god

tiri mangrove forests

tokatoka extended household

tualeita ancient pathway connecting villages

Turaga ni vuvale head of the house

Turanga ni koro head of the village

Turanga respected title donating the head of a group of people; old-fashioned address similar to "gentleman"

vanua land to which Fijians are spiritually bound

vasu the concept of a nephew or niece having privileges over an uncle

vesi popular wood for carving

voivoi leaf of the pandanus plant used for weaving

vude Fijian music blending folk and R&B

waqa *yaqona* roots in powder form

yaqona mildly narcotic ceremonial and social drink strained from the root of the *piper methysticum* plant

yavusa tribe

Travel store

D: Rough Guide
DIRECTIONS for
short breaks

Available from all good bookstores

For more information go to www.roughguides.com

ROUGH GUIDES

www.roughguides.com

nformation on over 25,000 destinations around the world

- **Read** Rough Guides' trusted travel info
- **Access** exclusive articles from Rough Guides authors
- **Update** yourself on new books, maps, CDs and other products
- **Enter** our competitions and win travel prizes
- **Share** ideas, journals, photos & travel advice with other users
- **Earn** points every time you contribute to the Rough Guide
  community and get rewards

Small print and

Index

A Rough Guide to Rough Guides

Published in 1982, the first Rough Guide – to Greece – was a student scheme that became a publishing phenomenon. Mark Ellingham, a recent graduate in English from Bristol University, had been travelling in Greece the previous summer and couldn't find the right guidebook. With a small group of friends he wrote his own guide, combining a highly contemporary, journalistic style with a thoroughly practical approach to travellers' needs.

The immediate success of the book spawned a series that rapidly covered dozens of destinations. And, in addition to impecunious backpackers, Rough Guides soon acquired a much broader and older readership that relished the guides' wit and inquisitiveness as much as their enthusiastic, critical approach and value-for-money ethos.

These days, Rough Guides include recommendations from shoestring to luxury and cover more than 200 destinations around the globe, including almost every country in the Americas and Europe, more than half of Africa and most of Asia and Australasia. Our ever-growing team of authors and photographers is spread all over the world, particularly in Europe, the USA and Australia.

In the early 1990s, Rough Guides branched out of travel, with the publication of Rough Guides to World Music, Classical Music and the Internet. All three have become benchmark titles in their fields, spearheading the publication of a wide range of books under the Rough Guide name.

Including the travel series, Rough Guides now number more than 350 titles, covering: phrasebooks, waterproof maps, music guides from Opera to Heavy Metal, reference works as diverse as Conspiracy Theories and Shakespeare, and popular culture books from iPods to Poker. Rough Guides also produce a series of more than 120 World Music CDs in partnership with World Music Network.

Visit www.roughguides.com to see our latest publications.

Rough Guide travel images are available for commercial licensing at www.roughguidespictures.com

Rough Guide credits

Text editor: Andy Turner
Layout: Nikhil Agarwal
Cartography: Rajesh Chhibber
Picture editor: Sarah Cummins
Production: Rebecca Short
Proofreader: Elaine Pollard
Cover design: Chloë Roberts
Photographer: Chris Christoforo
Editorial: **London** Ruth Blackmore, Alison Murchie, Keith Drew, Edward Aves, Alice Park, Lucy White, Jo Kirby, James Smart, Natasha Foges, Róisín Cameron, Emma Traynor, Emma Gibbs, James Rice, Kathryn Lane, Christina Valhouli, Monica Woods, Mani Ramaswamy, Joe Staines, Peter Buckley, Matthew Milton, Tracy Hopkins, Ruth Tidball; **New York** Andrew Rosenberg, Steven Horak, AnneLise Sorensen, April Isaacs, Ella Steim, Anna Owens, Sean Mahoney, Paula Neudorf, Courtney Miller; **Delhi** Madhavi Singh, Karen D'Souza
Design & Pictures: **London** Scott Stickland, Dan May, Diana Jarvis, Nicole Newman, Mark Thomas, Emily Taylor; **Delhi** Umesh Aggarwal, Ajay Verma, Jessica Subramanian, Ankur Guha, Pradeep

Thapliyal, Sachin Tanwar, Anita Singh
Production: Vicky Baldwin
Cartography: **London** Maxine Repath, Ed Wright, Katie Lloyd-Jones; **Delhi** Jai Prakash Mishra, Ashutosh Bharti, Rajesh Mishra, Animesh Pathak, Jasbir Sandhu, Karobi Gogoi, Alakananda Roy, Swati Handoo, Deshpal Singh
Online: Narender Kumar, Rakesh Kumar, Amit Verma, Rahul Kumar, Ganesh Sharma, Debojit Borah, Ravi Yadav
Marketing & Publicity: **London** Liz Statham, Niki Hanmer, Louise Maher, Jess Carter, Vanessa Godden, Vivienne Watton, Anna Paynton, Rachel Sprackett, Libby Jellie, Jayne McPherson, Holly Dudley; **New York** Geoff Colquitt, Katy Ball; **Delhi** Ragini Govind
Manager India: Punita Singh
Reference Director: Andrew Lockett
Operations Manager: Helen Phillips
PA to Publishing Director: Nicola Henderson
Publishing Director: Martin Dunford
Commercial Manager: Gino Magnotta
Managing Director: John Duhigg

Publishing information

This first edition published October 2008 by
Rough Guides Ltd,
80 Strand, London WC2R 0RL
345 Hudson St, 4th Floor,
New York, NY 10014, USA
14 Local Shopping Centre, Panchsheel Park,
New Delhi 110017, India
Distributed by the Penguin Group
Penguin Books Ltd,
80 Strand, London WC2R 0RL
Penguin Group (USA)
375 Hudson Street, NY 10014, USA
Penguin Group (Australia)
250 Camberwell Road, Camberwell,
Victoria 3124, Australia
Penguin Group (Canada)
195 Harry Walker Parkway N, Newmarket, ON,
L3Y 7B3 Canada
Penguin Group (NZ)
67 Apollo Drive, Mairangi Bay, Auckland 1310,
New Zealand

Cover concept by Peter Dyer.

Typeset in Bembo and Helvetica to an original design by Henry Iles.

Printed and bound in China

© Rough Guides 2008

312pp includes index

A catalogue record for this book is available from the British Library

ISBN: 978-1-85828-418-7

1   3   5   7   9   8   6   4   2

Help us update

We've gone to a lot of effort to ensure that the first edition of **The Rough Guide to Fiji** is accurate and up to date. However, things change – places get "discovered", opening hours are notoriously fickle, restaurants and rooms raise prices or lower standards. If you feel we've got it wrong or left something out, we'd like to know, and if you can remember the address, the price, the hours, the phone number, so much the better.

Please send your comments with the subject line "**Rough Guide Fiji Update**" to ℮mail @roughguides.com. We'll credit all contributions and send a copy of the next edition (or any other Rough Guide if you prefer) for the very best emails.

Have your questions answered and tell others about your trip at
ꝸ community.roughguides.com

Acknowledgements

Ian Osborn: my greatest thanks go to Sia, my beautiful, patient wife, and to my children, Tieri, Patrick and Safaira, who endured me being away for weeks at a time gallivanting around the islands and spending most of my time at home feverishly writing about my exploits.

I would also like to thank my old friend Robbie Rickman who shared his knowledge of living in Suva, Frederick Douglas for his fabulous insights and story telling, all the staff at Beautiful Pacific for helping out when called upon, especially Meli Titoka who assisted in ensuring my observations

on Fijian life and culture were accurate and Teresia Veresoni for providing the Rotuman vocabulary, Ronald Ritesh Kumar for assistance with Fiji-Hindi, John and Marilyn Milesi and Noby and John Foskett for their assistance on Ovalau, Talei and Hunter at Toberua, Nicolas Juet at Vatulele, Richard, Jeanie, Elizabeth, Isaac and Mark Mallaney on Kadavu, Noel Douglas and Patrick Bibi on Taveuni and JJ, Sharon and Lorna in Savusavu. Finally, special thanks to my editor, Andy Turner, for his unerring guidance and skill in adapting the text as you now read it.

Photo credits

Index

Map entries are in colour.

INDEX

Map symbols

maps are listed in the full index using coloured text

-----	International boundary	ⓘ	Information office
---	Chapter division boundary	⊠	Post office
===	Major road	⊞	Hospital
===	Minor road	⊛	Swimming pool
——	Unpaved road	★	Transport stop
-----	Path	⚑	Golf course
——	River	⚲	Lighthouse
—•—	Railway	⚭	Gardens
⊓⊓⊓⊓⊓	Steps	⚑	Mosque
⊔	Bridge	⚑	Hindu temple
⊠	Gate	⚑	Church
⌃⌃	Mountain range	⚑	Wind farm
▲	Mountain peak	⚑	Waterfall
⌂	Cave	∥∖	Volcano
✗	Domestic airport	⚓	Ferry/Boat stop
✈	Airport	▬	Building
♦	Point of Interest	+|	Church
⛽	Fuel station	░	Park/national park
⋀⋀	Spring	⣿	Beach
⌃⌃⌃	Reef	⌇⌇	Swamp/mangrove